Praise for
Wind Sprints: Shorter Essays

"The 143 essays in Epstein's entertaining new collection . . .are compulsively readable. . . . Epstein shows himself capable of writing engagingly at that brief length on just about any topic that strikes his fancy. . . .The essays are peppered with personal memories and quotes from literature and punctuated with bursts of humor—Epstein likens a bandleader's bellow to that 'of a man who has just been pushed off a cliff'—and they abound with pleasures that belie their brevity."

—*Publishers Weekly*

"A master of the essay form returns with a collection of brief pieces spanning nearly 20 years. . . . Another subtitle might have been *Healthful Snacks*, for these bite-size pieces are both enjoyable to ingest and good for you."

—*Kirkus Reviews* (Starred Review)

"This collection is the perfect introduction to the erudite and entertaining work of a prolific essayist. . . .Noted writer Joseph Epstein offers a smorgasbord of wit in the collection *Wind Sprints: Shorter Essays*."

—PETER DABBENE, *ForeWord Reviews*

"Epstein (emeritus lecturer of English, Northwestern Univ.), a frequent contributor to the *Wall Street Journal*, *Commentary*, and the *Weekly Standard*, is acclaimed for his witty, perceptive, and occasionally contentious essays, which he began during his editorship (1974–97) of *American Scholar*."

—LONNIE WEATHERBY, *Library Journal*

"In the 143 short essays, Epstein discusses his reading habits, language snobbery, his love of khakis and good ol' fashioned shoe shines, the need for a word to describe someone who is more than an acquaintance but less than a friend, the rise of hot dog prices, and the demise of the high five. . . .Generally acknowledged as one of America's foremost essayists, Epstein's short pieces are delightful and infuriating, endearing and aggravating."

—SEAN WEST, *San Francisco Book Review*

"I am purring, chortling and cursing my way through [*Wind Sprints*]. Cursing, because [the] wit, . . . erudition, . . . élan, panache, and . . . *je ne sais quoi* is just too depressing. There's treasure in every sentence. It's like spoon-eating caviar. I may have a stroke, but what a way to go."

—CHRISTOPHER BUCKLEY, author of *Thank You for Smoking*

"It has long been implausible to argue that there's a more engaging essayist on the planet than Epstein. . . . There are 143 pieces in *Wind Sprints*, with almost no repetition of subject. Perhaps because of the length of these pieces, Epstein takes on fewer literary questions and deals with more small, quotidian matters, though in ways to demonstrate that almost anything can be dealt with intelligently, and in an entertaining way."

—LARRY THORNBERRY, the *American Spectator*

"In *Wind Sprints*, his latest collection of essays, Joseph Epstein confesses to literary tippling—sampling bits of prose while in the supermarket line, during television commercials, or even in traffic. . . . He excels at lively, instructive, and often funny essays that sometimes run to 10,000 words. The only complication in starting them is that they're so charming and chatty that one cannot easily put them down. A reader who begins an Epstein piece behind the wheel is likely to be stalled on the freeway for a very long time."

—DANNY HEITMAN, the *Christian Science Monitor*

"Witty, common-sensical, civilized, reliably pleasure-giving, Epstein is solace."

—PATRICK KURP, *Anecdotal Evidence*

Praise for
A Literary Education and Other Essays

"Epstein follows up *Essays in Biography* (2012) with another collection of provocative and beguiling thought pieces. The range of his curiosity is exhilarating."

—*Publishers Weekly*

"[In *A Literary Education*] prolific essayist, biographer, and novelist Epstein ... delivers ... lots of erudition ... and ... fun."

—*Kirkus Reviews*

"Erudite, penetrating, and decisive ... Epstein's delivery is filled with thorough analysis, delightful allusions, and outright laughs. ..."

—PETER DABBENE, *ForeWord Reviews*

"Maybe it's time for a 'Joseph Epstein Reader' that would assemble the best work from his previous books for old and new fans alike. In the meantime, *A Literary Education* inspires hope that Mr. Epstein's good run [referring to the author's 24 books] isn't over just yet."

—DANNY HEITMAN, *Wall Street Journal*

"[This is a] wonderful book of summer reading that's [also] ... good for the cold, gray days ahead. ... [Epstein is] a man of his time and above his time. ..."

—SUZANNE FIELDS, *Washington Times*

"Joseph Epstein turns out the best essays—of the literary or familiar kind—of any writer on active duty today. ... Those who've reviewed Epstein's work over the years ... praise his humor, his erudition, his vast learning, and his elegance. ... Epstein's writing, like most French desserts, is very rich stuff."

—LARRY THORNBERRY, *American Spectator*

"Epstein's . . . *A Literary Education and Other Essays* . . . is his 24th book. This volume confirms that Epstein is not only the greatest living American literary critic, but also the country's foremost general essayist. He is, almost singlehandedly, holding aloft the flame for what used to be the honorable calling of 'the man of letters.'"

—JOHN PODHORETZ, *Commentary*

"[Epstein] writes sentences you want to remember. . . . His essays are troves of literary reference and allusion, maps between centuries, countries, genres. . . . [They] have personality and style, yes, but they also have something to say, and that's the pivotal distinction between Epstein and his bevy of imitators. . . . What's more, his wit is unkillable. . . ."

—WILLIAM GIRALDI, *New Criterion*

"Epstein is an essayist of the old school—learned, productive, and available to many occasions. A man gifted with a wit both cutting and self-deprecating, and an easy command of the many syntactic variations of the periodic sentence, he also has a fearless willingness to assert a view—and this, as any reader of the essay knows, is the drive wheel of the whole business, never mind if that view is widely shared or unpopular."

— SVEN BIRKERTS, *Los Angeles Review of Books*

Praise for
Essays in Biography

"Erudite…eloquent…opinionated…edifying and often very entertaining."
—*Publishers Weekly*

"The acclaimed essayist . . . presents a provocative collection of essays that [is] . . . guaranteed to both delight and disconcert."
—*Kirkus Reviews*

"[He] brings to biography a genius of discernment."
—*Choice*

"Mr. Epstein's essays are brilliant distillations. . . . "
—CARL ROLLYSON, *Wall Street Journal*

"*Essays in Biography* . . . is smart, witty and a pleasure to read."
—JONATHAN YARDLEY, *Washington Post*

"This . . . collection of biographical essays . . . [is] unabashedly personal, and flavored throughout by a wit that never stays in the background for long. [What Epstein calls a] 'heightened sense of life's possibilities' is . . . what a reader may take away."
—*Boston Globe*

"Joseph Epstein['s] . . . style and wit make his subjects come alive. . . . [He is] the dean of contemporary essayists."
—*Washington Times*

"Epstein is a gifted storyteller, a discerning critic, and a peerless stylist. . . . It's fair to say that a variety of over-used adjectives—witty, urbane, intelligent—are in this case quite appropriate."
—*Weekly Standard*

"[Joseph Epstein is] one of the few living writers whose every book I try to read promptly. He is never—really never—less than a pure thoughtful joy."
—BRIAN DOHERTY, SENIOR EDITOR, *Reason*

"Epstein writes suave, free-wheeling, charged essays."

—ROBERT FULFORD, *National Post*

"[Joseph Epstein's] personal mission statement, apparently, is to instruct and delight. . . . This is a book you can pick up and skip around in with pleasure and profit."

—CHRISTOPHER FLANNERY, *Claremont Review of Books*

The Ideal of Culture

Also by Joseph Epstein

Where Were We?: The Conversation Continues,
with Frederic Raphael (2017)
Wind Sprints: Shorter Essays (2016)
Frozen in Time (2016)
Masters of the Games: Essays and Stories on Sport (2015)
A Literary Education and Other Essays (2014)
Distant Intimacy: A Friendship in the Age of the Internet,
with Frederic Raphael (2013)
Essays in Biography (2012)
Gossip: The Untrivial Pursuit (2011)
The Love Song of A. Jerome Minkoff: And Other Stories (2010)
Fred Astaire (2008)
In a Cardboard Belt!: Essays Personal, Literary, and Savage (2007)
Friendship: An Exposé (2006)
Alexis de Tocqueville: Democracy's Guide (2006)
Fabulous Small Jews (2003)
Envy (2003)
Snobbery: The American Version (2002)
Narcissus Leaves the Pool: Familiar Essays (1999)
Life Sentences: Literary Essays (1997)
With My Trousers Rolled: Familiar Essays (1995)
Pertinent Players: Essays on the Literary Life (1993)
A Line Out for a Walk: Familiar Essays (1991)
The Goldin Boys: Stories (1991)
Partial Payments: Essays on Writers and Their Lives (1988)
Once More Around the Block: Familiar Essays (1987)
Plausible Prejudices: Essays on American Writing (1985)
Middle of My Tether: Familiar Essays (1983)
Ambition: The Secret Passion (1980)
Familiar Territory: Observations on American Life (1979)
Divorced in America: Marriage in an Age of Possibility (1974)

The Ideal of Culture

Essays

Joseph Epstein

The essays in this book were previously published
in journals and anthologies. Original publication
information can be found on page 541.

Axios Press
PO Box 457
Edinburg, VA 22824
888.542.9467   info@axiosinstitute.org

Library of Congress Cataloging-in-Publication Data

Names: Epstein, Joseph, 1937- author.
Title: The ideal of culture : essays / Joseph Epstein.
Description: Edinburg, VA : Axios Press, [2018] | Includes index.
Identifiers: LCCN 2017058772 (print) | LCCN 2018000088 (ebook) | ISBN 9781604191240
(ebook) | ISBN 9781604191233 (hardcover)
Classification: LCC PS3555.P6527 (ebook) | LCC PS3555.P6527 A6 2018 (print)
| DDC 814/.54--dc23

LC record available at https://lccn.loc.gov/2017058772

No page is more welcome to the Muses than that which
knows how to combine grave and gay, and to refresh
the weary mind with helpful trifles.

—Samuel Johnson

Of all the ways of acquiring books, the one
considered most reputable is to write them.

—Walter Benjamin

Contents

Part Three: Jewish

Part Four: Masterpieces

Part Five: Hitting Eighty

Introduction

MY FRIEND EDWARD SHILS held that there are four institutions of learning in modern societies. These are the classroom, serious magazines and newspapers, the conversation of intelligent friends, and new and especially used bookstores. I would add a fifth, though it is not open to everyone: writing for the public. I don't recall when I first heard the phrase, applied to writers, "getting one's education in public," or who originated it, but I have come to think it applies to me, a writer who did not come to the task of literary composition especially well equipped but, so to say, learned on the job. But then maybe all writers are essentially interns, perpetually on what was once called OJT, or on the job training.

An example: I was perhaps thirty-years old when I received a call from the editor Eve Auchincloss, at *Book World*, asking if I would like to review a new edition in four volumes of *My Past and Thoughts*, the memoirs of Alexander Herzen. After hesitating perhaps a nanosecond, I said, "Yes, I would." Eve prescribed the length of review wanted and said that the books would be in the mail. I thanked her, hung up, and asked myself, "Who is Alexander Herzen?" I subsequently read the four magnificent volumes of this great nineteenth-century Russian writer, read about him in books by Isaiah Berlin, E. H. Carr, and others, wrote my 1,500 or so words, and became perhaps a touch, if not smarter, more knowledgeable about things it is necessary for a person with intellectual pretensions to know.

So it has been for me over the past decades, widening my knowledge by fresh readings, and deepening it, as I like to think, by writing about them. For the act of writing is itself an act of education, perhaps even before it can be considered anything so grand as an act of creation. The way this works is that, at the outset, writing forces the writer to realize what he doesn't know.

Over the years, I have agreed to write about certain subjects in full confidence that I could do so interestingly. Only when I began tapping out my first paragraph did I often come to realize that my thoughts did not extend beyond the drabbest clichés. Since I prefer to think I have a strong revulsion for cliché, and a matching one for boredom, I find I must discover a new and interesting way to write about the subject. It is only in making the attempt to do so that I often come to realize that I knew things I didn't realize I knew. "How do I know what I think until I see what I say," an aphorism attributed to E. M. Forster, has long been, if not my mantra, then my motto.

For me a good part of the joy in writing—whether it be writing essays or short stories—is in this element of self-discovery. I am not saying here that writing is a form of therapy, that what I discover is myself. Not at all. What I am saying is that writing is a method of general discovery. The probes, the telescope and microscope used in this discovery is the English sentence. Its syntax juggled, precise words found, everything set in place, the English sentence can yield mysterious secrets. Or so I have learned.

Writing, like hanging the next morning for Dr. Johnson, tends to concentrate the mind. Having to write about a book or an idea is different from simply reading or thinking in general. Writing requires herding the wild cats of stray observations and inchoate notions, and forces the organization of one's thought, at least to the point where it is presentable for public inspection. I know some writers who are incapable of concentrated thinking without a pen in hand or a computer keyboard under their fingers. I happen to be one of them.

And so I beat on, like the man said, "boats against the current," continuing to attempt to further my education in public. I have been fortunate to have a small number of American and English editors abet me in the attempt, by finding things for me to write about or by agreeing to print things I have written and sent to them without their suggestion. As I look over the table of contents of *The Ideal of Culture*, I am mildly amused at the range of my interests, which run from Tacitus to Jewish boxers, from the concept of Cool to that of Cowardice, from Machiavelli to the Marx Brothers. Faith and begorrah, I seem to have got away with it.

A note of acknowledgement: I wish to thank John Podhoretz of *Commentary,* Philip Terzian of the *Weekly Standard*, John Kienker of the *Claremont Review of Books*, Abe Socher of the *Jewish Review of Books*, and Robert Messenger, David Propson, and Eric Gibson of the *Wall Street Journal.* I should also like to thank that unknown soul who invented the section of the weekend *Wall Street Journal* called "Masterpiece," in which unknown or forgotten or misunderstood works of literary, architectural, visual art, or music are remembered and revived, however briefly, in relatively short articles. Whoever that person is, he or she has provided me with the opportunity to revisit many of the great works that comprise the Masterpiece section of this book. Finally, a word of thanks to Jody Banks, my patient and thoughtful editor at Axios Press, and to Hunter Lewis, publisher of Axios Press, for encouraging me to persist.

Part One

The Culture

The Ideal of Culture

(2017)

URING MY TEACHING DAYS, along with courses on Henry James, Joseph Conrad, and Willa Cather, I taught an undergraduate course called Advanced Prose Style. What it was advanced over was never made clear, but each year the course was attended by 15 or so would-be—or, as we should say today, wannabe—novelists and poets. Usage, diction, syntax, rhythm, metaphor, irony were some of the subjects taken up in class. Around the sixth week of the eight-week term I passed out a list of 12 or so names and historical events—among them Sergei Diaghelev, Francis Poulenc, Mark Rothko, Alexander Herzen, the 1913 Armory Show, John Cage, the Spanish Civil War, George Balanchine, and Jean Cocteau—and asked how many of these items the students could identify.

The identification rate among my students was inevitably low, which did not much surprise me. I mentioned that, at their age (20 or 21), I should probably not have done much better, and then added:

> But if as writers you intend to present yourself to the world as
> cultured persons, you have to know these names and events
> and scores of others, and what is important about them.
> This is not something that one gets up as if for an exam, or

Googles and promptly forgets, but that must be understood in historical context—at least it must for those who seek to live a cultured life.

Oddly, no one ever asked what a cultured life was, and why it was worth pursuing. This may have been just as well for, though I believed I was myself by then leading (or earnestly attempting to lead) such a life, I'm not sure I could have answered either question. I'm going to attempt to do so now.

In 1952, the anthropologists Alfred Kroeber and Clyde Kluckhohn wrote a famous article, "Culture: A Critical Review of Concepts and Definitions," in which they specified no fewer than 164 definitions of culture. Culture can, of course, refer to whole civilizations, such as Western culture or Asian culture; it can refer to national, ethnic, or social-class cultures, such as Israeli culture or Irish Catholic culture, or working-class culture. In all these senses it refers to the overarching aspirations and assumptions that underlay the ways that different peoples and groups have of understanding and dealing with the world.

Kroeber and Kluckhohn might today have to expand their number of definitions, for the so-called "culture" of corporations, professions, and athletic teams has become among the leading cant phrases of our time. Princeton University Press recently published a book with the title *The Culture of Growth*, and the movie star Gwyneth Paltrow not long ago noted that her civilized break with her husband contributed to "the culture of divorce."

What I mean by the ideal of culture is high culture, as set out by Matthew Arnold in his 1867 essay "Culture and Anarchy." Arnold described this level of culture as "the best which has been thought and said," but in our day it has been enlarged to include the best that has been composed and painted and sculpted and filmed. Arnold believed that high culture had its "origin in the love of perfection" and the "study of perfection," and thought it an idea that the new democracy under the industrial revolution developing in his day needed "more than the idea of the blessedness of the franchise, or the wonderfulness of their own industrial performances."

Behind Arnold's notion of high culture was a program for the partial reform of human nature. Attaining the perfection of high culture, Arnold held, would bring about "an *inward* condition of the mind and spirit . . . at variance with the mechanical and material civilization in esteem with us." Properly cultivated, this elevated culture would lead to "an expansion of human nature" and release us from our "inaptitude for seeing more than one side of a thing, with our intense energetic absorption in the particular pursuit we happen to be following."

One might think Matthew Arnold's idea of culture is restricted to the well-born. He saw it otherwise. "In each class," he wrote,

> there are born a certain number of natures with a curiosity about their best self, with a bent for seeing things as they are, for disentangling themselves from machinery . . . for the pursuit, in a word, of perfection. . . . And this bent always tends . . . to take them out of their class, and to make their distinguishing characteristic not their [social origins, wealth, or status], but their *humanity*.

Make no mistake: High culture, culture in the sense in which Arnold speaks of it as an ideal, is an elite activity—but one potentially open to everyone with what Arnold calls a "bent" for it.

I SHOULD NEVER HAVE THOUGHT MYSELF to have had this bent, and might never have discovered it but for the somewhat fortuitous event of my having gone to the University of Chicago in the middle 1950s. Neither of my parents went to college, though both were highly intelligent and well-spoken. But anything remotely resembling high culture was simply not on their menu. My father was interested in politics and world events, my mother astute in her judgment of people; ours was a home with lots of newspapers and magazines but no books whatsoever—not even, as I recall, a dictionary. The only performing art of the least interest to my parents and their friends was musical comedy. They and their social set got on well enough without culture, preoccupied as they were with earning a living, raising families, maintaining friendships, and dealing with life's manifold quotidian matters.

Doubtless I should have, too, but for my having gone to college where and when I did. The University of Chicago was an institution, unlike the Ivy League schools, without the least taint of social snobbery: At Chicago, wealth, birth, good looks counted for nothing. (In fact, I once heard two distinguished professors there, the social scientist Edward Shils and the historiographer Arnaldo Momigliano, in conversation all but disqualify a male graduate student for being much too handsome to do serious scholarship.) All that mattered at Chicago was knowledge and intellect: what one knew, and how deeply and subtly one knew it.

Many of the most distinguished members of the faculty at the University of Chicago in the mid-1950s were European; several of these part of what one might call Adolf Hitler's gift to American intellectual life: that is, European Jews who fled the Nazi and fascist Jewish genocide. Among them were the political philosopher Leo Strauss, the physicist Enrico Fermi (whose wife was Jewish), the historian Karl Weintraub, the historian-philosopher of religion Mircea Eliade. Hannah Arendt was somewhat later a member of the university's Committee on Social Thought. These people gave a tone to the place—and the tone was that not merely of extensive erudition (merely, indeed!) but of an impressive density of culture probably not available anywhere else. I don't know about giants, but lots of highly cultured men and women walked the earth in those days.

From the deep abyss of my late-adolescent ignorance, I never for a moment thought I could hope to emulate such men and women. I nevertheless somehow sensed that there was something immensely impressive about them. The philosopher Eva Brann nicely captures my emotional reaction to the cultured men and women I glancingly encountered at the University of Chicago when, about her own students at St. John's College in Annapolis, she writes:

> Those students seem to me most admirable who are capti-
> vated by admiration, even adoration—who know what it is
> to lack and long, quail and emulate—to feel the exultation
> of being the lesser, bound by love to a greater, the pride of
> recognizing superiority, the generosity of pure delight in it.
> You have to be young; with maturity comes a more distant,
> more mordant view of even the finest of fellow humans.

Yet, if moments of being simply overcome by some magnificence or other have ceased altogether, you're not so much old as wizened.

At their best, these figures at the University of Chicago seemed above the fray, the everyday concerns of moneymaking, partisan politics, crude status gathering. (I would later learn that this was not always—in fact, was sometimes far from—the case.) The world might go about its business, but they were playing the game of life at another, a different and higher level. I yearned to play the game myself; I wondered, longingly, what it took to be allowed onto their court.

What it took to pass through the gates into the realm of high culture was years of thoughtful reading, listening, viewing, thinking. This would develop the critical sense needed to discern the difference between serious and *ersatz* culture, and a receptivity to the sublime in beauty. High culture critics, meanwhile, saw their job as that of gatekeepers, making certain that no inferior works were allowed to pass themselves off as the real thing. In the 1950s and early '60s, there was much written about highbrow, middlebrow, and lowbrow art—a distinction first made by the literary critic Van Wyck Brooks and, a generation later, expanded by the *Harper's* editor Russell Lynes—and the differences and distinctions among them.

The pursuit of high culture came with a price. Once hooked on it, one was no longer entirely at ease with popular culture—the culture, that is to say, most of us we grew up with and that remains the mainstream culture. Once one is devoted to the pursuit of high culture, the bestseller, the Oscar-winning movie, the highest-rated television shows— all uncomplicatedly enjoyed by one's contemporaries—are, if not of no interest, then thought somewhat out of bounds, with the enjoyment of them tending to fall under the category of guilty pleasures.

I had a friend, Samuel Lipman, a piano prodigy as a child, a student of the conductor and violinist Pierre Monteux, later a teacher at Juilliard, a powerful music critic, and publisher of the *New Criterion*, a magazine devoted to the arts. In the realm of culture, Sam was an immitigable, irretrievable highbrow. Once, after a meeting of the Council of the National Endowment for the Arts (of which we were both members), I said to Sam that I noted he rarely mentioned movies or television. "Oh,

I consider movies and television," he said, rather casually, "dog shit." Dog shit, I thought at the time, lower in dignity even than the excrement of bulls and horses.

Another friend of mine, Hilton Kramer, kept a comparably high standard. Hilton was an immensely amusing and witty fellow, but not a man you asked whom he liked in the World Series, or which he thought the best of Herman's Hermits' songs. When art critic at the *New York Times*, he was the only writer on the paper whom, in his exile, the great Russian dissident writer Alexander Solzhenitsyn would allow to interview him. Solzhenitsyn agreed to do so because—a great tribute here—he respected Hilton's seriousness.

Not everyone can live on the chaste cultural diets of Hilton Kramer and Sam Lipman. Two highly cultivated men of my acquaintance— the political thinker Irving Kristol and the historian of modern France Eugen Weber—were devoted to detective fiction; I only recently learned that Walter Benjamin, the metaphysician of language, was also addicted to detective fiction. And so was Gershom Scholem, the great authority on Jewish mysticism. William Phillips, the editor in its heyday of the intellectual quarterly *Partisan Review*, was an ardent New York Giants fan. I once saw the baritone Bryn Terfel perform at the Ravinia Festival in what I took to be a United Manchester soccer jersey.

Sam Lipman and Hilton Kramer were the aesthetic and intellectual equivalent of vegans—extremely cautious about what they consumed. As critics, which both men were, they saw their job as separating the serious from the pretentious, the genuine from the meretricious, the life-enhancing from the amusingly and sometimes perniciously trivial. Whence did their authority derive? What gave them the right to sit in judgment on, and find unacceptable, works that others had sometimes put years into making and which many others innocently enjoyed? Their authority came from their having thought about art for decades, and their passionate devotion to it. They were able to impose their views by the main force of the cogency of their arguments.

Culture is continuity with the past: A cultureless person knows only about, and lives exclusively in, the present. Few things are as pleasing— thrilling, really—as reading a classical author and discovering that he has had thoughts and emotions akin to your own. So I have felt, at times, reading Horace, Montaigne, William Hazlitt, and others who departed the planet centuries before my entrance upon it. Edmund Wilson writes splendidly on this point in a brief essay called "A Preface to Persius," in which he offers his observations on reading a late-18th-century edition of Persius, the first century CE Latin poet and satirist. Wilson read the preface to this edition in an Italian restaurant and speakeasy in Greenwich Village in 1927, and felt himself "warmed by this sense of continuity with the past, with Persius and William Drummond [the book's editor], by this spirit of stubborn endurance." This cultural connection put him, Edmund Wilson, however briefly, outside the politics and noisiness of the present, and forcefully reminded him that, for the man or woman of culture,

> there was nothing to do save to work with the dead for allies, and at odds with the ignorance of most of the living, that that edifice, so many times begun, so discouragingly reduced to ruins, might yet stand as the headquarters of humanity!

The edifice Wilson refers to is, of course, civilization.

DOES ALL THIS TALK OF HIGH CULTURE have a ring of snobbery? If so, I have badly misrepresented it. There is nothing snobbish about seeking out the best that has been thought and said. What it *is*, as noted earlier, is elitist, a word in our egalitarian age in even worse odor, perhaps, than snobbery. Cultural elitists, as do connoisseurs generally, like only the best and seek it out. But how do they determine what is best? From tradition, from the tastes of their culturally elitist forebears, from their own refined aesthetic and intellectual sensibilities. Along with Longinus, they identify as high culture those works of art and intellect that elevate the soul, stay in the memory, and appeal across different cultures. Elitist the cultural ideal certainly is, but with the difference, as noted by Matthew Arnold, that it is open to anyone who wishes to make the effort to attain that ideal.

Those opposed to the elitist impulse in art make the mistake of confusing the realms of culture and politics. To be a cultural elitist does not eliminate the possibility of one's simultaneously being a democrat in one's views politically, or even a man or woman determinedly on the left. The Australian art critic Robert Hughes claimed to be split in this way. Proof that the highbrow and the left-wing radical can live comfortably enough in the same person is illustrated—in fact, highlighted—in the last lines of Leon Trotsky's *Literature and Revolution*. Trotsky wrote that it was his dream that, under communism,

> man will become immeasurably stronger, wiser and subtler; his body will become more harmonized, his movements more rhythmic, his voice more musical. The forms of life will become dynamically dramatic. The average human type will rise to the heights of an Aristotle, a Goethe, or a Marx.

In other words, the end of the class struggle, as envisioned by the Communist revolutionary Leon Trotsky, would be the acquisition of high culture by all.

How, then, does one attain culture? Superior intelligence isn't the key. I have known high-level physicists and mathematicians—people whose IQs are doubtless stratospheric—who were, so to say, culture-proof. Even the most adroit teachers cannot hope to bestow culture on their students: the best they can do, if they are themselves cultivated, is provide a glimmer of what the real thing looks like. A university education is never sufficient in itself, though it can give its interested students useful guidance about where culture is available. In the realm of culture, as in all non-vocational education generally, we are all autodidacts—all on our own, that is. No approved method for acquiring culture is available: There is no useful list of the hundred most important books, 200 essential musical compositions, 300 significant paintings, 400 hundred best films. So far as I have been able to determine, no *Culture for Dummies* has yet been published, though one may well be on the way. No guides, no lists, no shortcuts to attaining culture exist; nor will they ever.

The sad truth, the bad news, is that one never really attains culture in the way one attains, say, a plumber's license or a CPA. If anyone says he is cultured, or even thinks himself cultured, which no truly cultured person ever would, he or she, like those who think themselves charming, probably is not. In striving after the attainment of culture, one invariably falls short.

Other people are soon enough discovered who have it in greater depth, and make one's own cultural attainments seem paltry.

One discovers, straightaway, that earlier eras had a higher standard for culture than our own. In the 19th century, without competence in ancient Greek and Latin, for example, no one could hope to be considered cultured. In the 18th century, George Washington was embarrassed to travel to France because he had no French. One is too clearly aware of the lacunae of one's own cultural shortcomings, the vast gaps in knowledge of the kind a person claiming to be cultured ought to possess: Knowledge of the history of the Byzantine Empire, of Gregorian chant, of the influence of Bauhaus, and so much more. To be cultured implies a certain roundedness of knowledge and interests. No one, of course, has all these things. No one is fully rounded—which is why no one is fully cultured and why culture, itself, remains an ideal and, like so many ideals, may well be ultimately out of reach, though still worth pursuing.

LET ME PAUSE HERE to mention a few of the people I have known who have come closest to this ideal. The first is Jacques Barzun, who was the figure one immediately thought of when thinking of Columbia University during its great days in mid-20th century America. Born in France in 1907 into a family with serious artistic interests—among his parents' friends were Guillaume Apollinaire, Marcel Duchamp, and Edgard Varèse—Barzun came to America in early adolescence and later returned to remain for the rest of his life. He was a cultural historian, who wrote with equal authority on Marx, William James, Hector Berlioz, Darwin, American university education, French prosody, English grammar and usage, and more. In his nineties, he produced a cultural synthesis called *From Dawn to Decadence: 500 Years of Western Cultural Life, 1500 to the Present*. In a dip into popular culture, he also knew baseball and edited anthologies about detective fiction. Jacques was formidable without being stuffy. He taught much of his adult life yet seemed—in his cosmopolitan culture, his metropolitan spirit—so much more than an academic.

I met Arnaldo Momigliano, long deemed to be the leading figure in the historiography of the ancient world, through my friend Edward Shils, who arranged to have him teach half the year at the University of

Chicago. He was at All Souls College, Oxford, the other half. Mussolini's fascist government caused him to flee to England from Turin, where he was born. I don't know how many languages Arnaldo had, but I once noticed, on the desk in his room at the University of Chicago faculty club, a Dostoyevsky novel—in Russian. He seemed to know everything.

I was having breakfast one morning with Leon Edel, the biographer of Henry James, at that same faculty club when Arnaldo came into the room. I introduced him to Edel who, I told Arnaldo, was currently writing a book about Bloomsbury. Had you joined us at that breakfast table, you would have thought Arnaldo had already written the definitive book on Bloomsbury—"The linchpin figure," he said in his Piedmontese accent, "was of course Duncan Grant"—so complete and penetrating was his knowledge of the subject, even though it was one that didn't remotely touch on what is called his "field." I once wrote that if there had been a game called not Trivial but Serious Pursuit, Arnaldo would have been its champion.

Hugh Lloyd-Jones was Regius Professor of Greek at Oxford and married to Mary Lefkowitz, a professor of classics at Wellesley and herself an estimable writer on classical subjects. Hugh was a charming man, witty, with a good laugh. Their love for each other, the joyousness of their relationship generally, made it pleasing to be in his and Mary's company. Hugh once told me that when Mary ironed his shirts, he, to relieve the tedium of the task, read Henry James or Marcel Proust to her—a high-culture version of "American Gothic."

My candidate for the most cultured American novelist of the past century is Willa Cather. Modern American writers have not been notably cultured. Hemingway wasn't, nor was Fitzgerald, nor Faulkner. Talented though all were, none could write beyond his immediate ken or *milieu*. Cather, born in 1873 in the small town of Red Cloud, Nebraska, through self-cultivation became a citizen of a much larger world. As a writer, she was above nationality, above politics and gender, androgynous as all the greatest artists are. Willa Cather, in effect, Europeanized herself: She admired the novels of Flaubert, the poetry of Housman, everything of Henry James, himself an American who had earlier acquired cosmopolitan culture, and had (as T. S. Eliot noted) "turned himself into a European but of no known country." Cather's personal culture allowed her to write not only about the Scandinavian immigrants she grew up with, and knew so well, but also about the life of the artist (*The Song of the Lark*), about late-17th-century European settlers in Quebec (*Shadow on the Rock*), about the lives of two 19th-century French priests, Fathers Latour and Vaillant, establishing a diocese in the newly formed territory of New Mexico (*Death Comes for the Archbishop*). Culture cannot make a writer, of course; but as in Cather's case, by expanding her horizons, it can vastly enlarge her reach.

A small detail from Cather's *Death Comes to the Archbishop*: Father (now Bishop) Latour is served a soup made by his companion Father Vaillant, an onion soup with croutons, upon which, after tasting it, Latour remarks:

> I am not deprecating your talent, Joseph, but, when one thinks of it, a soup like this is not the work of one man. It is the result of a constantly refined tradition. There are nearly a thousand years of history in this soup.

A soup with a thousand-year history—only a writer of deep culture could have written such a passage. Culture itself, one might add, is a soup thousands of years in the making.

FOR A CENTURY, AND MORE, the seat of culture for Americans was Europe. Europe had all the great writers, painters, composers, conductors, musical performers, the most magnificent museums and libraries and churches. Americans with cultural interests went to Europe as pilgrims to Mecca, and some with ample financial resources stayed on as expatriates. To be an American was, culturally, to feel oneself a yokel; and at 20 years old or so, even I, a true yokel, sensed that genuine culture lay on the other side of the Atlantic.

For a period of a few decades in the past century, however, this looked to be changing. In New York, the school of Abstract Expressionism became central in the realm of visual art. The important painters were Americans; so, too, earlier, in poetry, where the generation of Robert Frost, Wallace Stevens, the American-born T. S. Eliot, rivaled, if not surpassed in importance, the poetry of Yeats, Housman, and Hardy. The Englishman W. H. Auden, the leading poet of the following generation, chose to spend the years of his literary prime in the United States. European conductors led the Boston, Philadelphia, New York, and Chicago symphony orchestras. Was culture, itself, crossing the ocean *en masse*? Was America to be the new Rome to Europe's Greece? Alas, the hope now seems altogether too short-lived.

Today, high culture in America is in serious decline. (Nor is it doing much better in Europe, let me add, details on request.) Contemporary visual art, for example, scarcely exists—that is, it seems to be more about financial investment than about ideas or significant aesthetic experience. Poetry, once central to high culture, has become degraded to an intramural sport. Although the audience for poetry in America was never large, today even that audience has diminished, and the only people who seem to read contemporary poetry are those who write it or write about it. Are there substantial numbers of people awaiting the next novels of Michael Chabon, Jonathan Lethem, or Jonathan Safran Foer as they once eagerly anticipated the next novels of Bellow, Malamud, Katherine Anne Porter, and others? I don't believe there are.

In 1959, the novelist John O'Hara predicted that "the novel will be dead or moribund in less than a hundred years." This is beginning to look like a sound prediction. Contemporary American serious music has produced no Aaron Coplands, Virgil Thomsons, Samuel Barbers. The audiences for traditional classical music performance dwindle. The promise of American theater, the theater of Arthur Miller, Eugene O'Neill, and Tennessee Williams, now seems moribund, if not flat-out deceased. Contemporary philosophy, which I have seen described as attempting to discover where the flame of a candle went after it burned out, appears more and more (in the words of Michael Oakeshott) "devoted to creating riddles out of solutions." Theodor Mommsen, writing of culture during the reigns of the emperors Claudius, Nero, and Vespasian, noted that "the mark of the age is tedium." Might this also be true of the culture of the age we are now living in?

Before attempting an answer, perhaps it is worth reminding ourselves of the promise of high culture. What it offered was an escape from the tyranny of the present. Cicero wrote that not to remember your past— by which he meant "the past"—is to remain a child. High culture, even though it often traveled under the banner of the avant-garde, was always about tradition. A cultured person has a standard, a recollection, through literature and history and philosophy—if not necessarily through personal experience—of greatness. Without such a recollection, rising above mediocrity is difficult, if not impossible.

At the death of Winston Churchill in 1965, Leo Strauss wrote:

> The death of Churchill reminds us of the limitations of our craft, and therewith of our duty. We have no higher duty, and no more pressing duty, than to remind ourselves and our students, of political greatness, human greatness, of the peaks of human excellence. For we are supposed to train ourselves and others in seeing things as they are, and this means above all in seeing their greatness and their misery, their excellence and their vileness, their nobility and their triumphs, and therefore never to mistake mediocrity, however brilliant, for true greatness.

IF OURS IS, CULTURALLY, AN AGE OF TEDIUM, if the very notion of culture as an ideal is in doubt, how did this come about? Some would say that a digital age cannot be a rich age for culture. In the battle between pixels and print, pixels now seem well ahead. The smartphone, the iPad, the computer, for all their manifold benefits, do not encourage contemplation. They feature information over knowledge, and information is distinctly *not* knowledge. The skim, the scan, the tweet, the Wikipedia entry—they cater to, if they do not in fact breed, the shortened attention span. If I were to pass out a list of names and events of the kind I mentioned earlier to students today, they would wonder what the hell I was talking about: "The Spanish Civil War, the 1913 Armory Show—hey, no problem, I'll Google it." Google it up, gobble it up, we are in any case no longer talking about acquiring the necessary context, the delight in the power of making connections, that is the first step in acquiring culture.

The politics of the contemporary university, at least in its humanities and social sciences divisions, has not helped the nurturing of high culture. Quite the reverse. Academic feminists and multiculturalists, early in their rise to prominence, declared their impatience and boredom with (and anger at) the dominance of "dead white European males" in the curriculum. They might as well have declared war on high culture itself, for apart from a small number of notable examples—Sappho, Jane Austen, Madame de Stael, George Eliot—dead white European males *were*, and remain, the substance and pretty much the sum of high culture. In its striving for equality of interest for every culture and ethnic sub-group, the contemporary university has become an intellectual equal-opportunity institution, where the realm of art and intellect has little or nothing to do with equality. The result is that the American university, with a few notable exceptions, is less and less likely to purvey cogent samples of high culture, and provides fewer models of its benefits among its faculty.

In the early 1990s, I wrote an essay with the title "An Extremely Well-Informed SOB." In it I made the distinction among those who knew about the Now, such as the pundit on television, required to be *au courant* on everything in the news; the knowledgeable, which included people who knew both about the Now and a fair amount about the Then; the with-it, who prided themselves on knowing about the Next Big Thing and those myriad other things the rest of us are still in the dark about; and finally, the cultured, who insofar as possible, restrict themselves to knowing what is genuinely worth knowing.

Most people today prefer to spend their lives gathering more and more information. This plethora, this plague of information, now available to all—to what, precisely, does it lead? The best I can see, it leads to two things: The illusion that one understands the world, and to the formation of opinions, countless opinions, opinions on everything. Opinions are well enough, sometimes even required; but I have never quite been able to shake the capping remark made by V. S. Naipaul on a character in his novel *Guerrillas*: "She had a great many opinions, but taken together these did not add up to a point of view." Culture, true culture, helps form complex points of view.

Some years ago, the English political philosopher Michael Oakeshott was asked what he thought of England's entering the European Union. "I don't see," he answered, "why I should be required to have an opinion about that." An extraordinary thing for a contemporary political philosopher to say, or so I thought at the time. But later, reading Oakeshott's *Notebooks*, I came across two interesting passages that made clear the grounds on which he said it: First, "To be educated is to know how much one wishes to know and to have the courage not to be tempted beyond that limit." And second, that culture "teaches that there is much one does not want to know." I wonder if, in the current age, our so-called Information Age, knowing "what one doesn't want to know" isn't among the greatest gifts that the acquisition of culture can bestow.

To return to Matthew Arnold's supposition that culture holds out the promise of a change in human nature, one has to concede that the results, up to the moment, are not especially encouraging. But then, some people, quite without the aid of culture, have naturally good hearts; others have been brought to a high standard of goodness through religion. As for culture conferring virtue on those who possess it, it is impossible to forget that the Nazis played Beethoven at Auschwitz. Still, by removing oneself from the noise and vulgarities of the present, and lending oneself the perspective of the past, an engagement with high culture makes life richer—and thereby, immensely more interesting. And that, with apologies to Matthew Arnold, seems to me reward enough.

From Parent to Parenthood

(2015)

AS WITH LENGTHS OF SKIRTS, lapels on men's suits, breast-feeding, and other more or less important customs, there are also fashions in fatherhood. The institution changes from generation to generation. As a man of *un age certain*—if numbers be wanted, mine is 78—my experience of fatherhood, both from the receiving and giving end, is likely to be different from those of much younger men and women.

I had the good fortune to have an excellent father. He was fair, utterly without neuroses, a model of probity, honorable in every way. Born in Canada, my father departed Montreal to make his fortune in Chicago at the age of 17, without bothering to finish high school. Until his forties, when he came to own his own business, he was a salesman, but without any of the slickness or slyness usually associated with the occupation. He made his sales by winning over customers through his amiability, his reliability, and the utter absence of con in his presentation. He was successful, and became rich enough, in Henry James's phrase, "to meet the demands of his imagination," which weren't extravagant.

When, at the age of eighteen, it was time for me to go to college, my father told me that he would of course pay for my college education, but since I had shown so little interest in school, he wondered if I wouldn't do better to skip college. He thought that I would make a terrific salesman. This, you have to understand, was intended as a serious compliment; one of two I remember his paying me. The other came years later and had to do with my taking care of a complicated errand for him. After I had accomplished what he wanted, he said, "You handled that in a very businesslike way."

If this sounds as if I am complaining, the grounds being emotional starvation from want of approval, be assured that I'm not. Approval wasn't an item high on the list of emotional expenditure in our family. (When in my early thirties I informed my mother that I, who have no advanced degrees, had been offered a job teaching at Northwestern University, she replied, "That's nice, a job in the neighborhood," and we went on talk of other things.) I cannot ever recall seeking my parents' approval; it was only their disapproval that I wished to avoid, and this because it might cut down on my freedom, which, from an early age, was generous and extensive.

The not-especially-painful truth is that my younger brother and I— and I believe this is true of many families of our generation—were never quite at the center of our parents' lives. Their own lives—rightly, I would say—came first. So many in my generation, I have noticed, were born five or six years apart from our next brother or sister. The reason for this is that parents of that day decided that raising two children born too close together was damned inconvenient. The standard plan was to wait until the first child was in school before having a second.

My parents were never other than generous to my brother and to me. They never knocked us in any way. We knew we could count on them. But we also knew they had lives of their own and that we weren't, as is now so often the case with contemporary parents, everything to them. My mother had her charities, her card games, her friends. My father had his work, where he was happiest and most alive.

My father's exalted status as a breadwinner was central to his position in our household. The bread-winning function of men in those days, when so few married women worked, was crucial. Recall what a dim figure Pa Joad, in John Steinbeck's *The Grapes of Wrath*, is; the reason is that he is out of work, without financial function, and so the leadership in the novel is ceded to Ma Joad, the mother and dominant figure in the family. Although my father was the least tyrannical of men, my mother felt that he was owed many small services. "Get your father's slippers," my mother would say. "Ask your father if he'd like a glass of water." We were instructed not to "rumple up the newspaper before your father comes home."

As a Canadian, my father had no interest in American sports, so he never took my brother and me to baseball or football games. (He did like boxing, and on a couple of occasions he and I went to watch Golden Gloves matches together.) He certainly never came to watch me play any of the sports in which I participated. But then, in those days, no father did; his generation of fathers were at work—my father worked six days a week—and had no time to attend the games of boys. (I'm talking about pre-soccer days, and so girls in those days played no games.) Nor would it ever have occurred to me to want my father to watch me at play. One of the fathers among my friends did show up for lots of his son's games and was mocked behind his back for doing so; a Latinist among us referred to him as Omnipresent.

Although my father did not take me to sports or other events, or attend my own games, I nevertheless spent lots of time with him. From the age of fifteen through twenty, I drove with him to various Midwestern state fairs, where he sold costume jewelry to concessionaires. I was, officially, his flunky, schlepping his sample case and doing most of the driving. We shared hotel rooms. What amazes me now that I think about those many hours we spent together is how little of that time was given to intimate conversation between us. I never told my father about my worries, doubts, or concerns, nor did he tell me his. We never spoke about members of our family, except, critically, of dopey cousins or older brothers of his who had gone astray. We talked a fair amount about his customers. He offered me advice about saving, the importance of being financially independent, about never being a show-off of any kind—all of it perfectly sound advice, if made more than a touch boring by repetition.

Neither of us, my father or I, craved intimacy with the other. I wouldn't have known how to respond to an invitation to intimacy from him. I would have been embarrassed if he had told me about any of his weaknesses or deep regrets. So far as I could surmise, he didn't have any of either. Since I was a small boy I recall his invocation, often repeated, "Be a man." A man, distinctly, did not reveal his fears, even to his father; what a man did with his fears was conquer them.

THE GENERATION OF MY FATHER—men born in the first decade of the 20th century who came into their maturity during the Depression—was distinctly pre-psychological. In practice, this meant that such notions as insecurity, depression, or inadequacy of any sort did not signify as anything more than momentary lapses to be overcome by hitching up one's trousers and getting back to work. My father and I did not hug, we did not kiss, we did not say "I love you" to each other. This may seem strangely distant, even cold to a generation of huggers, sharers, and deep-dish carers. No deprivation was entailed here, please believe me. We didn't *have* to do any of these things, my father and I. The fact was, I loved my father, and I knew he loved me.

By the time I had children of my own, psychology had conquered with strong repercussions for child rearing. Benjamin Spock's book *Baby and Child Care* (1946), said in its day to be, after the Bible, the world's second-best-selling book, had swept the boards. Freudian theory was still in its ascendance. Under the new psychological dispensation, children were now viewed as highly fragile creatures, who if not carefully nurtured could skitter off the rails into a life of unhappiness and failure. As a young father, I was not a reader of Spock, nor was I ever a Freudian, yet so pervasive were the doctrines of Spock and Freud that their influence was unavoidable.

I was not a very good father; measured by current standards, I may have been a disastrous one. Having divorced from their mother when my sons were ten and eight years old, and having been given custody of them, I brought to my child rearing a modest but genuine load of guilt. I do not have any axiomatic truths about raising children except this one: Children were meant to be brought up by two parents. A single parent, man or woman, no matter how extraordinary, will always be insufficient.

Children, according to Dr. Spock and Dr. Freud, needed to be made to feel secure and loved. I couldn't do much about the first. But I proclaimed my love a lot to my sons, so often that they must have doubted that I really meant it. "You know I love you, goddamnit," I seem to recall saying too many times, especially after having blown my cool by yelling at them for some misdemeanor or other. Thank goodness I had boys; girls, I have discovered, cannot be yelled at, at least not with the same easy conscience.

Fortunately, my sons were fairly tough and independent characters. Neither of them as kids was interested in sports, so I didn't have to attend their Little League games. I took only a modest interest in their schooling. (My parents took none whatsoever in mine, which, given my wretched performance in school, was a break.) Nor did I trek out to Disneyland with them. My sons spent their Sundays with my parents, and my father, who turned out to be a fairly attentive grandfather, took them to the Museum of Science and Industry, the Adler Planetarium, the Shedd Aquarium, and other museums around Chicago. Raising children as a single parent, much of life during those years is now in my memory a blur—a blur of vast loads of laundry, lots of shopping, and less than first-class cookery (mine). "Dad, this steak tastes like fish," I remember one of my sons exclaiming, a reminder that I needed to do a better job of cleaning the broiler.

My oldest son, unlike his father, was good at school. When he was in high school he took to playing rock at a high volume in his room. I asked him how he could study with such loud music blaring away. "I seem to be getting all A's, Dad," he said. "Are you sure you want me to turn the music down?" He went on to Stanford, my other son to the University of Massachusetts. I drove neither of them on what is now the middle-class parents' compulsory tour of campuses while their children are in their junior year of high school. Nor did I tell them to which schools to apply. What I said is that I would pay all their bills, that I didn't need to look at their course selection or care about their major or grades, but only asked that they not make me pay for courses in science fiction or in which they watched movies. I visited each of them once while he was in college. I pasted no college decals on the back window of my car.

Some unknown genius for paradox said, "Married, single—neither is a solution." A similar formulation might be devised for the best time to have children: in one's twenties, thirties, forties, beyond—none seems ideal. In my generation, one married young—in my case, at 23—and had children soon thereafter. The idea behind this was to become an adult early, and thereby assume the responsibilities of adulthood: wife, children, house, dogs, "the full catastrophe," as Zorba the Greek put it. Now nearly everyone marries later, and women often delay having children, whether married or not, until their late thirties, sometimes early forties.

In one's twenties, one has the energy, but usually neither the perspective nor the funds, to bring up children with calm and understanding. Later in life, when one is more likely to have the perspective and the funds, the energy has departed. In my own case, along with having children to take care of, I had my own ambition with which to contend. I worked at forty-hour-a-week jobs, wrote on weekends and early in the mornings before work, read in the evenings, picked up socks and underwear scattered around the apartment, took out garbage, and in between times tried to establish some mild simulacrum of order in the household.

Because of this hectic life, my sons got less attention but more freedom than those of their contemporaries who had both parents at home; and vastly more freedom than kids brought up during these past two decades when the now-still-regnant, child-centered culture has taken over in American life in a big way.

I have a suspicion that this cultural change began with the entrée into the language of the word *parenting*. I don't know the exact year the word *parenting* came into vogue, but my guess is that it arrived around the same time as the new full-court press, boots-on-the-ground-with-heavy-air-support notion of being a parent. To be a parent is a role; parenting implies a job. It is one thing to be a parent, quite another to parent. "Parenting (or child rearing) is the process of promoting and supporting the physical, emotional, social, and intellectual development of a child from infancy to adulthood. Parenting refers to the aspects of raising a child aside from the biological relationship," according to the opening sentence of the Wikipedia entry on the subject. Read further down and you will find dreary paragraphs on "parenting styles," "parenting tools," "parenting across the lifespan," and more, alas, altogether too much more.

Under the regime of parenting, raising children became a top priority, an occupation before which all else must yield. The status of children inflated greatly. Much forethought went into giving children those piss-elegant names still turning up everywhere: all those Brandys and Brandons and Bradys; Hunters, Taylors, and Tylers; Coopers, Porters, and Madisons; Britannys, Tiffanys, and Kimberlys; and the rest. Deep thought, long-term plans, and much energy goes into seeing to it that they get into the right colleges. ("Tufts somehow feels right for Ashley,

Oberlin for Belmont.") What happens when they don't get into the right college, when they in effect fail to repay all the devout attention and care lavished upon them, is another, sadder story.

I BEGAN BY TALKING about "fashions" in fatherhood, but I wonder if *fashions* is the right word. I wonder if *cultural imperatives* doesn't cover the case more precisely. Since raising my sons in the hodgepodge way I did, I have become a grandfather, with two grandchildren living in northern California and one, a granddaughter now in her twenties, living in Chicago. My second (and final) wife and I have had a fairly extensive hand in helping to bring up our Chicago granddaughter, and I have to admit that, even though there is much about it with which I disagree, we have done so largely under the arrangements of the new parenting regime.

When this charming child entered the game, I had long since been working at home, with a loose enough schedule to allow me to bring up my granddaughter in a manner that violated just about everything I have mocked both in person and now in print about the way children are currently brought up. I drove her to school and lessons and usually picked her up afterward. I helped arrange private schools for her. I spent at least thrice the time with her that I did with my two sons combined. I heartily approved all her achievements. Yes—I report this with head bowed—when she was six years old, I took her to Disneyland. Worse news, I rather enjoyed it.

Not the "debbil," as the comedian Flip Wilson used to say, but the culture made me become nothing less than a hovering, endlessly bothering, in-her-face grandfather. (Pause for old Freudian joke: Why do grandparents and grandchildren get on so well? Answer: Because they have a common enemy.) The culture of his day condoned my father in his certainty that his business came before all else, allowing him to become an honorable if inattentive parent. The culture of my day allowed me to be a mildly muddled if ultimately responsible parent and still not entirely loathe myself. The culture of the current day dictated my bringing up my granddaughter, as I did with my wife's extensive help, as a nearly full-time job.

The culture of the current day calls for fathers to put in quite as much time with their children as mothers once did. In part this is owing to the fact that more and more women with children either need or want to work, and in part because, somehow, it only seems fair. Today if a father does not attend the games of his children, he is delinquent. If a father fails to take a strong hand in his children's education, he is deficient. If a father does not do all in his power to build up his children's self-esteem—"Good job, Ian"—he is damnable. If a father does not regularly hug and kiss his children and end all phone calls with "love ya," he is a monster. These are the dictates of the culture on—shall we call it?—"fathering" in our day, and it is not easy to go up against them; as an active grandparent, I, at least, did not find it easy.

Cultural shifts do not arrive without reason. Kids today, it is with some justice argued, cannot, owing to crime in all big cities, be left alone. They need to be more carefully protected than when I, or even my sons, were children. Getting into decent colleges and secondary and primary schools and, yes, even preschools is not the automatic business it once was. The competition for what is felt to be the best in this realm is furious; thought (and often serious sums of money) must go into it. Children are deemed more vulnerable than was once believed. How else to explain all those learning disabilities, attention deficits, and other confidence-shattering psychological conditions that seem to turn up with such regularity and in such abundance? The world generally has become a more frightening place, and any father with the least conscience will interpose himself between it and his children for as long as possible. One can no longer be merely a parent; one must be—up and at 'em— relentlessly parenting.

As a university teacher I have encountered students brought up under this new, full-time attention regimen. On occasion, I have been amused by the unearned confidence of some of these kids. Part of me—the part Flip Wilson's debbil controls—used to yearn to let the air out of their self-esteem. How many wretchedly executed student papers have I read, at the bottom of which I wished to write, "F. Too much love in the home."

Will all the attention now showered on the current generation of children make them smarter, more secure, finer, and nobler human beings? That remains, as the journalists used to say about the outcomes of Latin American revolutions, to be seen. Have the obligations of fathering made men's lives richer, or have they instead loaded men down with a feeling of hopeless inadequacy, for no man can hope to be the ideal father required in our day? How many men, one wonders, after a weekend of heavily programmed, rigidly regimented fun fathering with the kids, can't wait to return to the simpler but genuine pleasures of work? Only when the cultural imperative of parenting changes yet again are we likely to know.

"He that hath wife and children," wrote Francis Bacon, "hath given hostages to fortune, for they are impediments to great enterprises, either of virtue or mischief." Yet many centuries earlier, when Croesus, the richest man of his day, asked the wise Solon who was the most contented man in the world, thinking Solon would answer him—"You Croesus, of course."—Solon surprised him by naming an otherwise obscure Athenian named Tellus. The reason this was so, Solon explained, is that "he lived at a time when his city was particularly well, he had handsome, upstanding sons, and he ended up a grandfather, with all his grandchildren making it to adulthood."

Fathering children puts a man under heavy obligation and leaves him vulnerable to endless worry, not only about the fate of his children but of his children's children. This being so, the most sensible thing, one might think, is not to have children. But one would think wrong. Not to have children cuts a man off from any true sense of futurity and means that he has engaged life less than fully. Fatherhood, for all its modern-day complications, is ultimately manhood.

Death Takes No Holiday

(2014)

"I am, upon the whole, a happy man, have found the world an entertaining place and am thankful to Providence for the part allotted to me in it."

—SYDNEY SMITH

O
N A BOOKSHELF NEAR THE DESK on which sits my computer are a number of Penguin Classics, black bindings with yellow trim: Montaigne, Pascal, Stendhal, Cervantes, lots of Balzac, Turgenev, a two-volume edition of *War and Peace*. Am I likely to be around long enough to read *War and Peace* again? I have to wonder. My mother lived to 82, and my father to 91, dying of congestive heart failure, a fairly easeful death I think of as congestive heart success. So I hold decent cards, genetically speaking, but the Fates, as everyone knows, often deal off the bottom of the deck. People nowadays hope to make it past 80, at which point, honest people will acknowledge, they are playing on house money. If I were to peg out next month at 77, no one would be much surprised or remark that it was untimely.

In their development, human beings first grasp the concept of time, and not long after the certainty that it is running out. We are granted the mixed blessing of being the only species with foreknowledge of its mortality, an advantage in so many ways and yet one that complicates everything and, if allowed to get out of hand, can spoil nearly all one's days.

Homer held it was best not to be born at all or to die early. Most of us beg to differ, and long for life to be prolonged forever and perhaps just a bit beyond. (What else, after all, is all that running and healthy eating about?) Others, reconciled to death, wish to get the most of the time allotted to them, and feel, as the old blues song has it, "you're so beautiful, you've got to die some day / All's I want's a little lovin' before you pass away."

In reprinted versions of his best-known poem, "September 1, 1939," W. H. Auden omitted the stanza containing the most famous line he ever wrote: "We must love one another or die." We can love one another all we like, Auden concluded on further reflection, we're going to die anyway. The Persian King Xerxes, Herodotus reports, witnessing his more than 2,000 troops massed for the battle to conquer Greece, wept at the thought that "all these multitudes here and yet in 100 years' time not one of them will be alive." Then, as now, the mortality rate remains at 100 percent, with no likelihood of dropping soon.

Best not to ignore the most famous passage of Pascal in his *Pensées*:

> Imagine a number of men in chains, all under sentence of death, some of whom are each day butchered in the sight of the others; those remaining see their own condition in that of their fellows, and looking at each other with grief and despair await their turn. This is an image of the human condition.

E VERYONE WILL HAVE HAD a different introduction to death. For some it comes by way of the death of a pet, or, more tragically, of a parent, or of a young friend. Once death is on the board, the game is never quite the same. Some people from a fairly early age are able to think of little else; others, gifted with a short attention span, are able to hold the crushing fact of death at bay for long stretches. I am in the second group.

"Death is an old joke," wrote Turgenev, "that comes to each of us afresh." Death is nothing if not democratic. We try to remove the sting of it through euphemism, so that people do not die but "pass away," or "expire," or "go to a better place." All religions have had to accommodate the fact of death, some making more specific promises about its aftermath than others. Physicians are sworn to fight it off for as long as possible, though the phrase "pull the plug" by now qualifies as one of H. W. Fowler's "Vogue Words."

The great writers have understood that it provides the most serious theme in all of literature. No philosophy is complete without an explanation of the meaning of death, not excluding that it is a brute fact of nature and might have no further meaning than that.

The Greek philosopher Epicurus (341–270 BCE) provided a four-step program that, in one swoosh, eliminates any anxiety about death itself and worry about the prospect of an afterlife:

1. Do not believe in God, or the gods. There is no good evidence for their existence, and worrying about them and their judgments is therefore a waste of energy.

2. Do not give any thought to what happens after death. Oblivion follows death, in which you will return to the same state in which you existed before you were born.

3. Take your mind off pain. Two things only can follow from pain: Either it will go away, or it will get worse and worse and you will die, after which oblivion will follow.

4. Do not seek fame, power, money, or extravagant luxuries. All disappoint, and none finally yields satisfaction.

Follow these steps, and serenity, Epicurus holds, will be yours. I have no doubt that it would be. Pity, I find I am unable to follow any of these steps. I am no Epicurean.

OBLIVION IS MY PROBLEM. I cannot imagine it. Horace called it "eternal exile." Schopenhauer, like Epicurus, thought oblivion to be no different than life before we were born into it. For Schopenhauer, death, not life, was the constant. "Life can be regarded as a dream," he wrote, and "death as the awakening from it." Changing metaphors, he also claimed that "our life is to be regarded as a loan received from death, with sleep as our daily interest on this loan." Schopenhauer also believed that, on balance, suicide was not at all a bad idea. In *Speak, Memory*, Vladimir Nabokov wrote that "although the two [prenatal life and death] are identical twins, man, as a rule, views the prenatal abyss with more calm than the one he is heading for (at some forty-five-hundred heartbeats an hour)."

I write that oblivion isn't easy to imagine, but I suppose what I really mean is that I have no wish to imagine a world without me in it. George Santayana claimed that one of the reasons older people tend to grumpiness is that they find it difficult to envision a world of any quality in which they will not play a part. Life after I am gone will, of course, be exactly the same as when I was still on the roster of the living. I can think of four people who will truly mind, genuinely mourn, my death, no more. My absence from life will otherwise constitute no more than the removal of a single grain of sand from the beach. My death will not, as the Victorians used to say, signify. The only question is, When it will occur?

Death, unlike the railroads, publishes no schedule. *Untimely* is the adjective most often paired with death, but what would constitute a timely death? One, perhaps, that rescues a person from grievous pain, hideous scandal, unbearable guilt. With the exception of those formally pronounced terminally ill, the rest of us do not know when we are going to die. Would it help if we did? Would we act differently if we had precise foreknowledge of our demise? Would it make death any easier to deal with? On this matter of a (literal) deadline, Santayana thought that, no matter one's age, it is perhaps best to assume that one will live another decade. Yet, in his middle 80s, when his physician suggested he lose weight, Santayana noted that the man evidently wanted him in perfect health in time for his death. He died at 88 at the Convent of the Blue Nuns in Rome. Whenever I hear of someone who has died at 85 or above, I find myself saying, "I'd sign on for that," but, who knows, once there I should probably do all in my power to renegotiate the contract.

Putting death out of mind as best one can is a mistake, or so Montaigne thought. Wiser, he felt, to think constantly about death, not so much to confront it—how, in any case, would one do that?—but to get used to the idea of its ineluctability, and also of the suddenness with which it may visit. "How can we ever rid ourselves of thoughts of death," he writes, "or stop imagining that death has us by the scruff of the neck at every moment." Better to familiarize oneself with the idea. "Let us deprive death of its strangeness," he wrote, "let us frequent it, let us get used to it; let us have nothing more often in mind than death." Montaigne himself claims regularly to have been besieged by thoughts of death, "even in the most licentious period of my life."

Montaigne had a continuing curiosity about how great men died, as don't we all, down to wanting to know their last words. "When judging another's life," he wrote, "I always look to see how its end was borne; and one of my main concerns for my own is that it be borne well—that is, in a quiet and muted manner." All learning, he believed, was to make us ready for the end, to prepare us for death. "To Philosophize Is to Learn How to Die" is the title of his essay, and major statement, on the subject. He hoped that when death finally did appear, "it will bear no new warning for me. As far as we possibly can we must have our boots on, ready to go." His death at the age of 59 in 1592 was by quinsy, a disease caused by an abscess of tissue around the tonsils, which can be painful, and in his case had the side effect of rendering him, this most articulate of men, unable to speak.

Can one follow Montaigne's advice to keep death always in mind? I'm far from certain that any but a serious depressive can. F. Scott Fitzgerald, who died at 44, wrote that a state of mild depression is perfectly sensible for a man of middle age; what he has to be depressed about, of course, is the recognition that the clock is running. Philip Larkin, in his fifties, assuming a normal life span of 70, wrote to a friend that if each decade be taken as a day of the week, he, then in his middle 50s, was already up to Friday afternoon. Larkin, who may well have been a depressive, usually an amusing one, wrote the darkest modern poem about death, "Aubade," whose first stanza reads:

> I work all day, and get half-drunk at night.
> Waking at four to soundless dark, I stare.
> In time the curtain-edges will grow light.
> Till then I see what's really always there:
> Unresting death, a whole day nearer now,
> Making all thought impossible but how
> And where and when I shall myself die.
> Arid interrogation: yet the dread
> Of dying, and being dead,
> Flashes afresh to hold and horrify.

Philip Larkin checked out at 63.

If I could think about death with greater regularity, it would probably drag me down. "Act your age" was an old exhortation of parents and grammar-school teachers, but I find that, now as then, I am not easily able to act mine, or even to keep it for very long firmly in mind. Of course I know I am going to die, rather sooner than later, but what does that have to do with my needing a haircut, that there is a Bulls game on television tonight, or that I have to remember to pick up my dry cleaning on Thursday?

In his diary, Thomas Mann records the death of a friend named Jakob Wassermann, then adds, "No need to note the fact that the death of this good friend and contemporary raises with particular vividness the question of how much longer I myself will live." Mann was 58 at the time he wrote this, and would go on living until he was 80. Many of my dearest friends have been six or seven years older than I, and several of them are now dead, which causes me to ask the same question Mann poses: How much longer for me?

Thomas Mann is one of the writers that Victor Brombert, the cosmopolitan literary critic, considers in *Musings on Mortality*.* Brombert, born in France, has for many years taught comparative literature at Princeton. The writers he considers, in elegantly summarizing essays, are, along with Mann, Tolstoy, Kafka, Virginia Woolf, Albert Camus, Giorgio Bassani (author of *The Garden of the Finzi-Continis*), J. M. Coetzee, and Primo Levi.

An odd lot, these writers, when one considers that two of them (Woolf and Levi) committed suicide, one (Kafka) longed for death, another (Camus) died at 47 in a car accident, and J. M. Coetzee does not seem a writer near the caliber of the others. *Death in Venice*, the main work taken up in his Thomas Mann chapter, strikes me as more about decadence than about death, though in the novella the one leads to the other. The suicide of Adrian Leverkühn in Mann's *Doctor Faustus* is another artist's death. Gustav von Aschenbach of *Death in Venice* is a writer too enamored by beauty, Leverkühn a composer who has made a pact with the devil to advance his art, both of which suggest that high art and death

---

* University of Chicago Press, 200 pages.

are somehow allied. In his published *Diary*, George F. Kennan, who lived to 101, notes that "there comes a point, in fact, where beauty, for its reckless devotees, becomes the advocate of death against life."

The one writer relentlessly obsessed by death in Professor Brombert's study was Tolstoy. The death of Prince Andrei Bolkonsky in *War and Peace* is surely the most powerful such scene in all of Western literature. (The worst is in Dickens's *The Old Curiosity Shop*, about which Oscar Wilde remarked that "one must have a heart of stone to read the death of Little Nell without laughing.") No stronger extended fictional account exists than Tolstoy's story "The Death of Ivan Ilych." Brombert writes: "Tolstoy's singular achievement is that he conveys Ivan Ilych's terror in the face of death not in philosophical or abstract terms but as a subjective and visceral experience." Ivan Ilych's death provides the lesson that we all deceive ourselves when we forget about death, and only death gives us true insight into the meaning, or want of meaning, in our lives.

Tolstoy's own death came when he fled his family at the age of 82 over domestic turmoil between his wife and his disciples. He met his end in a station-master's cottage at the Astapovo train station, a day's journey from his estate at Yasnaya Polyana. His became one of the first celebrity deaths, with journalists and news cameras and gendarmes on the scene, hanging around awaiting word of his demise. A sad way to depart the planet, but then at the close of his own life, Tolstoy, who wrote a brief story called "Croesus and Fate," might well have recalled the Athenian statesman Solon's remark to King Croesus upon the latter's bragging about his wealth and well-being: "Call no man happy until he is dead."

Some of the best pages in *Musings on Mortality* are those in which Brombert conveys his own thoughts on death. At 91, he is (as they say in the NFL) hearing footsteps. His first encounter with death, he reports, was that of his pet canary when he was a little boy. The revulsion never left him; so strong was it that while serving as an American soldier in World War II, he "averted [his] eyes even when the dead soldier was a member of an SS unit." He went through the war with a heightened sense of his own vulnerability. He carries with him to this day the mental picture of the faces of his parents in their caskets. He refers to his *réveil mortel*, or mortal alarm clock, noting that he is the

last survivor of all the men in the two units with whom he landed on
a beach at Normandy. Each day he averages up the ages of those whose
names appear in the daily obituaries.

I myself not only read the obits, but do so before all else in the paper. A
good day in the obituaries for me is one in which everyone who has died
is above 90; a poor one is one on which everyone listed is younger than I.
Henry James remarked that, at the age of 50, someone he knows dies every
week. With the increased longevity since James's time to our own, I'd say the
age currently is closer to 70. I cannot say, like James, that someone I know
dies every week; someone I know dies every month is closer to it. Sometimes people I know die in clusters of three or four. My friend Edward Shils,
who died at 85, used to warn on such occasions, "Be careful, Joseph, the
machine-gunner is out." I find myself thinking of the dear friends who have
died, with foreknowledge that they will soon enough be followed by many
more. If one turns out to be long-lived, part of the deal is that of the friends
one most cares about, more are likely to be dead than alive.

At the end of his book, Victor Brombert writes:

> André Malraux's oracular pronouncements come to mind,
> as does his unverifiable, though inspiriting, notion that the
> first caveman who felt compelled to draw a bison on the
> stone wall of his cave knew that both he and the bison were
> mortal but that this first artificer also intuited that the act
> of depicting the perishable animal was somehow a way "to
> negate our nothingness."

Is art a stay of sorts against death, a consolation, a reprieve at least of a
philosophical kind? Not for most of us it isn't; it isn't for me, for whom
art has a high standing. Along with the absence of atheists, there are no
aesthetes in foxholes.

The only consolation for death that I know is the belief that one is
going on to something better. That conviction is not available to those
who feel they have outgrown religion or who have never been able to
achieve faith and have put what faith they possess in science. What comfort can a belief in science afford? In Willa Cather's *The Professor's House*,
Professor St. Peter remarks to a student:

I don't myself think much of science as a phase of human development. It has given us a lot of ingenious toys; they take our attention away from the real problems, of course, and since the problems are insoluble, I suppose we ought to be grateful for distraction.

Professor St. Peter continues:

Science hasn't given us any new amazements, except of the superficial kind we get from witnessing dexterity and sleight-of-hand. It hasn't given us any richer pleasures as the Renaissance did, nor any new sins—not one! Indeed, it takes our old ones away. . . . I don't think you help people by making their conduct of no importance—you impoverish them.

Professor St. Peter's view is that in losing religion we have lost the "gorgeous drama with God," in which men and women believed in "the mystery and importance of their own little individual lives." The drama of which he speaks is that of salvation, revolving around the question of whether one will have been found good enough in the eyes of God to be worthy of a happy afterlife. I'm not sure how many people I know believe in an afterlife. Serious Catholics still do. Seven or eight years ago, a neighbor of mine, a woman who had never married, told me that she didn't in the least fear death but only worried about dying with complications and in pain. As a Catholic, she was confident of her destination after death.

Without belief in an afterlife, there is only death, the anesthesia from which none come round. As for the dying, all one is left with is the hope against hope that one will have drawn one of the better exit cards, dying of old age, congestive heart failure, sudden heart attack, and not Alzheimer's or Lou Gehrig's, or Parkinson's or one of those cancers that leave slack for hope that, after the best efforts of chemistry, ultimately doesn't come to fruition.

NOT ALWAYS BUT OFTEN the people who most fear death are those who feel they have never begun living. These tend to be people who have not got much joy from work or who have little if anything invested in family life. The psychiatrist Leslie Farber noted that "death may be feared occasionally in maturity when life seems to have been unlived, when death would be seen as premature." Children, who often bring worry and sometimes sadness, also give one a sense of futurity, the feeling that a part of one goes on after one has oneself departed the planet, that one has left something behind, a trace of evidence, however imperishable itself, that one was oneself here.

In the 1970s, death, you should pardon the expression, was a hot topic. Courses were taught in thanatology, therapy for those left behind was on offer, a woman named Elisabeth Kübler-Ross wrote a book that told everyone about the five stages of grieving. Death was, in effect, being social-scientized. The point of all these exercises was to come to terms with death.

In a brilliant essay titled "O Death, Where Is Thy Sting-a-Ling-a-Ling?" published in *Commentary* in 1977, Leslie Farber demolished the notion that it could be done. His distaste for the experts on death was owing to their hubris in thinking they could be able to

> capture death—to tame it, domesticate it, draw it out of its absolute otherness into the realm of the living, where its mystery will be dispelled by the sweet, resolute counsels of enlightenment, and its significance will be revealed as just another, albeit a crucial, experience in life.

Death, Farber felt, could not be demystified. According to Farber,

> a death perspective, with its wholesale poignancy, cherishing everything temporal, therefore cherishing everything, will swallow up these meanings in an all-purpose "significance" which, valuing everything, cheapens all.

Such notions, like those promulgated by Kübler-Ross, that death is little more than a transition from one form of life to another, he properly mocks. "For myself," he concludes, "I don't think death has been brought down from the mountain. I can hear it howling up there on some dark nights, just as all men everywhere have heard it." The French philosopher Alain, visiting a friend who was suffering from depression after having recently undergone serious surgery, told him that it was natural to feel depressed. Surgery, after all, was an insult to the body, and it was perfectly natural to feel low after undergoing it. Alain advised his friend to give way to his depression, to let go, and feel as depressed as he liked—only, he added, not to let this depression get him down. Leslie Farber's advice on death, were he alive today—he died at 68 of a heart attack, four years after writing that essay—might not be dissimilar. Perfectly natural to think about death, to be befuddled and anxious and even terrified of it, but it would be a mistake to let it spoil your day.

Truth is, most of us don't. We keep our appointments, cherish our small victories, suffer our defeats; if moderately well-balanced, we recognize our true insignificance without letting it interfere with attempting to realize our dreams. If we are serious about our religion and we feel we have lived decent lives, the question of the afterlife will have been settled. For those of us—I include myself here—who do not closely follow the dictates of a religion yet believe in a higher power ruling the universe, we have to seek such wisdom on the subject of death where we can find it.

I must confess that I haven't found much, or at least not much that is reassuring. Plato devotes many pages to the subject of the afterlife, but provides little in the way of solace in settling the question. The *Phaedo*, Plato's main dialogue on death and the afterlife, remains unconvincing. The setting of the dialogue is the morning of the day that Socrates, having been found guilty by the Athenian democracy of undermining the gods and corrupting the youth of Athens, is awaiting the hemlock he is to take later in the day. Socrates, being the great philosopher he was, spends his last hours talking with some of his followers about the life he expects after being put to death, a life lived "more abundantly" than the one he is about to depart.

The argument of the *Phaedo* is that the man best prepared for death, by having "trained himself throughout his life to live in a state as close as possible to death," should be the last to be distressed by death. Such a man is likely to have been a philosopher, who has been initiated and enlightened, purified, and he "shall dwell among the gods," while "the uninitiated and the unenlightened shall lie in the mire." Because he himself has been among those who "have lived the philosophical life in the right way," Socrates says, "a company I have done my best in every way to join, leaving nothing undone which I could do to attain this end," he is confident that in the next life he will "find there, no less than here, good rulers and good friends." He will be in a place that is "invisible, divine, immortal, and wise" where, on arrival, his soul will find happiness awaiting and "release from uncertainty and folly, from fears and uncontrolled desires, and all other human evils and where, as they say of the initiates in the Mysteries, it really spends the rest of its time with the gods." Further talk in the dialogue, all of it extremely vague, has to do with transmigration of souls. Plato's eschatology is as richly complicated as it is unbelievable. Wouldn't it be a lot easier, one thinks after reading the *Phaedo*, to believe in the Trinity or await the Messiah and let it go at that.

66 NOTHING CONCENTRATES A MAN'S MIND more than the prospect of being hanged in the morning," observed Samuel Johnson. I'm not so sure. The night before my triple-bypass heart surgery in 1997, I remember, with the aid of a Valium, sleeping decently. I awoke the next morning and showered with a special surgical disinfectant soap. My wife drove me to the hospital. I joked with the nurse who gave me preliminary anesthesia, and the next thing I recall is waking to be told by my heart surgeon, at 2 a.m., that I had to be returned to surgery owing to a blood clot. "This sounds like a very bad idea to me," I remember saying. He answered that he was less concerned about me than about my wife, who was terribly worried when he told her. This is of course a story with a happy ending, as you will have gathered, but, though I greatly wanted to avoid this surgery, when the time for it arrived I went through it calmly enough. Was more than the Valium behind this calm?

The truth is that I have been waiting to die for quite some while now. I do not wish to die, certainly not until, as Socrates says, "life has no more to offer." I've not found that life has anywhere near run out of delight for me. I've never considered suicide, though I have, at different times, out of spiritual fatigue, thought I would welcome death. "All is finite," wrote Santayana, "all is to end, all is bearable—that is my only comfort."

Yet, though, contra Dylan Thomas, I hope to be allowed to go gently into that good night, I do not figure to welcome death when it arrives. Like everyone else, I take blood tests with my annual physical, and each year I expect the results to be disastrous, showing I have three different cancers, Parkinson's, incipient Lou Gehrig's, and what looks like Alzheimer's well on its way. I am waiting, in other words, for both shoes to fall.

When they do, I shall not be shocked or even surprised, but disappointed nonetheless. I have had a good and lucky run, having been born to honorable and intelligent parents in the most interesting country in the world during a period of unrivaled prosperity and vast technological advance. I prefer to think I've got the best out of my ability, and have been properly appreciated for what I've managed to accomplish. One may regard one's death as a tragic event, or view it as the ineluctable conclusion to the great good fortune of having been born to begin with. I'm going with the latter.

Unless the Dirty Tricks Department, which is always very active, gets to me, and makes my final years, months, days on Earth a hell of pain and undignified suffering, I shall regret my departure from life. On his deathbed, Goethe's last words are said to have been, "More light, more light." Gertrude Stein, on hers, asked, "What is the answer?" and when no one replied, laughed and asked, "Then what is the question?" I don't have a final draft of my own deathbed words, but I do have a theme, which is unembarrassed thanksgiving.

Wit

(2015)

True Wit is Nature to advantage dress'd,
What oft was thought but ne're so well express'd.
—ALEXANDER POPE, "An Essay on Criticism"

WIT IS ONE OF THE TEN WORDS investigated by C. S. Lewis in his *Studies in Words*. He tells us that "wit" was first used to connote "mind, reason, intelligence," fundamental good sense. Then its meaning changed to suggest a person's entire mental make-up. Then it rose in aesthetic significance to convey the imaginative skill of poets and other artists. "I take it that wit in the sense now current means that sort of mental agility or gymnastic which uses language as the principal equipment of its gymnasium," Lewis wrote. The word in our day describes all verbal cleverness, usually of the kind delivered orally. Pun, epigram, repartee, amusing paradox, surprising juxtaposition—these are among the verbal machines on which, to stay with Lewis's gymnasium metaphor, wit works out.

In imaginative writing—novels, movies, plays, poems—wit in this sense is most frequently found in clever dialogue; or in lyrics of the kind Ira Gershwin, Cole Porter, and Lorenz Hart wrote; or in works of non-fiction in amusing formulations. Falstaff, Shakespeare's wittiest character, was himself an artist of verbal wit, the Falstaff who said, "I am not only witty in myself, but the cause that wit is in other men." Written, or literary, wit had a good run in the 18th century: in the plays of William Congreve and Richard Sheridan, in the poetry of Alexander Pope, and in the various works of Jonathan Swift. Wit plays throughout Edward Gibbon's *Decline and Fall*, as in his footnote on the Emperor Gordian II:

> Twenty-two acknowledged concubines, and a library of sixty-two thousand volumes, attested the variety of his inclinations, and from the productions which he left behind him, it appears that the former as well as the latter were designed for use rather than ostentation.

Wit has come to find its consummation in conversation. Talk is now its main medium, unrehearsed talk in which someone says something so dazzling as to be memorable. Wit is not, as in writing, evoked in tranquility, but is instead, as Benjamin Errett defines it in *Elements of Wit*, "spontaneous creativity." Wit, though generally humorous, needs to be distinguished from humor, which can be created at leisure, polished through revision, and even tested upon focus groups to insure it works. "Unlike humor," Errett writes, "wit is a speed game."

That wit wasn't always what it is today, a form of brilliant and memorable talk, is attested by such idioms and words as "at wit's end," "dimwit," and "halfwit." All of these denote the connection between wit and common sense. The dimwit and the half-wit are of course deficient in such sense; to be at wit's end denotes finding oneself in a situation in which normal common sense is of no avail. Today, one is more likely to see wit applied as a label to public personalities who are thought to be clever; for example, that well-known wit . . . Joseph Epstein.

I have never thought myself a wit, but some years ago, in reviewing a book of mine on snobbery, William F. Buckley, Jr. called me "perhaps the wittiest writer (working in his genre) alive, the funniest since Randall Jarrell." The quotation has turned up as the last line in my Wikipedia entry, with the result that, on the rare occasions when I give a talk or lecture, I am generally introduced as—all qualifications dropped—"the wittiest writer alive." When this occurs, I hasten to tell my audience that I hope they will not be disappointed when, after four or five minutes into my talk, they come to find Mr. Buckley's generous contention not merely dubious but definitively disproved.

I wish it were otherwise, but I am not witty. What I believe I am is mildly charming. Charm is the ability to arouse approval for oneself, to seem socially adept. Wit is a more precise skill. Oscar Levant claimed never "to stoop to charm." Unlike charming people, witty ones can offend, and often don't care if they do. I myself prefer to be liked rather than admired for such shreds of wit as I do possess.

As a would-be charmer, I have over the years built up a store of anecdotes and fairly sure-fire jokes that I can trot out when needed. I can drop an interesting quotation with what I hope is lightness of touch. I am alert to the comedy of language, and often play off its absurdities, subverting clichés, twisting idioms, doing English in foreign accents. Like the character Sloppy reading the newspapers in *Our Mutual Friend*, I "do the police in different voices." I also have a taste for whimsy. Late one afternoon when my sons were growing up, I was at the stove making Italian meat sauce and asked them, as I put a spoonful of sugar into the pot, what movie my doing this reminded them of: the answer was *Absorba the Grease* after, of course, *Zorba the Greek*. (My children's upbringing, plainly, wasn't an easy one.) None of this, strictly speaking, is wit.

Wit, when available to me at all, is possible only when I can create it in tranquility, on the page, or now increasingly on the computer screen, where there is ample room for rehearsal, as aspiring but inadequate wits might think of revision. But wit in its sense of quick and amusing and often devastating riposte, is not my speciality. *Espirit d'escalier*, or staircase wit, the witty response that occurs to one too late, is for me rather closer to it.

During my last teaching days, in a course I taught on Henry James, I asked a student named Jonathan Stern to describe the character Gilbert Osmond from James's *The Portrait of a Lady*. Without the least intent to offend his teacher or evoke laughter from his classmates, he declared Osmond "an asshole." I seemed to be the only one in the room shocked by his response, and I told him, calmly, that I would allow each student in the course one such word, and he had now used up his allowance. Only later, leaving class, actually walking down the stairs, did it occur to me that what I should have said was, "I'm pleased, Mr. Stern, that I didn't ask you to describe Oedipus Rex."

I have been in the regular company of only one genuinely witty man, my friend Edward Shils. When I told Edward of a mutual acquaintance of ours having recently informed me that, in Prague, where he grew up, his father never shaved himself but always had a barber come in to do so, Edward replied, "You know, Joseph, the truth more likely is that his father shaved his mother." I once introduced Edward to the English journalist Henry Fairlie. Edward mentioned that he had heard Fairlie had become a socialist, and asked him to explain how this came about. Fairlie replied that he owed his conversion to hearing Michael Harrington speak in Chicago. "Michael Harrington in Chicago?" said Edward. "Surely a case of worst comes to worst." Of David Reisman, his colleague at the University of Chicago, who attempted to pass himself off as a WASP, Edward remarked, "I'll say this for David, he's never taken undue advantage of being Jewish."

Edward Shils taught half the year at Cambridge in England, a country where the tradition for wit is stronger than it has been in America. Maurice Bowra exemplified high-table Oxbridge wit. When someone told Bowra that the woman he was courting, the niece of Sir Thomas Beecham, was a lesbian, Bowra, himself reputed to be homosexual, replied, "Buggers can't be choosers." Noël Coward noted that "having to read footnotes resembles having to go downstairs to answer the door while in the midst of making love." Evelyn Waugh, surely the wittiest novelist of the past century, in World War II, coming out of a bunker during a German bombing of Yugoslavia, looked up at the sky raining enemy bombs and remarked, "Like everything German, vastly overdone." Kingsley Amis said that "laziness has become the chief characteristic of journalism, displacing incompetence." From *Beyond the Fringe* to *Monty Python*, English humor at its higher echelons featured wit.

Only a few traces of wit show up in Edward Shils's writing. No one knew about it who didn't know him personally; knowledge of his quick cleverness was restricted to his students and his friends. The great wits of the past century found means to have their witty remarks broadcast well beyond their social circle. Among the wits discussed in Errett's *Elements of Wit* are Sydney Smith, Mark Twain, Oscar Wilde, Dorothy Parker, Groucho Marx, Winston Churchill, Mae West, George Bernard Shaw,

Robert Benchley, and Oscar Levant. Missing are H. L. Mencken, W. C. Fields, Noël Coward, Billy Wilder, and George S. Kaufman. An obvious neurotic, Kaufman, when asked why he left psychotherapy after only a few sessions, claimed, "the guy asked too many goddamn personal questions." A relentless philanderer, Kaufman told Irving Berlin that he liked his song "Always," but would prefer it if he changed the title to "Thursdays."

I learned about these Kaufman quips from a biography of Kaufman by Howard Teichmann. Many of Churchill's best mots are recorded in other people's memoirs. Oscar Wilde made a show of his epigrams, paradoxes, and comic aphorisms ("A cynic is someone who knows the price of everything and the value of nothing.") while on tour in America. Traveling round the United States, he put himself perpetually on exhibit, his witty remarks picked up by the press that accompanied him; they accompanied him, in fact, chiefly because his remarks made good copy. The wittiest things said during the 1920s and '30s at the Algonquin Round Table found their way into Franklin Pierce Adams's "Conning Tower" column in the old *New York World* and later the *New York Herald-Tribune*. Oscar Levant, who let it all hang out before the phrase was invented, made many of his more outlandish remarks on the old *Jack Paar Show*, and on his own talk show before he was fired for going too far with a joke about Arthur Miller and Marilyn Monroe, oral sex, and keeping kosher. Wits without fame do not get their brilliant lines recorded, at least not in the past they didn't. The Internet, as we shall see, is changing this, at least somewhat.

Elements of Wit, like the Strunk and White book on composition after which it is titled, is pedagogical in intent. The book sets out on the project of teaching wit by precept and example. Along with offering mini-profiles of some famous wits of the past and present, Benjamin Errett (a Canadian journalist) provides discussion of the role of wit in improv theater; the effect of alcohol on lubricating and loosening wit; and the need for brevity, the soul, after all, of wit. He quotes from various studies on wit and humor; and, inevitably, as is de rigueur these days, he brings in far-from-convincing brain studies and ponders the connection of the physiology of the brain to the creation of wit.

At one point, Errett provides a list of 11 contemporary wits. The list includes Russell Brand, Gail Collins, Louis C. K., Nora Ephron, Tina

Fey, Christopher Hitchens, Fran Lebowitz, Steve Martin, Amy Poehler, Tom Stoppard, and Kanye West. The rapper Jay-Z, to whom he devotes several pages, is another of his models for wit in action.

Not all these contemporary wits pass Errett's definition of wit as "spontaneous creation." We learn that Steve Martin worked out his stand-up comedian's bits over time, so that little of the finished product of his wit can be said to have been spontaneous. Much of Tina Fey's wit was scripted for her television shows. Is Russell Brand sufficiently amusing to earn the title? Louis C.K. passes for witty if one's taste runs to masturbation jokes. Jay-Z's rap music, much of it created at the moment of recording, may be spontaneous, but does it truly qualify as witty? Lots of things—sarcasm, invective, obscenity—can be created spontaneously without being witty.

Would Christopher Hitchens have seemed witty without an English accent? Wasn't Hitchens, a man who gave the title *The Missionary Position* to his book-length attack on Mother Teresa, more a provocateur than a wit? Is there a great difference between Nora Ephron's complaining about age doing in her neck and the newspaper columnist Erma Bombeck's writing about the travails of being a housewife—any difference, really, apart from Ephron having had a fancier address and a flashier social set? In the few interviews I have seen with Tom Stoppard, his seriousness easily eclipses his wit. Are these cavils merely? Or do they suggest the lowering of standards on what passes for wit in our time?

Another of Errett's definitions of wit is "good sense that sparkles." He prefers cheerful wit; like Joseph Addison, whom he quotes, his taste runs to wit that "gives delight and surprise." Errett defines snark as wit that "scorches." Yet much wit is dark, and lots of the richest wit is outrageous. Think of the late Sue Mengers, the movie agent, who walked into a less than exclusive Hollywood party and remarked to a friend: "Schindler's B-list." After the Charles Manson murders, Mengers is supposed to have told her client Barbra Streisand, "Don't worry, honey, they're only killing bit players." Saul Bellow, whose propensity for saying witty things sometimes got him in trouble, wrote a story called "Him with His Foot in His Mouth," about a man who regularly wounded people because he could not control making offensively witty remarks. The wittiest remark in the story belongs not to the story's narrator but to an older scholar whose boredom is obvious when the narrator reads his scholarly article to him. The narrator asks if he is causing the scholar to fall asleep, to which the scholar answers, "No, you're keeping me awake."

Wit is meant to be pleasing, but as often as not it can be cruel. John Simon makes the point that humor is "basically good natured and often directed toward oneself," while wit is "aggressive, often destructive . . . and almost always directed at others." When Clare Boothe Luce held open a door for Dorothy Parker and said "Age before beauty," Miss Parker, passing through, replied, "Pearls before swine." Such examples of aggressive wit are generally the most memorable. What stays in the mind are the stabbing riposte, the ripping repartee, the punishing put-down.

Errett bridles at the thought that wit is no more than "clever nastiness." In his view "wit is the thought process that generates truly funny observations, as well as the most incisive comments, lasting quips and brilliant asides." Perhaps his cheerful outlook on the subject of wit compelled him to neglect entirely Gore Vidal, a figure often on the list of contemporary wits. If Vidal had had a motto, it might have been, "If you can't say something nasty, then say nothing at all." But Vidal fails the first test of wittiness, which is unpredictability. Predictability is death for wit, and Vidal's wit was always predictable. Apart from those of his mots devoted to slightly perverse sexual matters—"I am all for bringing back the birch, but only between consenting adults," is an example—most of the rest are about the crummy, inane, deceitful plutocracy that for him was America. Vidal paraded this merchandise on every talk show that would have him. "I never miss a chance to have sex or appear on television," is another of his mots. One knew what was coming before he opened his mouth; it was only a question of how mean he would be.

Defying anticipation in a way that is both amusing and causing one's auditors to take thought is one of the hallmarks of genuine wit. Of Doris Day, Oscar Levant remarked: "I knew her before she became a virgin." Fran Lebowitz, remarking that it's impossible not to notice that children in America are more and more protected and to a later and later age, claimed that "the man who invents the first shaving mirror for strollers is going to make a fortune."

If asked to choose an ideal, a perfect, wit, my candidate would be Sydney Smith, the early 19th-century clergyman who was one of the founders of the *Edinburgh Review*. Errett devotes a few sparse paragraphs to Smith in his book, but not enough to capture the splendor of a true wit at work. The actress Fannie Kemble wrote that "the fanciful and inexhaustible humorous drollery of his [Smith's] conversation among his intimates can never be adequately rendered or reproduced." A young Benjamin Disraeli, himself a famously witty man, was once seated next to Sydney Smith at a dinner party and found him "delightful. . . . I don't remember a more agreeable party." Others reported that they could not remember what he said because in his company they laughed so much. Sydney Smith spoke almost exclusively in mots, lovely metaphors, witty formulations. He said of the garrulous Lord Macaulay that his conversation contained "some gorgeous flashes of silence." He likened his life as a reviewer and sometimes polemicist to that of a razor, always "either in hot water or scrapes." Of two women screaming insults at each other from their apartments across a narrow street, he said: "Those two women will never agree. They are arguing from different premises."

Does wit come naturally or can one acquire it through effort and training? The assumption behind *Elements of Wit* is that it can be acquired. "Creative spontaneity," Errett writes, "takes practice." Yet his book casts doubt on the notion that wit, even among the most famous wits, really is created spontaneously. Winston Churchill, he informs us, was a reader of *Bartlett's Familiar Quotations* and in search of material for conversation sedulously read jokes columns in newspapers. "His magpie mind drew from books, film, media, and anywhere else he read, heard, or saw a line worth repeating." Errett does not mention La Rochefoucauld, the world's wittiest aphorist, who worked with his friend and lover Madame de Lafayette at burnishing his aphorisms before bringing them out for display in the salons of Mme de Rambouillet and Mme de Sablé, where they were further polished. Might it be that a great deal of what passes for wit—for, in Errett's term, "spontaneous creation"—isn't spontaneous at all but has been carefully worked up beforehand?

The leading forum for the display of wit in our days ought to be the television talk show. Yet one doesn't think of any of the talk-show hosts, now and in the past, as especially witty, if only because all employed or currently employ a cadre of writers who supply them with much of the material that passes for their own wit, though some among them ad lib cleverly. The same, one suspects, may well be true of ostensibly witty talk-show guests, who are often coached about what questions they will be asked and what subjects they can expect to discuss.

Are dazzling wits possible in our day? No reason why they shouldn't be, though how we might come to know about them is unclear. Might such a wit be someone out there sending witty tweets to friends? The form of the tweet, with its limit of 140 characters, could work to force a tweeter into concise wit. The closing pages of *The Elements of Wit* offer some amusing tweets. "So now Blagojevich has been double impeached, which sounds like a Ben & Jerry flavor," isn't at all bad; nor is this, "the most beautiful tweet ever tweeted," as chosen by Stephen Fry: "I believe we can build a better world! Of course, it'll take a whole lot of rock, water & dirt. Also not sure where to put it." I do not myself tweet—to do so would be unseemly in a man of my august age—but I have followed a couple of friends on Twitter, one of whose tweets are consistently amusing. If Twitter does create a new conveyance for wit, a new word for those who display their wit on it will be required—a twit-wit, perhaps.

As for whether wit can be taught, my own sense is that it cannot. Honed and sharpened it can be, but it has to be there to begin with. As Aristotle, in the *Poetics*, said about metaphor, so one might say about wit: "It is the one thing that cannot be learned; it is also a sign of genius." Wit, in other words, is a gift. But without an interesting point of view, a detached angle on life, a wide culture, the gift will come to naught. Wit is the expression of those who understand and are able to formulate and deflate in a pleasing way what they see as pretension, false self-esteem, empty ambition, snobbery, and much else worth mocking in life. We need wits on the scene, like doctors on the case. Without them to remind us how absurd we can be, we fall into the grave danger of taking ourselves altogether too seriously.

Genius

(2013)

A happy genius is the gift of nature: it depends on the influence
of the stars say the astrologers, on the organs of the body, say
the naturalists; 'tis the particular gift of heaven, say the divines,
both Christians and heathens. How to improve it, many books
can teach us; how to obtain it, none: that nothing can be done
without it all agree.

—JOHN DRYDEN, *A Parallel of Poetry and Painting*

I HAVE MET SIX NOBEL PRIZEWINNERS and none has come close in
my view to qualifying as a genius. Three won the prize for economics; all of these were supremely confident, no doubt highly intelligent, but, I thought, insufficiently impressed by the mysteries of life. One
of these Nobel laureates won his prize for physics, but in my company he
wished to talk only about Shakespeare, on which he was commonplace
and extremely boring. Another won a Nobel Prize for biology, yet seemed
to me, outside the laboratory, a man without the least subtlety. The last
won his Nobel Prize for literature, and the most profound thing about him
was the extent to which he had screwed up his personal life. Somehow it is
always sensible to remember that in 1949 the Nobel Prize in medicine was
given to Antonio Egas Moniz, a Portuguese surgeon, for developing the
procedure known as the lobotomy.

Genius is rare. Schopenhauer thought a genius was one in a hundred
million. In this realm if in no other, that most pessimistic of philosophers may have been optimistic. Distinguishing between a man of learning and a genius, Schopenhauer wrote: "A man of learning is a man who

has learned a great deal; a man of genius, one from whom we learn something which the genius has learned from nobody." A genius is not merely brilliant, skillful, masterly, sometimes dazzling; he is miraculous, in the sense that his presence on earth cannot be predicted, explained, or accounted for (at least thus far) by natural laws or scientific study. The definitions for genius may be greater than the actual number of true geniuses who have walked the earth. My own definition is as follows: Be he a genius of thought, art, science, or politics, a genius changes the way the rest of us hear or see or think about the world.

The word *genius*, like many another (superstar, icon, fabulous), has undergone much inflation in recent decades. Football coaches are called geniuses, so too successful hedge-fund operators and chefs. "We are lucky to be living in an age of genius," the editors of *Esquire* proclaimed in 1999 when they ran an issue devoted to the subject. Their candidates for genius included, among others, the actor Leonardo DiCaprio, the basketball player Allen Iverson, the designer Tom Ford, the foreign policy pundit Fareed Zakaria, the chef Thomas Keller, a computer scientist named Bill Joy, and Jeff Bezos of Amazon.com. Handsome, skillful, talented, fraudulent, immensely successful, whatever else they are, none of these men is a genius, not even close.

The first question about genius is, in the root sense, existential: Does genius truly exist? Although he had himself earlier fallen for what he took to be the genius of Richard Wagner, in his later writings Friederich Nietzsche thought not. In his *Late Notebooks*, Nietzsche referred to "the superstition of our [the nineteenth] century, the superstitious belief in genius." In *Human, All Too Human*, he wrote:

> Because we think well of ourselves, but in no way expect that we could ever make the sketch to a painting by Raphael or a scene like one in a play by Shakespeare, we convince ourselves that the ability to do so is quite excessively wonderful, a quite uncommon accident, or, if we still have a religious sensibility, a grace from above.

The genius, whether in science or art, was for Nietzsche not in the least miraculous if only because he didn't really exist.

Nietzsche held that the belief in genius, along with being irrational, was of most danger to those who come to believe in their own genius. As a case in point, he cites Napoleon, whose belief in his own genius "turned into an almost mad fatalism, robbed him of his quick, penetrating eye, and became the cause of his downfall." Nietzsche's own dubiety about genius did not stop a cult of genius from forming around him, with many acolytes in the approved German manner, even before he was dead.

A distinction needs to be made between genius and talent. "Talent is like the marksman who hits a target, which others cannot reach," wrote Schopenhauer, "genius is like the marksman who hits a target, which others cannot see." Mere talent cannot hope to rival genius, but neither can genius dispense with talent. "Talent without genius isn't much," wrote Paul Valery, "but genius without talent is nothing whatsoever." On good days, I am talented. Shakespeare was a genius every day.

Who and who is not an authentic genius is a question always up for dispute. Dante, Shakespeare, and Tolstoy are on most lists of geniuses. So, too, among the ancients, Homer, Socrates, Plato, Aristotle. Bach, Beethoven, and Mozart are the indisputable musical geniuses. Leonardo da Vinci and Michelangelo and Raphael make the cut in the visual arts. So in science do Euclid, Galileo, Kepler, Newton, and Darwin. In politics Pericles, Alexander the Great, Julius and Augustus Caesar, Napoleon, Winston Churchill, Mahatma Gandhi would seem to qualify, with Lenin and Hitler and Stalin and Mao Tze-tung falling into the category of evil geniuses.

Secondary geniuses may be added into the mix, those figures who, however glittering their brilliance, have not affected the world in the same fundamental way as have primary geniuses: figures such as Descartes and Pascal, Spinoza and Kant, Titian and Rembrandt and possibly Picasso, Haydn and Handel and Schubert, Dostoyevsky and Dickens. Was Balanchine a genius? Was Matisse? Stravinsky? Or were they merely—some *merely*—great artists?

With the names Karl Marx and Sigmund Freud we enter the murky waters of geniuses who are today perhaps better thought the intellectual equivalent of false messiahs. Marx and Freud each made people see the world very differently than before they wrote, but we now know that they made them see it falsely—most people no longer believe in either the Class Struggle or the Oedipus Complex—and so their license to genius has, in effect, expired.

If you think you are a genius, you probably aren't. "I have nothing to declare except my genius," Oscar Wilde is supposed to have told the agent at customs on Ellis Island when he visited America in 1882. Gertrude Stein announced that the Jews produced only three geniuses, Jesus, Spinoza, and herself. Neither Wilde nor Stein of course was a genius, not even close, and certainly not by any strict definition. Such genius as they possessed was chiefly for self-promotion.

Most people would cite Albert Einstein as the last modern genius, and those with an interest in professional philosophy might add Ludwig Wittgenstein to the relatively recent genius list. As candidates for genius status, Einstein and Wittgenstein have the added allure of having been, not to put too fine a point on it, goofy, for the modern taste in geniuses seems to run to the goofy. In an earlier era, geniuses were felt to be not goofy but strange if not mad. Nietzsche's last years were cloaked with insanity, which seemed to add to his authority. The world's first acknowledged genius, Socrates, was of course himself in many ways strange. An exceedingly ugly man, with astonishing powers of concentration, he was entirely uninterested in honor, wealth, or even minimal material comforts, risked his life in battle, chose to spend his days arguing that he knew nothing while demonstrating that his interlocutors knew even less, and accepted the verdict of the Athenian assembly that he was the enemy of the state and therefore willingly took the hemlock.

Albert Einstein, sockless, in his sweatshirt, with his wild hair and doofus mustache, walked the streets of Princeton looking like nothing so much as the fifth Marx Brother. Wittgenstein, the scion of a wealthy and neurotic Viennese family, shed his personal fortune and went in for corporeal punishment when he taught young children in Austria. Jewish, homosexual, hot-tempered, he was, as Bertrand Russell averred, "the most perfect example I have known of genius as traditionally conceived; passionate, profound, intense, and domineering."

Genius as traditionally conceived is the subject of Darrin M. McMahon's *Divine Fury, A History of Genius*, a work at once erudite and intellectually penetrating and immensely readable. An historian at the Florida State University, McMahon has written what he terms "a history in ideas," by which he means "a long-range intellectual history that examines concepts in multiple contexts across broad expanses of time." Tracing the history of how people have thought about genius from the ancient world to our day, he has, in his own words, teased "out genius's intimate connection to the divine, a connection that few analysts of the subject have explored." Providing many mini-portraits of genius figures along the way, he persuasively argues that genius has never been entirely shorn of the notion of divinity, even in boldly secular ages, and how central the conception of genius has been to the way that different ages have apprehended the world.

Socrates never spoke of his genius, but he did refer to his *daimon*, a spirit that resided within him offering instruction only on what he must not do. For the ancient Greeks, thinkers and artists were believed neither to discover nor create but to find what already existed. Their genius led them to these unveilings. No one was a genius, but a privileged few *had* genius, which was in the providence of the gods, and functioned, as it did for Socrates, as a guardian spirit. As such, genius could be good or evil. One was either born with genius or not; it could not be acquired, but inhabited only those souls the gods inspired—inspire, Professor McMahan notes, means to breath into—to extraordinary deeds.

Professor McMahon doesn't quite say so, but geniuses tend to emerge in those areas of life dominant in specific cultures at specific times. For the Greeks, the main games were philosophy and art. For the Romans it was military exploits and administration, and the only two Romans up for genius whom McMahon mentions prominently are Julius and Augustus Caesar. During the middle ages, devotion and piety, with an emphasis on asceticism and personal sacrifice, won the genius laurels, and the genius that occupied the souls of men and women were thought to be imbued by angels. Augustine and Thomas Aquinas were both made saints. ("Genius," wrote the Russian philosopher Nicolai Berdiaev, "is another kind of sainthood.") For the Renaissance it was art, chiefly visual art, painting and sculpture and architecture, that rang the genius gong. For the modern age, beginning with the 18th century, scientific geniuses predominate. For our own age the main game, once thought to be invention—Thomas Edison,

Henry Ford held genius status for a while—has yet to be determined, especially with so much science now being done not individually but in teams. Hence the paucity of agreed upon geniuses in our day. Those master marketeers of the digital age, Bill Gates and Steve Jobs, need not apply.

The dividing line for our understanding of genius was the eighteenth century. In an emerging secular age, Descartes and Voltaire removed the tutelary angel aspect from the conception of genius. MacMahon reminds us that it was only "in the eighteenth century that Shakespeare was declared a genius." Men were no longer thought to *have* genius but to *be* geniuses. John Locke and Thomas Hobbes took things a step further, arguing that geniuses were not born but made. The English essayist Joseph Addison divided geniuses between natural geniuses (Homer, Pindar, Shakespeare) and what he called "imitative" geniuses, or geniuses of learning (Aristotle, Francis Bacon, John Milton).

The Enlightenment, operating on the suppositions of liberalism, held that if the educational franchise were only sufficiently extended, genius was a possibility for all. "To improve social conditions, widen access to education, and enhance human possibilities," according to Professor MacMahon, "was to extend the frontiers of the republic of genius, enhancing the potential of all." Being in the right place at the right time was thought a necessity for establishing one's genius. Genius, in other words, was being demystified.

The cult of genius was central to the French Revolution. Voltaire, Mirabeau, Rousseau were taken as geniuses by the revolutionaries, and Napoleon was later thought to be the genius child of the revolution. Hegel came up with the notion of "the world-historical individual," of whom Napoleon fitted the mold perfectly. Goethe kept a bust of Napoleon in his study. Beethoven wrote the *Eroica* with Napoleon in mind, though subsequently bailed out of the Napoleon genius cult.

The romantics preferred their geniuses daring like Lord Byron, mystical like William Blake; and tragic like poor John Keats. For them geniuses, simultaneously heroes and martyrs, were blessed with gifts for revelation, and cursed by being at odds with the culture of their time. The ideal type of the genius for the romantic was the poet. Shelley called poets "the unacknowledged legislators of the world"; they were also prophets, who showed and revealed the sacred. Romantic critics—Hazlitt, Coleridge, in America Ralph Waldo Emerson—made the genius out to be above the law, a law unto himself, and in his own way a god.

For the romantics, so for the Germans, where God had been, genius now stood. Genius for Germans became religion by other means, in the sense that the German people took their bearings from their supposed geniuses. Goethe, Schiller, Hegel, von Humboldt, Wagner, Nietzsche, the candidates for genius among them were not few. The one work of fiction with a genius as its hero, Thomas Mann's modern composer Adrian Leverkuhn in *Dr. Faustus*, was of course a rich product of German culture.

The worship of genius on the part of the Germans would one day exact a heavy price. Some of Professor MacMahon's most brilliant pages persuasively set out how the genius cult helped pave the way to power for Adolf Hitler. Even Hitler's failure as an artist played into his reputation and self-regard as a genius. "Far from abandoning his interest in art," MacMahon writes, "Hitler, via politics, pursued aesthetics by other means." In *Mein Kampf*, Hitler announced his own entrance onto the world stage as a genius: "Geniuses of an extraordinary kind do not admit consideration of normal humanity." Even Hitler's madness tended to certify him as a genius, for by the early decades of the twentieth century, everyone knew that geniuses were "touched," in all meanings of the word.

The next obvious step in the demystification of genius was to attempt scientifically to measure it. Here the conflict was between those who took geniuses as miracles of nature and those who took them as the product of their nurture. Eugenicists and others began studying genius, attempting to locate and then quantify it. Much nuttiness followed: the measuring of skulls and brainpans (cranioscopy) and the studying of bumps on heads (phrenology) were for a time thought to supply the key. People even began grave robbing to secure the skulls of long-dead geniuses. The Italian criminologist Cesare Lombroso studied the interrelation of genius, madness, and degenerative disease, producing wild conclusions about the longevity of geniuses and the paucity of the production of genius in topographically flat countries. Genius and climate conditions were added into the mix; in one such treatise, the cold northern European countries were said to be more productive of genius than the warm southern European ones.

In the second half of the nineteenth century, the eugenicist Francis Galton, a cousin of Charles Darwin, sought and failed to prove that genius was hereditary. If it were, then we should have to regret the many geniuses who were childless, when they might have created a rich gene pool. (In the 1980s, an American optometrist named Robert K. Graham, himself distinctly no genius, began a Nobel Prize-winners sperm bank, known as the Repository for Germinal Choice, which, as McMahon notes, "closed it vaults in 1997.") In fact no two geniuses—if one holds to a strict standard—have ever showed up in the same family. A nature trumps nurture man, Galton's ideas for breeding higher intelligence, and hence increasing the prospects of genius, never really got off the ground, though as we sadly know Hitler, in later years, ran with them.

Professor MacMahon calls all these various social- and pseudo-scientific attempts to understand genius "geniology." The best known, of course, was the invention, by the Frenchman Alfred Binet in 1906, of the educational diagnostic tool known as Intelligence Quotient, or IQ. MacMahon writes:

> The immediate goal was to classify those falling below normalcy, but it was readily apparent that an exam of this sort could be used to do the opposite, too, identifying and ranking individuals whose mental ages were above average.

IQ was arrived at by dividing mental age by actual age and then multiplying by 100. What IQ chiefly showed was a propensity, or want thereof, for solving abstract problems. (The Scholastic Aptitude Test, the SAT, similarly, predicts nothing more than one's chances of doing well in college.) Chess players, mathematics wizards, and memory freaks seemed to score highest on IQ tests.

IQ, those who believed in it felt, was innate, and derived from heredity. A man named Lewis Terman was a true believer in the accuracy of IQ. He believed that through using the results of IQ testing carefully, society, in a bit of finely tuned social engineering, could be improved by early marking out the brightest of children and encouraging and ultimately utilizing their talents. "It should go without saying," Terman wrote, that a nation's resources of intellectual talent are among the most precious it will have. The origins of genius, the natural laws of its development, and the environmental influences by which it may be affected for good or ill are scientific problems of almost unequaled importance in human welfare.

In what is known as a longitudinal study, Terman discovered 1,000 children who scored 140 or more on IQ tests—140 was thought to be potential genius level—and arranged to track them through their later lives. None did anything extraordinary, while two children tested at the same time who did not make the 140 IQ cut went on to win Nobel Prizes. In his acknowledgements, Professor MacMahon notes that he was someone who early in life was told his intelligence test results showed him "not the recipient of gifts." He goes on to write:

> There is evidence to suggest that an exaggerated belief in the strength of one's innate capacities can actually harm a child's development, sapping motivation and initiative. And there is even more evidence to show how damaging it can be to tell young people that, according to the numbers, they just don't measure up.

Intelligence, as anyone who has thought at all about it will long ago have concluded, is multi-valent, or of many kinds. Howard Gardner, the Harvard developmental psychologist and the leading investigator of intelligence in our day, has concluded that there are at least seven types of intelligence: linguistic, logical-mathematical, musical, bodily-kinesthetic, spatial, interpersonal, and intrapersonal. (He later added an eighth, naturalist intelligence, or that of people with a gift for observing nature.) Each of us is likely to be better endowed in one or another of these than in the others. "No two people," Gardner concludes, "have exactly the same intelligence in the same combination."

Genius, meanwhile, remains the least understood of all kinds of intelligence. The explanation for the existence of geniuses and accounting for their extraordinary powers have thus far eluded all attempts at scientific study. The intelligence of genius is still, so to say, off the charts. "As yet little is known about the genetics and neurobiology of creative individuals," writes Howard Gardner. "We know neither whether creative individuals have distinctive genetic constitutions, nor whether there is anything remarkable about the structure and functioning of their nervous systems."

I, for one, find it pleasing that science cannot account for genius. I do not myself believe in miracles, but I do have a strong taste for mysteries, and the presence, usually at lengthy intervals, of geniuses is among the great mysteries. Schopenhauer had no explanation for the existence of geniuses, either, but, even while knowing all the flaws inherent in even the greatest among them, he held that geniuses "were the lighthouses of humanity; and without them mankind would lose itself in the boundless sea of error and bewilderment." The genius is able to fulfill this function because he is able to think outside himself, to see things whole while the rest of us at best see them partially, and he has the courage, skill, and force to break the log-jam of fixed opinions and stultified forms. Through its geniuses the world has made what serious progress it has thus far recorded. God willing, we haven't seen the last of them.

Cowardice

(2015)

TWO JEWS before a Nazi firing squad. The officer in charge approaches the first of the Jews and asks if he wants a blindfold. "Go to hell, you Nazi pig," he says, and spits in his face. The second Jew whispers to the first, "Shhh. Don't! You'll get him angry."

Is the first Jew in this story courageous? Is the second Jew a coward, or instead comically prudent? As for the Nazi officer, is he, with the force of his squad of soldiers behind him, the true coward?

These questions, it turns out, are not so easily answered. According to *Webster's New World Dictionary*'s definition of a coward—"a person who lacks courage, especially one who is shamefully unable to control fear and so shrinks from danger or trouble"—none of these men qualifies. The first Jew certainly isn't cowardly; the second Jew isn't either, but is merely reverting to traditionally temporizing methods that apparently worked for him in the past. As for the Nazi, his behavior isn't cowardly, but is instead wicked and cruel. Cowards are perhaps rarer than one might have thought. And, with a substantial push from modern psychological theory and medicine, they are becoming rarer all the time.

Cultures devoted to the cultivation of courage, which is also to say to the avoidance of cowardice, have existed. Perhaps the most famous was that of Sparta. As a warrior culture, Spartan training of the young was almost exclusively devoted to making them fit for battle. Spartan boys, according to Plutarch, were put on a regimen of relentless competition intended to conquer fear and instill courage. This regimen included a sparse diet, which implicitly encouraged them to steal food. Those who were caught were whipped; only successful thieves went unpunished. (Ethics in Spartan training was of a much lower priority than acquiring the skills of survival necessary for victory in battle.) The entire education of Spartan boys, Plutarch writes, "was aimed at developing smart obedience, perseverance under stress, and victory in battle." The success of this upbringing, judged by its own terms, was illustrated at Thermopylae, where 300 Spartans, with the aid of small bands of other Greeks, held off tens of thousands of Persians for days until all the Spartans were finally killed. Among Spartans, the most honorable life was concluded by death on the battlefield. Much of Spartan poetry is divided between praise for those who died for the country and contempt for those who showed cowardice.

Japan, with its samurai tradition of honor, obedience, and self-sacrifice, provided another culture devoted to courage that lasted well into the 20th century. Death before dishonor was integral to the Japanese military ethos. Banzai charges during World War II were emblematic of this culture. Kamikaze pilots, sent out to crash into Allied ships, were nothing less than human missiles. (An old joke tells of a kamikaze pilot who had been on twelve flights before being discharged owing to an insufficient death wish.) Defenders of the American use of the atomic bomb to end the war have argued that the Japanese would otherwise never have surrendered.

In certain sports—football, hockey—the tradition of physical courage runs deep. Doug Plank, for eight years the almost suicidally aggressive safety of the Chicago Bears, claimed that the first thing one must jettison if one is to play in the National Football League is one's sense of self-preservation. Hockey is a sport where playing with pain is less a notable than it is a reigning assumption. I once saw a Chicago Blackhawks game in which a player in the first period suffered an injury to his face that required 33 stitches who then returned to play in the third period. For high-serotonin types—mountain climbers, skydivers, aerial tightrope walkers—cowardice does not exist as a possibility. For the rest of us, concerned about pain, shame, death itself, cowardice awaits just outside the door.

Until relatively recently, when parents began supervising much of the play of children, Spartan training (diminished a thousand fold) reigned among young boys in America. My own boyhood, between the ages of 10 and 14, was spent on the playground, competing at the three major American sports of the day. Two of these sports—baseball and football—provided ample opportunities for cowardice. (Basketball had not yet become the physical game it now is.) In baseball, there was the fear of being hit (*beaned* was the word) by a fast pitch in the head or face in a day when boys did not wear batting helmets, or of being spiked by a base runner. In football, fear came in the form of being brutally tackled, or missing tackles one should have made, or dropping passes lest one be clobbered upon catching them ("hearing footsteps" is the catch-phrase here). Then there was tree-climbing, doing risky tricks on bicycles, hitching onto the backs of cars on snowy streets, minor shoplifting from five-and-ten-cent stores. Fights broke out, and to walk away from a challenge to a fight was a disgrace.

Cowardice, also known as "chickening out," was disdained, courage admired. The greatest courage on exhibit at the Boone School playground was that of Marty Sommerfield. Marty was small, well-coordinated, intelligent about sports and much else (in high school he won a Westinghouse science award), but what distinguished him above all was his fearlessness. He would crash into walls going after fly balls, race out into the street to catch foul balls. At least twice that I can remember he suffered concussions as a running back playing without a helmet. Although not pugnacious, in later years he took on guys six inches taller and 40 or 50 pounds heavier than he in fist fights. Although I was never guilty of chickening out on the playground, I knew that there was a distinct difference between Marty and me. I considered the prospect of pain and injury; Marty Sommerfield apparently never did. I haven't read Tom Brokaw's *The Greatest Generation*, but I gather what made the generation great for Brokaw was that its members risked their lives in World War II. I, too, admire the men who fought in that war, as I do those soldiers who faced death in our country's subsequent wars. Every man of the least imagination surely wonders how he would have fared in battle. I've wondered about it for years. Would I, as the British say, have cacked my pants, or would I have come through admirably? I shall never know, but how splendid it would be to walk the streets knowing that I had faced death bravely on the battlefield.

COWARDICE: A BRIEF HISTORY by Chris Walsh, a university teacher with an interest in military history, examines the changing nature of cowardice over the past 200 or so years. His emphasis is on America, the home, as our anthem has it, of the brave. Not a great deal has been written on cowardice, for, as Walsh notes, it "is not a pleasant topic." Among the reasons for this is that "contemplating other's cowardice can push us to contemplate our own." Yet cowardice, a subset of shame, is a moral category, and all such categories, insofar as they constitute a piece in the great unsolved puzzle of what constitutes human nature, are worthy of study in and of themselves. "Thinking more clearly about cowardice," Walsh writes, "can help us think more critically, more realistically, about fear and how society should respond to it." Walsh writes clearly, with a sardonic point of view and a sure grasp of the issues raised by his subject.

Cowardice concentrates chiefly on military cowardice. "The cowardly soldier," its author writes, "remains the poster boy, so to speak, for cowardice." Walsh examines the word *coward* in its every nuance. He distinguishes between courage and recklessness, cowardice and prudence. Although the meaning of cowardice has changed over time, what hasn't is the word's continuing force as an insult. In America, politicians and journalists called the terrorists who flew the planes into the Pentagon and the Twin Towers cowards. In their own eyes, of course, the terrorists were warriors, ready to die for Allah. The fear associated with cowardice had nothing to do with their acts. The immensely unattractive Bill Maher made this point on his television show and threw in, at no extra charge, the accusations that we Americans, killing Serbs with cruise missiles, were the true cowards. In both cases, *cowardice* is the wrong word. Terrorists are not cowards, but they are indubitably villainous because they have no compunction about killing innocent people. As for killing without risk by missile or drone, cowardice doesn't really enter into this new advance in the technology of modern warfare. A drone, after all, is little more than a javelin hurled at great distance and powered by computer.

The grave mistake here derives from the notion that all bullies are at bottom cowards. In his *Modern English Usage,* which Walsh quotes, H. W. Fowler notes:

> The identification of coward and bully has gone so far in the popular consciousness that persons and acts in which no trace of fear is to be found are often called *coward(ly)* merely because advantage has been taken of superior strength or position.

My father, who bought me boxing gloves when I was six years old and used to spar with me in our living room, was fond of saying of bullies that the bigger they are, the harder they fall. I recognized that this may have a certain truth in physics, but the problem, I thought even then, was how to get them to fall in the first place.

The literary chronicling of cowardice begins with Shakespeare, whose Falstaff held that "discretion is the better part of valor" and who in *Cymbeline* wrote, "Plenty and Peace breed cowards." In the *Inferno*, Dante placed cowards, those who refused to take stands in life, who feared life itself, in the anteroom to hell. There they dwelled for all eternity

> and all about were stung
> By stings of wasps and hornets that were there.
> Because of these, Blood, from their faces sprung,
> Was mingled with their tears and flowed to feast
> The loathly worms that about their feet clung

The great American novel of cowardice is Stephen Crane's *The Red Badge of Courage*, set in the Civil War, and from which Walsh quotes generously. Joseph Heller's *Catch-22*, on the other hand, is given but a single paragraph. But then it is a novel that lends cowardice justification, through arguing, in effect, that war is on the face of it absurd, and no war, not even one against Hitler, is worth dying for, which, if it is to be believed, closes the books on military cowardice.

The shame of cowardice, Walsh reports, was regularly preached from the pulpit during the Revolutionary War. The motive of avoiding shame has always functioned as a great deterrent against cowardice. Shame in this realm takes many forms, from fear of letting down one's fellow soldiers to that of bringing disgrace on one's family. Honor and saving face have always been the chief antidotes to cowardice. In his book, Walsh reprints a British World War I poster that shows a man, his son playing on the floor before him, and his daughter on his lap asking, "Daddy, what did YOU do in the Great War?" In marked contrast, he reprints a poster, during the Vietnam War, of Joan Baez, her sister, and Mimi Farina, all showing lots of leg, under a sign reading, "Girls Say Yes to Boys Who Say NO," an inducement to draft resisters.

During the Civil War, Walsh recounts, there were roughly 500 courts martial for cowardice. The last, and the only, American soldier to be executed, by firing squad, for cowardice (he deserted) was Eddie Slovik during World War II. Some 15,000 Germans during the same war were executed for dereliction of duty, and the Russians under Stalin are thought to have killed hundreds of thousands of their troops for the same reason.

Courts martial for cowardice in England and in the United States decreased radically when the cowardice shifted categories from the moral to the medical, from, in other words, being thought a sin to being thought a sickness. "The link between the moral and the medical," in Walsh's phrase, greatly lessened if it did not altogether remove the onus on cowardly behavior. One cannot, after all, accuse a man in shell shock of cowardice, nor can one, in our day, feel anything but sympathy for soldiers claiming to have Post-Traumatic Stress Disorder, which long ago made it into the American Psychological Association's *Diagnostic and Statistical Manual* of mental illnesses. In the brave new world department, Walsh mentions that work is in progress on a pill to defeat fear. The age of therapy, the age in which we currently live, is doing all it can to eliminate cowardice as an act of moral failure.

With an all-volunteer army in place, fewer and fewer Americans will have their courage tested by the fire of war, which, as Walsh points out, has taken the question of cowardice, at least in its military context, off the big board of pressing issues. A lingering doubt nevertheless remains. In this connection, he prints a photograph of a graffito scribbled on a wall in the city of Ramadi in Iraq that reads: "America is not at war. The Marine Corps is at war. America is at the mall." If that doesn't leave a touch of citizenly guilt, nothing will.

Boosters of military courage, once ubiquitous, are no longer prominent. Walsh reminds us that Teddy Roosevelt accused Woodrow Wilson of being the leader of "a cult of cowardice"; General George S. Pat-
ton caused a public-relations crisis when he slapped two enlisted men in
psychiatric wards whom he accused of goldbricking; Ernest Hemingway
wrote to his publisher Charles Scribner accusing James Jones of cowardice for even bringing the subject up in his novels; and Richard Nixon,
during the Cold War, called Adlai Stevenson an "appeaser." Today, when
politicians who have not themselves served in the armed forces suggest
the need for a greater military presence in the Middle East, they are written off, at least on the left, with the contemptuous phrase "chickenhawks."

Not all courage has a military context. Walsh mentions Gandhi and
Martin Luther King, Jr., the first the founder, the second the foremost
American proponent of non-violent resistance, both of whom, interestingly, declared violence a lesser evil than cowardice. (Gandhi fought in
the Boer War.) Those who have had the courage to face down violence
other than on the battlefield seem, at least to me, quite as impressive as
those who succeeded in doing so in war. In my twenties, living in the
south and working as the director of an anti-poverty program in Arkansas, I met a man two years younger than I named Bill Hansen, who was
the head of the local chapter of the Student Non-Violent Coordinating
Committee, at that time the leading edge of the civil-rights movement.
Hansen was married to a black woman, which was then against state law,
and had been arrested for sit-ins and protest demonstrations no fewer
than 45 times; on one of these occasions, a prison trustee, viewing him
as a race traitor, broke his jaw and some of his ribs. Once, at lunch in a
black dinner in Little Rock, after I picked up the check, he left a tip; but
when I informed him that Trotsky never tipped, he picked up the three
quarters he had left on the table. Not high on humor, Bill Hansen—who
is currently working in Nigeria at the American University as a professor
of international relations and comparative politics—yet I admired him
unstintingly for his physical courage, and still do.

Is physical courage also required of women? Some women in the
military are lobbying to insert themselves in combat missions, and some
are already fighting. If this continues, cowardice may soon, if it is not

already, arise as para-sexual issue. "Eligibility for cowardice," Walsh writes on this point, "is eligibility for courage," by which I take him to mean that courage consists in good part of the avoidance of cowardice. Outside a military context, I should say that any woman who has gone through the tribulations of pregnancy and the pain of childbirth can never be thought cowardly.

Not all courage of course is in the realm of the physical. In his final chapter, Walsh takes up, glancingly, cowardice preventing love, the energy for entrepreneurship, the engagement of moral imagination, and much more. The German people of the World War II generation, he charges, apropos of the Holocaust, with "the unavoidable example of the cowardice of silence." Aligned with this, all death-camp survivors, in my view, qualify as courageous for not letting go of life under such extended heinous torture as they went through. He mentions the extended use of irony as a screen for cowardice. He cites Henry James's story "The Beast in the Jungle" as an example of the cowardice of hesitation. Hamlet suffered from this same cowardice, and Walsh quotes Kierkegaard on this point to good effect:

> What cowardice fears most of all is resolution, for a resolution instantly dissipates the mist. The power cowardice prefers to conspire with is time; for neither time nor cowardice finds any reason for haste.

In 1979, my friend Edward Shils gave the Jefferson Lecture at the University of Chicago on the subject of government interference in the contemporary university. After it was over, I stood near him on the podium when a young man came up to tell him how courageous he was for speaking truth to power. "I'm not in the least courageous," Edward said. "Fighting apartheid in South Africa is courageous. Alexander Solzhenitsyn is courageous. No one is coming after me for what I said in this lecture, and, not only that, but I've been paid ten thousand dollars for saying it."

Yet cowardice can and often has played a strong role in intellectual life. Out of cowardice, fewer and fewer intellectuals and academics are prepared to go against the grain of their times. Cowardice of this kind today is found among those who defend or go along with the program of political correctness in our universities, or who are terrified (not too strong a word) to comment on the shoddiness of victim studies in higher education. Fear of unconformity reigns in large sections of university life.

The only person I have ever accused of being a coward was a colleague, and a close friend for more than a quarter of a century, in the English department at Northwestern University. He supported a radical woman who was on record for being against free speech. I told him that I could see only two reasons for his doing so: one, he was fearful of alienating his fellow teachers in the department and the university at large; and, two, he was equally fearful of losing his following among graduate students. "Are you calling me a coward?" he asked. "Since you don't deny it, I guess I am," I replied. We've not spoken since, and probably never shall speak again.

Old Age and Other Laughs

(2012)

What shall I do with this absurdity—O heart, O troubled heart—this
caricature, Decrepit age that has been tied to me As to a dog's tale.
—W. B. YEATS, "The Tower"

I RECENTLY BOUGHT SOMETHING called catastrophe health insurance for my college-student granddaughter—a policy that has a high
deductible but is in place lest, God forfend, she needs to undergo a
lengthy and expensive hospital stay. The insurance agent who sold it to
me is a man named Jack Gross, whom I occasionally see walking around
the streets of my neighborhood and who always greets me, often with a
new joke. Being an insurance salesman and having me there in his office,
Jack couldn't resist asking me if my wife and I have assisted-living insurance, a policy designed for older people that pays for caregivers (or mind-
ers, as the English, more precisely, call them), thus allowing those suffering from dementia or other devastating conditions to avoid nursing
homes. Assisted-living insurance is very expensive, especially if one first
acquires it in one's seventies, which my wife and I are.

"Thanks all the same, Jack, but we have no need for assisted-living
insurance," I said. "We have pistols."

"Great," he replied, nicely on beat. "I just hope when the time comes to
use them you are able to find them."

The problem with that amusing response is that it has an uncomfortably
high truth content. Memory lapses, sometimes significant ones, but often

quite as maddening trivial ones, are, as everyone knows, a standard part of the problem of getting old. Why the other day could I not recall the name of an old Expos and later Mets catcher (Gary Carter), or the hotel in San Francisco that my wife and I favor (the Huntington), or the actress I used to enjoy talking with occasionally when we were both on the Council of the National Endowment for the Arts (Celeste Holm)? Where are my glasses? Why have I come into this room? I opened the refrigerator door for . . . what, exactly?

The word "old," I have been informed, is now politically incorrect. I recently read a book on the aging of the baby-boomer generation, *Never Say Die: The Myth and Marketing of the New Old Age* by Susan Jacoby, that introduced me to the words "wellderly" and "illderly." Not very helpful. "Aging" isn't much help either, for newborn babies are, *ipso facto*, aging the moment they emerge from the womb. "Old," "getting old," "being old"—these are words I prefer, and in this essay I'm sticking with them.

The difficulty enters in deciding who qualifies as old. Unless brought badly down by serious illness, in the United States one isn't any longer considered old at 62 or 65, the years Social Security allows a person to begin collecting what used to be considered old-age benefits. Some people, owing to a good ticket in the gene-pool lottery, or through being scrupulously careful about their health, begin to get old ten or so years later than do others. But old we all get, that is if we are lucky enough not to have been crushed by disease, accident, or war, and taken out of the game early. Next only to death itself, old age is the most democratic institution going— nearly everyone gets to enjoy it.

Enjoy is not the word most people would use in connection with old age. Many fight off old age through cosmetic surgery, strict exercise and stringent diet regimens, pills beyond naming, hair plugs, penal implants, even monkey glands (the useless remedy attempted by W. Somerset Maugham and W. B. Yeats). More struggle against old age with the aid of one or another form of positive thinking: keep your mind active, look on the bright side of things, remember life is a journey, you're only as old as you feel, and all that malarkey.

The first physical signs that one is getting old are those slight alterations in your body that remain permanent. Sometime in my late fifties,

I lost the hair from my shins and calves, to which it has never returned. Not much later a few brown spots appeared on my forehead, never to depart. Capillaries burst, leaving parts of one's body—in my case, my ankles—nicely empurpled. Bruises take longer to disappear than when one was young, and the scars from some of them never quite do. Time is a methodical and cruel sculptor.

Conversations among friends take up new subjects. When young, my male friends and I talked a fair amount about sports and sex. Later, conversation about food and movies came to loom large. Nostalgia—"the rust of memory," Robert Nisbet called it—began to set in around 60. Sleep is currently a hot topic, and by sleep I do not mean whom one is sleeping with, but instead how long is one able to sleep uninterruptedly.

The first time one cannot make love twice in one night, I have heard it said, is disappointing, the second time one cannot make love once in two nights can be the cause for despair. Viagra and other aids have helped solve this problem, but pharmacology has yet to come up with the pill to make one physically appealing. Few things sadder than to watch a man in his seventies, forgetting what he looks like, flirting with a waitress in her twenties. Women are not without their own problems in this realm. I once heard a woman roughly my age tell a female friend that her bra size was now 34″ long.

Things once done easily, even blithely, suddenly require taking second thought. Coming down a staircase, I seek the banister. Walking on slightly uneven pavement, I remind myself to lift my feet. Don't drive too slowly, I say to myself. The safety bar in the shower is there for a reason. Put on sunscreen. Virtue consists of ordering a salad for lunch; disappointment, in eating it.

I used to consider myself a Jewish Scientist, like unto a Christian Scientist, if only in my avoidance of physicians. Proust says that to believe in modern medicine is insane, and that the only thing more insane is not to believe it. My body forced me out of the church of Jewish Science in my late fifties. When once I had a single doctor—a primary and in my case only physician—I now have what feels like a medical staff: a gastroenterologist, an ophthalmologist, a cardiologist, and a dermatologist. In the past fifteen years, I have been diagnosed (not always correctly) with Crohn's Disease, auto-immune hepatitis, Celiac Disease; have had a triple-bypass surgery (though not a heart attack), cataract surgery, and a detached retina; and finally a charming skin disease called—and best pronounced in a W. C. Fields accent—bulous pemphigoid. Such a rich buffet of health problems eats into one's former feelings of personal invincibility.

At 70, in fact, one awaits both shoes to drop: the tumor to form, the strange pain not to disappear, the aneurysm to show up on the CAT scan. Hypochondria, at this age, is the better part of valor, for as paranoids sometimes have real enemies, so do hypochondriacs sometimes drop dead. One awaits the results of "blood work" like a prisoner on death row awaits a governor's reprieve. Preventive medicine, with its various specialists and panoply of tests, in old age can be as exacting as an illness.

Fatal illnesses often strike older people without clear—make that *any*—reason. An acquaintance of mine who spent his life staying in shape—weight lifting, jogging, competing in triathlons, the works— recently died of lymphoma. Everyone knows of someone who never smoked getting lung cancer. Alzheimer's blasts the most active and well-stocked minds. Immune systems break down, causing major problems no one could have predicted; body parts wear out, not all of them replaceable. It's a minefield out there, with deadly darts falling from the sky.

Physical change is accompanied by mental change. When old, time begins to register differently. Did this or that incident happen eight or was it 11 years ago? Years back, I met a long-unseen uncle, then about my age now, and asked him how old his son was. "Thirty-seven," he said confidently. "He's 45," his wife corrected him. I ask an acquaintance if his daughter got into Stanford, and he tells me that she graduated two years ago from the Yale Law School. The minutes, the hours, the days, weeks, and months seem to pass at roughly the same rate; it's only the decades that fly by.

Then there is the matter of repetition. Have I done this, said that, written the other before? Some things refuse to stick in the mind. Movies are high on the list. I seem to have arrived at the place in life where I can watch *The Pelican Brief* as if seeing it afresh every eighteen months. One of the saddest things an old person can hear is a younger friend saying, "You already told me." Friends one's own age are more likely to say, "You may have told me, but I've forgotten, so tell me again."

One begins to notice that contemporaries have, in their garrulity, become bores. As there is no fool like an old fool, neither is there any bore quite as tiresome as an old bore. How close am I myself to having achieved accreditation in this line? In too many conversations, I note that I wait patiently to slot in one of my standard jokes or sure-fire (I think) anecdotes. Have I arrived at my anecdotage, the stage of mental decomposition that precedes full dotage? Do I break into too many of other people's monologues? Have I become like the man who, returning from a party, when asked by his wife if he enjoyed himself, replies: "Yes, but if it wasn't for me, I would have been bored to death."

Crankishness, complaint division, sets in. How is it no man born after 1942 carries a handkerchief in his back pocket? Why is the membership of the entire U. S. Senate so bloody undistinguished? Might it be because the vast majority of its members are younger than I? One of the reasons the old complain about the world, Santayana wrote, is that they cannot imagine a world being any good at all in which they will not be around to participate.

One of the standby subjects of the old is how much richer, less gruesome, altogether better life was when they were young. The problem is that, when old, things genuinely do seem this way, and, who knows, they may well have been. Forty years ago, in my own line of work, universities seemed more serious, intellectuals more impressive, culture more weighty. I do not allow myself to lecture the young on how much better life used to be. I only talk about the old days with contemporaries, which is to say, with fellow cranks.

With age, curiosity is curtailed, attention attenuated. This is especially so in the realm of advancing technology. I have friends my age who, even ten or fifteen years ago, could not make the jump to learning how to use computers. Even among those of us who love e-mail and have a heavy reliance on Google and adore smartphones, the continual refinements on digital technology tend to swamp us. Do I really require Apple's new app that will allow me to replay the entire Russian Revolution on my phone and store all my photos in my navel?

In classical music concerts, my mind, like musical notes in a hall with poor acoustics, wanders all over the place, though the fact that the median age of the audience for classical music appears to be roughly 114 does make me feel refreshingly youthful. My stamina for museums and art galleries is now almost non-existent. Less than halfway through a play, I ask myself why I have paid 85 dollars to listen to the lucubrations of a fellow even more stupid than I. Confronted with the prospect of travel, the effort seems greatly to outweigh the prospects of pleasure. More and more I feel like the poet Philip Larkin, who when asked if he wished to visit China, answered yes, indeed, if he could return home that night.

I live within a block of two large retirement homes. The people who reside in them, most older than I, are part of my everyday *mise en scène*. Many are in good enough fettle: straight and kempt and cheerful, they have made the decision that living on their own has, for one reason or another, become too lonely or otherwise burdensome. Others have funny walks, or are bent with osteoporosis; a few have slightly vacant looks in their eyes. An occasional resident, in a wheelchair pushed by a Filipina minder, is deep into dementia, and is not so much out for a walk as for an airing. I have watched some of these people go from walking confidently to using a metal cane to requiring a walker to disappearing. Doubtless you have yourself already heard the ugly rumor that the mortality rate at present is at 100 percent.

For all that can be said on its behalf, *Losing It*, William Ian Miller's book on the subject of old age, is not a gift one wants to present to a friend or relative on his or her eightieth birthday. Professor Miller is an historian of the medieval world, with a special interest in Icelandic sagas, who teaches in the law school at the University of Michigan. Years ago I read—and reviewed in the *New Yorker*—an earlier book of his called *The Anatomy of Disgust*. He has written other books on revenge, fraudulence, and humiliation, and obviously has a penchant for darkish subjects. Self-described as "halfway between an essayist and an historian," he writes well, with a slightly macabre sense of humor, with irony added, shoring up his arguments with rich historical comparisons and analogies.

Writing a book called *Losing It* puts one in danger straightaway of giving evidence that one has oneself begun to lose it. Professor Miller's premise is that he hasn't quite lost it but is well on his way to doing so. "It" stands for one's intelligence, wit, intellectual penetration, verbal agility, physical prowess, and strength, all the powers that one felt confident of when younger but feels slipping away with age. Miller's *bête noir* in this book is the school of positive psychologists who claim that old age is the time of our lives, those serene golden years, all wisdom and tea (also tee) times. Miller's own view is closer to that of a friend of mine who recently turned 90 and, to the question of what is the best thing about old age, answered: "It doesn't last long."

Professor Miller laces his book with autobiographical bits, touching on his own experience of growing old. He is Jewish, despite that suspicious middle name of Ian, born and brought up in Green Bay, Wisconsin. (*Losing It* contains several references to the Green Bay Packers.) He was 65 when he began writing this book, 66 at its completion, a tad too young perhaps to claim the complaining privileges of old age. As a university teacher, his being around students may aid in making him feel old; nothing adds years on a person more than being regularly around the young. Miller worries, in fact, that in his book he may have exaggerated his decrepitude. He is, after all, a man who continues to teach, works out on an exercise bike, has a mother still alive (at 90), drives a motorcycle—not, clearly, everyone's idea of an *alte kocher*.

Intimations of mortality are what Miller has begun to feel, but, I should say, intimations merely. He speaks of memory lapses, of thinning hair, of no longer being quick in response, of his more attractive female students grasping that he is not really in sexual contention: "Oh, Professor Miller, he's such a cute old man," a colleague reported one such student saying of him. At the close of his book, he mentions a memory blackout he suffered—Transient Global Amnesia is its clinical name—before a Packers game. But where are his surgical scars? Where his white hair or baldness? He admits to taking Zoloft and Paxil, anti-depressant and anti-anxiety drugs, but so far as I know, he doesn't even have a plastic weekly calendar pill box, that badge of the older player.

Where *Losing It* is most valuable is in its author's recounting of stories of growing old in warrior societies (such as the Vikings, Norsemen, and Icelanders) and religious communities. In warrior, or honor, societies, a good death was one in which one went down in battle, preferably with one's enemies defeated, a ticket for Valhalla under your shield. In a religious, or at any rate a Christian community, martyrdom is the speediest way to heaven, there to dwell among the angels. In warrior societies, one dies with a sword in hand; in religious communities, with a Bible in one's bed and a priest by one's side. In secular societies, one is more likely to die with an IV on one's wrist and a tube up one's nose. The best death in a secular society is one in which one expires in one's sleep—in other words, a death, next to birth the major element in one's life, that one isn't even around to witness.

Professor Miller relishes retailing the problems of old age. He describes the shrinkage that takes place in the human brain. Dubious about old age bringing wisdom, he holds that wisdom is rare at any age, and no more likely to be found among the old than any other group. He even cites studies that conclude the old are stupider than the young, in relying more on stereotypes and appearances to make judgments. He is quite properly skeptical about the official wise men and women of our day: "I still find the wise dead considerably wiser than those we hold to be modern-day wise men and women, who, the more famous they are, the more likely they are to be charlatans." Sounds right to me.

No one gets Miller's heart racing more quickly than those who find the prospects of old age cheerful. A book called *Successful Aging* he describes as advocating "staying spunky, thinking positively, and then dropping dead quickly when thinking positively finally succumbs to reality." F. Scott Fitzgerald claimed that the sensible state for the older man was mild depression. Miller wouldn't disagree: "As a general rule," he writes, "critical intelligence—mental acuity—wars with happiness."

Miller takes after a Stanford professor named Laura Carstensen, whose optimism on the subject of being old drives him up and nearly over the nursing home wall. For Professor Cartensen, everything in old age presents an opportunity for contentment. For her, even "brain rot," according to Miller, has its upbeat side. When Cartensen reports a sense of well-being among the elderly respondents to a study she has done, Miller asks, "Did she interview any old Jews? She couldn't have, unless we have become more assimilated than I would ever have thought possible." The work of Professor Cartensen and her followers, he characterizes as "suspect science" and selling "snake oil bearing the Stanford label."

Miller's own view of old age is that it is downhill all the way, a journey that leads ultimately back to a second infancy, replete with diapers, hairlessness, loss of locomotion—a ride from goo-goo to ga-ga. In old age Miller sees only diminishment, humiliation, the curtailment of pleasure. Old age, he writes, "made it hard for several of the deadly sins to operate," though here La Rochefoucauld beat him to the punch by more than three centuries, writing: "Old people like to give good advice as a consolation for the fact that they can no longer set bad examples."

Live long enough, Miller warns, and even an exemplary career can be done in during one's dotage. "You end up remembered," he writes, "for your doddering vacancy . . . for your former self is now redefined in light of your drooling present." Think of Bertrand Russell, a genius when young, a political fool in old age, hostage as he was at the end of his life to nutty left-wing movements.

When I began teaching at Northwestern University, the great figure there was Bergen Evans, the lexicographer who had earlier been the host of a television show on ABC called *Of Many Things*. His courses drew six or seven hundred students, his lexicographical works were best-sellers. A student in one of my classes who was taking Bergen Evans's course in American usage told me that three times during the current quarter, Professor Evans took a letter out of his suit-jacket pocket, announced it arrived in the previous day's mail, and read it to the class—and all three times it was the same letter. Oops!

Finding nothing good to say about old age, Miller does not ease up, either, on life after death. "Death does not lock in a reputation," Miller writes.

> What if ten years after you die it turns out that your son is a serial killer, your daughter a positive psychologist [I say, that's a joke, son], your grandchildren drug addicts and in

prison? You are not safe, your virtue, your life, will be reevaluated, and . . . there is no relaxing, no satisfaction in a life once thought well lived if you have spawned a line of losers.

Not a speaker much in demand at Ann Arbor Rotary Club meetings, Professor Miller, I should guess.

Do I need here to confess that I rather like my current age? I of course recognize, *pace* Yeats, that this is "no country for old men"; none, after all, is. Yet old age confers, if not wisdom—I would never claim that for myself, especially if I had it—then a certain amused perspective. From the parapet of 75 I can see the trajectory and final shape of the careers of my contemporaries, including the insignificance of my own. With the sense old age gives of time passing quickly, I find myself more patient now than in earlier years; old age has helped, if not entirely to defeat, then at least to quieten the traditional Jewish disease of *schpilkosis*.

My age has released me from the need to be *au courant,* or even moderately with it. I am no longer responsible for knowing much about Madonna, Lady Gaga, and the young women who will inevitably follow them. With the grave yawning, surely I cannot be expected to read the 600-page novel about the assistant professor of English who discovers his father is a transvestite? The imminence of death may or may not concentrate the mind wonderfully, as Samuel Johnson had it, but it does provide a few clues about how to expend what remains of one's mental energy.

At 75, I feel I am playing with house money—the rest of my life, as people used to say before the worry about cholesterol set in, is gravy. Lovely it would be to stay in the game for another ten years or so, and I hope to be able to do so. But if before then some bright young oncologist or grave neurologist informs me that the time has come for me to cease flossing, I shall be mightily disappointed but scarcely shocked or even much surprised. On such an occasion I hope to retain the calm to count my blessings, which in my case have not been few. Among them will be that I have lived in freedom during a time of unprecedented prosperity, been allowed to do work of my own choosing that has been appreciated and decently rewarded, while never having been called upon to betray my friends or my ideals. Another blessing has been that thus far I have dodged the landmines, the flying darts, and the machine-gunner, and arrived at old age.

Day, day, enu, as the Hebrew chant has it, *dayenu, dayenu.*

What's So Funny?

(2014)

THE MOTIVES FOR HUMOR are as manifold as those for murder. Among them are the raucous physical misfortunes of others (slapstick), grotesque incongruities (between reality and appearance), ethnic abuse (Polish, Irish, anti-Semitic, and other), subtlety elegantly deployed (through irony and understatement), release of inhibition (blue jokes), witnessing the mighty fallen (the revered made to look ridiculous). Laughter itself comes in multiple forms: smiles, sniggers, grins, giggles, belly laughs, falling-off-the-couch laughs, and what Mel Brooks once called heart-attack laughter. The realm of jokes encompasses the entire world in its subject matter and appears in such varying forms as puns, one-liners, epigrams, witty ripostes, practical jokes, comic commercials, and elaborate narratives requiring foreign, often Jewish-greenhorn, accents.

Various, often contradictory theories about humor have been devised—from the notion that humor is little more than a form of hidden aggression to those that hold humor is a cure for all sorts of illnesses. Given the range of motives for humor, its varying kinds and occasions and forms, can it be usefully studied and codified in the way of other phenomena?

Whether it can or not, it already is, in universities, in scholarly journals, at comedy clubs, at improv studios, and elsewhere. The University of Southern California provides students a "concentration" in humor.

The University of Colorado has a Humor Research Laboratory. The international Society for Humor Studies publishes *Humor: The International Journal of Humor.*

Henri Bergson is perhaps the greatest name to write a full treatise on the subject, *Laughter: An Essay on the Meaning of the Comic*, a work that brings to mind the comedian Chris Rock's remark after seeing the movie *The Last Temptation of Christ*, "Not many laughs." Freud's *Jokes and Their Relation to the Unconscious* (1905) contains a few decent jokes but it, too, fails to light up the subject, except perhaps for that minuscule portion of the population that continues to believe in the doctrines of the man Vladimir Nabokov never failed to call "the Viennese Quack."

THREE PEOPLE, IT HAS BEEN SAID, are required for the successful consummation of a joke: one person to tell it, another to laugh at it, and a third not to get it. If you have to explain it, as everyone knows, it isn't funny.

Without spontaneity—even well-rehearsed spontaneity—humor is sadly crippled. I once told a joke through a translator to the Soviet dissident hero Andrei Sinyavsky. The translator had come up to me at a party to say Mr. Sinyavsky had heard I knew lots of jokes. He, Sinyavsky, loved jokes, and would be pleased if I would tell him one. I proceeded to do so. The translator translated me line for line. At the punchline, Sinyavsky smiled faintly, and told the translator, in Russian, "Very nice." But it wasn't, really. All rhythm was lost, literally, in translation, and by the time I came to the joke's end I myself was slightly bored by it.

"Analyzing humor," E. B. White wrote, "is like dissecting a frog. Few people are interested and the frog dies." This sentence appears toward the end of Peter McGraw and Joel Warner's *The Humor Code: A Global Search for What Makes Things Funny.* Interesting they would include it, since their book is about little else than the dissection of humor to learn how it works, when it is effective, and what are its uses. The authors propose to answer such questions, among others, as:

> Do comics need to come from screwed-up childhoods? What's the secret to winning the *New Yorker* cartoon caption contest?

Why does being funny make you more attractive? Who's got a bigger funny bone—men or women, Democrats or Republicans?

They do answer them, but for the most part in the largely unsatisfactory manner of social science—with, that is, poll results, surveys, and focus-group findings.

McGraw, the director of the Humor Research Lab at the University of Colorado, supplied the theoretical expertise for the book. The notion of a Humor Research Lab is itself amusing. One imagines a large, well-lit room with mice and monkeys falling over with laughter while watching videos of Rodney Dangerfield.

Much legwork went into the making of *The Humor Code*. The authors interviewed the cartoon editor of the *New Yorker* and a founding editor of the *Onion* and many other experts. They investigated one or another aspect of humor in Sweden, Denmark, Africa, Japan, and Palestine; and talked with stand-up comics and humor theorists in New York, Los Angeles, Montreal, and elsewhere. Many studies are cited (some are called "compelling") and the word *science* often comes into play when social science, a much less stringent activity, is meant. All of which leads into a poor joke of my own creation: How many social scientists does it take to change a lightbulb? Answer: Difficult to say. They'll first need a grant to do a study of the problem.

McGraw's studies have led him to endorse something called the benign-violation theory, which holds that "humor only occurs when something seems wrong, unsettling, or threatening (i.e. a violation), but simultaneously seems okay, acceptable, or safe (i.e., benign.)" The form this takes in most jokes and comic situations is to begin with the threat of a violation of some sort and save the uneasiness this causes by its turning benign at its end.

The theory does work with a great many jokes. In 1962 I heard Lenny Bruce, a man not overly concerned with seeming benign, tell a joke whose premise was that Sophie Tucker, still alive at 75 and then thought one of the great ladies of show business, was a nymphomaniac requiring the services of an unending supply of Puerto Rican busboys working in the nightclubs in which she performed. Bruce then staged a dialogue between Mr. Rosenberg, the (naturally) Jewish owner of such a nightclub, attempting to persuade Manuel, one of his busboys, to attend to Miss Tucker in her room. In a heavy Hispanic accent, Manuel protests vigorously, citing Miss Tucker's age, her looks, the outrageous impropriety of the whole business. Rosenberg offers him 50 dollars. Manuel claims it's impossible, he cannot do it. Rosenberg assures him it will all be over in 10 minutes. This back and forth conversation continues until, finally, Manuel says, "I don't care what you say, Mr. Rosenberg, I cannot, I cannot, I will not [brief pause here] *schtup* her."

The joke turns out not to be about Sophie Tucker's putative nymphomania but about Manuel's use of the word *schtup*, which picks up on the point that the minority employees of Jewish bosses often acquire odd bits of Yiddish.

Another such joke has a man and woman necking passionately on their banquette in a French restaurant, when suddenly the woman slides under the table. (You should be a bit nervous at this point.) A moment or two later the waiter approaches the table and informs the man that his wife is missing, to which he replies: "No, she's not. She just walked in the door." Relief follows; it's not a fellatio joke with a high yuck quotient.

In both jokes, benignity wins out over violation. But not always, however. Not even all that often, actually. The benign-violation theory has its limits.

For example: A woman comes to her physician to announce that her husband, a Christian Scientist, has been behaving strangely of late, but, owing to his religion, refuses to see a doctor. The physician suggests she give him a list of her husband's symptoms. After she does so, he says that there are two distinct possibilities here: her husband has either AIDS or Alzheimer's. When the woman asks what is she to do, the physician offers a simple solution. "Drive your husband thirty miles out of town and drop him off. If he returns home, don't sleep with him." (A more forceful word than "sleep," unfit for a family magazine, was used when I first heard it.) No redemption in the benign here; quite the reverse.

Sometimes a joke will offer no hint of violation whatsoever, but will instead be a story with an amusing ending. The conductor of a great symphony has a heart attack an hour before performance. The assistant director is on sabbatical. The artistic director asks if there is anyone in the orchestra who has any experience conducting. A modest man from the viola section steps up to say that he had some minor experience conducting a student orchestra in Vienna. He'll have to do. That night he conducts, and at the end his performance is greeted with a 20-minute standing ovation and raves in the next day's press. He conducts again the next night and the night after to similar acclaim, and takes over the job. Only at the close of the season does the regular conductor, now recovered from his heart attack, resume the podium. The violist returns to his old seat in the viola section. "Good to see you," the violist seated next to him says. "Where've you been?" Nothing violative here in this joke about overrating the importance of symphonic conductors.

No wonder that, when asked about the benign-violation theory, the comedian Louis C. K. replied, "I don't think it's that simple. There are thousands of jokes. I just don't believe there's one explanation."

Without wishing to put the various humor labs, institutes, journals, societies, and independent humor gurus out of business, thus increasing unemployment in America, why, one wonders, would anyone need to have an all-purpose explanation of how humor works anyhow? The authors of *The Humor Code* try to understand a laughing epidemic that took place in a high school in Tanzania, but are unable to discover what, exactly, brought it about. They go to Denmark to learn about the extreme Muslim reaction to the book of cartoons mocking Mohammed, but conclude very little. They fly down to the Amazon in clown costumes, joining Patch Adams and his troop of clowns, in the hope of cheering up the lives of wretchedly poor South American children, and the main result appears to have been that it allowed co-author Joel Warner to lose many of his inhibitions while playing a clown. They visit Palestine and write about humor among the Palestinians, but come up with scarcely any interesting examples. In this last venture one is reminded of Albert Brooks, in his movie *Looking for Comedy in the Muslim World*, attempting his twitchy, neurotic humor before an audience of dour Muslim men, and dying on stage.

Which brings up the question of how well humor translates from one country to another, from one culture to another, from one social class to another, from one generation to another. Imagine Jackie Mason doing stand-up before the Boko Haram, Sarah Silverman before a Tea Party meeting, Alan King at a Sunday morning session of Jesse Jackson's PUSH organization.

Bob Mankoff, the cartoon editor of the *New Yorker*, tells McGraw and Warner that to be merely funny is insufficient for a cartoon to qualify for publication in the magazine. "A great *New Yorker* cartoon," according to Mankoff must also "have a point" and provide "an insight"—must have an "'aha!' moment, alongside the 'ha-ha.'" How many such cartoons the magazine publishes that meet this criterion is difficult to say. Most weeks the majority fail. Am I guilty of insufficient subtlety, or are Mankoff and the magazine's editor, David Remnick (who also has a hand in choosing each week's cartoons), and I on different wavelengths, they on FM, I on cruder AM? Might it be that *New Yorker* cartoons, like New York itself, always seems better when one was younger? For me the golden age of cartoons in the magazine were those of Peter Arno, Helen Hokinson, James Thurber, Charles Addams, extending up through Edward Koren, whereas I have long ago ceased bothering to read the small print balloons in the celebrated Roz Chast's cartoons, failing to find the pay-off worth the effort.

Todd Hanson, a longtime writer for *Onion*, the satirical weekly newspaper, raises the question with McGraw and Warner of historical timing and humor, chiefly connected with the question of when it is permissible to make jokes about national tragedies. The example they discuss is 9/11. Thirteen years later the time still hasn't come to make this subject fit for comedy. The *Onion* never took on the subject directly, but instead made jokes about the terrorists, among them the headline, "Hijackers Surprised to Find Selves in Hell." I am not a regular reader of the *Onion*, but two of its headlines stick in my mind: "[Bill] Clinton Vaguely Disappointed by Lack of Assassination Attempts" and, soon after the 2008 presidential election, "Black Man Gets Worst Job in America."

Humor changes from generation to generation, but at some times more quickly than at others. I suspect we are currently in one of those times. I have a repertoire of jokes that require what used to be called a greenhorn, or a Jewish immigrant, accent, but a generation has now come of age that may never have heard that accent since Eastern European Jewish emigration to America essentially ended nearly 70 years ago. But for many jokes the accent is necessary. A man returns from his annual checkup, and his wife asks if the doctor found anything wrong with him. "He says I have something called herpes?" the man says. "Nu," says his wife, "so what is herpes?" The man says he was embarrassed to ask. The wife tells him she'll look it up in the dictionary, and leaves the room. "Nothing to worry," she says on her return, "the dictionary say herpes is a disease of the gentiles." Without the accent, the joke disappears.

The great Jewish waiter jokes clearly will obviously have less force for generations who have never seen a Jewish waiter. I'm fond of a joke about a man who leaves a pair of shoes with a cobbler and forgets them when he goes off to World War II. When he returns to his old neighborhood 50 years later, the shoe repair shop is still in business, the same Jewish owner is still running it. The veteran inquiries about his shoes; the repairman remembers and describes them and then says "dey'll be ready Vendsday." Apart from the accent problem, though there are still shoe-repairmen— in my neighborhood they are almost all Russian émigrés—nowadays people more and more wear sneakers and fewer and fewer bother to have leather shoes repaired; they just toss 'em. *Autre temps, autres moeurs, autre plaisanteries.*

HUMAN NATURE MAY NOT CHANGE, but human rhythms do. I have tried Laurel and Hardy movies, a great favorite of mine when young and a favorite still, on a number of kids and they don't find them very funny. The action is too slow; that they are filmed in black and white doesn't help. W. C. Fields movies produced even sadder results. In the time that it takes Fields to do one of his double pregnant pauses, my young interlocutors can send off two, maybe three text messages.

The Humor Code does not take up the matter of comedians using language once considered risqué. A small band of comedians always did "work blue": Buddy Hackett in nightclubs was one of them, and Belle Barth another ("From me," she used to say, "you won't hear the Gettysburg Address."). On cable television and YouTube, of course, anything goes. Turn on Comedy Central and there is a good chance you will find a woman comedian doing a riff on tampons or the etiquette of fellatio. The political comedian Bill Maher will get a laugh calling someone with whose politics he disagrees an asshole. Not funny, though his audience, sympathetic with his politics, laughs. Has the removal of censorship increased the Gross National Humor, or only enlarged the Gross part?

A great potential source of humor, or so one would think, would be the targets open to comedians by political correctness. Not many, though, seem to have taken advantage of it, which suggests that, despite all the bravura of using once outlawed words or taking up sexual subjects, not all that many contemporary comedians are courageous, at least in this line. Fifteen or so years ago I heard a comedian named Bobby Slayton, also known as Yid Vicious, complain about the dropping of language requirements in high schools. In his day, he noted, one had to take a language. "I took Spanish," he said. "I figure the Puerto Ricans can learn it, how tough can it be?" That joke today just might get him a lawsuit.

Sarah Silverman is a comedian who bucks political correctness, though not quite directly. Through the persona of a faux naïve Jewish princess, she gets away with jokes that would be disallowed if told straightforwardly. In one she begins by remarking that her biological clock is ticking, but there seems never to have been a good time for her to have had children. She then runs through the inappropriateness of her having done so at various times in her life: in her early twenties she was still immature, an airhead; in her late twenties her career was finally getting underway, and there was no time; in her early and middle thirties that same career absorbed all her energy. "I guess," she concludes, "the best time to have a baby is when you're a black teenager."

More daringly, she jokes about what she calls "the alleged" Holocaust. One such joke has her "lesbian niece" report to her that in Hebrew school she learned that they killed sixty million Jews during the Holocaust. She corrects the niece by saying that it was "only" six million. "What's the difference?" the niece asks. "The difference" Silverman replies, "is sixty million is unforgiveable, young lady." These jokes, please notice, reverse the violation-benign formula. They start out benign and end up in full flame violation.

Sarah Silverman is a liberal—a potty-mouthed liberal, for she gets most of her laughs using what one can only call naughty (to the highest power) words. But, then, the most commercially successful comedians of the current day are also liberal: Jon Stewart, Stephen Colbert, John Oliver, Bill Maher. The only authentically conservative comic I know of is Dennis Miller. Liberalism, based on hope, should offer more fodder for humor than conservatism, which prides itself on reality, but in our time it does not—though the authors of *The Humor Code* quote a study done at Duke University showing that conservatives responded more generously to a wider range of jokes than did liberals. Another of the mysteries of humor, this, that cannot be decoded.

Can a person enjoy humor that rubs too harshly against the grain of his or her politics? The short answer is probably not. Perhaps the most successful political comedian of the past half-century was Mort Sahl. I met Sahl one night coming out of the long-defunct Chicago nightclub called Mr. Kelley's and could not resist asking him if the then racist governor of Arkansas, Orval Faubus, took over William Fulbright's senate seat, as he threatened to do, would this mean that students would study abroad on a Faubus? "Not bad," he said, and then told me that a recently planned meeting between Adlai Stevenson and Dwight David Eisenhower had to be cancelled because the translator didn't show up.

Mort Sahl was a fairly standard liberal, but as a comedian he was prepared to abandon his politics for a laugh. One night on Jack Paar's *Tonight Show* he avowed that he had had a most disturbing letter from the NAACP, informing him that, as a man of the left, he ought to be ashamed not to have a Negro (as the term then was) in his act. Sahl allowed that the NAACP had a point. "So I've hired this brilliant young negro comedian," he said. Pausing, he looked down at his watch, and added: "He ought to have been here by now." It took the audience fully 15 seconds to get the joke, and break out in ripple effect laughter.

THE FIELD FOR HUMOR has also expanded in my lifetime. Mel Brooks made bad taste not only acceptable but amusing. The flatulent cowboys sitting around a fire after a meal of beans in his 1974 movie *Blazing Saddles* is only one notable example. The play within a play, "Springtime for Hitler," in his 1968 movie and 2002 Broadway musical *The Producers* is another. On *60 Minutes*, Brooks, interviewed by Mike Wallace, broke into Wallace's first question by asking him what he paid for his wristwatch. He broke into the second question by feeling the lapels of Wallace's sportjacket and asking what a garment like that cost. He was playing the pushy, the utterly materialistic, Jew, and, so egregious was he, he got away with it.

Woody Allen, in his stand-up days and also in his movies, made self-debasement and hypochondria into subjects for humor. The television show *Seinfeld* did something similar with selfishness—the defining quality of nearly every character on the show was his disregard for the feelings or interests of others—thus playing an ostensibly deplorable vice for laughs. Larry David, along with Jerry Seinfeld the principal creator of *Seinfeld*, has done the same thing with insensitivity on his HBO show *Curb Your Enthusiasm*.

Christie Davies, a man described in *The Humor Code* as "the Indiana Jones of hilarity," notes that "nearly every country has stupidity jokes." This means that every country finds someone, usually within its borders, to select for comic abuse. The Polish joke has receded in popularity in America in recent years, replaced by the less ethnically offensive blonde jokes. In India, the Sikhs are the victims of such humor, as the Irish have long been for the English. (What do you call an Irish homosexual? A man who prefers women over whiskey.) Uzbeks, Davies claims, "get made fun of in Tajikistan, while in France it's the French-speaking Swiss. . . . Brazilians joke about the Portuguese, Finns knock the Karelians, Nigerians rib the Hausas." In the realm of international humor, the French used to ask what was the difference between America and yogurt, the answer to which is yogurt has culture.

Of course it has long been understood that minority members can tell jokes, often brutal ones, against their own people in the same way that they can use otherwise banned words to describe them. Richard Pryor and the early Eddie Murphy did humor about blacks; Pryor had a bit about being the first black president that is all too prescient about our current president. Keegan Michael Key and Jordan Peele, a very funny team, do wildly amusing bits about ghetto-named athletes, a black teacher mispronouncing all the conventional names in a white suburban school, and gay black gangstas. I hope they will one day do Jesse Jackson confronting Al Sharpton, but that is perhaps too much to ask.

Jews are famous for jokes about Jews, not all of them likely to pass the anti-Semitism test of the Anti-Defamation League. (What happens when a Jew with an erection runs into a wall? Answer: He breaks his nose. What is the ultimate Jewish dilemma? Answer: Ham—on sale.)

Only Jews could have devised Gentile jokes, two of which run: A Gentile goes into a men's shop and enquires about the price of a suede jacket. When told it cost $1,800, he replies: "I'll take it." The same Gentile calls his mother on Thanksgiving to say that he'll be three hours late for dinner. "I understand," she says. These jokes are of course not about Gentiles at all, but about the supposed Jewish propensity for haggling and about neurotically demanding Jewish mothers.

Humor ought never to be too general, or at least the best jokes never are. Warner and McGraw cite what a humor expert concluded, by way of survey, to be the world's funniest joke. This is it: Two hunters are out in the woods when one of them collapses. He doesn't seem to be breathing and his eyes are glazed. The other guy whips out his phone and calls emergency services. He gasps, "My friend is dead! What can I do?" The operator says, "Calm down. I can help. First, let's make sure he's dead." There is a silence, then a gunshot. Back on the phone the guy says, "Okay, now what?"

Not that funny, and, as Warner and McGraw suggest, it can only have qualified as the world's funniest joke because it offends no large group (with the exception, perhaps, of animal-rights activists opposed to hunting) and is general in its context and frame of reference; it could, presumably, have taken place in almost any country in the world. But more particular humor is better; and private humor, between two or three persons, can sometimes be best of all.

Gallows humor is not taken up in *The Humor Code*, that humor which comes into play when situations are so dour that there is nothing left but to laugh. The humor that came out of the Soviet Union is a notable case in point; the heritage of Soviet Communism, of 75 years of murder, useless suffering, and general gloom, produced little of value except perhaps a dozen good jokes. A characteristic one is about the man who goes into a Soviet car dealership to learn that there is only one model of car for sale, that this model has no extra features, comes in only one color, and cannot be delivered for 10 years. The man says that he'll take it but would prefer to have it delivered in the afternoon 10 years from today. When the car salesman asks why in the afternoon, the man says that he has the plumber coming in the morning. If there were good German jokes within the briefer Nazi era, none has come down to us. But, then, in the joke that lists the world's five shortest books, the first volume is titled Great German Stand-up Comedians.

What of the healing effects of laughter, a theory given wide publicity by Norman Cousins, then the editor of the *Saturday Review,* in a series of books published in the 1970s and early '80s about the relief he gained from laughing while suffering illness. Cousins used Marx Brothers movies to relieve pain. "I made the joyous discovery that 10 minutes of genuine belly laughter had an anesthetic effect and would give me at least two hours of pain-free sleep," he reported. "When the pain-killing effect of the laughter wore off, we would switch on the motion-picture projector again and not infrequently, it would lead to another pain-free interval." McGraw and Warner do not hold with Cousins's ideas on the curative effects of humor. The most they concede is that "while science doesn't yet support the idea that humor improves people's physical health, there is evidence that it improves emotional health." Humor, they hold, "helps people cope with their problems, it distracts from dispiriting thoughts, it creates an escape from what ails you, whether that be the loss of a loved one, a diagnosis of Parkinson's, a lifetime of suffering in a place like Belsen, or just a crummy day." I'm not sure this isn't overstatement; Parkinson's is no laughing matter, nor is the death of a loved one, or a lifetime of suffering anywhere. Even laughter has its limits.

Havelock Ellis, the pioneering psychologist and a less than notably funny man, thought that laughter had a religious basis. "Even the momentary expansion of the soul in laughter is, to however slight an extent, a religious exercise," Ellis wrote. There is something appealing about the notion that laughter is an expansion of the soul, allowing fleeting moments in which all one's troubles are dismissed and one feels an elevation of spirit. The notion suggests that laughter is a gift, possibly a divine gift. I say "possibly divine" because, when viewing the human comedy, in its full range of preposterousness, its endless ironies and unexpected pratfalls, one is forced to conclude that God Himself must love a joke.

The Fall of the WASPs

(2013)

THE UNITED STATES once had an unofficial but nonetheless genuine ruling class. This class was drawn from what came to be known as the WASP Establishment. Members of this establishment dominated politics, economics, education, but they do so no more. The WASPocracy, as I tend to think of it, lost its confidence, and with it its power and interest in leading. The United States at present is without a ruling class, and it is far from clear whether this is a good thing.

The acronym WASP of course derives from White Anglo-Saxon Protestant, but as acronyms go, this one is more deficient than most. Lots of people, including prominent powerful figures, among them U.S. Presidents, have been white, Anglo-Saxon, and Protestant, but were far from being WASPS. Jimmy Carter and Bill Clinton were both white, Anglo-Saxon, and Protestant, but neither was a WASP.

WASPs were a caste, and as such closed off to all not born within the caste, with the possible exception of those who crashed the barriers by marrying into it. WASP credentials came with lineage, and lineage, that is proper birth, automatically brought connections to the right institutions. Yale, Princeton, Harvard were the great WASP universities, backed up by Choate, Groton, Andover, Exeter, and other prep schools. WASPs tended to live in exclusive neighborhoods: on upper Park and Fifth Avenue in

New York, on the Mainline in Philadelphia, Back Bay in Boston, Lake Forest and Winnetka in Chicago, though WASP life was chiefly found on the eastern seaboard. WASPs had their own social clubs, and did business with a small number of select investment and legal firms such as Brown Brothers Harriman and Sullivan & Cromwell. Many were thought to have lived on inherited money soundly invested.

The State Department was dominated by WASPs and so, too, was the Supreme Court, with one seat left unoccupied for a Jew of proper mien. Congress was never preponderantly WASP, though a number of Senators—Henry Cabot Lodge, Leverett A. Saltonstall come to mind—have been WASPs. Looking down on the crudities of quotidian politics, Henry Adams, a WASP to the highest power, called the dealings of Congress, the horse-trading and corruption and the rest of it, "the dance of democracy." In one of his short stories, Henry James has characters modelled on Henry and Clover Adams, planning a social evening, say, "Let's be vulgar—let's invite the President."

So strong, so dominant was WASP culture that wealthy families who did not qualify by lineage attempted to imitate and live the WASP life. The most notable example was the Kennedys. The Kennedy compound at Hyannis Port, the sailing, the clothes, the touch football played on expansive green lawns—pure WASP-mimicry, all of it. Except that true WASPs were too upstanding to go in for the unscrupulous business dealings of Joe Kennedy or feckless philanderings of him and his sons.

That the Kennedys did their best to imitate WASP life is perhaps not surprising, for in their exclusion the Irish may have felt the sting of envy for WASPocracy more than any others. The main literary chroniclers of WASP culture—F. Scott Fitzgerald, John O'Hara—were Irish. (Both Fitzgerald and O'Hara tried to live their lives on the WASP model.) But not the Irish alone. To this day, the designer Ralph Lauren (né Lifshitz) turns out clothes inspired by his notion of the WASP life lived on the gracious margins of expensive leisure.

The last WASP President was George H. W. Bush, but there is reason to believe he was not entirely proud of being a WASP. At any rate, he certainly wasn't featuring it. When running for office, he made every attempt to pass himself off as a Texan, declaring a passion for pork rinds and a love for the music of the Oak Ridge Boys. (George W. Bush, even though he had gone to the right schools, and can claim impeccable WASP lineage, seems otherwise to have shed all WASPish coloration and is an authentic Texan, happily married to a perfectly middle-class librarian.)

That George H. W. Bush felt it strategic not to emphasize his WASP background was a strong sign that the decline of the prestige of the WASP in American culture was well on its way. Other signs had arisen much earlier. During the late 1960s, some of the heirs of the Rockefeller clan openly opined that they felt guilty about their wealth and how their ancestors came by it. By the 1970s, exclusive universities and prep schools began dropping their age-old quotas on Catholics and Jews and contorted their requirements to encourage the enrollment of blacks. The social cachet of the Episcopal Church, a major WASP institution, drained away as its clergy turned its major energies to leftish causes.

Elite, which was how WASPs of an earlier era preferred to think themselves, became a buzz, and a bad, word. Being a WASP was no longer a source of happy pride, but distasteful if not slightly disgraceful—the old privileges of membership now seeming unjust and therefore badly tainted. An old joke has one bee asking another bee why he is wearing a yarmulke. "Because," answers the second bee, "I don't want anyone to take me for a WASP."

The late 1960s put the first serious dent into the WASPs as untitled aristocrats and national leaders. The word WASP did not come into play so much for the student protestors as the word Establishment, heretofore chiefly an ecclesiastical term. The Establishment was the enemy and the target of much 1960s protest. The Establishment was thought to have sent the country into Vietnam; it was perfectly content with the status quo, with all its restrictions on freedom, tolerance for unjust social arrangements; it stood for uptightedness, and repressiveness generally.

The Establishment took its place in a long tradition of enemies of American life. On this list of enemies at various times have been Wall Street, Madison Avenue, the military-industrial complex—vague entities all. But there was nothing vague about the Establishment. They were alive and breathing, and they had such names as John Foster and Allen Dulles, Averell Harriman, McGeorge Bundy, Dean Rusk, Townsend

Hoopes, Joseph Alsop, C. Douglas Dillon, and Robert McNamara. The WASPs ruled the country, and for those who didn't much like the country, or the directions in which they saw it tending, the WASPs were the great and easily identifiable enemy.

The last unashamed WASP to live in the White House was Franklin Delano Roosevelt, and he, with his penchant for reform of American society, was considered by many a traitor to his social class. He is also likely to be the last to reside there. WASP culture, though it exists in pockets of private life—country clubs, neighborhoods, a few prep schools and law firms—is finished as a phenomenon of public significance.

Much can be—and has been—said about the shortcomings of WASPs. As a class, they were exclusionary, and hence tolerant of social prejudice, if not often downright snobbish. Tradition minded, they tended to be dead to innovation and social change. Imagination was not high on their list of admired qualities. Yet they had dignity and an impressive sense of social responsibility. In a book of 1990 called *The Way of the Wasp*, Richard Brookhiser held that the chief WASP qualities were "success depending on industry; civic-mindedness placing obligations on success, and anti-sensuality setting limits to the enjoyment of it [sensuality]; conscience watching over everything." Under WASP hegemony, corruption, scandal, incompetence in high places were not, as now, regular features of public life. Under WASP rule, stability, solidity, gravity, a certain weight and aura of seriousness suffused public life.

For better or worse, we don't at present have anything like an unofficial ruling class that older generations of WASPs provided. What we have instead is a meritocracy, a leadership thought to be based on men and women who have earned their way not through the privileges of birth but by merit.

La carrière ouverte aux les talents, careers open to the talented, is what Napoleon Buonparte promised, and it is what any meritocratic system is supposed to provide. America now fancies itself under a meritocratic system, under which the highest jobs are open to the most talented people, no matter their lineage or social background. And so it might seem, when one considers that our 42nd President, Bill Clinton, came from a broken home in a backwater town in Arkansas, while our 44th President, Barack

Obama, was himself also from a broken home, biracial into the bargain, and with a background in radical politics.

Both men arrived at their high posts through political savvy, paid staff expert in arranging their images, and the usual American electoral she-nanigans. But none of this would have been possible if they—and their wives—hadn't had their mettle tested in the fire of the American educational system. Meritocracy in America starts, and for many ends, in colleges and universities, really a small number—perhaps eight or ten—colleges and universities. On the meritocratic climb, one must first succeed in getting into these institutions, then do well within them, to be considered among the talented to whom all careers are open.

Bill Clinton had Georgetown, Oxford (as a Rhodes Scholar), and Yale Law School on his resume; Barack Obama had Columbia and Harvard Law School. Their wives had, respectively, Wellesley and Yale Law School and Princeton and Harvard Law School. They are players all, high rollers in the great American game of meritocracy. Their initial merit resides, presumably, in their having been superior students.

David Brooks once wrote a column in the *New York Times* on the brilliance of the Obama cabinet and support staff. His only evidence was that so many of them had gone to ostensibly splendid schools. A "vale-dictory," he called the collectivity, suggesting so many must have been perennial valedictorians of their various schools on their climb to such powerful jobs.

A meritocracy in America, in this reading, means people who are best in school go right to the top. But is the merit genuine? One is reminded that of the two strongest American presidents since 1950—Harry S. Truman and Ronald Reagan—the first didn't go to college at all and the second went to Eureka College, a school affiliated with the Disciples of Christ Church in Eureka, Illinois. The notion of Harry Truman as a Princeton man, Ronald Reagan as a Yalie somehow diminishes them both.

Apart from mathematics, which demands a high IQ, and science, which requires a distinct aptitude, the only thing that normal undergraduate schooling prepares a person for is . . . more schooling. Having been a good student, in other words, means nothing more than one was good at school: one had the discipline to do as one was told, one learned the skill of quick response to oral and written questions, one psyched out what one's professors wanted and gave it to them. Having been a good student, no matter how good the reputation of the school, is no indication of one's quality or promise as a leader. It might even suggest that one is more than a bit of a follower, a conformist, standing ready to give satisfaction to the powers that be, so that one can proceed on to the next good school or step up the ladder of meritocracy.

What our new meritocrats have failed to evince that the older WASP generation prided itself on is character. Character embodied in honorable action is at the heart of the novels and stories of Louis Auchincloss, America's last unembarrassedly WASP writer. Doing the right thing, especially in the face of temptations to do otherwise, was the WASP test par excellence.

Trust, honor, character—these are the elements that have departed American public life with the departure from prominence of WASP culture. Rule by meritocrat has not thus far been able to replace them. For all his suavity and cunning, and for all her vast ambition, does anybody really doubt that at bottom Bill and Hillary Clinton are ultimately in business for themselves? However articulate he may sound, and reasonable he may seem, why do Barack Obama's words lack weight and conviction?

A moral component is absent in the culture of meritocracy. A financier I know, who grew up under the WASP standard, not long ago told me he thought that the subprime real estate collapse and the continuing hedge-fund scandals have been directly brought on by men and women who are little more than greedy pigs without a shred of character or concern for their clients or country. Naturally, he added, they all have MBAs from the putatively best business schools in the nation—meritocrats, in other words.

Meritocrats, those earnest good students, are about little more than getting on, getting ahead, above all getting their own. The WASP leadership, for all that may be said in criticism of it, was better than that.

The WASP day is done. Such leadership as it provided is not likely to be revived. But recalling it at its best is a sad reminder that what has followed from it is far from clear progress. Rather the reverse.

The Virtue of Victims

(2015)

Our virtues lose themselves in selfishness
as rivers are lost in the sea.

—LA ROCHEFOUCAULD

F HILLARY CLINTON wins the presidency in 2016, she will not only be the nation's first woman president but our second affirmative-action president. By affirmative-action president I mean that she, like Barack Obama, will have got into office partly for reasons extraneous to her political philosophy or to her merits, which, though fully tested while holding some of the highest offices in the land, have not been notably distinguished. In his election, Mr. Obama was aided by the far from enticing Republican candidates who opposed him, but a substantial portion of the electorate voted for him because having a bi-racial president seemed a way of redressing old injustices. They hoped his election would put the country's racial problems on a different footing, which sadly, as we now know, it has failed to do. Many people voted for Mr. Obama, as many women can be expected to vote for Mrs. Clinton, because it made them feel virtuous to do so. The element of self-virtue—of having an elevated feeling about oneself—is perhaps insufficiently appreciated in American politics.

How have we come to the point where we elect presidents of the United States not on their intrinsic qualities but because of the accidents of their birth: because they are black, or women, or, one day doubtless, gay, or disabled—not, in other words, for themselves but for the causes they seem to embody or represent, for their status as members of a victim group? It's a long but not, I think, a boring story.

In recent decades, vast numbers of people have clamored to establish themselves or the ethnic group or sexual identity or even gender to which they belong as victims of prejudice, oppression, and injustice generally. E. M. Forster wrote of "the aristocracy of the sensitive, the considerate, and the plucky." Owing to the spread of victimhood, we have today a large aristocracy of the suffering, the put-upon, and the unlucky. Blacks, gays, women, American Indians, Hispanics, the obese, Vietnam veterans, illegal immigrants, the handicapped, single parents, fast-food workers, the homeless, poets, and anyone else able to establish underdog *bona fides* can now claim to be a victim. Many years ago, on television, I watched a show that invited us to consider the plight of unwed fathers. We are, it sometimes seems, a nation of victims.

Victims of an earlier time viewed themselves as supplicants, throwing themselves on the conscience if not mercy of those in power to raise them from their downtrodden condition. The contemporary victim tends to be angry, suspicious, above all progress-denying. He or she is ever on the lookout for that touch of racism, sexism, homophobia, or insensitivity that might show up in a stray opinion, an odd locution, an uninformed misnomer. People who count themselves victims require enemies. Forces high and low block their progress: The economy disfavors them; society is organized against them; the malevolent, who are always in ample supply, conspire to keep them down; the system precludes them. Asked some years ago by an interviewer in *Time* magazine about violence in schools that are all-black—that is, violence by blacks against blacks—the novelist Toni Morrison, a connoisseur of victimhood whose novels deal with little else, replied, "None of those things can take place, you know, without the complicity of the people who run the schools and the city."

Public pronouncements from victims can take on a slightly menacing quality, in which, somehow, the role of victim and supposed antagonist is reversed. Today, it is the victim who is doing the bullying: threatening boycott, riot, career-destroying social media condemnation, and frequently making good on their threats. Victims often seem actively to enjoy their victimhood—enjoy above all the moral advantage it gives them. Fueled by their own high sense of virtue, of feeling themselves absolutely in the right, what they take to be this moral advantage allows them to overstate their case, to absolve themselves from all responsibility for their condition, to ask the impossible, and demand it *now*, and then to demonstrate virulently, sometimes violently, when it isn't forthcoming.

Evidence of the taste for victimhood is abundant, and one sometimes discovers it in peculiar places, even among the rich, the famous, and those who have access to publishers. One finds it often in the spate of victim memoirs that have been published in recent decades. These memoirs are at bottom declarations of the victim status of their authors, whose stories are about their having been raised with abusive or alcoholic parents, having been sexually abused, having struggled against a debilitating mental illness. If the only standing higher than victimhood in contemporary America is celebrity, the celebrity victim book—starting years ago with *Mommie Dearest* by Joan Crawford's daughter—rings both gongs simultaneously to make the greatest public noise.

A relatively new sub-genre of the victim memoir are books and essays about that ultimate victim status, those who are about to die, but aren't ready to depart the planet without first announcing it, often at book length. Christopher Hitchens's last book was about his encounter with esophageal cancer. The historian Tony Judt was able to compose a book about his dying from ALS, or Lou Gehrig's Disease, while in the grip of that nightmare affliction. The critic and poet Clive James announced his forthcoming death in 2010, and has been publishing several poems and giving interviews about it in the interval between then and now; the neurologist Oliver Sacks took to the *New York Times* op-ed page to announce his own imminent death by melanoma. All this as if death, that most democratic of institutions, didn't make victims of us all, and wouldn't continue to do so as long as the mortality rate remains at an even 100 percent.

THE CONTEMPORARY UNIVERSITY, where so many misbegotten ideas find fertile ground and ample watering, has been especially hospitable to the culture of victimhood. Two of the most consequential of these ideas, both catering directly to victims, have been multiculturalism and its twin sister, enforced diversity. Multiculturalism, with its insistence that all cultures are equal, has tended to diminish the centrality of western culture, with its dominance of white male writers, artists, philosophers, and to push what one might call victim studies, or victimology, to the forefront of university curricula. The result has been the emphasis on race, class, and gender and the concomitant politicalization—some would add trivialization—of much that goes on in the humanities and social sciences departments.

Universities are proud of their diversity; some have deans of diversity. Every college catalogue shows blacks and Asians lounging languorously on their lush green lawns. Today, the rarest item at Northwestern University, where I taught for many years, is a photograph of its current president unaccompanied by at least one black, an east Indian, a Chinese, Japanese, or Korean, and, any other minority-group student with a few free minutes to kill on a photo op. Affirmative action itself was of course from the outset a victim compensation program.

Now that so many different minority groups have become part of the contemporary university, the sensibility of their members, it became evident, must at all costs not be offended, their self-esteem in no way deflected, let alone deflated. In their putative defense, political correctness inevitably followed multiculturalism and diversity in universities as what psychologists might term a support system. In classrooms, the pronoun police were soon on the prowl, making certain no professor used such proscribed words as "lady" or "oriental" or failed to use "she" at least as often as "he" when citing examples, even if some seemed more than a bit forced: Every construction worker knows she can readily be laid off. As both a prefix (mankind) and a suffix (chairman), "man" had to go. If a teacher mentioned Shakespeare or Tolstoy in class, he had better find a way to drag in, under an unspoken equal-opportunity pedagogy rule, Jane Austen or Virginia Woolf. If he used the word Negro instead of African-American, or homosexual instead of gay, he acquired an instant reputation as a racist or a homophobe. Tell a slightly off-color joke, or make an indirectly sexual allusion, he could be hauled in for sexual assault. Victims, even if self-appointed ones, must be protected at all costs, and political correctness was there to do the job.

Meanwhile the already ample glossary of political correctness grows, with many old words proscribed daily. The most recent is "thug" or "thugs." The reason is that many people, including President Obama, have referred to the violent rioters and looters in Ferguson, Missouri, and Baltimore as thugs. Thugs, it is now understood, means young, riotous black men, and therefore using the word marks its user as racist. The addition of newly politically incorrect language hastens apace; soon a daily bulletin will be required instructing which once commonly used words are now ruled *verboten*.

If the rigidities of political correctness were limited to universities, it might not be so bad. The inmates in the bedlam that has become the contemporary university, after all, seem to get on cheerily enough with one another under this tyranny. Alas, these rigidities aren't so limited. Students graduate, and many, if they take little else with them from their years in college, acquire the censorious sensitivities learned under the reign of political correctness experienced during those years.

I had lunch a few weeks ago with a lawyer in his late seventies who told me that, owing to the retirement of several of his partners, he planned to close his office and move in with a large firm where he would become, in the trade phrase, "of counsel." The deal was set, but before the actual move, he took 12 of what were to be his new firm's associates to lunch, to explain to them how he worked with his clients. The day after the lunch, he was called by a senior partner of the firm and informed that the move couldn't be made after all. When he inquired why, he was told that, at the lunch, he apparently made a joke about a fat man and more than once referred to women who had worked for him as "my girls." The associates, as a body, found this unacceptable, and wanted no part of him. "When I was in college, there were certain words you couldn't say in front of a girl," Tom Lehrer remarked. "Now you can say them, but you can't say 'girl.'"

I happen to know that the lawyer in fact paid these women well, treated them respectfully, and as a result they were as loyal to him as he to them over the decades they worked together. None of which, though, signified, since the associates made their judgment of him on grounds of political correctness, and from the kangaroo courts of political correctness there is no reprieve, no time off for good behavior, and no parole.

IN 1970, SOME 45 YEARS AGO, I wrote an essay in *Harper's* on the subject of homosexuality. The chief points of my essay were that no one had a true understanding of the origins of human homosexuality, that there was much false tolerance on the part of some people toward homosexuals; that for many reasons homosexuality could be a tough card to have drawn in life; and that given a choice, owing to the complications of homosexual life, most people would prefer their children to be heterosexual. Quotations from that essay today occupy the center of my Wikipedia entry. In every history of gay life in America, the essay has a prominent place. When I write something controversial, this essay is brought up, usually by the same professional gay liberationists, to be used against me. That I am pleased the tolerance for homosexuality has widened in America and elsewhere, that in some respects my own aesthetic sensibility favors much homosexual artistic production (Cavafy, Proust, Auden), cuts neither ice nor slack. My only hope now is that, on my gravestone, the words Noted Homophobe aren't carved.

Political correctness excludes candor, or even complexity, in discussion of public problems, questions, issues. Might one bring up the high crime rates of blacks and black-on-black crime in the recent publicity of police shootings of black criminals without being called racist? Is it possible to mention the matter of potential pregnancy when hiring young married women for high-level jobs without being thought anti-woman? If one says sex-change operation instead of gender reassignment surgery, is one hopelessly insensitive? The answer in each case is plain enough: to ask or to say any of these things disqualifies one instanter.

Thus has political correctness, the vigilantism of the victim, squashed discussion and in many realms of public life replaced ethics. Stefano Gabbana, of the clothing firm of Dolce & Gabbana, in an interview with the Italian magazine *Panorama*, recently made the mistake of criticizing in-vitro births. "Wombs for rent," he called such arrangements, "sperm selected from a catalog. . . . Who would agree to be the daughter of chemistry? Procreation must be an act of love, now not even psychiatrists are prepared to deal with the effects of these experiments." The singer Elton John, who with his companion is raising two such children, shot back,

> How dare you refer to my beautiful children as "synthetic"!
> And shame on you for wagging your judgmental little fingers
> at IVF—a miracle that has allowed legions of loving people,
> both straight and gay, to fulfill their dream of having children.
> Your archaic thinking is out of step with the times, just like
> your fashions. I shall never wear Dolce & Gabbana ever again.

In an Instagram, Sir Elton called for a boycott of Dolce & Gabbana clothes, in which he was presently joined by Ricky Martin, Martina Navratilova, and Ryan Murphy, the producer of *Glee*.

Stefano Gabbana, who is himself gay, apologized profusely, claimed that his views are those of someone brought up in the traditional Sicilian family, that he wished all gay couples with children well. His partner Domenico Dolce even chimed in that he loved Elton John's music. "Boycott Dolce & Gabbana for what?" Gabbana asked. "They don't think like you? This is correct? This is not correct. We are in 2015. This is like medieval. It's not correct."

That there is a genuine issue up for serious discussion in IVF births—that it often requires women so hard pressed for money that they agree to carry other people's children in what is a form of modern bondage—is ignored in this exchange. Political correctness, though, isn't about issues, about items in the flux of controversy. It's about denouncing people who don't think as you do, and as such it is a key weapon in the arsenal of victims.

Because virtue is at the heart of so many political questions in our day, in victim culture things get to the contempt stage and beyond fairly fast. Elton John does not strongly disagree with Stefano Gabanna; he wants to put him out of business. Nor does one have oneself to be a victim to claim virtue for one's position. Many bask in the warm virtue of victims by coming out strongly on their side. These are the virtucrats, or those people whose political opinions are propelled by their strong sense of self-virtue. They are people who judge others, mercilessly, by their opinions. Some years ago, a journalist with whom I found myself in a political argument closed off the discussion by claiming that the chief difference between us was that I did not care about people anywhere near as much as he, thus positioning himself as a much finer person than I. An old fellow traveler, a Stalinist in his day, once told me that he was of course wrong about Soviet communism, adding that nonetheless in his heart he was right, while I, who may have been correct in never falling for communism, owing to having early read George Orwell, Arthur Koestler, and Sidney Hook on the subject, in my heart was ultimately wrong for failing to have been moved by the promise of communism.

One of the hallmarks of the virtucrat is his taste for underdogs, or what he takes to be underdogs, no matter how egregious their actions. With the underdogs, after all, is where virtue lies. The true virtucrat lines up with the oppressed (if rocket-launching) Palestinians against Israel, with black and Hispanic criminals apprehended by police, most recently against the French satire magazine *Charlie Hebdo* for mocking terrorists, who after all have feelings, too. In a presidential election between Al Sharpton and Mitt Romney, the virtucrat would have to go for Sharpton. In an earlier election between Louis Farakhan and Ronald Regan, he would, after much moral hand-wringing, probably have taken the high ground and abstained from voting. One of the reasons that virtucrats tend to be anti-American, is that America, however correct its position in foreign affairs, however clearly on the side of justice and generosity, is never—at least not yet—the underdog and therefore can never have virtue on its side.

H OWEVER REPELLENT the professional victims, those who make a nice living off their victimhood— the race hustlers, the academic feminists finding a phallus in every chalice, and others—there is of course a core of truth to the oppression most victims have felt. Everyone knows of the travails of slavery and beyond, the battles of women for equality in the workplace and elsewhere, the mocking and shunning of homosexuals, and the degrading of other victim groups; it was genuine, and painful—its victims truly were victims, and a blot, though one would hope far from an ineradicable one, on our country. Anyone with a conscience in decent repair recognizes and regrets this.

Yet the victims of our day make their appeal not to conscience but to guilt. An appeal to guilt is almost entirely negative; rather than awaken the best in one, it insists those who disagree with one are swine. An appeal to conscience, on the other hand, is an appeal to one's ethical feeling, to one's sense of fair play; it is fundamentally an appeal to act upon the best that is in one, one's better nature.

The brilliance of Gandhi and Martin Luther King, Jr., was their appeal to conscience, reinforced by their non-violent means of achieving their respective ends of Indian independence and the abolishment of vile segregation laws. The victims of our day work at inducing guilt, exacting punishment where possible through boycott and disqualification, and above all capturing, as they have no doubt they do, the high ground of superior virtue. God love them, for it is all but impossible for ordinary men and women to do so.

Cool

(2017)

I don't blow but I'm a fan.
Look at me swing, ring-a-ding-ding.
I even call my girlfriend "man" . . . .

Every Saturday night with my suit
Buttoned tight and my suedes on
I'm getting my kicks digging arty French
Flicks with my shades on.

—"I'm Hip," lyrics by DAVE FRISHBERG

THE FIRST DISTINCTION required in treating Joel Dinerstein's exhaustive—and slightly exhausting—book is that between hip and cool. To be cool is, in Dinerstein's words, "associated with detached composure as well as artistic achievement," while to be hip "is to be knowledgeable and resourceful," above all about those who are cool. Something there is a touch uncool about being hip, a camp follower or chronicler of cool. Joel Dinerstein is the hippest of the hip. To paraphrase Dave Frishberg, he was doubtless "hep when it was hip to be hep."

The Origins of Cool in Postwar America is a lengthy work, 25 years in the making. Its author was curator of a 2014 Smithsonian exhibition called "American Cool" (see "Strike a Pose: The Unbearable Lightness of Being Cool," July 28, 2014) and has written *Coach: A Story of New York Cool* (2016), which is not a book about the New York Knicks under Red Holzman but about the luxury brand of purses and leather goods. During the past 15 years he has taught a course on the history of cool at

Tulane, and is interested in (as he puts it) "the intersections of modernity and popular culture, race and American music, and literature and ethnicity." How cool is that? I'll leave it for you to decide.

A larger, more complex question that Dinerstein's book raises is: How cool is cool itself? Is the phenomenon of cool at all significant in our day? Was it ever? For Joel Dinerstein, cool is an apotheosis, elevating those who possess it to the secular equivalent of near divine status. The major figures in his cool pantheon are the jazz musicians Lester Young, Miles Davis, and Charlie Parker; the film noir actors Humphrey Bogart, Alan Ladd, and Robert Mitchum; the writers Richard Wright, Jack Kerouac, and Ralph Ellison; the existentialist thinkers Albert Camus, Jean-Paul Sartre, and Simone de Beauvoir; the singers and actors Frank Sinatra, Marlon Brando, James Dean, Clint Eastwood, and Elvis Presley; and the playwright Lorraine Hansberry, whose career, for Dinerstein, in some ways marks the end of postwar cool.

In its origin, cool was a creation of African-American jazz musicians to face the pressure of Jim Crow arrangements during a time when the United States was an unembarrassedly racialist white society. At various points in its history, cool was, in Dinerstein's language, "the aestheticizing of detachment," "an emotional mask, a strategy of masking emotion," "a public mode of covert resistance," "a walking indictment of society," "relaxed intensity" played out through the jazz musician, who was "global culture's first nonwhite rebel."

The first figure of cool Dinerstein takes up is Lester Young, the great tenor saxophonist. Born in Mississippi, Young met with Jim Crow at its most intense. He later moved on to Kansas City, where he played in Count Basie's orchestra. Drafted during World War II, he was caught with marijuana and booze in his possession and clapped into a brutal Army jail in Alabama, from which, after a year, he was dishonorably discharged.

Lester Young is the first to have invoked the word "cool" to mean "relaxed and under control." Young also used it to apply to a musical aesthetic that Dinerstein describes as combining "flow and understatement, minimalism and relaxed phrasing, deep tone and nonverbal narration." The guitarist B. B. King, greatly influenced by the playing and personal style of Lester Young, called him the "King of Cool." The blues singer Billie Holiday referred to him as "Prez." Dinerstein provides a telling anecdote about Young remarking to the young drummer Willie Jones III: "You have good technique, Lady Jones, but what's your story?" What he meant, Jones recounted, is that the jazz musician uses music "to project the particular philosophy he subscribes to." Whitney Balliett, that most lyrical of writers on jazz, wrote of Lester Young in performance that "his relation to the band in a solo was that of a migrating bird to a tree: he circled, perched briefly, preened, and moved on; he enhanced the band, but it did not alter him." Every jazz solo, as Dinerstein puts it, "is an artistic transmutation of personal experience processed into sound." Lester Young died at 49, of liver disease and malnutrition brought on by alcoholism.

The incarnation of cool Dinerstein considers after jazz is film noir, those stark movies, some about Western outlaws and urban gangsters, most of them detective stories—many made from Raymond Chandler or Dashiell Hammett novels—whose representative actor was Humphrey Bogart. Cool is of course not a word that the Bogart—or the Alan Ladd or the Robert Mitchum—character in film noir would ever use, let alone call himself; but cool he indubitably was, though in a distinctly different way from the jazz musician's notions of cool.

In his film noir roles, Bogart was usually a private detective, with a dreary office, a furnished room, a single suit, and, of course, his ubiquitous fedora, kept on even during fist fights. His form of cool had nothing to do with adapting a mask to confront an unjust society but everything to do with retaining his integrity in a society that was thought to work against integrity itself. The noir films are distinctly short on happy endings: "Well, I'll have some rotten nights after I've sent you over [to the police]," the Bogart/Sam Spade character says to the Mary Astor/Brigid O'Shaughnessy character at the conclusion of *The Maltese Falcon* (1941), "but that'll pass." And we are confident it will. What will remain intact, though, will be Bogie's ironclad integrity. Cool.

So big was Humphrey Bogart in his day that, Dinerstein reports, Albert Camus was pleased to be told he resembled the actor, not knowing apparently that Bogie wore a hairpiece and, according to Billy Wilder, emitted spittle when he spoke. (Jean-Paul Sartre, I was amused to learn from Dinerstein's book, fantasized that he was Gary Cooper. A better example of what is known as "a stretch" is unavailable.) Camus, who as a member of the French Resistance to the Nazis was a genuine, and not merely a movie, hero, was frequently photographed in the standard film noir trench coat, a half-smoked cigarette pending from his mouth—pure Bogie *à la française*.

Camus, Sartre, & Co. get a lengthy chapter in *The Origins of Cool in Postwar America*, under the title "Albert Camus and the Birth of Existential Cool." But how cool was existentialism, which had a vogue in the 1950s, a time when American intellectuals looked to France for their cultural enrichment? "Existentialism was a theory," Dinerstein writes, lapsing into the abstraction to which he too often falls victim, "of individual response to both religious hypocrisy and the randomness of the universe, both the failures of European superiority and the collateral damage of corporate capitalism."

As a body of philosophy, if anything so muddled and vague could qualify as such, existentialism "found resonance in the United States with intellectuals, artists, rogue leftists, college students, theatergoers, and self-conscious rebels." Existentialism, the philosophy of the absurdity of existence, provided grist for the darkness of Samuel Beckett's plays, Richard Wright's later novels (Ralph Ellison thought Wright "had lost himself, his art, and his culture by casting his lot with the alien philosophy of existentialism"), and much of the higher-falutin' gibberish of Norman Mailer. Dinerstein labors, not entirely successfully, to connect what he calls "an organic American existentialism" to African-American blues, soul, later jazz, and rock 'n' roll.

Women get short shrift in *The Origins of Cool in Postwar America*. But then, cool is not a standard female quality, nor a much desired (or for that matter needed) one. Dinerstein mentions, almost in passing, Barbara Stanwyck, Lauren Bacall, Lena Horne, and Anita O'Day as exemplars of female cool. He gives more attention to Billie Holiday—first called Lady Day by Lester Young—whose life, much sadder than it was cool, ended when she was 44, cirrhosis her killer.

Simone de Beauvoir is the woman who gets more attention than any other. She and Jean-Paul Sartre were, of course, in Dinerstein's phrase, "existentialism's first couple." But the closer the camera bears in on their lives, the less cool they seem. Dinerstein neglects to mention that Sartre was one of the world's true savant-idiots: one of those brilliant minds that gets all the important things wrong, in his case the beneficence of the Soviet Union, the cure for anti-Semitism, and much else. He was also, in his spare time, an earnest lecher: five feet tall, with a bulging right eye and less than scrupulous about hygiene, with Beauvoir's help Sartre lured various young women into his untidy bed; some first had lesbian affairs with her. Sartre and Beauvoir, though never married, were thought to have an open arrangement; but in later years her job was to lure young women, students, and others who had fallen under her influence into sexual relations with the troll-like Sartre. They would later recount these adventures in detailed letters to each other. Simone de Beauvoir, in fact, functioned as (in the cant phrase) Sartre's "enabler." More precisely, she was his pimp—not cool, not in the least; squalid, rather, sordid in the extreme.

The Beats, for Dinerstein, are notably cool, with Jack Kerouac's writing, a form of "blowing," or jazz performance. Dinerstein is high, if such an adjective may be called into service on this subject, on Jack Kerouac. "Kerouac," he writes, "brought together Zen concepts, jazz practice, blues poetics, and European modernist ideals into a new synthesis for American literature." He holds that the literary success of the Beats was due in part to their calling out

> the West's dysfunction: the distinction between its claimed religious precepts and its immoral actions, between its soapbox morality and pragmatic capitalism, between its abstract Enlightenment values and its seeming technological death wish.

The fact is that the Beats formed no "synthesis for American literature," and they achieved nothing like a literary success. Taken up by *Time* as gaudy good copy, they belong (as was said of the Sitwells) less to the history of literature than to the history of publicity. Surely no single figure was less cool than the boisterous, needy, publicity-hungry Allen Ginsberg humming Zen mantras in a soiled sheet.

Joel Dinerstein has a regrettably strong taste for abstraction. Such a taste is needed to commit such sentences (and many similar ones pop up in his pages) as "With the temporary evisceration of economic uncertainty came a rejuvenation of national confidence and American triumphalism" and

"Here we see the rise of a neoliberal ideology that combines or conflates technological rationalism with a neo-Christian ethos and telos." He is big on Marxian "commodification" and seems to be much worried about "the consumer society," as if in the modern world there were any other kind. The words "charisma" and "valorization" get a good workout in his pages, and if I had $10 for every time Dinerstein uses the word "iconic," my great-grandchildren would never have to work.

"Frank Sinatra," he writes, "became the primary avatar of cool renewal for the wartime generation and shifted its cultural imagination from past to future with the onset of national prosperity." Dinerstein has gathered much amusing material about Sinatra. The bandleader Harry James, for example, wanted him to change his name to "Frankie Satin." Sinatra became the hero of "swingers"—not an entirely enviable, let alone cool, audience to have in thrall.

"Dean Martin," Dinerstein writes, "played an equal role in shifting a generation's ideal from the solitary consciousness of Hemingway's existential cool to the swinger's playboy bacchanalia." On the cool scale, Dean Martin weighs in more heavily than Sinatra: Utterly independent, he genuinely seemed not to have given a rat's rump about anything. This would include his friend Frank Sinatra's propensity to suck up to the powerful—the Mafia, the Kennedys, finally the Reagans—which Martin pointed out and claimed simply not to understand. But anyone with any knowledge of Sinatra's life without a microphone in his hand will find it difficult to think well of him, for the stories of his bullying, his meanness, and cruelty, are manifold. "Frank saved my life one night in a parking lot in Las Vegas," Don Rickles joked. "He said, 'That's enough, boys.'"

The next wall in Dinerstein's gallery of the cool consists of Marlon Brando, James Dean, and Elvis (last name available on request). Cool, in other words, is now to be found in jeans and leather jackets and often seated on motorcycles (*varoom, varoom*). Cool becomes openly, though not very precisely, rebellious. When in *The Wild One* (1953), the Brando character is asked what he is rebelling against, he answers, "Whaddya got?" James Dean's great breakthrough was in *Rebel Without a Cause* (1955). The problem, according to Dinerstein, now shifts to "the tensions of [the] inner life." Cool suddenly has a psychotherapeutic side. Marlon

Brando cries in *A Streetcar Named Desire* (1951)—something, surely, Humphrey Bogart never would have done. Dinerstein refers to Brando as "therapeutic man," noting that, among the cool, "neurosis was no longer suppressed but expressed, a sign of how deeply psychoanalysis had penetrated aesthetic and intellectual communities."

James Dean and Elvis apparently were in awe of Marlon Brando, as Bob Dylan and John Lennon would come to be of Elvis. Brando and Dean, Dinerstein reports, "were gay icons and had bisexual relationships." Brando would in later years take on enough weight to pass as Orson Welles's twin; Elvis ended his days a pillhead nearly too fat to squeeze into his glittering stage costumes. These new cool rebels did not grow old coolly. James Dean, after appearing in three dud movies (*Rebel Without a Cause, East of Eden, Giant*) made the savvy career move of dying at 24 by crashing his speeding Porsche, and thus allowing Dinerstein to call him "postwar cool's Keats or Rimbaud"—minus, he neglects to add, the talent. Cool would henceforth remain an option open exclusively to the young.

T HE STRONGEST CHAPTER in *The Origins of Postwar Cool* is that on Lorraine Hansberry, author of *A Raisin in the Sun* (1959), who sounded the buzzer signifying the end of cool. She attacked the Beats, saying "they have made a crummy revolt, a revolt that has not added up to a hill of beans." She wrote a play, *Les Blancs*, mocking Jean Genet's *The Blacks* for its ultimate emptiness. And while she was at it, she claimed that Samuel Beckett, Norman Mailer, and Albert Camus, with their literary existentialism, were artistic failures. She felt that the *angst* about the specter of nuclear war, which supposedly affected entire generations, was a fraud: "As a playwright, civil rights activist, and feminist," Dinerstein writes, "Lorraine Hansberry represents the end of existential cool and the onset of a period of participatory social change often just called the '60s." Perhaps only a black, bisexual woman married to a Jewish husband could have brought all this off.

If one didn't look too closely at the squalor behind the scenes during his White House days, John F. Kennedy would seem to have qualified as cool. In a famous-in-its-day *Esquire* article, Norman Mailer, who perhaps wrote and said more stupid things than any writer in the past century, styled Kennedy "Superman Comes to the Supermarket." Dinerstein calls Kennedy's death "the most transformative" of all in the postwar era. It now begins to look as if all that John F. Kennedy (who preferred to go hatless) transformed was the sale of men's fedoras.

The hippie revolution was implacably youthful—"Never trust anyone over 30" was one of its shibboleths—and the heir of the coarser remnants of cool. "In the mid-1960s," Dinerstein writes,

> the mask of cool exploded out of its black and Beat phases [and] the inflection of rebellion moved away from African-American culture towards a new counterculture and its emphasis on drugs, a value on personal authenticity, and an earthier lifestyle.

Yet the leaders of the counterculture—Abbie Hoffman, Jerry Rubin, Tom Hayden, Rennie Davis—were not cool in any way that Lester Young, the phenomenon's inventor, would have recognized.

Dinerstein's final definition of cool is the muzzy one of "a subconscious method for negotiating identity in modernity through popular culture." Yet in the realm of popular culture, perhaps the last figures to qualify as cool were Steve McQueen and Paul Newman. Brad Pitt, with his sloppy marriages, certainly isn't cool, nor is George Clooney. No rapper I know of qualifies as cool, including the fellow who calls himself LL Cool J. Yet, Dinerstein holds,

> Cool has not faded, but its meanings have morphed with every generation . . . and to consider or call someone cool remains the supreme compliment of American and global culture—even as it has been nearly emptied of generational and ideological conflict, of artistic risk and vision, of old transgressions and social change.

The Origins of Cool in Postwar America, though written to vaunt the richness of the concept of cool and its possessors, has had, at least on this reader, quite the opposite effect. Apart from those early black jazz musicians who required the mask of cool to face a cruelly hostile world, cool turns out to have been the preoccupation, chiefly, of less-than-first-rate writers, shoddy thinkers, and poseurs generally. Undreamt of in the philosophy of those who have ardently strained after the appearance of cool, courage, kindness, generosity, and natural refinement are the things that are, and always have been, truly cool.

The Sixties

(2017)

I**T'S A RORSCHACH TEST**: Say what you think of the 1960s and you reveal a great deal about yourself.

For some, the sixties were a time of splendid creative disorder, in which a rigid cultural and impossible political life underwent critical and long-needed change. The Establishment, that congeries of social, economic, and political power connections, was everywhere under attack. During these years civil rights were expanded, especially for blacks in the segregated south. Women's rights beyond the suffrage were beginning to be recognized. Sexuality (with the important aid of the birth-control pill) was freed from its old middle-class constraints and straitjacketed morality. Windows were everywhere flung open. People could at last breathe in the fullness of life.

For others, the sixties were hell on earth. Disruptive protest was endemic. Drug experiments often brought permanent derangement or death by overdose to the young. In the sexual realm, orgiastic squalor was deemed normal and sex itself became a trivial act. Authority was everywhere undermined, as tradition was spat upon under the banner of glib shibboleths: do your own thing, change the paradigm, don't trust anyone over 30. All this in the name of . . . what—anarchy, a misguided notion of democratic values, revolution itself? The sixties, in this view, put an end to dignity, seriousness, a middle-class way of life that made the United States the splendid country it only recently was.

The first problem confronting anyone contemplating the sixties is that the decade shows up the thinness of accounting for history by the all-too-tidy decennial category. An argument can be made that the sixties really began in 1965, with the Free Speech Movement at the University of California at Berkeley. One can just as easily maintain that it began in the late 1950s with the black student sit-ins at lunch counters in the south in protest of immoral segregationist accommodations. Some would set the beginning of the sixties with the election in 1960 of John F. Kennedy, who ushered in a new spirit of youthfulness; for others his assassination marked the start of the sixties. The journalist Christopher Hitchens, despite his later political change, always identified himself as a *soixante huitard*, or man formed by 1968, the apex of sixties agitation and excitement. Many would hold that the great watershed event of the sixties was the Vietnam War, though that war was not fully engaged until 1969 and not officially ended until 1973.

The motives behind the "student unrest"—my favorite of all euphemisms—that set its seal on the sixties are also in contention. Some argue that moral revulsion was behind the protest movements of the decade: genuine hatred of injustice in nearly all realms of American life, culminating in the deadly injustice of asking young men to die in a needless war in Southeast Asia. Others claim this is tosh, that the anti-Vietnam protests were about little more than prosperous college students protesting to save their own bottoms, perfectly willing to let working-class whites and poor blacks die in their place. As proof of their argument they note that, once the draft was abolished, the protests immediately simmered down, then ceased. Isaiah Berlin thought that the student protests in America and Europe, were chiefly the product of *ennui*:

> The Welfare State, prosperity, security, increasing efficiency, etc. do not attract those young who feel the need to sacrifice themselves for some worthy ideal, if possible in company with other like-minded persons, and that they are desperately searching for some form of self-expression which will cause them to swim against some sort of stream and not simply drift in a harmless way, too comfortably with it.

At one point Berlin refers to these young as "barbarians."

Some say the sixties haven't ended yet, and that the overall cultural effect of the sixties far exceeds that of the thirties, the other crucial twentieth-century decade in American life. They point to the fact that many of those who had a good sixties are now in power: in the universities, in politics, in the bureaucracy, the media, throughout the culture generally, exerting a strong sixties influence on current events. Identity politics, the prominence of victim groups (blacks, LGTBQ, *et alia*), the rise of multiculturalism, the democratization of the university, the ready turn to street protest, the radical change in both the constituencies and the nature of the Democratic and Republican Parties, and so much more—all of it, without great difficulty, can be accounted for as a direct legacy of the sixties.

The key figures of the sixties are now either dead or easing into old age. Allen Ginsberg, Paul Goodman, Stokely Carmichael, Norman Mailer, Timothy Leary, Jane Fonda, Bob Dylan, Tom Hayden, Joan Baez, Gloria Steinem, James Baldwin—figures of protest all. Joseph Heller's antinomian novel *Catch-22*, the hippie musical *Hair*, the movie *Easy Rider*, the druggier songs of the Beatles and of the Rolling Stones, all these, the most famous artistic products of the sixties, were in the main in opposition to mainstream culture. Art, though, was never the leading *motif* of the sixties; the politics of protest was, together with the undermining of middle-class values.

One's reaction to the sixties is likely to have been conditioned by one's own personal situation during the time. Perhaps the best time to have been going through the period was in one's twenties and the best place in one or another graduate school; to be, in other words, of an age that put one fully in the stream of life, open to physical—sexual, pharmaceutical, political—freedom and experiment, with little or nothing at stake in taking radical positions. Best, surely, during the sixties to have been unmarried and without children.

I was myself married and with four children. I was 23 when the 1960s began and 28 in 1965, with two stepsons and two sons of my own. My stepsons were in adolescence as the decades proceeded. Lots of talk about various drugs bruited about among them and their friends; on occasion, listening in on their conversation, one might have thought them passionate chemistry majors. One of the boys living in our apartment building died from drug overdose. Pot was standard fare, the Hershey bars of the sixties generation. Schoolwork wasn't where the action was, nor athletics. Adulthood could be put off, apparently endlessly. As a parent, responsible for bringing children safely into harbor, it was a frightening time, or so to me it seemed. I remember often thinking I was glad not to have had daughters.

I considered myself a strong liberal, leaning to the radical, in politics. I thought John F. Kennedy, for example, a sell-out; another pretty face but business as usual, little more. I thought American society deeply philistine. Backed by the books of H. L. Mencken and Sinclair Lewis, I thought the middle class, though it was the class of my origin and upbringing, hollow and hypocritical. If you had said to me, as my father used sometimes to say that "you can't argue with success," if you meant success in America, I would have answered that I knew of nothing better to argue with.

Living in the South in 1963–64, I was, at the age of 26, director of the anti-Poverty Program for Little Rock, Arkansas, and its surrounding county. As such I befriended and worked with the local chapter of the Student Non-Violent Coordinating Committee (SNCC), the courage of whose members in facing down angry southern police and their German police dogs I much admired. When I say "worked with" I mean I gave local SNCC leaders advice on how to secure federal funds for their own political causes. I felt myself on their side as I did on the side of all blacks whose lives in the south were clearly stunted by inferior education and other segregationist arrangements. I was impressed by Lyndon Johnson, whom I thought of as John F. Kennedy minus the Camelot baloney and with real political savvy added.

The first inkling I had of feeling uncomfortable with the sixties was when graduate students from Columbia, Barnard, and NYU came down to Little Rock, supposedly to aid the black cause. A few taught at the city's two impoverished Negro colleges, Philander Smith and Shorter; others worked on SNCC projects. They were fundamentally unserious, I thought, spending a summer doing moral tourism. One among them, a young woman, called me at my anti-Poverty office to notify me that a protest march was planned that afternoon at the state capital building and that I was expected to attend.

"If I do," I said, "I would have to give up my job and with it any possible further usefulness I might have."

"You're either with us or not," she replied, and hung up.

Not long after I left Little Rock, Stokely Carmichael, one of the leaders of SNCC, announced that the time had come for the Civil Rights Movement to declare for Black Power, which meant white participation was no longer welcome and which put an end to the integrated movement that had until then had such splendid momentum. Thus the first and last great moral movement of my lifetime—"moral" in the sense that it set out to right clear wrongs and its appeal through moral suasion was to the best nature of Americans—ended, heartbreakingly, in shambles, never to regain its former strength or standing.

I would encounter something of this same moral righteousness that I found in the New York students come down to join the civil rights movement among the young at my next job. This began in 1965 in Chicago, where I was a senior editor of *Encyclopaedia Britannica*. The spirit at *Britannica* was preponderantly liberal, in a largely admirable way. One editor there remained in his home in the South Shore neighborhood long after the neighborhood had become nearly all black. Another, an older woman, had moved into a deliberately and carefully integrated apartment complex on the near South side called Prairie Shores to show that not only her heart but her entire body was in the right place.

The younger editors at *Britannica* were differently disposed, keener on symbolic behavior than on committed actions. The smell of pot wafted in the back stairwells at Britannica. Anti-Americanism was part of coffee-break conversation. One among these younger editors used to say about anyone he found loathsome, "He's a great American."

I began teaching in the English Department at Northwestern University in 1973. The Vietnam War was over, and so, one might think, was the sixties. But the universities, where much of the tumult had begun, was among the first of the country's institutions to continue to feel the effects of the era in a powerful way. The significance of the university in keeping alive the spirit of the sixties can scarcely be overestimated. The reason, of course, is that members of the sixties generation for the past 40 or so years have been the preponderant teachers of college students, and have imbued many of these students with their own sixties-formed views.

The university culture I entered as a teacher in 1973 was vastly different than the one I had known as a student two decades earlier at the University of Chicago. An almost militant informality now reigned. Younger professors taught in jeans and tee shirts. They called their students by their first names, and in some instances their students returned the compliment. Student evaluations, one of the small victories of the student uprisings, were now installed, so that at the end of every term a professor was, in effect, graded by his students. This put being lively, as opposed to be being thorough or serious, at a premium.

Course titles—"Television Commercials as Poetry," "Science Fiction in the Real World"—began to sound more like uninteresting magazine articles than university courses. Marxism, disqualified elsewhere in the world, found a home in contemporary English departments. Fresh political interpretations of traditional works were everywhere on offer. Shakespeare turned up gay in one classroom, a running dog of 17th-century English imperialism in another. A graduate student once came to me to ask if I thought David Copperfield "a sexual criminal." She went on to explain that the man who taught the Victorian novel in our department thought he was because he had contributed to his first wife's death in childbirth—contributed, that is, by making her pregnant in the first place. Not nice to knock a colleague, no matter how nutty or stupid he might be. "We sleep tonight, Ms. Jones," I replied, "criticism stands guard," and walked off.

"Question Authority," another shibboleth of the sixties, took a direct toll on universities, where intellectual authority was formerly, quite properly, at the heart of things. In an earlier era, the chairman of an academic department was the most distinguished man, less often woman, in the department. In what the sixties academic rebels would view as the bad old days, he set the tone and more important the standard, in scholarship, conduct, seriousness generally. If a young instructor wished to teach a course in, say, the Beat Generation or the novels of Kurt Vonnegut, the chairman, was likely to say sorry, but such subjects fall below the line of serious literary study. Besides, students could read such stuff outside the classroom on their own without pedagogical aid.

Now, with the chairman being someone who has agreed to take on the job, with all its pettifogging administrative tasks, only because it meant as a reward he could lighten his teaching load or take an earlier sabbatical, no one, really, is at the helm. Now there is unlikely to be anyone to tell a teacher he can't do the course in "Star Wars and the Literature of Apocalypse." Owing to the sixties, conduct became, and has remained, free-floating, with everyone in business for himself. Any outside interference with what goes on in the classroom or outside of it with students is likely to be viewed, incorrectly but firmly, as an infringement of academic freedom, as if the right to egregious behavior and politicizing courses were what academic freedom is about.

MIDWAY IN MY TEACHING CAREER at Northwestern, a woman named Barbara Foley arrived to teach in the English Department. She was a no-bones-about-it Marxist. At Northwestern she openly proselytized undergraduate students, ushering them into a group she called INCAR, or International Committee Against Racism. Everyone knew about this proselytizing; nobody stood ready to object. Only when she allowed, after organizing a shout-down of a Nicaraguan Contra speaker, that the man didn't have a right to speak—in fact, she said he deserved to die—and that First Amendment rights didn't apply to him did she get into difficulties. None of this, not even her turgid Marxist writings, got in the way of her being offered tenure by the Northwestern English Department. When the university's provost, an honorable and earnest traditional liberal named Raymond W. Mack, denied approval of her tenure on the grounds of her uncivil behavior, many of her colleagues among the faculty protested. The Modern Language Association, by this time itself vastly politicized, beseeched Northwestern to reverse its decision, though under another man of principle, the school's then-president Arnold Weber, the school did not back down. It held that anyone who acted on the belief that he or she didn't believe in free speech was not a worthy citizen of a serious university. Foley is still in business, now a distinguished professor at Rutgers, unaltered in her politics, still arising each morning hoping to greet the revolution.

A few of Foley's converted students wandered into one or another of my courses at Northwestern, and a rigid and dreary cadre they were, little lunatics of one idea, seeing the exploitation of the workers, blacks, not least themselves, everywhere. Soon enough they were joined by the academic feminists, whose one idea was that current arrangements were everywhere stacked against women, with the cure for this being more courses featuring Virginia Woolf, Kate Chopin, and other women writers, and a more thoughtful disposition of pronouns and suffixes, and an end to what they called "phallocentrism." I retired from university teaching before the Queer Theorists took hold, multiculturalism kicked in, and victimology became the real and staple subject of so many university courses in the humanities and social sciences. But of course the way had been prepared for all this by what you might call the enforced tolerance of the sixties.

IN THE SIXTIES, the adversary culture, a term first used by Lionel Trilling, and standing for an academic milieu opposed to the prevailing mainstream, itself came close to becoming the mainstream. One of the chief inheritances from the sixties was the death of traditional liberalism, a liberalism devoted to public justice, political equality, economic opportunity, and honorable disagreement with opponents—the liberalism of such politicians as Hubert Humphrey, such writers as John Steinbeck, such intellectuals as Lionel Trilling himself.

If the sixties killed liberalism, it also did a pretty good job on adulthood. Most men and women who went through the sixties even now find it difficult to oppose any doctrine or behavior that is leftist in its origins or inspirations, for to do so would be to betray their youth. Among his many wise political apothegms, Orwell wrote that liberals fear few things more than being outflanked on the left. In the 1930s, this fear brought many liberals into the Communist Party, put them on the side of the Stalinists in Spain, caused them to overlook the monstrousness of Lenin and sanitize the cruelty of Trotsky, and turn the Democratic Party over to identity politics. History has never been an effective teacher, and so 30 and more years later, liberals, out of fear of being outflanked once again, everywhere gave way to radicals, so that dogmatic academic feminism, victimological African-American Studies, and the rest found a secure place in the first watering and then dumbing down and thorough politicizing of university study that eventually seeped through the general culture.

Scratch a man of the sixties, who now himself may well be in his seventies, and you will discover someone who feels a continuing, if in however lingering a form, allegiance to the era of his youth. Youth is the keyword here. The great promise of the sixties was to snatch the world from the stodgy and dodgy old, and make it anew for the ebullient young. I occasionally see men I taught with who are now in their late sixties and early seventies who dress as if still students. They carry backpacks, wear baseball hats backwards, are in jeans and gym shoes—in what I think of as in youth drag. But for their lined faces, gray hair—and the occasionally heartbreakingly sad gray ponytail—they might themselves be students. Clearly they intend to go from juvenility to senility, with no stops in between.

The price of the sixties was the death of a once-admirable liberalism and the eclipse of adulthood. Some would say, considering the broadening of American society overall, it was well worth it. Your call. Rorschach Tests, after all, aren't graded.

University of Chicago Days

(2017)

"Everyone was neurotic, weird, bizarre—it was paradise."
—MIKE NICHOLS

THE FORTUITOUS, happening by accident or chance and not by design, a word never to be confused with the fortunate, plays a larger role in people's lives than they might think. Certainly it has in my own.

When I was in the Army, stationed at Fort Hood, Texas, I learned that there were openings for typists at recruiting stations in Little Rock, Arkansas, and Shreveport, Louisiana. I applied, and one morning soon after was told that I had been selected for one of these jobs. I met with a southern staff sergeant, a man I judged to be not long on patience, who said, "Take your choice, Shreveport or Little Rock." I had a nano-second to reply. Shreveport, I thought, Louisiana, good food, Catholic, possibly interesting illicit goings-on; Little Rock, Governor Faubus in power, politically volatile, closer to Chicago. "Little Rock, Sergeant," I said. Subsequently, in Little Rock, I met and married and had two children with my first wife. What, I have often wondered since, if I had said "Shreveport, Sergeant?"

I had more time to think about going to the University of Chicago, but my thoughts about the place were scarcely more informed than my thoughts about Little Rock and Shreveport. Even though I lived in Chicago all my life, I had never seen the place, with its fake but nonetheless grand gray Gothic buildings. In Chicago one lived in one's neighborhood as if in a village, and my village, West Rogers Park, in the far north of the city was as far from the University of Chicago and still in Chicago as it was possible to be. The University of Chicago was reputed to be radical, some said "pinko," meaning vaguely communist. This reputation derived, I learned much later, from the school's president, Robert Hutchins, making it clear that he wasn't going to be pushed around by Senator Joseph McCarthy and his crude anti-Communism. Hutchins had also eliminated the school's Big Ten football team and installed a program, known jokingly as Hutchins's Children's Crusade, that allowed students as young as fifteen to matriculate at the university. The word "nerdy" not yet having come into existence, people who went to Chicago were in those days thought "brainy."

Brainy was the last thing I would ever have been called. A thoroughly uninterested high school student—I graduated 169 in a class of 211—my high school years were spent playing basketball and tennis, pursuing girls, and establishing myself as a good guy, which is to say, as a genial screw-off. When it came time to go to college, my father, a successful businessman who left high school in Montreal at seventeen to move to Chicago, told me he would pay for my college, but he wondered if my going to college weren't perhaps a waste of time. He thought I would be a terrific salesman. Since that is what he was, there was a compliment implicit in the thought. He may well have been right on both counts, but I decided that, like most of my friends, I should give college a shot.

In those days, the University of Illinois at Champaign-Urbana, had, in effect, open enrollment, at least if you were a resident of the state. You could have three felonies and graduate last in your class and the school still had to take you, on probation, to be sure, but take you they did. So, without anything resembling study habits, having read no book of greater complexity than that of *The Amboy Dukes,* without a single intellectual interest, with no goal in mind but, hope against hope, to avoid flunking out, in 1955 I mounted the train at Chicago's Twelfth Street station for Champaign-Urbana.

I had never heard the term liberal arts until I arrived at the University of Illinois. And then I heard of it as a way out of majoring in business, which most of the boys I hung around with did, no doubt to establish their seriousness, both to their families and to themselves. I did know enough about myself to realize that the dreariness of accounting courses and the rest of it would have paralyzed me with boredom. ("Lloydie," the successful immigrant father of a friend of mine is supposed to have said to his son, who evinced an interest in accounting, "don't be a *schmuck*. You don't study accounting. You hire an accountant.")

My first year courses at the University of Illinois included Biology, French, Rhetoric (really freshman composition), physical education, and ROTC, the latter two being requirements at a land grant college. Biology in those pre-DNA days meant little more than distinguishing among and memorizing the phyla. French meant memorizing, too, irregular verbs and the rest. I was too unsophisticated to known that my instructor, a man named Philip Kolb, was the editor of the French Plon edition of Proust's letters, for which he won a prize from the *Academie Francaise* and the legion of honor. I made it through Rhetoric by steering clear of anything tricky; and tricky at that time meant using a semi-colon or dash or attempting a sentence longer than twelve words. I got mostly Bs.

Bs were good enough to get me into the University of Chicago. This was in part because my generation—those of us born late in the Depression—was a small population cohort, so small that the universities actually wanted us. Then, too, Chicago, for reasons I've mentioned, was not a particularly popular place for undergraduates. When I was there, I believe there were fewer than 2,000 undergraduates alongside more than 6,000 graduate and professional students. I remember awaiting word about my admission, and when, by late April, none arrived, I drove to the university to inquire about it from the dean of students, a man named Robert Strozier. "Wait a minute," he said, went to a file cabinet, pulled out a folder that he quickly glimpsed, and said, "Yes, you can come if you like."

I began that summer (1956) at the University of Chicago taking what was called the Math Course. I was living at home, and somehow made a connection with another University of Chicago student from West Rogers Park who was also taking the course. He drove me down for the first day's class. When the three-hour class was over, I suggested we alternate driving each other down each day.

"I won't be here," he said.

"What do you mean?" I asked.

"I'm going to Europe for the summer. I'll be back in time to take the comp [the six-hour examination given at the end of the College's year-long courses, an exam that counted for one-hundred percent of your grade]."

I gulped and said no more. At the end of the summer, there he was, seated for the exam, and looking a lot more confident than I felt.

The course itself, I should say, was most impressive. The first two-thirds were pure logic in which no numbers were mentioned ("if p, then not q equals?"). The last third was analytical geometry, and, based on what one learned in the first two thirds, seemed easy.

The College at the University of Chicago was devised of fourteen year-long core courses, in all of which one took a single comprehensive examination, known as "comps," at the end of the year. (By the time I arrived at Chicago, one also had to declare a major outside the College.) Some kids were so well prepared and good at taking examinations that, during placement exams on entering the school, they "placed out," or got credit for, fully two years' worth of courses. No attendance was ever taken in any of the College courses. Essays might be assigned, but one's grades on them counted only to show students how they were doing. I recall no quizzes. Most mystifying of all, one's teachers, like tutors at Oxford and Cambridge, did not grade students. Something called the College's Examiner's Office did. This simultaneously removed the whole matter of playing up—sucking up—to teachers, and it gave one's grade a more objective feel. During my own university teaching days a few decades later, I longed for an Examiner's Office, so that all emotion would be divested from grading my own students. I think especially of those perfectly mediocre students who nonetheless tried so very hard that giving them a grade less than B- seemed an act of cruelty. On such kindly emotions has the current endemic phenomenon of grade inflation been built.

At the University of Illinois I was a member of a fraternity, Phi Epsilon Pi, the leading Jewish fraternity on campus. Fraternities and sororities in those days at most schools were strictly segregated by religion, an arrangement about which no one complained. The University of Chicago had nine fraternities and no sororities whatsoever. I moved into one called the Phi Psi house, not as a member but as boarder, because an acquaintance of mine who was a member told me the fraternity had plenty of extra rooms, which it rented out for $35 a month. (Tuition at the University of Chicago in those days was $690 a year; at the University of Illinois it was $90 a semester.)

Phi Psi was a shambles, less a fraternity than a hot-sheet joint. People moved in an out. A fellow in medical school lived there with a beautiful biracial girlfriend with the wonderful name of Arizona Williams, who audited the occasional course at the university and was said to dance at a black-and-tan club on the edge of the Loop. Another graduate student, working on a PhD in bio-chemistry, lived with his fiancé and a German Shepherd. A few fellows at Phi Psi were in their middle twenties and who dropped out of school but didn't want to leave the university's Hyde Park neighborhood, an enclave, an island, of culture in philistine Chicago. Years later, I had a call from a man named Robert Lucas, a Nobel Prizewinner in Economics, asking me for a donation for our class gift. "What do you mean 'class'?" I said. "There were no 'classes' at the University of Chicago. You entered at 15 and left at 27, often without a degree."

An enormous fellow, perhaps 6'5", a Korean War vet at the university on the GI bill named Bob Bruhn, held a full-time job at Commonwealth Edison while going to school, boarded at Phi Psi. He once came into my room to ask if he might use the phone. During his call, to his recently divorced wife, he listed all their possessions that he no longer needed: furniture, appliances, linen, and ended by saying, in a plaintive voice, "If you still have that recording of 'Tenderly,' I'd be grateful if you would save it for me, sweetie."

A scruffy bohemianism obtained among University of Chicago students of those days. On campus, an even moderately well-dressed person would have looked strikingly out of place. A militant unkemptness ruled, as if to divagate from the pursuit of truth and beauty for the mere niceties of respectable grooming were to demonstrate one's puerility. The university, I used to say, had a single quota, that on attractive young women: among undergraduates only four were allowed in at any time. A joke of the day had it that a panty raid on Foster Hall, the women's dormitory, rendered a field jacket and a pair of combat boots.

In later life I met a number of my teachers at the University of Chicago—a few sent me manuscripts for the *American Scholar*, which I then edited—and none recognized me as a former student. No reason they should have done. My classroom strategy was to hide out. Not coming from a bookish home, I did my best to conceal my ignorance, which was substantial, and looked above all to avoid embarrassing myself. The possibilities for embarrassment were manifold. Had you not seen nor heard them before, how would you have pronounced the names Thucydides, Proust, Wagner? No doubt wrongly.

Most of my classmates seemed confident in their views, aggressive in their opinions. Many of them were New Yorkers, and, it later occurred to me, were probably reading the *Nation* and the *New Republic* from about the age of thirteen. Their parents and friends no doubt argued about Trotsky, Bakunin, Max Schachtman, the Moscow Trials, the Soviet-Nazi Pact. In my family, politics wasn't a serious subject; all politicians were crooks until proven innocent, which, in Chicago, few were. Many of my fellow students had doubtless been in psychotherapy. I recall with a slight shudder during the course called Social Science Two, when we read Ruth Benedict's *Patterns of Culture,* a classmate blithely describing her own experience with menstruation and comparing it with those of the women of the Kwakiutl Indian tribe. Many among my fellow students also had a fair amount of musical culture, whereas musical comedy was as high as musical culture reached in West Rogers Park. In her memoir *A Backward Glance*, Edith Wharton notes that the great thing as a young person is never to be considered promising. So many of the promising young men of her acquaintance who began life soaring, under the burden of their early promise, went down in flames. I qualified nicely here. Promising is not something I was ever considered.

By my second year at the University of Chicago, I had a acquired a modest cultural literacy. I remember sitting in a modern poetry class taught by Elder Olson, and his mentioning Baudelaire. By then I knew that Charles Baudelaire was a French poet, nineteenth century, dark in subject matter, author of *Les Fleurs du Mal*—and that exhausted my knowledge of Baudelaire. Olson began to chant, "*Hypocrite lecteur!—mon frère, mon semblable . . .*" when he was joined in his chant by Martha Silverman, the girl sitting next to me. Which meant she, Miss Silverman, not only knew Baudelaire's poetry, but had it by memory and in French. At that moment

I felt the sharp stab of hopelessness, and wondered whether they might be taking job applications at Jiffy Lube?

Among students at the University of Chicago, brilliance, not solidity was the goal. Three names of notable students at the school, George Steiner, Allan Bloom, and Susan Sontag, all somewhat older than I, might stand in as representative University of Chicago graduates, each brilliant, all crucially flawed. How many Chicago undergraduates went on to distinguished careers I do not know. Not so very many, I suspect. Too many, perhaps, were promising.

I never tried for brilliance myself, and wouldn't have come close to achieving it if I had done. My body may have been in the classroom, but my mind frequently deserted it. I remember concentrating a fair amount of time on the perilously long ash of Elder Olson's cigarettes. Another teacher might remark on the way one's eye follows a certain sweep in a painting, though my eye never did. A teacher might set out eight reasons for the Renaissance, and I wondered what possessed him to buy that hopeless necktie. For grades I received chiefly Cs with a light scattering of Bs, and, best memory serves, not a single A. I have since come to take a perhaps unseemly delight in great figures in literature and philosophy who were less than stellar students, some indeed dropouts: a roster that includes Pascal, Tolstoy, Henry James, Paul Valery, F. Scott Fitzgerald, and others. Mike Nichols, from whom I take my epigraph, entered the University of Chicago in 1950 as a pre-med student, and dropped out in 1953 without a degree.

I did better outside the classroom with the bookish offerings at the university. One of the best things about the College was that no textbooks were used. So one didn't read that "Freud said . . . ," "Plato held . . . ," "Marx stipulated . . . ," "J. S. Mill believed. . . ." Instead one read Freud, Plato, Marx, and Mill. Heady stuff, for a nineteen-year-old with only *A Stone for Danny Fisher, The Hoods,* and *Knock on Any Door* under his belt. I remember the deep aura of gloom I felt while reading Freud's *Civilization and Its Discontents* and the excitement of noting the dazzling connections made by Max Weber in *The Protestant Ethic and the Spirit of Capitalism.*

Everywhere through the undergraduate curriculum at Chicago in those days one ran into Aristotle and Plato: *The Poetics, The Rhetoric, The Ethics,*

The Politics, The Phaedrus, The Symposium, The Crito, The Apology. When it came time to declare a major, I decided on English, only to learn that the university's English Department in those years was heavily Aristotelian in its approach to literature.

In my last year at the university, looking for a soft fourth course, I signed up for something called "History of Greek Philosophy." Thales, Prythagoras, Democritus, Heraclitus, I figured, learn a few of their key concepts, fill in the rough dates of the narrative of the history—how tough could it be? First day of class the teacher, an exceedingly tidy-seeming man named Warner Arms Wick, announced that there really isn't an impressively coherent history of Greek philosophy before Plato and Aristotle, so we would chiefly be reading Plato and Aristotle during the quarter.

Harvard, it was said, was tougher to get into than the University of Chicago, but Chicago was tougher to get out of. (Another saying had it that the University of Chicago was where fun went to die.) No soft spots anywhere for an undergraduate at the University of Chicago in those years. In the English Department, which might have been thought such a soft spot, undergraduate students, along with their regular course work, were examined at the end of their junior and senior years on two extracurricular reading lists that contained perhaps seventy-five items each. The items on the lists were precisely those that any young person should prefer, if at all possible, to avoid reading: Hobbes's *Leviathan,* Milton's *Paradise Regained,* Spenser's *The Faery Queen,* Richardson's *Pamela,* Locke's *Second Treatise on Civil Government.* A better organized student than I might have read them over the regular academic quarters; I needed to forfeit my summer vacations to do so. In fact, I only finished my second, or senior, reading list while in the Army, and took the examination on it on a pool table at Headquarters Company at Fort Hood, Texas, proctored by an ROTC second lieutenant from Alabama, the passing of which allowed me to graduate, A.B. *in absentia* from the university in 1959.

What the University of Chicago taught, even to a student with little preparedness and a wandering mind, was a standard of seriousness. This standard continued long after my departure from the school. In my early thirties, I became a close friend of Edward Shils—I would not have been prepared for him any earlier—for decades one of the great figures at the university. I recall Edward saying, "You know, Joseph, I fear that my colleagues on the Committee on Social Thought labor under the misapprehension that Richard Rorty is an intelligent man." (This at a time when every university in the country was seeking Rorty's services.) On another occasion, Edward said, apropos Hannah Arendt, "No great *chachemess* [wise women], our Hannah." Toward the end of his career, Edward brought Arnaldo Momigliano, the great historiographer of the ancient world, to teach at the University of Chicago. After the loss of a gifted graduate student to Princeton, Arnaldo, himself Jewish, noted: "A Jewish boy. The Ivy League beckons. He is gone." Teachers such as Edward, Arnaldo, Christian Mackauer, Enrico Fermi, Leo Strauss, many of them Europeans, gave the university a cosmopolitan tone and serious feeling unavailable anywhere else.

No trivial books were taught at the University of Chicago during my time there. The only books by living writers I encountered were in a course on the modern novel taught by Morton Dauwen Zabel: *Howard's End* by E. M. Forster, *Brighton Rock* by Graham Greene, and *A Handful of Dust* by Evelyn Waugh. This was of course long before multiculturalism, feminist studies, political correctness, and the rest kicked in, and so there was no need to teach, or for students to read, secondary writers to show they were on the side of the progressive political angels.

The University of Chicago in those years favored, in Max Weber's distinction, "soul-saving" over "skill-acquiring" education. If there were then undergraduates majoring in economics, I never met them. The university in those days seemed outside the orbit of capitalism itself. A graduate business school was housed in the main campus quadrangle, but in the era before the MBA became the golden key to open corporate doors, it seemed anomalous, besides the point. The knock on the University of Chicago Law School then was that it was "too theoretical," which really meant too philosophical; if one's aim was to get a job with a Chicago law firm, it was said one did better to go to Northwestern Law School.

Job-getting wasn't what the University of Chicago was about. Only careers in the arts, scientific research, politics practiced at the highest level, with, at second remove, the teaching of artists, scientists and statesmen also being acceptable, were thought worthy of serious people. A conventional success ethos, such as Santayana discovered early in the last century at Yale, was never in force at Chicago. To be lashed to money making, even if it resulted in becoming immensely wealthy, made a person little more than one of Aristotle's natural slaves, a peasant raking gravel in the sun. No surprise, then that great economic success has not been notable among the school's graduates. Not without reason has the University of Chicago, compared with other major universities, had a comparatively small endowment.

In the mid-1960s, while working at *Encyclopaedia Britannica*, I would occasionally meet Robert Hutchins, under whose youthful presidency (begun in 1929 when he was twenty-nine years old), the radical institution that was the University of Chicago College had been set in motion, and found him an immensely handsome but weary and sad man. Hutchins had earlier ardently wished to become a Supreme Court justice, a job Franklin Delano Roosevelt dangled before him but cruelly withdrew. He had instead since 1959 been running the Ford-Foundation-Fund-for-the-Republic-sponsored think tank in Santa Barbara, California called The Center for the Study of Democratic Institutions—also known derisively as The Leisure of the Theory Class—which wasted its time on such hopeless projects as devising a constitution for a world government. At lunch one day at the Tavern Club in Chicago, he, Hutchins, knowing I had gone to the University of Chicago, asked me if I knew whether they had restored football there, a remark witness to his sense of defeat and disappointment and suggesting that his one great accomplishment, founding the College with its Great Books centered learning, had also come to nothing.

I should have but neglected to assure him that, as far as I was concerned, it had come to a great deal, at least for me. Under the influence of Robert Hutchins' College at the University of Chicago, I set out on a life of high culture, which I may never have attained yet never regretted. Because of the values fostered at Chicago, I determined to become a writer with a confidence in the rightness of my decision that I was unlikely to find anywhere else.

Not long ago my son reminded me that when it was time for him to go off to college, I told him that I hoped he would be able to get into a school that the world, "that great ninny" (as Henry James once called it), thought a good school. He would, I told him, probably discover that the school wasn't so good as all that, but at least he would not spend his life feeling that if only he had gone to a good college his life would have been happier. This advice was of course based on my own experience, except that I found the University of Chicago in the mid-1950s better than I had ever imagined, and owe it more than I can hope to repay.

"Little Rock, Sergeant," why not the University of Chicago, out of such rash decisions are lives shaped.

Part Two
Literary

Eric Auerbach

(2014)

T. S. ELIOT THOUGHT that the first requisite for being a literary critic is to be very intelligent. The second, I should say, is to have a well-stocked mind, which means having knowledge of literatures and literary traditions other than that into which one was born; possessing several languages; and acquiring a more than nodding acquaintance with history, philosophy, and theology—to be, in brief, learned. To be both highly intelligent and learned is not all that common. Eliot claimed for himself—and this by implication, for he was a modest man—only the former.

Erich Auerbach (1892–1957) had both great intelligence and great learning. Born in Germany, Auerbach, along with other Jewish scholars of his time, was another of Adolf Hitler's intellectual gifts to the United States. After being expelled from his academic post as professor of Romance Philology at the University of Marburg during the Nazi purges, he spent eleven years, between 1935 and 1946, at the University of Istanbul. Arriving in the United States in 1947, he first taught at Penn State, was briefly at the Institute for Advanced Study at Princeton, and ended his career at Yale.

While in Istanbul, Auerbach wrote *Mimesis: The Representation of Reality in Western Literature*, which is the greatest single work of literary criticism of the 20th century. Auerbach worked on the book between 1942 and

1945, and it was first published in 1946. Part of the mythos of *Mimesis* has been that he wrote it without the aid of a serious library. This is somewhat exaggerated. The University of Istanbul was far from academically primitive, and Auerbach was in touch with friends who could send him such literary materials as he required.

That he didn't have access to a library that stocked scholarly periodicals probably worked in his book's favor. *Mimesis* is a scholarly work unencumbered by footnotes or other critical apparatus. At the close of the penultimate paragraph of the epilogue, Auerbach writes,

> [I]t is quite possible that the book owes its existence to just this lack of a rich and specialized library. If it had been possible for me to acquaint myself with all the work that has been done on so many subjects, I might never have reached the point of writing.

Erich Auerbach was a philologist. Once a standard academic discipline, philology is no longer in currency, let alone in vogue. In its traditional form, philology dealt with the structure—the grammar, syntax, and semantics—of language and its historical development. Philology has always seemed a more Continental than English or American enterprise. In America, scholars who in an earlier era might have taught philology taught, instead, what became known as comparative literature. In time, comparative literature fizzled out, taken over by literary theorists who turned out to be not all that much interested in literature in any language.

What distinguished philologists and comparativists was their polyglotism. They knew multiple languages, and an article of belief among them was that literary works can only be truly comprehended in the languages in which they were composed. If you read works in translation, you are, from the philological standpoint, a *schmoozer*, a *potzer*, a *kibbitzer*, and fundamentally unserious. In the prologue to his recent *Musings on Mortality: From Tolstoy to Primo Levi*, Victor Brombert, who for many years taught comparative literature at Princeton, notes that "in all cases, I have discussed only authors whose works I have read in the original."

Erich Auerbach read eight languages: Greek, Latin, German, Italian, French, Spanish, Portuguese, and Hebrew. In *Mimesis* he remarks that he scanted a detailed discussion of the rise of realism in Russian literature because "this is impossible when one cannot read the works in their original language." (I, the reader should know, read *Mimesis* in the excellent English translation from the German by Willard R. Trask.)

In his 1952 essay "Philology and World History," Auerbach asserted that

> the intellectual and spiritual history of the last several millennia is the history of the human race as it has achieved self-expression. It is with this history that philology concerns itself as a historical discipline.

The task of philology, he held, was to evaluate literature and language in such a way that it might contribute to that history, "and thus to realization of a unified vision of the human race in all its variety." Auerbach felt this task all the more pressing given "the impoverishment of understanding associated with a concept of education that has no sense of the past"—an impoverishment, he added, that threatens to become "hegemonic." He also accepted as "inevitable that world culture is in the process of becoming standardized." About this, at a time when people are claiming the nation-state an anachronism, he was surely correct. Every time I hear the word "globalization," I reach for my copy of *Mimesis*.

The publication of *Time, History, and Literature: Selected Essays of Erich Auerbach* provides an excellent opportunity to witness a master philologist at work. This book includes: five essays on Giambattista Vico, the philosopher of history and an important influence on Auerbach, who translated Vico's *Scienza Nuova* (1725); four essays on Dante, the subject of Auerbach's first book (*Dante: Poet of the Secular World*, 1929); and essays on Montaigne, Pascal, Racine, Rousseau, and Proust. Two of the essays, "Figura" (1938) and "*Passio* as Passion" (1941), are more traditionally philological in subject matter and treatment.

In the first of these essays, Auerbach considers the meaning of the word "*figura*," its history, and its import in medieval Christian literature, where it denoted foreshadowing and prophecy. The Old Testament, in this regard, was thought to prophesy the New Testament, and Virgil to prophesy Dante. This essay shows, as Auerbach writes,

> how a word branches out from its semantic meaning and into a world-historical situation and how the structures that emerge out of this situation can remain effective for many centuries.

In his essay on the word "*passio*," Auerbach demonstrates how, over the centuries, it elided into the word "passion." At its inception, *passio* denoted passiveness and suffering, which is how it was understood in its religious sense—hence, the Passion of Christ—and went on to become associated with erotic passion, or "a heightening of human existence worth pursuing." In a brilliant essay not in this book titled "La Cour et La Ville" (1951), Auerbach does a similar workup of the changing meaning of the word "public," setting out its differing meanings at different times.

Serious scholar though he was, Auerbach was no less impressive as a literary critic. In fewer than six pages, he places, describes, and explains the power of Marcel Proust's great novel *À la recherche du temps perdu* (*In Search of Lost Time*). "Next to it," writes Auerbach, "all the other works we know seem to be no more than novellas." Better than anyone I have read, Auerbach is able to convey the experience of reading Proust's novel:

> No story of the centuries past seems so overwhelmingly historical, so covered with patina, so finally and irrevocably over, so mummified, antique, and eternal as the one he gives to us in his representation of Parisian society around 1900 and of the intelligent and sickly young man who inhabits it.

ALTHOUGH AUERBACH finds the novel's astonishing cast of characters ultimately beyond description, he writes:

> This chronicle of the inner life flows along with a kind of epic uniformity, for it is only memory and self-examination. The novel is the authentic epic of the soul; truth itself ensnares the reader in a long, sweet dream in which he suffers a great deal, to be sure, but in which he also enjoys a release and sense of calm.

In Search of Lost Time is, in short, a work of "ever-flowing pathos that at once oppresses us and sustains us without end."

Auerbach's knowledge of the historical circumstances under which literary works were written allowed him exceptional insights into how these works came into being. He characterizes Rousseau, for example, by stating that

> of the men who are well known in European intellectual history, [he] is the first who, despite a thoroughly Christian constitution, was no longer able to be a Christian.

In intellectual circles, the Enlightenment of the second half of the 18th century had scotched the notion of original sin, and with it the belief in evil, thus freeing writers of the time to believe in the more preposterous notion of the perfectibility of human beings. Rousseau, Auerbach notes, "could no longer find a place in any Christian church, and also failed to found a new one."

Michel de Montaigne was, for Auerbach, the first generalist in literature, and next to him every other important figure in the 16th century was "a mere specialist." Montaigne claimed to write for himself; yet in doing so, he created an educated public. It was Montaigne, Auerbach writes, who "created a community of lay people and his book became the lay book par excellence." The pleasure one takes in reading Montaigne is unique; his work is neither aesthetic nor didactic, nor always logical in direction, but is nevertheless always compelling. It is the pleasure of witnessing a man beholden to no one, never lapsing into cliché or bromide, writing truthfully about life, and never forgetting its ineluctable conclusion. Auerbach formulates the message of Montaigne thus:

> I am alone, I have to die. This world is not my home, I am only passing through, but where I have come from and where I am headed—I do not know. What is the only thing that is mine? My self.

Montaigne also gets a chapter in the center of *Mimesis*. The book is divided into 20 chapters, each illustrating the advance of literature as it finds ways of capturing more and more of the actuality of life.

Auerbach averred that his "purpose is always to write history," but literary history usually confines itself to a period or is conducted within
national borders. In *Mimesis*, Auerbach covers nearly 3,000 years and
vast stretches of Western literature. English literature tends to get short
shrift, and American literature isn't even mentioned; yet somehow one
scarcely notices.

While realism is Auerbach's subject, he doesn't provide an elaborate
or exact definition of it. In traditional literary studies, realism comes
down to works of literature that deal with common, often even inar-
ticulate, people and their struggles and inchoate desires. One thinks of
Frank Norris or Theodore Dreiser. Auerbach's idea of realism is simultaneously much more widely gauged and cuts much deeper. Realism,
for him, stresses the actuality of peoples' lives and the way in which literature, through the art of mimesis, raised man (as Auerbach writes in
his book on Dante) "out of the two-dimensional unreality of a remote
dreamland or philosophical abstraction, and moved him into the historical area in which he really lives."

In *Mimesis*, Auerbach demonstrates why, at certain periods, writers were
not able to deal with many social questions and psychological problems
that later became central to literature. They weren't able to, in part, because
they didn't have the stylistic resources to do so; in part, because entire sec-
tors of the population were considered out-of-bounds to literature. One of
Auerbach's most suggestive chapters is on the rise of Christianity, with its
emphasis on the drama of salvation that included kings and peasants and
everyone in between. Before Christianity, literature was the equivalent of a
chess game played only among kings, queens, and knights.

Literature, unlike science, does not operate on a script of progress, every
day in every way getting better and better. Yet history is far from negligible
in literature. Auerbach understood that precursors made the existence of
great works possible, and that great works, in their turn, extended the literary possibilities for successors. *Mimesis* is a dazzling exercise in tracing this
phenomenon.

The first of Auerbach's 20 chapters, "Odysseus' Scar," takes up two
passages, one from *The Odyssey*, the second from the Old Testament,
through which he demonstrates that, unlike characters in the Old

Testament, characters in Homer do not develop. Hector remains Hector and Achilles remains Achilles; but Abraham, Isaac, and Jacob undergo radical changes over their lengthy lives.

Classical literature, for all its strength and beauty, excluded social or historical explanations for the behavior of its characters. Classical historians—Tacitus, for example, whom Auerbach rightly considers "a great artist"—were much more interested in vice and virtue than in political forces and general ideas. Like kings, classical poets and dramatists, writing from on high, looked down upon their subjects. Their ethical and rhetorical approach, Auerbach writes, is "incompatible with a conception in which reality is a development of forces" acting upon individuals. In classical literature, order, clarity, and dramatic impact take precedence over the sometimes scruffy, but often interesting, details of quotidian life. The elevation inherent in classical style, the words available to classical writers, and the syntactical limitations on their deployment made it impossible to write about everyday things in a natural way.

Auerbach's method in *Mimesis* is to choose a passage a paragraph or two long from an important or representative literary work and examine how it is made. An example is Emma Bovary's discomfort, bordering on disgust, regarding her husband's slow and methodical eating habits. These are passages that, Auerbach writes, "contain the whole." With his customary brilliance at comparison and making connections, Auerbach denotes how these passages signify the expansion or retardation of literary sensibility. *Mimesis* recounts the story of how literature went from Priam to Proust, from an invocation to the gods to Mrs. Ramsay's stream of consciousness while darning a pair of brown socks.

Making literary judgments in an authoritative yet never dogmatic way, Auerbach does riff-like analyses of the boundaries that history, at different times, set on literary works. "Augustine," he writes, "masters the stylistic contrast of classical and Christian world-view." Gregory of Tours's language "is but imperfectly equipped to organize facts . . . but things come to Gregory directly; he no longer need force them into the straitjacket of an elevated style." Of the figures in the *Chanson de Roland*, he notes that they "have no reality; they have only signification." Francis of Assisi, along with being a saint, was

> a great poet . . . an instinctive master of the art of acting out
> his own being, [who] was the first to awaken the dramatic
> powers of Italian feeling and of the Italian language.

Voltaire's genius is for tempo. The Duc de Saint-Simon, in his all-inclusive method, his

> synthesis of a human being which is so entirely free from
> traditional harmonizing, which presses so unswervingly on
> from the random data of the phenomenon itself to the ultimate depths of existence,

is a writer at least a century ahead of his time.

After *Don Quixote*, Auerbach writes, "so universal and multilayered, so noncritical and nonproblematical gaiety in the portrayal of everyday reality has not been attempted again in European letters." The tradition of knightly adventure and chivalric romance, which Cervantes devastatingly satirized in his great novel, had exerted

> a restrictive influence upon literary realism, . . . [for] courtly
> culture was decidedly unfavorable to the development of a
> literary art which should apprehend reality in its full breadth
> and depth.

Once *Don Quixote* came into the world, the genre of courtly romance could no longer be written with a straight face.

Dante is the key figure in *Mimesis*, because Auerbach felt his stylistic advances were such that "we come to the conclusion that this man used his language to discover the world anew." Dante was the great bridge between the medieval and modern worlds: "He gave us," Auerbach writes, "for the first time in literature, the history of man's inner life and unfolding." His presuppositions may have been Christian, harking back to Thomas Aquinas, but his poetry was thoroughly modern.

Dante was a writer of the highest skill: His language was precise, his metaphors were elegantly concrete, and his masterly syntax allowed him to form sentences of sublime construction. Here is Auerbach, not in *Mimesis* but in *Dante: Poet of the Secular World*, describing what the poet achieved in the *Divine Comedy*:

Nearly every line of the *Comedy* reveals enormous exertion; the language writhes and rebels in the hard fetters of rhyme and meter; the form of certain lines and sentences suggests a man frozen or petrified in a peculiarly unnatural position: they are monumentally clear and expressive, but strange, terrifying and superhuman. That is why Dante is associated with Michelangelo in the popular mind.

Cervantes and Dante were literary geniuses, and no one, not even so brilliant a critic and scholar as Erich Auerbach, can account for genius. Cervantes and Dante greatly advanced the history of realism in literature; other literary geniuses—Marcel Proust, James Joyce—did not. Shakespeare's genius is admitted, but being *sui generis*, his influence on realism was less than significant—so much the worse for realism, some might say. Auerbach avers that "Shakespeare embraces reality but he transcends it."

Modern realism sets in for Auerbach in 19th-century France, with Stendhal and Balzac, both of whom used "contemporary political and social conditions as the context" for their novels:

Insofar as the serious realism of modern times cannot represent man otherwise than as embedded in a total reality, political, social, and economic, which is concrete and constantly evolving—as is the case today in any novel or film—Stendhal is its founder.

Auerbach favors the realism of Stendhal and Balzac over that of Victor Hugo and Gustave Flaubert. Of the novels of Flaubert and the Goncourt brothers, Auerbach writes that they exhibit "something narrow, something oppressively close." The novels of Émile Zola, "one of the very few authors . . . who created their work out of problems of the age," in Auerbach's mind, marks the apogee of realism for the 19th century. Auerbach is, perhaps, too high on Zola, and predicts (thus far mistakenly) that "his stature will increase as we attain distance from his age and its problems—the more so because he was the last of the great French realists."

Moving into the modern—really, the modernist—era: Proust, Joyce, and Virginia Woolf may not be realists in the strict sense of the term, but the development of realism made it possible for these authors to concentrate in the richest possible detail on the interior lives of the narrator of *In Search of Lost Time*, Stephen Dedalus and Leopold Bloom, and Mesdames Ramsay and Dalloway.

Mimesis is a book by a man with little interest in theory, setting out definitions, or laying down laws. Yet so suggestive, so rich in understanding and insight, so useful in teaching one how to read more deeply and appreciatively is the book that it is difficult to believe that anyone will ever again have the intellectual resources to write another book about literature anywhere near as powerful. Written while the Nazis were marching across Europe, *Mimesis* is a strong reminder of the glory of Western literature, and by extension of Western civilization, and of what is at stake in the battle against those who would simplify, politicize, or otherwise degrade it.

Kafka

(2013)

THE FORMIDABLE LITERARY CRITIC Edmund Wilson claimed that the only writer he could not read while eating his breakfast was the Marquise de Sade. I, for different reasons, have been having a difficult time reading Franz Kafka with my breakfast. So much torture, description of wounds, appearance of rodents, beetles, vultures, and other detestable creatures, settings of disorientation, sado-masochism, unexplained cruelty, all set out before a background of utter hopelessness—distinctly not a jolly way to start the day. Kafka doesn't make very comforting reading at bedtime, either.

Hypochondraical, insomniac, food faddist, cripplingly indecisive, terrified by life, horrified by death, Franz Kafka turned, as best he was able, his neuroses into art. As a character in Isaac Bashevis Singer's story "A Friend of Kafka" says, he "showed *homo sapiens* in his highest degree of self-torture." Still, the consensus remains that Franz Kafka is a modern master—a master, more specifically, of modernism, housed in the same pantheon as Joyce, Picasso, Stravinsky, Mallarmé, and other modern artists who have radically altered contemporary understanding of the world.

Kafka's wrote in what Erich Heller called "lucid obscurity," adding that "his is an art more poignantly and disturbingly obscure than literature has ever known." One thinks one grasps his meaning, but does one,

really? All seems so clear, yet is it, truly? One of Kafka's famous aphorisms reads: "Hiding places there are innumerable, escape is only one,
but possibilities for escape, again, are as many as hiding places." Another
runs: "A cage goes in search of a bird."

With Kafka's aphorisms, so with his parables. Walter Benjamin wrote
that "Kafka's parables are never exhausted by what is explainable; on the
contrary, he took all conceivable precautions against the interpretation
of his writing." Whatever these precautions may have been, they were
inadequate, for the works of Franz Kafka, apart perhaps only from the
Bible and Shakespeare, may be the most relentlessly interpreted, if not
over-interpreted, in the modern world.

The September 12, 2012 issue of the London *Times Literary Supplement*
ran a review of no fewer than five new interpretive books on Kafka. *Franz
Kafka, The Poet of Guilt and Shame* by Saul Friedlander is the latest entry
in the Kafka interpretive derby. Mr. Friedlander is not by trade a literary
critic but an historian. His affinity for Kafka is historical and genealogical.
His family origins, like Kafka's, are in Prague, German-speaking and Jewish. His father went to the same law school that Kafka did, though fifteen
years later. As Kafka lost his three sisters, so did Mr. Friedlander lose his
parents, in Nazi death camps.

Mr. Friedlander is well aware of the competing theories about the
meaning of Kafka's small body of work. This includes three uncompleted novels, fewer than two dozen short stories, an assemblage of
fragment-like shorter works, his diaries, collections of letters mostly to
fiancées whom he never married, and his famous *Letter to My Father*,
which he never sent. Mr. Friedlander's method in this short book is to
work back and forth from the life to the work in the attempt to explain
Kafka's significance. His own view is that Kafka was "the poet of his
own disorder." He has no doubt about his greatness, though he resists
explaining in what, exactly, it resides.

"The issues torturing Kafka most of his life were of a sexual nature," Mr.
Friedlander writes. Although he doesn't say so straight out, he appears to
believe that Franz Kafka was a repressed homosexual—that the guilt and
shame of his subtitle were chiefly over his hidden sexuality. He offers no
clinching proof of Kafka's homosexuality, and at one point goes so far as

to say "it is highly improbable that Kafka ever considered the possibility of homosexual relations."

Yet in Kafka's stories, Mr. Friedlander finds, "there is a secret to be discovered, something that the protagonists attempt to hide. Doesn't this recurrent metaphor bring us back to Kafka's constant effort to hide his sexual leanings?" In the unending critical Easter-egg hunt for the secret meaning in Franz Kafka's fiction, Mr. Friedlander has retrieved the gay egg.

At one point Mr. Friedlander remarks on Kafka's interest in young boys (Death not in Venice but in Prague). At another he remarks that "Kafka's representation of women is grimacing at best." A youthful "homoerotic" interest on Kafka's part in friends is noted. In the story "A Country Doctor," the wound in the side of the boy the doctor has been called out to heal, a wound suppurating worms, is, Mr. Friedlander agrees with another critic, symbolic of the vagina. Ah, we sleep tonight; criticism stands guard.

Kafka, the critic Jeremy Adler holds, is "less dazzling than Proust, less innovative than Joyce, [but his] vision is more stark, more painful, more obviously universal than that of his peers." Kafka's universality derives from his operating at a high level of generality. Places are not named, characters often go undescribed, landscapes sere and menacing appear as they might in nightmares. Joyce and Proust work from detail to generality, Kafka from generality to detail, giving his fiction the feeling of parable, of something deeply significant going on, if only we could grasp what precisely it is.

"The vicinity of literature and autobiography could hardly be closer than it is with Kafka," wrote Erich Heller, "indeed, it almost amounts to identity." The broader lineaments of Kafka's autobiography are well-known. Taken together they comprise a life of nearly unrelieved doubt and mental suffering.

From his *Letter to My Father*, we know that Kafka's father Herrmann Kahn was strong and oppressive, a man who left his son with a permanent feeling of inadequacy. We know of the drudgery of Kafka's work as a lawyer at the Workmen's Accident Insurance Institute in Prague, and the first-hand acquaintance it gave him of the hideous entanglements of bureaucracy (that now go by the name Kafkaesque). Perhaps most pertinent are his misfired love affairs. Kafka made four different marriage proposals, and never made good on any of them. He died in 1924 at forty-one, of tuberculosis, without having quite lived except during those solitary nights that, in trance-like exaltation, he devoted to his writing. Before his death, he instructed his stalwart friend Max Brod to destroy much of his work, but against Kafka's wishes Brod chose not to do so, thereby becoming a minor hero of literature.

The crushing father figure comes in for a good workout in such Kafka stories as "Metamorphosis" and "The Judgment." In other stories, one is presented with pure, unexplained *Angst*. These are the stories whose characters are being severely punished for petty crimes ("In the Penal Colony"), or even for crimes they are unaware of having committed (*The Trial*). Conveying nightmares in lucid detail, chronicling the unravelling of lives in which illogic becomes plausible, guilt goes unexplained, and brutal punishment doled out for no known offense, such is the art of Franz Kafka.

In his *The Tremendous World I Have Inside My Head, A Biography of Franz Kafka,* Louis Begley, one of the best interpreters of Kafka's life, especially of his relationships with women, claims that in his fiction he "wrote about the human condition." Erich Heller, in his Modern Masters book on Kafka, held that his writing transcended "most realities of the age." Neither man, though, tells quite how he did these things.

Benjamin, Begley, Heller, Friedlander, and other critics who take Kafka's greatness as an artist as self-evident hold that he cannot be either explained or judged in the same way as other literary artists. Walter Benjamin believed that

> Kafka's entire work constitutes a code of gestures which surely had no symbolic meaning for the author from the outset; rather, the author tried to derive such a meaning from them in ever-changing contexts and experimental groupings.

"In Kafka's fiction," writes Mr. Friedlander, "the Truth remains inaccessible, and is possibly non-existent." Mr. Begley, remarking on an object referred to as "Odradek" in a five-paragraph exercise called "The Cares of a Family Man," writes: "Some things cannot be explained." Of "Metamorphosis," Kafka's most famous story, Erich Heller writes that it defies any established intellectual order and familiar form of understanding, and thus arouses the kind of intellectual anxiety that greedily and compulsively reaches out for interpretation.

Gabriel Josipovici, noting that one hundred years have passed since Kafka wrote his story "The Judgement," writes:

> We are probably no nearer to understanding that or any other of his works today than his first readers were, nor should we expect to be.

In other words, Kafka is given a pass on criticism. The argument is that he cannot finally be explained, but merely read, appreciated, re-read until his meaning, somehow, washes over one. But what if this meaning seems oddly skewed and even outmoded in the way great literature never is?

Claustral was Kafka's life, and claustral is the feeling that accompanies reading him today. As Mr. Friedlander underscores, Kafka came into his maturity as a German-speaking Jew in anti-Semitic Czechoslovakia—as a minority, in other words, within a minority—a condition that was to worsen after the death of the relatively benign rule of Emperor Franz Josef. Kafka's fiction was created in the closing years of the Austro-Hapsburg Empire, where Otto Weininger, author of *Sex and Character*, and even more Sigmund Freud, emphasized the centrality of family and the sexual life in human development. Touching on the hot-house intellectual atmosphere of this time, Mr. Friedlander quotes the German critic Willy Haas (1891–1972): "I cannot imagine how any man can understand him [Kafka] at all who was not born in Prague in the period 1880 to 1890."

And much, it is true, isn't easily understood. For a man who claimed to be under the lash of a tyrannical father, Kafka nevertheless lived at home until he was nearly forty. He strung women along for years—poor Felice Bauer, his longest standing fiancée for five years—holding out hopes for marriage on which he could not deliver.

Kafka felt that his "talent was for portraying his inner dream-life." But dreams, however gripping they can be, are aesthetically unsatisfying, especially in their endings. Kafka himself did not find the ending of "Metamorphosis," his greatest and most famous story, satisfying. Perhaps for the same reason, he was unable to complete his novels: dreams, especially nightmares, have no artistic endings. Another character in Singer's story "A Friend of Kafka's" says of *The Castle*, "It's too long for a dream. Allegories should be short."

Kafka is credited with powers of prophesy in predicting, through his novels *The Trial* and *The Castle*, the totalitarian regimes that would arise after his death, especially that of the Soviet Union with its arbitrary, insane, yes Kafkaesque, crushing bureaucratic apparatus for killing. But today, the stories of fatherly tyranny carry too strong an odor of the now moribund doctrine of Sigmund Freud—Oedipus Complex and all that. His break-through story, "The Judgement," about a father who sentences his son to death by drowning, causing the young man to jump off a bridge in suicide, he claimed to have written under the influence of the doctrines of Sigmund Freud. The centrality of dreams in his stories also reflects Freud's certainty about the significance of the dream life. The spread of Freudianism and the rise of Kafka's reputation ran, not without good reason, parallel. Kafka often reads like Freud fictionalized. Freud's reputation is now quite prop-erly in radical decline, Kafka's, somehow, lives on undiminished.

All of which brings one round to the question of whether Franz Kafka was truly a major writer. His greatest proponents among critics, insist-ing that he is, cannot say why he is, and ask a permanent moratorium on conventional criticism of his writing. His detractors, a distinct minority, feel that what he left us was, in the words of Edmund Wilson, a "half-expressed gasp of a self-doubting soul trampled under." In the end, wrote Henry James in his essay on Turgenev, we want to know what a writer thinks about life. Kafka found it unbearably complicated, altogether daunting, and for the most part joyless—not, let us agree, the best pre-scription for a great artist.

Orwell

(1990)

IX YEARS AFTER the heavily over-Orwelled if otherwise unfateful year of 1984, and fully forty years since his death in 1950, one still feels that nothing like a clear picture of the precise quality of George Orwell has yet to emerge. Fame—a great, billowy, international cloud of fame—has got in the way. Ozone-like layers of controversy, chiefly having to do with conservative and left-wing claimants to Orwell's political legacy, have further obscured the atmosphere. The highly uneven nature of Orwell's writing has sent up yet more in the way of mist. Q. D. Leavis, for example, who early praised Orwell's essays and criticism, asked that he write no more fiction. Then there is Orwell's life, which from one standpoint appears so seamless, an unblemished sheet of uninterrupted goodness, and then from another makes him appear a cold and rather tasteless fish indeed, whose first wife felt that her husband's work came before her and in fact before everything else in life and who died during an operation for an illness—presumably cancer—he scarcely knew about.

Fame of the kind enjoyed by performing artists, politicians, and other public figures is rarely available to writers and creative artists generally. Whenever he was in danger of thinking himself famous, Virgil Thomson used to say, he had only to go out into the world to disabuse himself of the notion. Soon after the burial of Balzac, a writer always keenly interested in fame, the bookkeepers at the Père-Lachaise Cemetery sent their bill for services to the family of "M. Balsaque." Surely there must be a lesson here somewhere.

George Orwell's fame—which has been largely a posthumous phenomenon—has been not only extraordinary but across the board: popular, academic, intellectual. What put Orwell on, in fact all over the map were his two international best-sellers, *Animal Farm* (1945) and *Nineteen Eighty-Four* (1949). These books have been translated into more than thirty languages and have by now sold scores of millions of copies. In the English-speaking world, they are nearly unavoidable; for some years now students have generally encountered *Animal Farm* in junior high school or its equivalent and *Nineteen Eighty-Four* in secondary school and are frequently asked to read an Orwell essay or two in university composition courses: "A Hanging" (1931) or "Shooting an Elephant" (1936), perhaps, or "Politics and the English Language" or "Why I Write" (both 1946). Among schoolchildren nowadays, the name George Orwell may be better known than William Shakespeare. George Orwell's fame has been not only extraordinary but across the board: popular, academic, intellectual.

Unfortunately for Danielle Steel and Euclid, it is neither number of books sold nor number of children forced to read an author that confers upon him true literal fame. Instead it is the currency of his ideas that matters. Here Orwell has scored, and scored heavily. "Orwellian" has clearly left "Kafkaesque," "Chekhovian," and other literary eponyms far behind. Partly, of course, this is owing to recent decades having been—if you will allow the expression—highly Orwellian. But partly it has to do with the stark clarity of Orwell's ideas, or at least the chief ideas of *Animal Farm* and *Nineteen Eighty-Four*. So much is this less so in Orwell's other writings—his essays and nonfictional books—despite the lucidity of each discrete work, that the question of whether Orwell was finally a man of the Left or not will probably never be entirely settled.

Between the "finer grain" and the "broader outline" writers, Orwell was surely among the latter—among, that is, those writers whose work can be reduced to its essential ideas, as the work of Henry James, Marcel Proust, and George Santayana cannot. So much have the ideas extracted from Orwell's writing been in the air that one needs scarcely to have read him to have a strong notion of what these ideas are. Just as one need not have read through Marx to be aware of the class struggle and economic determinism, or have read much of Freud to know about the Oedipus complex and the importance of dreams, slips, and early sexuality, so one does not really have to have turned a page of Orwell to know that "some pigs are more equal than others," that "Power is Knowledge," and that Big Brother (the creep) is watching you.

In personal testimony to this fact, I can report that, toward the end of 1984, the year of the great Orwell glut, I was asked to add to the slag heap by giving a little talk on *Nineteen Eighty-Four*, which I glumly agreed to do. It was only when I sat down to prepare this talk that I realized that I had never read *Nineteen Eighty-Four*. I had seen the American movie version, with the impressively sweaty-faced Edmund O'Brien playing Winston Smith; I had for years heard bandied about—no doubt bandied about myself—such terms as "newspeak" and "doublethink"; I had read a number of essays on the novel; but as for actually having read the novel itself, nope, I couldn't rightly say that I had. When I did get around to reading it, I found it rather disappointing; like most of Orwell's fiction, it was thin on detail, and the working-out of the plot seemed unconvincing. As a dystopian novel, I thought it less prescient than Aldous Huxley's *Brave New World* (1932); as a specifically Cold War novel, it couldn't lay a glove on Arthur Koestler's masterpiece, *Darkness at Noon* (1940). But the more interesting point is that, such has been the fame of *Nineteen Eighty-Four*, one not only can come to believe one has read the novel when one hasn't but, more amazing still, such has been the spread of the novel through the general culture, it may well be that one doesn't really have to have read the novel at all, so long as one doesn't agree to go about giving talks on it.

Not only does Orwell's fame spread wide and cut deep, but there has become, somehow, something sacrosanct about him and his works. This, too, is a posthumous phenomenon. While he lived, Orwell had more than the normal allotment of enemies. Chief among them were political intellectuals, and in the 1930s, when Orwell came to literary maturity, to be intellectual was by definition to be political. One of Orwell's specialties was attacking intellectuals, and especially catching them out at disseminating left-wing cant, upon which he, Orwell, loved to stomp. ("All left-wing parties in the highly industrialized countries are at bottom a sham," he wrote in his essay "Rudyard Kipling" [1942], "because they make it their business to fight against something which they do not really wish to destroy.") Orwell was much better at influencing people than at making friends, at least when alive. Now the situation appears nearly to be reversed. Excepting only the most artery-hardened Marxists and academic feminists, everyone is Orwell's friend nowadays. Devotion to Orwell has become no laughing matter. Or so I conclude from the fact that, after all these years, no one so far as I know has published a parody of Orwell—an easy enough job, one would think, given the many strongly characteristic tics and turns of Orwell's readily recognized prose style, with its aggressively commonsensical spin. Here is my attempt at the job:

> As I write, this room is rapidly filling up with the stench of smelly little orthodoxies, and they are all about me. Every neo-con, lib-lab, beard-bearing student-humping academic, every *Nation*-reader, language snob, think-tank barnacle, priest, admiral, Harvard child-psychologist, CEO is aware that I am high on the list of entirely O.K. writers. "Orwell" has become one of those magic words, like "Art"; say it and everything is fine. You have only to quote me and your case is made. The grandchildren of people who fifty or sixty years ago would have been pleased to wipe their boots on me are now forced to read me in paperback. It's no use pretending that the sheer power of my writing has brought this about, or that such a diversity of admirers have all come round to my general views. The last man you want to trust is the man whom everyone thinks is admirable. "Saints," I once wrote, "should always be judged guilty until they are proven innocent." The same holds true for writers, except that, as any writer worth his salt will tell you, no good writer is ever innocent.

In one of those complex, less-than-straightforward letters of rejection that publisher's editors frequently find themselves writing to authors, T. S.

Eliot, after rejecting *Animal Farm* on behalf of the firm of Faber & Faber, wrote to Orwell that he regretted the rejection and that "I have a regard for your work, because it is good writing of fundamental integrity." My guess is that Orwell would have had no difficulty accepting that as a fair description of the quality of his writing. It strikes me as dead on target: "good writing of fundamental integrity." Nowhere did Orwell suggest that he thought himself a writer for the ages, a universal genius, a figure of the kind that, posthumously and through the vagaries of circumstance, he has become: translated into all languages, required reading for schoolchildren, quoted approvingly by natural enemies.

How intricate and never quite arbitrary a thing is reputation in literature! In one instance it can be aided immensely by early death (James Agee), in another by longevity (Robert Penn Warren). Unpopular politics have crushed a writer's reputation (Wyndham Lewis), while careful radicalism can elevate another writer's reputation (Robert Lowell). Some writers appear to have gained as greatly by withdrawing from the scene (Thomas Pynchon) as others have by clever self-promotion (Truman Capote). Reading the recent obituaries for Mary McCarthy, one of the more famous serious writers of our day, it occurred to me that Miss McCarthy's fame had always depended upon her being alive to reinforce it. Her early rise in reputation depended in part on her youthful good looks, no matter how clever she was as a critic. In the fiction of her early and middle years, she sustained her reputation by her continuing ability to outrage through gossip and scandal. In her later years, a doyenne now, it was her being outraged that people tended to be concerned about, for she could be enormously disapproving and had ample supplies of anger for those of whom she disapproved. But now that Mary McCarthy is dead, good looks, outrageousness, disapproval, anger—all count for nothing. Only the work remains—much of it in her case, as has been said before, destructive and marred by a falsely moral snobbery—and since this gives so little in the way of pleasure or instruction, it is likely soon to dissipate, then disappear.

Mary McCarthy was among those who attacked Orwell. In 1969, she thought that he left no generative political ideas, that his concept of decency was badly in need of definition, that he was conservative by temperament and thus almost instinctively opposed to fashion, change, and innovation—that, finally and in 1969 devastatingly, he probably would have been on the wrong side in Vietnam. Others have written against Orwell: Anthony West attempted to diminish him by psychoanalyzing him; Kingsley Martin claimed that in *Animal Farm* he had lost faith not merely in the Soviet Union but in mankind; D. A. N. Jones felt that he unfairly blackened the picture against left-wing intellectuals and was father of the bashing of feminists, pacifists, homosexuals, and other left-minded groups that Jones views as part of the political distraction and irrelevance of the current day. Firing away with Howitzers, Uzis, and squirt guns, Raymond Williams, Conor Cruise O'Brien, and Terry Eagleton have all, in their turn and in their different times, taken their shots at him. Still others have spat upon, bepissed, and whacked away at the statue of Orwell, but without in any serious way staining it, let alone tipping it over.

No critic of high standing has ever claimed that George Orwell was a first-rate novelist, though John Wain, Kingsley Amis, Philip Larkin, and other distinguished writers have written approvingly of his novels. Orwell did not write enough literary criticism to qualify, strictly speaking, as a literary critic. When he did write about writers—as he did about Dickens, Kipling, Tolstoy, Henry Miller—his impetus was generally extra-literary. A number of his familiar and personal essays are immensely impressive, but the quantity of these essays is not great. As with every journalist who works on weekly and fortnightly deadlines— as Orwell did on the *Tribune* and the London *Observer*—some weeks he was much better than others, and on many of those other weeks he could be pretty thin. He was splendid as a critic of popular culture— was something even of a pioneer in this field—but he could also come near ruining his work here through the intrusion of his own often rather coarse politics. After his admirably lucid account of the widely read sub-literature known as boys' weeklies, and a measured analysis of their social import, Orwell could not refrain from remarking that the stories in the boys' weeklies lead their readers to believe "that there is nothing wrong with laissez-faire capitalism" and he ended his essay, most disappointingly, by suggesting that, given the significant impression that youthful reading tends to leave for life, it is surely time to develop left-wing stories for the boys' weekly market.

Orwell died, of tuberculosis, in 1950 at the much-too-early age of forty-six. In a relatively brief writing career, he produced a vast amount of work. Except toward the end of his life, when the royalties from *Animal Farm* began to arrive, he produced what he did under considerable financial strain. His wretched health increased the strain. Although Orwell much admired craft, and more than once wrote of the importance of the aesthetic element in his own writing, the circumstances under which he worked were always arduous and scarcely allowed for Flaubertian meticulousness. If not altogether by choice, he was much less the artist than the professional writer. He was also, as he came to learn, chiefly a political writer.

> When I sit down to write a book, I do not say to myself, "I am going to produce a work of art." I write it because there is some lie that I want to expose, some fact to which I want to draw attention, and my initial concern is to get a hearing.

Cyril Connolly later seconded this point, remarking that Orwell was "a political animal" who "reduced everything to politics. . . . He could not blow his nose without moralising on conditions in the handkerchief industry."

"Good prose," Orwell famously wrote, "is like a window pane," and the absence of artful window dressing in his own prose has been part of Orwell's attraction for many readers. He commanded a prose style that strongly implied truth-telling ought to take precedence over art. In some of his work—one thinks of the chapter on the role of the POUM in *Homage to Catalonia* (1938) that he acknowledges may ruin his book but must nevertheless be included to set the record straight—this seemed to set Orwell above art, which, from a certain point of view, isn't a bad place to be.

Not, however, in the opinion of everyone. Conor Cruise O'Brien, reviewing the four-volume *Collected Essays, Journalism and Letters of George Orwell* when it appeared in 1968, interestingly noted that "plain language has a tendency to become extreme—which is why the other kind of language is generally preferred—and thus a laudable peculiarity of style made Orwell seem more extreme than he was." It has also made arriving at anything like a consensus about his true literary quality difficult. No agreement exists, for example, about which of Orwell's books is his best. Some profess admiration for *Homage to Catalonia*; some say the first, others the second half of *The Road to Wigan Pier* (1937) represents his best work. Mary McCarthy called *Down and Out in Paris and London* (1933) Orwell's "masterpiece"; Cyril Connolly felt the same book was not more than "agreeable journalism" done much better by Henry Miller. Most sophisticated readers, when asked where the best of Orwell is to be found, reply, the essays; but even here consensus never quite arrives. Edmund Wilson, while admiring Orwell generally, thought that in his literary essays he had "the habit of taking complex personalities too much at their face value, of not getting inside them enough." Newton Arvin thought Orwell, as an essayist, "an excellent writer on certain sorts of subjects," but not up to writing on figures of the high cultural complexity of Yeats. Evelyn Waugh noted of Orwell: "He has an unusually high moral sense and respect for justice and truth, but he seems never to have been touched by a conception of religious thought and life." Apart from showing how discrepant opinions about Orwell can be, these views show how apt other writers were to read into Orwell, or discover missing from him, those qualities they thought most important in their own work. What was the quality in George Orwell that made other writers read him as if he were a Rorschach test? And might not this quality, too, be connected in some central way to the unflagging prominence of Orwell's reputation?

To get at the complex nature of Orwell's reputation, clearly something like a book-length study is required, or so at least Professor John Rodden, who teaches rhetoric at the University of Virginia and who has recently written such a book, must have felt. *The Politics of Literary Reputation,* which carries the subtitle *The Making and Claiming of "St. George" Orwell,* is a vast production. The book is easily double the length of any single book its subject ever wrote, and carries behind it, in a giant academic caboose, more than twelve hundred footnotes, most of them discursive. Professor Rodden has to have read nearly everything ever written about or connected with or even loosely tangential to George Orwell, popular and academic, English, American, and European. The small-type index feels like the telephone directory of a small town. It is an exhaustive study.

Professor Rodden writes well enough, in a style that combines intellectual journalism with a heavy though not deadly admixture of academic locutions. There is little about his book, like so much current academic criticism, that bears the unmarked but unmistakable legend "TO THE TRADE ONLY." And yet there is something about *The Politics of Literary Reputation* that makes it the near reverse, in the cant phrase, of "a good read." It is instead a rough and rambling read. Less like a "read" at all, it feels like a long career, in which all one's movement is lateral. Professor Rodden views Orwell from every possible angle—as Rebel, as Prophet, as Common Man, as Saint—but somehow the portrait that emerges from all these angle shots comes out less rounded than blurred. Pace and progress seem to play no part in the argument. The struggle to get in everything is paramount. Rodden seems perpetually to be reconstructing "foil phases of Orwell's reputation in postwar Germany," or demarcating his "three *Tribune* 'lives' between 1937–47," or noting that this or that critic's "history of reception of Orwell's work can be divided into four or five parts." Near the close, Rodden refers to his book as "this project," and project is how the reader—including the entirely interested reader—comes to view it, too. An exhaustive study, as I say.

Yet, for all Professor Rodden's labors, one feels that the job has not been done—that is, if the job has been to account for why a writer of George Orwell's particular quality has loomed as large as he has in the contemporary world. We get a great deal of background on the issues, questions, and problems connected with Orwell's career. We learn much about what he meant to his contemporaries, the generation immediately following them, and to the left-wing intellectuals of the current day. We are filled in on the dispute over the ultimate character of Orwell's politics and hence over the matter of his political legacy. Professor Rodden takes positions, is not shy about announcing his own politics ("left-of-center white male of working-class origins, a post-Vatican II Catholic liberal"), or fearful of speculating upon why one critic found Orwell attractive and another finds him repulsive. Rodden glues literally hundreds of small mosaics to the wall, but, somehow, a picture refuses to cohere. What one is left with are data, a vaster collection of facts about the career of a single writer than has perhaps ever before been gathered in a single place. But data, however interesting, remain data.

What is missing, I believe, is a stronger element of literary criticism than the author of *The Politics of Literary Reputation* chooses to provide. The choice was a deliberate one—"This book," writes Professor Rodden, "aims chiefly to describe the making and claiming of a reputation, rather than to argue a specific case for its upward or downward revaluation"—but it is not clear that the two activities, criticism and description, are so easily separable. Insofar as one of the tasks of criticism is to establish the quality of a writer with a view toward placing him among his contemporaries and predecessors, the reputation of any serious writer is almost always best understood from the perspective of criticism. Another of the tasks of criticism—one of the major ones, surely—is to confer just reputation. An unjust literary reputation, as ought by now to be well-known, can be as easily built on a writer's defects as on his strengths; see, not merely passim, the last thirty or so years of American novelists. In the case of Orwell, one wonders if the question of how he arrived at his extraordinary reputation isn't bound up with the answer to the literary critical question of what kind of writer he was, strengths, defects, ambiguities, and all.

George Orwell has become a hero of culture. Other literary men have been heroes of culture over the past century, Henry James, James Joyce, T. S. Eliot among them. But these men derived their status from their art, for which they made heroic sacrifices and on which they left a permanent impress. But Orwell is extraordinary among heroes of culture in not being exclusively an artist, or even, strictly speaking, a figure whose most strenuous efforts were invested in high culture. One might even say that Orwell's status derives in good part from his very artlessness. Max Beerbohm once declared that "to be interesting, a man must be complex and elusive," citing the examples of Byron, Disraeli, and Rossetti as among the most interesting men in nineteenth-century England. But Orwell's power, much of his interest to us, comes from the reverse qualities: his simplicity and straightforwardness, at least as these are exhibited in the character he projected in his most powerful writing.

George Orwell has become a hero of culture. From the standpoint of reputation, character has always been Orwell's strongest asset. It was imputed to him early and continued to be conferred on him posthumously. "I was a stage rebel," wrote Cyril Connolly, who went to St. Cyprian's and then Eton with him, "Orwell a true one," adding: "The remarkable thing about Orwell was that alone among the boys he was an intellectual and not a parrot for he thought for himself." The imputation of strong character would heighten over the years. When Lionel Trilling came to write about Orwell, in an introduction to a 1952 edition of *Homage to Catalonia*, character had turned into virtue. Trilling allowed that Orwell was "not a genius," but emphasized that Orwell's virtue comprised "not merely moral goodness, but also fortitude and strength in goodness." That he was not a genius made him, in Trilling's view, all the more important, "for he communicates to us the sense that what he has done any one of us could do." (In Trilling's essay there follows a paragraph of extraordinary qualification that begins, "Or could do if we but made up our mind to it," which suggests most of us cannot; and here one senses how Lionel Trilling, that academic Demosthenes, his mouth filled not with pebbles but perpetual qualifications and hesitations, must have achingly envied Orwell's plainspokenness and readiness to act on his views.) From boy of character to man of virtue, Orwell was next (though not in strict chronological order) transmuted into "the wintry conscience of a generation," in V. S. Pritchett's obituary article in the *New Statesman* of January 28, 1950, "a kind of saint," a "Don Quixote" whose "conscience could be allayed only by taking upon itself the pain, the misery, the dinginess and the pathetic but hard vulgarities of a stale and hopeless period." One would like to think that George Orwell, reading all this, would have been mildly amused.

Yet these have been the terms in which, for the vast most part, Orwell has been judged. As Professor Rodden puts it,

> If we see Pritchett's obituary [which also appeared in a somewhat different version in the *New York Times Book Review*] as one of those reception moments to which readers have repeatedly returned—like Trilling's introduction to *Homage to Catalonia* and Connolly's characterization of Orwell in *Enemies of Promise* (1938)—it offers further insight into the reputation process.

Cyril Connolly, Lionel Trilling, and V. S. Pritchett make for a pretty fair triumvirate of testimonials, representing English and American literary criticism at its best from its aesthetic through its morally serious strain. Yet can the terms for judging Orwell that they have set down be sustained in our day?

I do not, myself, think that they quite can be. I say this with no great glee, for Orwell has been one of a small number of modern writers from whom my own way of viewing the world derives. Although one is trained, in judging literature, to ignore the life of a writer and concentrate on the work, anyone with any normal human feeling is always secretly delighted to learn that a writer he admires is also a man or woman he can respect. Part of the attractiveness of Orwell has of course been the respect that the integrity of his life invites. No finality in biography is available, and it may yet turn up that Orwell perpetuated some hideously caddish acts. But just now it does seem that a good part of the reason for the reverence in which he is held is the stupidity-ridden, disgrace-laden, generally shameful history of intellectual life of the past half century or so, against which Orwell's relative normality, common sense, and decency stand out.

At the same time, it ought not to stand in the way of a clear judgment of Orwell's work. Orwell was himself much concerned about what it is that makes for survival in literature and about the changing nature of literary reputation. In "Inside the Whale" (1940) he took up the change that had swept over the remains—that is to say, the poems—of A. E. Housman, who had been an important figure in his own generation when Orwell was young but seemed less so later. With typical good sense, he writes: "There is no need to under-rate him now because he was over-rated a few years ago." I don't mean to imply that Orwell, too, was over-rated; he said things crucial to his day, and in so saying helped form not only the terms of the discussion but the history of that day and became one its central writers. Rereading Orwell in our day, one's admiration for his insight and intellectual courage do not lessen; quite the reverse, much that he wrote then seems no less pertinent now, and not as prophesy but as simple truth. Yet much in Orwell can also seem thin, or oddly skewed, inadequate, or simply wrong. George Orwell has reached that privileged position of high reputation where his weaknesses can be openly dealt with because his strengths are no longer in serious dispute. The time, surely, has come for a fuller portrait.

It will not, for example, any longer do to consider George Orwell principally as a Cold War writer. He was partly that, of course, one of the best and most important, possibly the primary anti-totalitarian writer of the late 1930s and 1940s, a time of great denial of the murderousness of left-wing totalitarianism. Orwell was a strong and straightaway anti-Communist. It was an honorable and lonely position, and one which a man who earned a small living by his writings paid for by being denied entry into many magazines. The significance of this strain in Orwell cannot be gainsaid; nor is it quite time, at least in the gardens of the Third World, to shuck it all off as once pertinent but no longer. But Orwell's anti-Communism grew not alone out of his historical experience—with his self-acclaimed talent for facing unpleasant facts—but also out of his exposure to intellectuals under political pressure. He repeatedly said that "the intellectuals are more totalitarian in outlook than the common people." He said it in dozens of different ways, and none of them tactful. "The truth is, of course," he wrote in "Raffles and Miss Blandish" (1944), "that the countless English intellectuals who kiss the arse of Stalin are not different from the minority who give their allegiance to Hitler or Mussolini."

Although Orwell described himself in *The Road to Wigan Pier* as "a semi-intellectual," he was among modern writers the fiercest anti-intellectual going. Perhaps he was just enough of an intellectual—bookish, someone interested in the play of ideas—to have understood and despised the type. Having gone to Eton but not on to university, Orwell was nicely positioned to feel no inferiority toward the general class of English intellectuals and yet not quite feel himself of that class, either. To become an intellectual was, for Orwell, to become deeply out of it, hypocritical, stupid, inhumanly corrupted, spiritually bankrupt. Here is a small bouquet of Orwell's prime remarks about intellectuals:

> They take their cookery from Paris and their opinions from Moscow.
>
> —*The Lion and the Unicorn* (1941)

It is only the "educated" man, especially the literary man, who knows how to be a bigot.

—*The Road to Wigan Pier*

One has to belong to the intelligentsia to believe things like that [that America had entered World War II to prevent an English revolution]; no ordinary man could be so stupid.

—"Notes on Nationalism" (1945)

[The leftish politics] of the English intellectual is the patriotism of the deracinated.

—"Inside the Whale"

England is perhaps the only great nation whose intellectuals are ashamed of their country.

—*The Lion and the Unicorn*

Orwell wasn't much cheerier on the subject of what one might think of as intellectual auxiliaries. "A humanitarian is always a hypocrite," he wrote, "and Kipling's understanding of this is perhaps the central secret of his power to create telling phrases." Of Ezra Pound in particular, but of the conduct of artists generally, he noted: "One has the right to expect ordinary decency even of a poet." And of course his devastating shot at the grotesque unreality of those who flocked to contemporary Socialism, which appears in the second half of *The Road to Wigan Pier*, once read can scarcely be forgot: "The fact is that Socialism, *in the form in which it is now presented*, appeals chiefly to unsatisfactory or even inhuman types." Details not withheld:

One sometimes gets the impression that the mere words "Socialism" and "Communism" draw towards them with magnetic force every fruit-juice drinker, nudist, sandal-wearer, sex-maniac, Quaker, "Nature Cure" quack, pacifist and feminist in England.

It gets worse, wilder, and, if you happen to be sitting on the right side of the aisle, even funnier.

Having declared intellectuals poison—and "the modern English literary world, at any rate the highbrow section of it, a sort of poisonous jungle where only weeds can nourish"—Orwell was thrown back on the figure he frequently referred to in his writing as "the common man." Sometimes this "common man" is assumed to be of the working class, a man who, quite rightly in Orwell's view, is entirely uninterested in the philosophical side of Marxism, with its "pea-and-thimble trick with those three mysterious entities, thesis, antithesis, and synthesis." Sometimes he is the "ordinary man," who "may not flinch from a dictatorship of the proletariat, if you offer it tactfully; [but] offer him a dictatorship of the prigs, and he gets ready to fight." People of "very different type can be described as the common man," Orwell wrote in his essay on Dickens.

But what marks this common man above all for Orwell is "a native decency," a distaste for abstraction, and an appreciation of the small pleasures and surface delights of life. When Orwell writes that "the common man is still living in the mental world of Dickens, but nearly every modern intellectual has gone over to some or other form of totalitarianism," he means that the common man retains a bred-in-the-bone respect for loyalty and kindness, courage and freedom, a hatred of unfairness and oppression, and a love for life in its everyday quality that the intellectual has bred out of himself. Mary McCarthy, it will be recalled, felt Orwell's concept of decency needed refining, but then she was herself almost the perfect type of intellectual and wasn't, in Orwell's view, likely to have understood it in any case.

Orwell understood it and tried by his best lights to live it. After his youthful years in the British imperial police in Burma, after his days of deliberately going down and out, he tried to live like the common man, at least in the outward appurtenances of his life. Bernard Crick's biography of Orwell, the most complete we now have, recounts several of the details of Orwell's almost aggressive anti-bohemianism. On the other hand, he was blocked off from living in an easy middle-class way not only by his meager earnings as a freelance writer but even more by his strong antipathy to the bourgeois life from which he had come. ("To have a horror of the bourgeois," said Jules Renard, "is bourgeois.") The result was that Orwell and his wife Eileen tended to muddle along somewhat grimly between working- and lower-middle-class living arrangements, with Orwell affecting proletarian habits. He smoked shag cigarettes, slurped his tea out of the saucer, cared not at all about clothes. In the last years of his life, with the royalties that were beginning to come in from *Animal Farm*, he bought a farm in Jura, in the Scottish Hebrides, where, with his sister and adopted son under his roof, he attempted to live the life of the hardscrabble farmer. As best he could, Orwell attempted, to use the French phrase he himself would doubtless have abjured, to live *dans le vrai*.

He attempted to write, too, *dans le vrai*, and one of his working assumptions, though so far as I know he never put it straight out, was that the truth of life has been distorted by much literature. As a literary critic, he was best as a revisionist—revising the received opinions about other writers that felt wrong to him. Allowing for Kipling's worst thoughts, he goes on to make the points that "Kipling deals in thoughts which are both vulgar and permanent," that "few people who have criticized England from the inside have said bitterer things about her than this gutter patriot," that he wrote "with responsibility" and knew that "men can only be highly civilized while other men, inevitably less civilized, are there to guard and feed them." (W. H. Auden, in his political phase during the 1930s, Orwell called "a sort of gutless Kipling.") He de-Marxified Dickens, showing how little interested in politics Dickens was, and asserted that "he was popular chiefly because he was able to express in comic, simplified and therefore memorable form that native decency of the common man." Brilliantly, he notes: "The outstanding, unmistakable mark of Dickens's writing is the unnecessary detail." In what is Orwell's best literary essay, "Lear, Tolstoy and the Fool" (1947)—an essay that anticipates and is superior to Isaiah Berlin's "The Hedgehog and the Fox"—he sides against Tolstoy, whose "main aim, in his later years, was to narrow the range of human consciousness," and with Shakespeare, who "loved the surface of the earth and the process of life . . . [and whose] main hold on us is through language."

George Orwell was half an artist. This was not sufficient to make him a memorable novelist, but it did put him in the class of the best English essayists, all of whom have also been, in their various ways, half artists. Serious visual art and music never come in for mention in Orwell; he is dead to the artistic significance of religion, toward which he was generally—and in the case of Roman Catholics particularly—antagonistic. But about literary art he was passionate:

> So long as I remain alive and well I shall continue to feel strongly about prose style, to love the surface of the earth [the same phrase he uses in connection with Shakespeare], and to take a pleasure in solid objects and scraps of useless information.

In another time, he might have been able to give way to this side of himself. But not in that in which he lived. In his own time, politics was unavoidable, and he saw his job as reconciling "my ingrained likes and dislikes with the essentially public, non-individual activities that this age forces on all of us." As for his own ambition, about this he is entirely clear: "What I have wanted to do throughout the past ten years," he remarked in "Why I Write," "is to make political writing into an art."

How successful was Orwell at turning political writing into an art? Very, is one's unhesitating first response. A tradition of sorts was there. Burke, Paine, Cobden, Hazlitt, Macaulay had each produced political writing that—sometimes in flashes, sometimes in sustained patches—remains powerful, beautiful, greatly moving. In this tradition, political writing that aspired to art tended to go for the searing and the soaring, flamethrowers followed by French horns. Part of Orwell's distinction as a political writer is that he departed from this tradition by playing it flat and playing it straight. He described the indecency of shooting a Fascist when the man is running while trying to hold up his trousers; he described the loathsomeness of tripe on a coal miner's table; always and everywhere he described smells and filth, discomfort and disgust, and made plain that in war and in poverty "physical details always outweigh everything else." When he took on a political subject, Orwell regularly warned against his bias, he struggled on the page before the reader to be as honest as possible within that bias, and his interest in any political event or issue had nothing to do with his establishing his own superiority to it. This was, in political writing, revolutionary, and, since Orwell's death in 1950, it remains without parallel.

Yet the limitations built into making political writing an art, and thus giving it a chance for survival, are considerable. For one, political writing is called into being by events and issues, and events and issues are in the fullness—sometimes in the leanness—of time settled, dissolved, simply forgotten. Of the writing about them, only the rhetoric remains, trailing the stale odor of once-strong opinion. For another, in politics, unlike in art, it is important that one be correct, or at the very minimum not altogether wrong. In "Politics vs. Literature" (1947), his essay on Swift, whom he called "one of the writers I admire with the least reserve," Orwell asks: "What is the relationship between agreement with a writer's opinions, and enjoyment of his work?" Orwell doesn't quite get around to answering this question, so let me answer it for him by saying that, in politics, where agreement exists it is usually immensely improved.

As for Orwell's own politics, a subject of much contention, it can be said that all interpretations are equal, but some are more equal than others. In "Why I Write" he set them out in a single sentence: "Every line of serious work that I have written since 1936 [since, that is, his experience of international betrayal in the Spanish Civil War] has been written, directly or indirectly, *against* totalitarianism and *for* democratic Socialism, as I understand it." That sounds plain enough, but a twist is added: the progressive party of Orwell's time so revolted him—as, he notes, Swift was revolted by the progressive party of his own—that Orwell's most penetrating and original writing is about the detachment from political reality of left-wing intellectuals and its serious consequences in a world where horror, suffering, and organized murder are real enough. Yet, throughout his work there is a persistent rattling against the evils of "the utter rottenness of private capitalism"—for leftists of Orwell's generation, capitalism was a weigh station directly on the road to fascism—clichéd references to the filthy rich ("The lady in the Rolls-Royce car is now more damaging to morale than a fleet of Goring's bombing-planes," he wrote in *The Lion and the Unicorn*), false assertions ("Laissez-faire capitalism is dead"), and much else that one could pop into print in next week's issue of the *Nation* without anyone noticing.

On his deathbed, apropos of Evelyn Waugh, in his journal Orwell wrote: "One cannot really be a Catholic and grown up." In *Homage to Catalonia*, he wrote: "when I see an actual flesh-and-blood worker in conflict with his natural enemy, the policeman, I do not have to ask which side I am on." (The man could be a rapist, George; better ask.) Israel was for him just another variant of nationalism, and he despised nationalism in all its forms, case closed. "The opinion that art should have nothing to do with politics is itself a political attitude," he wrote, in a sentence that not only illustrates Conor Cruise O'Brien's remark that "plain language has a tendency to become extreme" but has caused great mischief by being interpreted to mean that, at bottom, everything in the world is political in any case, so let 'er rip. Orwell was wrong about many things, and about some things not merely wrong but crudely, callowly wrong.

But on many important things Orwell was right. He was right to trust his instincts over his political opinions whenever the two clashed. He was right in recognizing that the major political question of his time was how best to confront totalitarianism and all its deceptions; and right again to do so head on, with all his art and all his heart and the vast quantity of courage at his command. He was right in his impatience with intellectual cant, and percipient in early underscoring the connection between totalitarian habits of thought and the corruption of language. Orwell was scarcely a genius, nor even, in any striking way, an original thinker. What he was was honest, and what he had was unshakable integrity, and these qualities, working their magic, lent his writing great force and made him a figure crucial for his time and left him a model for our own. However high George Orwell's reputation may have risen, no matter how low it may one day fall, all this is finally part of the history of publicity. What matters is that through moral effort, he made himself into a good writer. That is permanent, not subject to fluctuation, and can never be taken away.

Proust

(2012)

FIVE OR SIX YEARS AGO, I found the seats at classical music concerts becoming uncomfortable. I blame the seats, but in fact I had lost the *Sitzfleisch*—in German literally "seat meat," in looser translation "bottom patience"—to sit through a concert. In concert halls, my mind wandered. I counted the people around me who had fallen asleep, searched the audience for anyone under 40, frequently checked my watch. Time seemed to pass more slowly than in a laundromat.

I used to go to from 12 to 20 concerts a year. With my loss of attention at concerts, and given the expense of concert tickets, it finally occurred to me that I was wasting time and money in dragging myself to these events. I love serious music; it was only at concerts that I couldn't seem to enjoy it. My condition was not unlike that of the English journalist Malcolm Muggeridge, who once wrote that he couldn't take his mind off thoughts of God, and it was only when he entered an Anglican church and the vicar began speaking that for him God was gone.

George Santayana late in life also found he could no longer bear to attend concerts. Going to hear serious music, he reports in one of his letters, had come to resemble an act of piety instead of one of pleasure. In Rome, where Santayana was living at the time, there was lots of good street music, and he achieved a useful compromise by listening to this music, out-of-doors and standing up. I listen to most of my music on CDs driving around the city in my car.

I recently attempted a concert-hall comeback. An all-Mozart program was scheduled a few weeks ago by the Chicago Symphony Orchestra, with Mitsuko Uchida, the foremost Mozart interpreter of our day, playing and conducting two Mozart concerti. Uchida was splendid, the CSO turned in its usual smooth performance, and as the program ended to a standing ovation for Uchida, I said to myself, "Please don't let her play an encore."

Two weeks later, I went to a Dame Myra Hess concert at the Chicago Cultural Center. The concert, played by a youthful woodwinds quintet, was roughly 45 minutes long. The crowd, like most classical music audiences, was less than spritely. The man seated to my left fell asleep just before the performers were introduced and woke—refreshed, I assume—only at their finish. I found myself rising to my feet to applaud, and went happily off to lunch with friends afterwards. Successful as this outing was, I feel no urge to return, at least not soon.

No, the best arrangement for me is what I think of as the Proustian solution. Marcel Proust was a regular concert-goer, and his interest in music was intense and highly intelligent; his fictional composer Vinteuil in *In Search of Lost Time* attests to that. He was especially enamored of the music of Beethoven and César Franck, and in particular of Franck's String Quartet in D as played by the Poulet Quartet.

One night around 11 o'clock in the winter of 1916, wanting eagerly to hear the Franck quartet, Proust paid a call on Gaston Poulet, the leader of the Poulet Quartet. When Poulet came to the door in his pajamas, Proust informed him that he would like very much to hear his group play the Franck composition that very night in his apartment on the Boulevard Haussmann. Lured by the high fee Proust offered, Poulet agreed, and he and Proust in a cab rounded up the other members of the quartet. They arrived at Proust's apartment near 1:00 A.M.

As they began the César Franck quartet, Proust listened with his eyes closed. He enjoyed it so much that he asked the musicians to play it again, and then went to a small Chinese box from which he extracted a stack of notes redeemable for 45,000 ordinary francs, a sum grand enough for the Poulet Quartet to play the piece a second time without

diminution of energy. In subsequent months, Proust called on the Poulet Quartet to play others of his favorite compositions in his apartment,
Mozart, Ravel, and Schumann among them, each time one assumes for
a similarly lucrative fee.

I should mention that when Proust's mother died, in 1905 at the age of
56, she left her son the equivalent of roughly $4.6 million in current dol-
lars, a sum that allowed him to tip waiters at the Ritz 100 percent and more
and to listen to live music in the ideal conditions of his own apartment.

If only I could adopt Proust's solution to my concert-hall problem.
How I should like to have the Chicago Symphony perform for me alone
in my living room! And perhaps someday I shall, once I figure out how
to do so without dipping into capital.

C. K. Scott Moncrieff

(2015)

WITHOUT TRANSLATORS, all but the omniglot among us would be rendered hopelessly parochial. Even after having lived off their labors, one struggles to name more than half a dozen or so laborers in this ill-paid field. One begins with Constance Garnett who brought the great Russian writers into the Anglophone world; Willard Trask, who did superior work in both German and French; Gregory Rabassa, who translated Latin American writers; William Weaver for modern Italian literature; Richard Lattimore, David Grene, Robert Fitzgerald, and Robert Fagles for Greek and Latin, with Benjamin Jowett still the main man for Greek philosophy.

The supreme figure in the annals of modern translation is C(harles). K(enneth). Scott Moncrieff (1889–1930), the translator into English of Marcel Proust's monumental seven-volume novel *Remembrance of Things Past*. When Scott Moncrieff began his translation in 1920, Proust, who died in 1922, was still correcting the typescript for *La Prisonnière*, the fifth volume in his vast novel. Scott Moncrieff began translating the novel without knowing how long the completed work would be. Roughly, it turned out, a million and a quarter words and more than 3,200 pages, the whole dealing with some 2,000 different characters. Scott Moncrieff spent nine years translating Proust, while simultaneously working on translations of Stendhal, Pirandello, and (in medieval Latin) *Abelard et Heloise*.

Scott Moncrieff's Proust translation has never been free of controversy. The controversy began with the title he gave his English version of the novel. Proust's overarching title, *A la rechere du temps perdu,* translates as "In Search for Lost Time"; Scott Moncrieff took his title from a phrase in Shakespeare's Sonnet #30:

> When to the sessions of sweet silent thought/I summon to remembrance of things past/I sigh the lack of many a thing I sought,/And with old woes new wail my dear time's waste...

In his only letter to his English translator, Proust criticized Scott Moncrieff's title as well as his calling the first volume of the novel *Swann's Way* (the French is *Du Côté de chez Swann*). *Swann's Way,* Proust felt, gave the book an unwanted double meaning, suggesting that it was not alone about the milieu of Charles Swann but also about his general manner. He died fearing that Scott Moncrieff would make a frightful botch of his masterwork.

Translations, like lovers, the old saw has it, are either beautiful or faithful, but they cannot be both. In his translation of Proust, Scott Moncrieff went, without hesitation, for the beautiful. Jean Findlay, in her elegant and even-handed biography of Scott Moncrieff, who was her mother's great-uncle, does not intricately examine the character of her ancestor's translation. She does provide a single example of the difference between it and the more literal 2004 translation of *Swann's Way* by Lydia Davis, one of the six different translators who have done a new English version of Proust's novel for Penguin Press. Here is the last sentence in a paragraph rendered by Ms. Davis: "He [Charles Swann] brushed against all those dim bodies as if, among the phantoms of the dead, in the kingdom of darkness, he were searching for Eurydice." Scott Moncrieff's version of the same sentence runs: "Anxiously he explored every one of these vaguely seen shapes, as though among the phantoms of the dead, in the realms of darkness, he had been searching for a lost Eurydice." Among other touches, Scott Moncrieff has added the penultimate word "lost," which does not appear in Proust's French text. This is known as taking liberties, and the question before any reader is whether they are liberties worth taking.

As Ms. Findlay's biography makes plain, Scott Moncrieff, given his character, could scarcely have produced a literal translation. Once one knows the facts of his life and how his mind was tuned, the thought of his having done so is unthinkable. Although not so eccentric or unconventional as Marcel Proust, C. K. Scott Moncrieff was himself a raffish character in whom wildly contradictory qualities resided quite comfortably.

As an English officer in World War I, Scott Moncrieff was fearless and heroic. He was awarded the Military Cross, though the men who served under him and who greatly admired him thought he should have been awarded the higher Victorian Cross for his bravery and coolness of command under fire. The masculine military leader was also a cruising homosexual, a member in good standing of the English homintern of his day, which included Robert Ross, Norman Douglas, Reggie Turner, E. M. Forster, Noel Coward, Harold Acton, and others.

Scott Moncrieff chose to keep his homosexuality from his parents, whom he much loved, and who, he felt, would have been saddened by knowledge of it. His mother held out hopes he would marry up to the time of his death; and so, according to his biographer, did he. Born into the Calvinist Church of Scotland, as a young man he became a serious Catholic: confession allowed him to live more easily with what he felt the spiritual complexities of his sexuality. Before he died he received, as Ms. Findlay notes, the last sacraments of confession, viaticum, and extreme unction.

Jean Findlay speculates that Scott Moncrieff was drawn to Proust in part because both men had in common homosexuality and a great fondness for their mothers. Charles Scott Moncrieff was the youngest of three sons born into a middle-class Scottish family. His father was a judge; his mother, whom he adored, read books to him well in advance of his age. Until he was three, his nanny, a Belgian, spoke to him only in French. He displayed intellectual precocity from an early age, and won a scholarship at Winchester, one of the great English public schools. In perhaps the major disappointment of his life, he failed to gain entrance to Oxford or to Cambridge. He went instead to the University of Edinburgh, where he studied—"read," as the English say—law and literature, the latter under George Saintsbury, who imbued him with a love of French literature.

Scott Moncrieff's active military service ended when a bomb blast broke his leg in two places and left shrapnel in his thigh, resulting in one of his legs being permanently shorter than the other, and bestowing upon him a permanent limp. After the war, he eased into London literary life. Among his close friends were Robert Graves, Wilfred Owen, and Vyvyan Holland, the son of Oscar Wilde; the last, it seems necessary to add, a notorious heterosexual. Scott Moncrieff had written poetry from as early as his Winchester days, many of his youthful poems masking his homosexual yearnings. He edited an anthology of Georgian poets. He published the occasional negligible poem, but the superior poems of Wilfred Owen persuaded him that poetry was not his line. "I don't write good poetry," he wrote to his friend Edward Marsh, "and fortunately I know it."

He took up reviewing, writing weekly for the *New Witness*, a magazine founded and edited by G. K. Chesterton and described by Osbert Sitwell as "a queer bastard socialist-ultra-Conservative paper." As a reviewer, Scott Moncrieff was often acerbic, and never more so than when writing about the Sitwells, Edith, Osbert, and Sacheverell, whom T. S. Eliot, giving way to his bawdy side, referred to as "the Shitwells." Jean Findlay writes that the Sitwells "regarded a failure to admire their poetry as an affront to their aristocratic status." In Scott Moncrieff's view, they were neither poets nor aristocrats, thereby anticipating F. R. Leavis's remark that what the Sitwells really belonged to was "the history of publicity."

Scott Moncrieff seems not so much to have planned as to have backed into translation, which was to be his literary legacy. One day in a London bookshop, he discovered a student copy of *Chanson de Roland*, and, despite not having Old French, set out to translating it into English. In doing so he discovered that the key to successful translation was assonance, the repetition of vowel sounds in non-rhyming syllables. The sound of a translated text, its cadence, he felt was of primary significance. Once he began his Proust translation, his regular procedure was to read aloud to friends his Englished version of the novel to get a feel for its sound. In this he would have agreed with Robert Frost, who wrote: "The ear is the only true writer and the only true reader."

In the early decades of the last century, Marcel Proust was a hard sell for English publishers. When in 1919 Scott Moncrieff proposed a translation of Proust to Constable & Company, the publishing firm's editors replied that they saw little point in publishing a translation "of Prevost." The following year he wrote to J. C. Squire, who worked on Hilaire Belloc's magazine *Land and Water*, to inquire whether it "would consider for a moment running Marcel Proust's book (which recently got the *Prix Goncourt*) as a serial in English." Apparently it would not. Edmund Gosse, the English man of letters, tried to discourage him from doing a translation of Proust and suggested he attempt instead a translation of the *Roman de la Rose*, another medieval text. In the end, Scott Moncrieff decided to take on the Proust translation on his own.

During the years Scott Moncrieff worked on his Proust translation, he held other jobs, among them at the British War Office; as a private secretary to Lord Northcliffe, the febrile owner and publisher of the London *Times;* and, finally, under cover of working for the British passport control department in Italy, as a spy reporting on the disposition of Mussolini's troops and naval forces and on British subjects in Italy thought to be fascist sympathizers. As the work on Proust progressed, he took time out to translate Stendhal, whose prose, next to the complexity of Proust's, was a bite of madeleine, for he could translate Stendhal directly from the text to the typewriter. Although he claimed neither to speak nor write Italian well, he also began to translate Pirandello, plays, novels, stories, and claimed he wanted to do the entire *oeuvre,* which ran to 218 volumes.

While in Italy, Scott Moncrieff entertained family and friends in his various Italian apartments and hostels, chased boys, engaged in a vast correspondence that, to selected friends, often included hilariously obscene limericks. He also helped pay for the schooling of his various nephews and nieces. (In his *Who's Who* entry under the rubric Recreation, he wrote: Nepotism.) When he worked at his Proust translation, however, nothing was allowed to interfere. "He may have developed a Catholic soul," Ms. Findlay writes, "but he always had what we understand as a Protestant work ethic, the legacy from his father and the Church of Scotland."

Jean Findlay recounts obstacles that Scott Moncrieff incurred along the long and rocky road to completing his Proust translation. Censorship was not least among them. Laws against homosexuality were still on the books in England, and Proust's fourth volume *Sodome et Gomorrhe*, with its account of the homosexual adventures of the Baron de Charlus, had to be toned down, through euphemism and innuendo, for the English version of the novel. The title of the volume in itself presented a problem. Scott Moncrieff came up with the splendid substitute of *Cities of the Plain*, which to friends he referred to as "Cissies of the Plain."

Of his own French, Scott Moncrieff said, "I know comparatively few French words and no grammar, so when I come to a frightful howler, like the German musician on whose score a fly alighted, 'I play him.'" Yet he turned out a translation of Proust that most Proustolaters—this reviewer among them—find unsurpassed, and probably unsurpassable. The polyglottal Joseph Conrad, a friend of Scott Moncrieff's, held that he preferred his translation to Proust's original. Virginia Woolf wrote to Roger Fry that reading Scott Moncrieff's translation was for her, in Ms. Findlay's paraphrase, "akin to a sexual experience," and she apparently lifted a number of his English phrasings for *To the Lighthouse*. George Painter, Proust's best English biographer, called it "a masterly recreation of the original." F. Scott Fitzgerald claimed that "Scott Moncrieff's Proust is a masterpiece in itself."

Scott Moncrieff was able to bring off his astonishing translation because he was attuned to the sensibility of Proust in a way that perhaps no contemporary translator can be. The two, author and translator, were temperamentally suited to each other. Scott Moncrieff had an instinctive sense of Proust's cast of mind, and a strong appetite for the subtlety of observation and analytical intricacy behind the layered sinuosities of his prose. His translation succeeded above all because Scott Moncrieff, too, was an artist (however otherwise *manque)*, who discovered his mission in life in vastly widening the audience for the work of a much greater artist.

Consumer note: For those ready to make their first literary ascent up Mount Proust, from which, be assured, the views are dazzling, the best edition in English is the three-book 1981 Random House version, with revisions in C. K. Scott Moncrieff's translation by Terence Kilmartin. Kilmartin's revisions correct the many mistakes found in the original Gallimard French version of Proust's novel from which Scott Moncrieff had of necessity to work, but which were eliminated in a later Pleiade edition. Mr. Kilmartin sometimes drains the purple from Scott Moncrieff's prose

and corrects his occasional errors—"elemental but unimportant errors,
" George Painter calls them—especially in translating idiomatic French.
The 1981 Random House edition is also generously leaded, leaving ample
space between lines of the text, a mercy in reading a novel that can itself, in
French or in English, sometimes seem crowded by too teeming brilliance.

The Young T. S. Eliot

(2015)

READERS OF THE CURRENT DAY, no matter how young, will not in their lifetimes, and quite possibly in the lifetimes of their children and grandchildren, encounter another poet who achieved the fame and had the literary authority of T. S. Eliot. That fame and authority ranged through the Anglophone world roughly between 1922, with the publication of *The Waste Land*, and Eliot's death in 1965. If an example of its magnitude is needed, Eliot, in 1956, lectured on the subject of "The Frontiers of Criticism" in a gymnasium at the University of Minnesota before a crowd of 15,000. He exchanged amusing letters with Groucho Marx. His approval or disapproval of writers, living or dead, could elevate or deflate their standing instantly. While still young, he had the confidence to declare *Hamlet* a flop—"So far from being Shakespeare's masterpiece, the play is most certainly an artistic failure"—lightly scolding Goethe and Coleridge for their misapprehension of the play's true meaning.

At the close of his brief essay on the failure of *Hamlet*, Eliot wonders why Shakespeare attempted this play for whose central problem—the guilt of a mother in the eyes of her son—he, Shakespeare, could find no objective correlative. The phrase "objective correlative," which Eliot brought over from philosophy into literary criticism, refers to "a set of objects, a situation, a chain of events which shall be the formula of that *particular* emotion; such that when the external facts . . . are given, the emotion is immediately evoked." In order to understand this failure, Eliot claims, we should have to know a great many facts about Shakespeare's life that are unknowable. "We should have to understand things which Shakespeare did not understand himself."

MIGHTN'T SOMETHING OF THE SAME be said not about T. S. Eliot's failure but of his extraordinary success? How did this success come about? On what was it based? What was his own estimate of it? Biography, with all its limitations and inadequacies, is our only resource in pursuit of the answers to these questions. To understand them, to paraphrase Eliot, we should have to understand things which T. S. Eliot himself did not understand.

To begin with, there is the interesting circumstance of Eliot's turning himself from a Midwestern American into an Englishman, in some ways even more English than the English. His model here was his fellow American Henry James, whom Eliot much admired, and whose cosmopolitanism he hoped to emulate. "It is the final perfection, the consummation, of an American," Eliot wrote apropos of James, "to become, not an Englishman, but a European—something which no born European, no person born of any European nationality, can become." Eliot also drew inspiration from James's double talent as artist and critic, which is of course what Eliot himself would become: a powerful critic, the most influential of his day, and an avant-garde poet of the highest rank and power. The combination of the two, poet and critic, conduced to the great *réclame* that Eliot enjoyed.

Thomas Stearns Eliot, born in 1888, was half Midwesterner, half New Englander. He grew up in St. Louis, the youngest of six children, but his well-established genealogical origins were in New England, where, in Gloucester, Massachusetts, the family spent its summers. A cousin, Charles Eliot, was president of Harvard. His grandfather was the founder of Washington University in St. Louis. His father was a successful businessman, owner of the Hydraulic-Press Brick Company. His mother was a published—in church magazines—poet. The family, among the first in St. Louis, was Unitarian, and took its religion seriously.

T. S. (then Tom) Eliot loved his parents, without complication, his life long. As the youngest child he was coddled. He was sent to the best, which is to say the most exclusive, schools in St. Louis. He had, it would seem, all the advantages: money, birth, a loving family. Yet he was born with a double hernia, and had to wear a truss early in life, which prevented him from participating in football and other games, and was in itself an embarrassment. He didn't like his own looks: his teeth came in crooked, his nose was big, with flared nostrils, he was sensitive about his too-large ears. He was bashful generally, and especially shy with girls. While not unhappy, his boyhood was a somewhat isolated and bookish one, without close friends among his contemporaries, always slightly on the periphery of things.

THE CONTENTION OF ROBERT CRAWFORD in *Young Eliot* is that T. S. Eliot's early years, which have tended to be scanted by earlier biographers, were formative in the root sense. These years have been scanted because there is little documentary evidence to help biographers in filling them out. For five years in his late teens and early twenties, for example, the only surviving Eliot correspondence is a single postcard. T. S. Eliot was not eager for a biography, and to this day no official biographer has been appointed. Valerie Eliot, his second wife, asked Richard Ellmann, the biographer of James Joyce, to undertake her husband's biography, but, put off by the anti-Semitic streak in Eliot, Ellmann, a Jew, demurred.

Robert Crawford, who has published several collections of his own poetry, in addition to his many other books, is a professor of English at the University of St. Andrews. His is not the official biography of T. S. Eliot, nor does he claim, despite its length—a second volume is planned, taking up his subject's life after 1922—that it will be definitive. What is most impressive about *Young Eliot* is the insistent pressure its author keeps on the attempt to show how Eliot's experiences impinged on his poetry and the ideas propelling his criticism. Eliot's reading, both as a boy and later as a student, is underscored and highlighted, its use in his later poetry persuasively indicated.

Of his prep school reading, for example, Crawford writes:

Extended study of Xenophon's *Anabasis* in Greek when he
was 14 and 15 set him up for his much later translation of
Saint-John Perse's *Anabase. Julius Caesar* and *The Merchant
of Venice* yielded phrases used in his mature verse.

In Palgrave's *Golden Treasury*, a famous poetry anthology of its day, he
picked up, from Shakespeare, the line "Those are pearls that were his
eyes," which became part of *The Waste Land*. Crawford is aware that, to
a writer of sensitive antennae, such as Eliot possessed, reading can be as
vivid and significant as the most direct experience offered by life.

The boy Tom's first hint of genuine poetic talent showed up in a pas-
tiche of Ben Jonson in a lyric he wrote for an admired teacher at Smith
Academy in St. Louis. So proficient was it that his teacher asked if he
had had any help in writing it. His mother, who was always in his corner, told Tom that it was better than anything she could have written.
"I knew what her verse meant to her," Eliot later wrote. "We did not
discuss the matter further." He would later remark that he had been
"forced into poetry by my weakness in other directions. . . . I took this
direction very young, and learned very early to find my life and my
realisation in this curious way, and to be obtuse and indifferent to my
reality in other ways."

EDITH WHARTON, in her memoir *A Backward Glance*, remarks that
one of the great mistakes a young person could make was to be thought
promising. So many of her young contemporaries so judged couldn't abide
the pressure of expectation and petered out early in their lives. She and
others, left to their own devices without any ballyhoo about their promise,
went on to impressive achievement.

The young Tom Eliot did not suffer from the pressure of having been
considered promising. He was a less than stellar student. He required an
additional year of prepping at Milton Academy in Massachusetts before
entering Harvard. His shyness continued at Harvard, and his social entrée
card was ribald verse, which he could turn out on demand. At the end of
his first semester he was put on probation, owing to lower than mediocre
grades. His second year he was a C student.

In those years, under the recently installed elective system, Eliot's main course of study was what would in a later day, as Crawford suggests, be called comparative literature. He took courses in Latin, Greek, French, and German, and in philosophy, history, and government. Barrett Wendell and George Santayana and Irving Babbitt were among his teachers; Babbitt, he claimed, was the "one teacher at Harvard" who "had the greatest influence on me." The journalist John Reed (*Ten Days That Shook the World*) was in his class of 1910; so, too, was Walter Lippmann. Van Wyck Brooks, whose book *The Wine of the Puritans* was to influence Eliot in his decision to depart America for England, was at Harvard at the same time, but in the class of 1908.

Only in his last years at Harvard did Eliot catch intellectual fire. His lingering interest in a poetic career was reignited, Crawford reports, by his coming upon the poetry of Jules Laforgue in Arthur Symons's *The Symbolist Movement in Literature*. Laforgue taught him the possibility of combining the traditional and the new, the profound and the profane, in verse in a way he hadn't hitherto thought possible. ("Without [Laforgue's] . . . intoxicating example, however," Crawford writes, "Tom might have stalled forever [as a poet].") He was elected to the editorial board of the *Advocate*. George Herbert Palmer, a popular teacher of Ancient Philosophy, introduced him to the poetry of George Herbert, an interest that would later issue in Eliot's writing about, and thereby reviving interest in, those 17th-century poets that Samuel Johnson called the Metaphysical poets. Palmer was perhaps the first of his teachers to recognize something extraordinary about the young T. S. Eliot.

TWO TRIPS TO EUROPE further widened Eliot's intellectual range, applying the polish to the blacking of his undergraduate years. On the first, taken in 1910, shortly after his graduation, he attended the lectures of Henri Bergson at the Sorbonne. Travel in France turned him Francophiliac; at one point he even thought he might write exclusively in French. He acquired an interest in Charles Maurras, one of the leading figures in *Action Française* and an anti-Semite, and perhaps an influence in sustaining Eliot's own home-grown WASP anti-Semitism.

Returning to Harvard as a graduate student, he studied Sanskrit and began a thesis on the idealist philosophy of F. H. Bradley. The Sanskrit would later be of use in *The Waste Land*. He studied with Josiah Royce. From another philosophy professor, J. H. Woods, he acquired the notion that philosophy and poetry could be welded together, much to the advantage of poetry. "No other major twentieth century poet," as Crawford notes, "was so thoroughly and strenuously educated." As a graduate student, he was thought sufficiently promising to be awarded a Sheldon Fellowship, which allowed him a second, and decisive, trip to Europe—a trip from which, it might be said, he never returned.

In 1914, the year World War I began, Eliot was at the University of Marburg. With the war underway he found it difficult to leave Germany. He next traveled on to London; there he had his fateful meeting with Ezra Pound, who had read his first major poem, "The Love Song of J. Alfred Prufrock," and immediately sensed the potential of its author. (Eliot took the name Prufrock, Crawford informs us, from a St. Louis furniture manufacturer.) With his unerring radar for spotting authentic poetic talent, Pound took up the cause of, and proved immensely helpful in, promoting Eliot's career. Pound it was who later, through extensive cutting, edited *The Waste Land* into its final form.

From London, Eliot went on to Merton College, Oxford, which was neither to his temper nor to his taste. "Oxford is very pretty," he wrote to Conrad Aiken, "but I don't like to be dead." He considered a career in university teaching, though when the prospect arose of a teaching job at Harvard, if he would return to America to defend his doctoral thesis, he had no hesitation in turning it down. At Oxford, Eliot encountered an important influence in the person of Harold Joachim, a philosopher who "taught me in the course of criticizing weekly essays with a sarcasm the more authoritative because of its gentle impersonality." The ideal of impersonality would loom large in Eliot's writing, and especially in his most famous essay, "Tradition and the Individual Talent," where he wrote: "Poetry is not a turning loose of emotion, but an escape from emotion; it is not the expression of personality, but an escape from personality," to which he added the biographically supercharged coda: "But, of course, only those who have personality and emotions know what it means to want to escape from these things."

THE EMOTIONAL QUAGMIRE to which those sentences ever so indirectly allude began to form when Eliot returned from Oxford to London. There he began to make further literary connections; among them was Wyndham Lewis, the novelist who published some of Eliot's poetry in his magazine *Blast*. He picked up relations with Bertrand Russell, whom he had first met at Harvard, and who introduced him at Garsington, home of Lady Ottoline Morrell, whose salon attracted the figures of what had by then become known as Bloomsbury: Lytton Strachey, Roger Fry, Virginia and Leonard Woolf, Clive and Vanessa Bell, & Co. He began reviewing books for the *New Statesman*, the *Manchester Guardian,* and, later, the *Times Literary Supplement.*

But the crucial event, not merely of the year but in some ways of Eliot's life, was his rather sudden marriage to a woman named Vivien Haigh-Wood, daughter of a little-known painter and herself a major-league neurotic, with more troubles than the Middle East. Eliot had earlier declared his love to an American of his own WASP cast named Emily Hale, who turned him down for his want of prospects; and Vivien Haigh-Wood had had her hopes of marrying Scofield Thayer, a wealthy American and later editor of the *Dial*, scotched. Each, then, was on the rebound. Both were emotionally fragile. Eliot, at 26 still a virgin, brought to the marriage his sexual inexperience. Although he presented them with a *fait accompli*, his parents disapproved of the marriage.

Robert Crawford quotes Eliot, writing nearly half a century later, on his reason for marrying:

> I think all I wanted of Vivienne [she spelled her name in different ways] was a flirtation or a mild affair; I was too shy and unpractised to achieve either with anybody. I believe that I came to persuade myself that I was in love with her simply because I wanted to burn my boats and commit myself to staying in England. And she persuaded herself . . . that she would save the poet by keeping him in England.

Shouldn't, as the Jews say, be a total loss. Of this marriage made in hell Eliot noted, "To me it brought the state of mind out of which came *The Waste Land*."

THE EARLY YEARS of Eliot's married life were an unrelenting round of work and worry. He taught at two different boys' schools, and lectured to adult audiences in the evenings. He reviewed books. He worked at his poetry. He was from the outset a conscious and careful careerist, writing to his Harvard teacher J. H. Woods that there were two ways to succeed in the literary life in England, one being to appear in print everywhere, the other to appear less frequently but always dazzle. He chose the former for his criticism, the latter for his poetry.

Beginning in 1917, Eliot worked at Lloyds Bank in the Colonial and Foreign Department, translating documents and analyzing foreign financial reports. While at the bank, he signed on as an assistant editor for Harriet Shaw Weaver's magazine the *Egoist*. Miss Weaver was a patron to James Joyce; Eliot himself thought Joyce "the best English prose writer alive" and *Ulysses* "the greatest work of the age." He was offered but turned down a full-time editorial job at John Middleton Murry's *Atheneum*, his justification being that "if one has to earn a living, the safest occupation is that most remote from the arts."

Vivien's mental stability was never to be counted upon, and her myriad illnesses included neuritis, neuralgia, colitis, and heavy depression, with tuberculosis as a child thrown in at no extra charge. Her belief in Eliot's high fate as a poet was unflagging, but this didn't stand in the way of her cuckolding him with that family friend and paragon of political virtue, Bertrand Russell.

The pressure of all this must have seemed to someone of Eliot's delicate nervous organization insuperable. Lady Ottoline Morrell upon meeting him described him as "The Undertaker," adding that he was "dull, dull, dull." Virginia Woolf, noting his repressed behavior, referred to him as "the man in the four-piece suit." I. A. Richards, who saw him at work at Lloyds, described him "stooping, very like a dark bird in a feeder, over a big table covered with all sorts and sizes of foreign correspondence." At one point, Eliot suffered a breakdown, and went off to Lausanne to be treated by a famous mentalist of the day named Roger Vittoz, who diagnosed him as suffering from fatigue and anxiety, though assuring him that his mind was not disordered.

Eliot thought himself the victim of *aboulie*, or want of will. Self-diagnosis couldn't have gone further astray. Under the onslaught of personal problems and career ambitions, his will had held up, and he had begun to win through. Earlier, he had written to his mother about his place in contemporary English letters: "There is a small and select public which regards me as the best living critic, as well as the best living poet, in England," and he was not wrong.

A T THE CLOSE of Crawford's first volume, T. S. Eliot has just published *The Waste Land*, the most famous of his long poems. The poem set the seal on his position, maintained into our day, in the first rank of modern poets. A large portion of *The Waste Land* appeared in the *Criterion*, the magazine, underwritten by Lady Rothermere, whose editor was Eliot. The *Criterion* added to his literary luster, and was widely considered the most distinguished magazine of its time. He would eventually leave Vivien, who in her madness would sometimes show up at his lectures and readings with a sign on her back reading, "I Am the Wife He Abandoned." Having lost interest in his family's Unitarianism, he found his interest in Anglo-Catholicism deepening and his faith grew stronger with the passage of years. When he died in 1965, at the age of 76, Eliot was easily the English-speaking world's most famous poet and influential critic.

Young Eliot is festooned with infelicities in prose style: people in its pages are "bonding," students "gifted" Eliot with *The Oxford Book of English Verse*, Eliot becomes one of "the best networked younger figures in London literary publishing," "Tom and [Wyndham] Lewis decided to excurse to France together," and more. Egregious examples of elegant variation crop up: Paris in one sentence becomes "The French capital" in the next. "Reinvent," one of the leading cant phrases of our day, is too often pressed into service.

B UT THESE MINOR MISSTEPS do not diminish the book's many virtues. Crawford admires Eliot without ignoring his flaws; the anti-Semitism that Eliot picked up from his parents and upper-crust WASP milieu, and that has marred his reputation in the eyes of many, is neither overlooked nor in any way scanted, though Crawford mentions Eliot's horror at the revelations of Auschwitz. Crawford understands that Eliot is only of interest as the man who wrote the poems and the criticism, and everywhere he weighs the events in his life, both social and intellectual, on the precise scale of their importance to his writing. "Ultimately," Crawford writes, in a characteristic sentence, "Tom became a great poet through learning how to access and articulate unforgettably the wide spectrum of his inner life, his experience and his voracious reading."

T. S. Eliot was not a genius—not a poet of the grandeur of Dante, Shakespeare, Pope, Keats—but a great talent, and his life is an example of how far talent, with the aid of a first-rate intelligence and wide learning, can take one. More than anyone else who has written about him, Robert Crawford has shown how Eliot brought it all off.

Philip Larkin

(2014)

THE OTHER MORNING ON C-SPAN I saw at the Library of
Congress our current poet laureate, a man of nearly 80, long
white hair parted in the middle, reading incomprehensible verse
in a deep southern accent to an audience bored periwinkle blue, and at first
wondered whether this might be a skit from *Saturday Night Live* or a bit
from an old Ernie Kovacs show.

Which is another way of saying we live in a distinctly unbardic age, in
which poetry itself often seems, not to put too fine a point on it, preposterous. The last half century or so has not seen poetry, nor many serious poets,
flourish, at least not outside universities. Poets worthy of the attention
of serious readers, and not merely of that captive audience that shows up
under duress every September in classrooms, have been a small minority:
Elizabeth Bishop, L. E. Sissman, Donald Justice, Richard Wilbur, Howard
Nemerov, Anthony Hecht, Philip Larkin, and that is about it.

Of this group, only Philip Larkin passes the ultimate test of having written poetry that is memorable. Only Larkin understood how inhospitable
to poetry is the current age. Only he in his poems set out to give his readers
neither puzzles nor punishment but pleasure. Poetry, like all art, he held, "is
inextricably bound up with giving pleasure, and if a poet loses his pleasure-
seeking audience he has lost the only audience worth having . . ." Larkin

never gave poetry readings, never taught poetry, never wrote about it at significant length. He turned down opportunities to be the Oxford Professor of Poetry and to be Poet Laureate of England. He was content to write unforgettable poems and never play the official role of poet.

Larkin's poems at first reading may seem dark, depressive even. "Deprivation is for me," he said, "what daffodils were for Wordsworth." The imperfection of life was his subject, the inadequacy of his own endowments for living it his context. Sometimes the darkness can be overdone. In the poem "Dockery and Son" (1964), he writes, "Life is first boredom, then fear," to which one wants to reply, "So stop complaining, have a beer." The next line in this poem reads, "Whether or not we use it, it goes," to which the only proper response is, "Stop your blubbering and wipe your nose."

Yet, for the vast most part, far from being depressing, Larkin's poems, written with a wondrous precision and lucidity, and a comic élan that can produce outright laughter, have the effect of lifting one's spirits, as truth-telling often does. Not only aesthetically but in just about every other way, Larkin was a man set against his time: modernism in the arts, left-wing politics of the kind that appeals to academic intellectuals, admiration of youth—none of it was to his taste. This, as we shall see, has cost him.

Philip Larkin was haunted by death, as perhaps all of us with normal attentions spans are, but more than most. Fear of marriage, or what it would do to him personally, was another major inhibitor in his life. In his poem "Love" (1962) he wrote: "How can you be satisfied / Putting someone else first / So that you come off worst? / My life is for me. / As well ignore gravity."

"I think writing about unhappiness is probably the source of my popularity, if I have any—after all most people are unhappy, don't you think?" he told an interviewer. Self-depreciation, self-mockery, self-doubt came naturally to him. Aging, depression, failure, senility, mortality, from these unpromising subjects he made riveting poems. "The ultimate aim of a poet," he wrote, "should be to touch our hearts by showing his own."

Monica Jones, the woman with whom Larkin had a relationship that spanned decades, wrote to him after the publication of *The Less Deceived*, the collection of poems that in 1955 made his reputation, with prophetic correctness: "I'm sure that you are the one of this generation! . . . I feel more sure of it than ever before, it is you who are the one." He, too, was confident of his own future fame. When he missed a visit from the Queen at the opening of the Hull University Library, of which he was chief librarian, he wrote to his mother: "Ah well, one day I shall meet her as Philip Larkin, not the paltry librarian of a piffling university." He knew his quality. "I don't think I write well—just better than anyone else," he wrote to Anthony Thwaite.

Philip Larkin died in 1985, at 63, the same age as his father, a parallelism he prophesied. His last years were not easy ones. He lost much hearing, suffered impotence, both sexually and artistically. The year before his death, he wrote to his friend Kingley Amis:

> So now we face 1982, sixteen stone six, gargantuantly paunched, helplessly addicted to alcohol, tired of livin' and scared of dyin', world famous unable-to-write poet, well you know the rest.

He was not exaggerating his fame. A television profile of him was done on the BBC. Honorary degrees rolled in. He was awarded the Queen's Medal for Poetry. His portrait was commissioned by the National Gallery. He had a carefully cultivated oeuvre that included a dozen or so imperishable poems, one among them, "This Be The Verse" (1971), the funniest poem in the English language. At his death, Philip Larkin's reputation seemed solid and secure.

Not long after the house came down. 1993 was an *annus horribilis*. The previous year had seen the publication of *Selected Letters of Philip Larkin, 1940–85* edited by Anthony Thwaite, and *Philip Larkin: A Writer's Life* by Andrew Motion. (Both men had been chosen by the poet as his literary executors.) The letters were filled with jokes about women, put-downs of labor politicians and student radicals, an interest in pornography, regret over the loss of the British empire and more. He compared getting a woman into bed as "almost as much trouble as standing for parliament." The critic A. Alvarez, who badly misread Larkin's poetry, he called "El Al"; the novelist Salman Rushdie, "Salmagundi." He referred to *Catch-22* as "the American hymn to cowardice," the IRA as "these mad, murdering, Irish swine." The word "wog" often appears in these letters. The publication of these letters laid Larkin open to the kind of critics and biographers who cherry-pick unacceptable opinions in order to attack him.

In Mr. Motion, poet laureate of England between 1999 and 2009, he found such a biographer. If there was anything ostensibly degrading, however derisory, to be said about Philip Larkin, Mr. Motion found it and worked it into his biography. He claimed Larkin detested his parents; he made him out to be a racist, a right-winger, an exploiter of women. In the Motion biography, Larkin is nailed to the cross of political correctness. How could a man holding such views, the reasoning ran, be a great poet?

Not the least value of James Booth's biography of Philip Larkin is the antidote it supplies to Andrew Motion's. James Booth takes a few swipes at Mr. Motion's obtuseness, but his *Philip Larkin* is, far from a polemic, true to its subtitle, exploring Larkin's *Life, Art, and Love*. The author has achieved a proper balance, rare in books about writers, between the life and the art, always intent on showing how the life influenced the art, which in the end ought to be the only reason for interest in the life.

Mr. Booth is wise enough to distinguish between indiscretions in letters to friends and actions in the world. He also has the sense of humor required of anyone who writes about Larkin and which is so evidently missing in Andrew Motion. James Booth's biography reveals a Philip Larkin more complex, three-dimensional, and subtler in every way than Andrew Motion ever dreamed possible.

Larkin may have written the immortal line about how one's mum and dad fuck one up, but he nevertheless liked his parents and was himself the model of the good son. He admired his father's competence—he was a civil servant in Coventry—and appreciated that he introduced him, at any early age, to literature of a sophisticated kind. Larkin cared for his mother through her long widowhood (she died at 91), and wrote to her at least twice a week; Mr. Booth notes that there are more than 4,000 of his letters to her in the Larkin archive. His parents, meanwhile, according to his 10-years-older sister, "worshipped him."

"I wouldn't want it thought that I didn't like my parents," Larkin told Miriam Gross, who interviewed him for the *London Observer*. "I did like them. But at the same time they were rather awkward people and not very good at being happy." Their marriage caused him to see in marriage a kind of mutual prison, reducing the potentialities of both parties. If Larkin was in any way disappointing to the five or so women with whom he had serious relationships, it was owing to his inability to assent to marriage. Not that he was entirely happy with his bachelor life. He often wrote, in poems and in letters, of the possibility that he had missed out on the fuller life provided by wife and children. But he couldn't pull the trigger on marriage. Married or single, neither, for Larkin, was a true solution, but he went with single.

That the three women with whom he had continuous affairs wished to marry him is not alone a sign of a nesting instinct in women but a testament to Larkin's decency, tenderness, kindness as a lover. Whatever he may have said jokingly in his letters, many of them to Kingsley Amis and to Robert Conquest, in his actual treatment of women he was as far as possible from being a brute. When Monica Jones became ill he brought her to Hull, established her in his apartment, and cared for her in a devoted husbandly way. When the seriously Catholic Maeve Brennan, another of the women with whom he had a lengthy relationship, made plain that she held strong views on pre-marital sex, Larkin seems by and large to have acceded to these views. No one did more than he to revive the reputation of the novelist Barbara Pym. Despite the misogynist bluster of his letters, he was charming and attentive to women, around whom, his biographer avers, he always felt most at ease.

As for Larkin's politics, they were scarcely central to his art or his personality. He was supposed to be an ardent nationalist in politics, yet Mr. Booth quotes a letter he wrote to Monica Jones in which he remarks that "my God, surely nationalism is the surest mark of mediocrity." Larkin was not a right-winger; he was instead anti-left, which is not at all the same thing. As for his alleged racism, this is a label that should not be stuck upon a man who adored the music of Fats Waller and Duke Ellington and thought Louis Armstrong a genius.

"Books are a load of crap," from his poem "A Study of Reading Habits" (1964), is another of Larkin's best-known lines, and one that went a long way to establishing his reputation as a philistine. The notion is absurd for any poet whose major influences were Auden, Yeats, Hardy, and the French symbolist Jules Laforgue. What he was opposed to, as he made perhaps too plain in the introduction to *All What Jazz* (1970), his collection of writings on jazz, was modernism in the arts, as represented by such figures as Ezra Pound, Pablo Picasso, and Charlie Parker. He disliked such arts "not because they are new, but because they are irresponsible exploitations of technique in contradiction of human life as we know it." He could be amusing about such art. He called Kafka's *The Trial* "that gloomy convincing piece of bullshit." He thought Robert Lowell "balmy," and never passed up a chance to mock Ted Hughes, whom he thought "no good at all."

Larkin's views have been too often conflated with the coarser views of Kingsley Amis. The two men, James Booth shows, were not as close as Andrew Motion and others believed. At Larkin's funeral, Amis remarked, "I sometimes wonder if I really knew him." The answer was that he didn't. Until now, with the publication of Mr. Booth's biography, no one did. James Booth's *Philip Larkin* is a salutary reminder that biography need be neither iconoclastic nor reveal dark secrets to help readers understand the subtle richness of a complex man.

Willa Cather

(2013)

WILLA CATHER'S LITERARY reputation is even now, nearly 70 years after her death, less than clear. In her day—born in 1873, she published her main novels and books of stories between 1912 and 1940—she was regarded as insufficiently modernist, both in method and in outlook. She was later found to be a poor fit for academic feminism, for she wrote about the great dignity of female strength and resignation in the face of the harshest conditions. Advocates of gay literature who inhabit universities under the banner of Queer Theory have attempted to adopt her, taking her for a lesbian—she never married and had no serious romantic relationships with men—but her lesbianism remains suppositious at best. The powerful critics of her day and of ours have never lined up behind her. All she has had is readers who adore her novels and stories.

I am among them, and if pressed I should say that Willa Cather was the best novelist of the 20th century. Not all of her novels were successful: *One of Ours*, *Lucy Gayheart*, *Sapphira and the Slave Girl* don't really come off. But those that do—*O Pioneers!* (1913), *The Song of the Lark* (1915), *My Antonia* (1918), *A Lost Lady* (1922) *The Professor's House* (1925), *Death Comes for the Archbishop* (1927), and *Shadows on the Rock* (1931)—do so with a grace and grandeur that show a mastery of the highest power.

Willa Cather's great subject was immigration to America, chiefly among northern Europeans, their endurance in the face of nature's pitiless hardships, and what she calls "the gorgeous drama with God." Her prose was confidently cadenced and classically pure, never—like that of Hemingway or Faulkner—calling attention to itself, but instead devoted to illuminating her characters and their landscapes. (No one described landscape more beautifully than she.) Snobbery, egotism, politics never marred her storytelling. She wrote with a fine eye for the particular without ever losing sight of the larger scheme of the game of life.

Cather's favorite of her own novels, *Death Comes for the Archbishop*, her account of two missionary French priests settling what will one day be New Mexico, strikes so exquisite a note of reverence that many people took its author for a Catholic. She wasn't. Born a Baptist, she later became an Episcopalian. In one of the letters in the recently published collection *The Selected Letters of Willa Cather*, Cather writes to a sociologist at the University of Miami named Read Bain that she was not a Catholic nor had she any intention of becoming one. "On the other hand," she wrote,

> I do not regard the Roman Church merely as "artistic material." If the external form and ceremonial of that Church happens to be more beautiful than that of other churches, it certainly corresponds to some beautiful vision within. It is sacred, if for no other reason than that it is the faith that has been most loved by human creatures, and loved over the greatest stretch of centuries.

THAT WE HAVE *The Selected Letters of Willa Cather* at all is a point of interest in itself. Willa Cather intensely disliked having her private life on display. She carefully promoted her books, frequently chiding publishers for their want of effort at publicizing them and stocking them in book stores. But she didn't think that promoting and publicizing extended to promoting and publicizing herself. She eschewed writing blurbs for the excellent reason that "sometimes the best possible friends write the worst possible books." She gave few interviews, and when she wrote something about another person in a letter, she not uncommonly asked that her recipient keep it in confidence. Like Henry James, she burned many of the letters sent to her.

"We fully realize that in producing this book of selected letters," write the editors of *The Selected Letters*, "we are defying Willa Cather's stated preference that her letters remain hidden from the public eye." Their justification is that now, 66 years after her death in 1947, with her artistic reputation secure, "these letters heighten our sense of her complex personality, provide insights into her methods and artistic choices as she worked, and reveal Cather herself to be a complicated, funny, brilliant, flinty, sensitive, sometimes confounding human being." The letters, in their view, flesh out in a useful way the skeletal figure of the pure artist that Cather preferred to project.

Nothing in *The Selected Letters* touches directly on the vexed question of Willa Cather's sexuality—on, that is, whether or not she was a lesbian. The reason is the paucity of the letters to the two women with whom Cather was closest during her adult life. The first was Isabelle McClung, in whose family's house she lived while a journalist and high-school teacher in Pittsburgh. Isabelle later married a violinist named Jan Hambourg from a Jewish family of musicians, which was painful for Cather, who didn't much care for him. When Isabelle died, in 1938, Cather felt it as a great subtraction. The second, Edith Lewis, with whom Cather shared apartments in New York and vacation homes in Grand Manan Island in the Bay of Fundy and in Maine, worked in publishing and later as a copywriter. She assisted in innumerable ways, from proofreader to nurse during Cather's many late-life ailments. Lewis survived Cather and wrote a rather anodyne memoir of her after her death.

Hermione Lee, Cather's least tendentious biographer, refers to Edith Lewis's status as that of "wife" to Willa Cather. But she also allows that there is no evidence of the novelist ever having been the lover of either Isabelle McClung or Edith Lewis. If Cather's and Isabelle McClung's had been an active lesbian relationship, it is highly unlikely that Isabelle's father, a judge known for his conservative outlook, would have permitted Cather to live in his house. Nor would Cather have traveled and lived so openly with Edith Lewis if theirs was a lesbian relationship, for there were few things that Willa Cather more greatly contemned than scandal.

Case closed, or so one would like to think, though it probably never will be, for, as La Rochefoucauld had it, dirty minds never sleep.

Willa Cather was born in Virginia and, fortunately for her art, her family moved to Nebraska when she was nine. The move was jolting in every sense, physically and psychologically. The Nebraska landscape was barren, conventional cultural life there nearly non-existent. Her father, a gentle man of great dignity, arranged farm loans, at which he was only moderately successful. Her mother did not easily take to life on the prairie.

Cather was the oldest in a family of seven children, with two sisters and four brothers. The town of Red Cloud, where the Cathers settled, was without many amenities, but she found there an Englishman named William Drucker who instructed her in Greek and Latin. German-Jewish neighbors kept a decent library to which they allowed her access. Her initial impulse was to become a physician. She dressed boyishly, was called Willie. In some of her letters in later life she writes of her insensitivity to her family, but in regard to her surroundings she was one of those children on whom not much was lost. Great writers are in training for their art long before they are even aware they wish to be writers.

Willa Cather grew to know the Bohemian, Swedish, Norwegian, German farmers with whom her father did business, and to love the land despite its droughts, scorching sun, brutal winters, and unforgiving severity. She would later come to love the Colorado of the cliff dwellers, of whom she wrote in *The Professor's House*, and the Southwest even more. "I do not think my heart ever got across the Missouri river," she wrote to an old Nebraska friend. To her publisher, Alfred A. Knopf, she wrote during a holiday in Red Cloud: "I get more thrills to the square mile out of this cornfield country than I can out of any other country in the world."

Some of Cather's more interesting letters are to publishers and editors. The first major publisher for her novels was Houghton Mifflin, where she dealt with an editor named Ferris Greenslet. She felt her books treated as second-class merchandise there, and in 1919 she left Houghton Mifflin for the firm of Alfred A. Knopf, Inc. Knopf, who was then 26 years old and who had begun his firm four years earlier, was eager to have Willa Cather's books on his list. The move was providential, and profitable to both author and publisher. The young Knopf brought out her books in handsome editions, and always treated their author as the literary equivalent of a *grande dame*, which was, one learns from her letters, the least she expected.

For a girl raised in the outback of North America, Willa Cather, once out of Nebraska, quickly took on the cosmopolitan qualities of the highly cultivated writer. She worked eight years for *McClure's*, the New York magazine where Ida Tarbell and other muckraking writers of the day regularly wrote. Cather herself ghost-wrote for the magazine the biography of Mary Baker Eddy, the founder of Christian Science. She made a number of trips to Europe. Her experience widened, her insights deepened.

WILLA CATHER's TASTES in literature, music, food, travel were all impressively refined. She favored Balzac, Tolstoy, and Henry James, and claimed the last two as influences on her own writing. She preferred French over English novelists, because they dispensed with congeniality and their range of interests was much wider. Her love of music ran strong, and she later befriended the Menuhin family, whose son Yehudi was the great violin prodigy of his day. Food was important to her, in and for itself and for what it conveyed about civilized culture. In a scene in *Death Comes for the Archbishop*, the novel's main character, Bishop Latour, is served an onion soup by his assistant Father Vaillant, about which the bishop remarks:

> I am not deprecating your individual talent, Joseph, but, when one thinks of it, a soup like this is not the work of one man. It is the result of a constantly refined tradition. There are nearly a thousand years of history in this soup.

Willa Cather hated vulgarity, in art and in life. She wrote to Alfred Knopf, on the death of his father, of "that delicate instrument inside one which knows the cheap from the fine. The recognition of the really fine is simply one of the richest pleasures in life." In life so in art: "As one grows older," she wrote to the Nebraska editor Will Owen Jones, "one cares less about clever writing and more about a simple and faithful presentation." She chose not to have her novels published in school editions, for she didn't want them to be "assigned to students as part of the grind"; forced to read her in school, she felt, they would be unlikely to do so in later years when they were mature enough to appreciate her.

Cather had published five books—a volume of verse, another of short stories, and three novels—before *My Ántonia* (1918), the novel of life on the prairie as told by Jim Burden, who arrives in Nebraska on the same train as the novel's heroine, the Bohemian immigrant Antonia Schimerdas. Randolph Bourne, one of the powerful critics of the day, said of the novel: "Here at last is an American novel, redolent of the Western prairie, that our most irritated and exacting preconceptions can be content with." Not all the criticism of the novel was positive; nor was its commercial success immediate. But its achievement as a work of art convinced Willa Cather of her own standing as an artist of high seriousness.

The rest of the world soon followed her in this opinion. Her World War I novel, *One of Ours,* a book that peters out sadly in its second half, won a Pulitzer Prize. (Pulitzer Prizes in the arts, as everyone knows, go to two kinds of people: those who don't need them and those who don't deserve them.) Universities began lining up to give her honorary degrees, a queue that lasted throughout her life. Her novels, under the publishing orchestration of Alfred A. Knopf, had a reliably steady sale.

Sarah Orne Jewett, the author of *The Country of the Pointed Firs*, had once advised the young Willa Cather to

> write to the human heart, the great consciousness that all humanity goes to make up. . . . And to write and work on this level, we must live on it—we must at least recognize it and defer to it at every step. We must be ourselves, but we must be our best selves.

"To write well," Cather wrote to her brother Douglas, "you have to be all wrapped up on your game and think it awfully worthwhile." For her there was no better game. She steered clear of politics in her writing, feeling that those with "zeal to reconstruct and improve human society seem to lose touch with human beings and with the individual needs and desires which make people what they are." Not even Tolstoy could win through as a reformer, she notes in one of her letters, and "certainly no one ever took the puzzle of human life more to heart or puzzled over it more agonizingly,—not even the *New Republic.*"

"People say I have a 'classic style,'" Cather wrote to Roscoe, another of her four brothers. "A few of them know it's the heart under the words that counts." A feeling for the English sentence, she felt, was "the beginning of everything." Style, she believed, was "merely the writer, not the *person* himself; what he was born with and what he has done to himself." Admiration and love for her subjects were strong ingredients in her writing. "I can write successfully only when I write about people or places that I very greatly admire; which, indeed, I actually love." Real feeling was at the heart of great writing for her, though of course it took "skill to get that feeling across to many people in many languages, but the strong feeling that comes out of the living heart is the thing *most necessary—and most rarely found.*"

THE TOUGHEST THING TO ARRANGE IN LIFE is a smooth exit. *The Selected Letters* shows that Willa Cather could not arrange one. Illnesses kicked in as she grew old. An inflamed sheath of the large tendon in the thumb of her right hand kept her from writing for months at a stretch. The death of friends and members of her family threw her off course to the point of near-nervous breakdown, for she felt things deeply. As she wrote to Thomas Masaryk, the founder and president of Czechoslovakia, she felt, as people of a certain age will, that "the times are out of joint." Elsewhere, in the preface to *Not Under Forty* (1936), her collection of essays, she wrote that no one under the age of 40 was likely to understand her essays, for "the world changed in 1922, or thereabouts," by which she meant that the world was no longer producing men and women with the solidity of character of the immigrant generations. The world seemed a more garish yet dreary place than the one she grew up in, filled with such vulgarians as Ivy Peters, a character whose coarseness she described in *A Lost Lady.*

A note of complaint works its way in the late-life letters; the editors note that she could sometimes play the "drama queen." But this tends to be blotted out by the many passages of insight and good sense. She is wonderful on child-raising, and the penalties attaching to too much mother love.

There is also the solace of accomplishment recognized. She is delighted to find herself the subject of an article in *Encylopaedia Britannica*. When she learns that Thomas Hardy and J. M. Barrie thought well of her novels, she writes to William Lyon Phelps, the Yale professor and literary critic: "I think there is nothing so satisfying as having given pleasure, in their old age, to some of the writers who fascinated one in one's youth."

Skeptical of modernity, Cather had a low view of "the cold pride of science [which] is the most devilish thing that has ever come into this world. It is the absolute enemy of happiness. The human mind, not the spirit, has disinherited human nature." In *The Professor's House*, she formulates this precisely when she has the novel's eponymous hero Professor Godfrey St. John tell a student:

> No, Miller, I don't myself think much of science, as a phase of human development. It has given us a lot of ingenious toys; they take our attention away from the real problems, of course, and since the problems are insoluble, I suppose we ought to be grateful for the distraction. But the fact is, the human mind, the individual mind, has always been made more interesting by dwelling on the old riddles, even if it makes nothing of them. Science . . . hasn't given us any richer pleasures, as the Renaissance did, nor any new sins—not one! Indeed it takes the old ones away. It's the laboratory, not the Lamb of God, that taketh away the sins of the world. . . . I don't think you help people by making their conduct of no importance—you impoverish them. . . . The king and the beggar had the same chance at miracles and great temptations and revelations. And that's what makes men happy, believing in the mystery and importance of their own little individual lives. It makes us happy to surround our creature needs and bodily instincts with as much pomp and circumstance as possible. Art and religion (they are the same thing in the end, of course) have given man the only happiness he has ever had.

In one of the last of her letters, she writes to E. K. Brown, one of her early biographers:

. . . we learn a great deal from great people. The mere information doesn't matter much—but they somehow strike out
the foolish platitudes that we have been taught to respect
devoutly, and give us courage to be honest and free. Free to
rely on what we really feel and really love—and that only.

When Willa Cather wrote that, did she know that she herself had become
one of those great people? One hopes so, for she indubitably was.

George Kennan

(2014)

THE CAREER OF GEORGE F. KENNAN (1904–2005), the diplomatist whose name is chiefly associated with the Cold War, peaked when Kennan was in his early forties. On February 22, 1946, working at the time as a foreign service officer at the State Department, he wrote a "long telegram" of 5,540 words explaining the motive force behind the behavior of the Soviet Union and how best to deal with it. The gist of the telegram was that the Soviet Union, pressed by economic failure and hemmed in by Marxist-Leninist ideology, needed and found a perfect enemy in the United States, and therefore was uninterested in diplomatic negotiation or compromise. This being so, the best way for the United States to deal with the Soviet Union was to build up the still free countries of Western Europe and do all it could to contain Soviet expansionism. This policy became known as "containment," and its immediate result was the massive aid program to post-war western Europe known as the Marshall Plan, in whose organization Kennan had a major hand.

In a 1947 article signed "X" in *Foreign Affairs* titled "The Sources of Soviet Conduct," Kennan expanded upon and consolidated these views, declaring that "the main element of any United States policy toward the Soviet Union must be that of a long-term, patient but firm and vigilant containment of Russian expansive tendencies." Despite the anonymity under which the article was published, it became known that George Kennan was its author, and this lent added luster to his reputation. He would soon be made head of the State Department's Policy Planning Committee, and in 1952, he was appointed the United States ambassador to Moscow by Harry Truman. Puffing on power and fame, George Kennan was riding high.

KENNAN'S BEST DAYS were under Harry Truman, who respected his advice, if he didn't always follow it. His worst days were under John Foster Dulles, who as secretary of state during the Eisenhower presidency was dismayed at Kennan's recommendation that the United States accept Soviet domination of eastern Europe, instead of attempting to roll it back. Dulles failed to appoint Kennan to a serious post and left him dangling without work for months. In 1953, after twenty-seven years in the foreign service, Kennan retired from government and moved to Princeton, where he was given a place at the Institute for Advanced Study. Apart from his brief stint as Ambassador to Yugoslavia (1961–1963), he remained at Princeton for the remainder of his long life, writing and lecturing but chiefly seeking influence for his views on foreign policy.

Influence was the name of George Kennan's desire. After the Truman years, he never regained it. Once out of the foreign service, he had nearly fifty years to complain about the loss. The foreign policy for which he sought influence was, with qualifications, essentially isolationist. For Kennan, foreign policy was never a moral but always a practical matter. Apart from honoring treaties and alliances, foreign policy, he held, ought to be "guided strictly by consideration of national interest." Our entanglements in other nations, in this reading, ought to be limited only to "those aspects of [their] official behavior which touched our interests—maintaining, in other words, a relationship with [them] of mutual respect and courtesy— but distant." Government generally, he wrote in *Around the Cragged Hill: A Personal and Political Philosophy*, "is simply not the channel through which men's noblest impulses are to be realized. Its task, on the contrary, is largely to see that its ignoble ones are kept under restraint and not permitted to go too far."

As for the United States, Kennan believed it had no business following an aggressive foreign policy. As a foreign service officer stationed in Moscow and later as an ambassador there, he had a close view of the brutalities of the Soviet regime. But the eradication of human rights in one country were not, he believed, the business of any other country. Whole continents and vast territories—Latin America, Africa, most of the Middle East—seemed to him not yet arrived at a state of civilization such as admitted of complex diplomatic negotiation. Foreign aid, most likely to be wasted and never really appreciated by its recipients, was little more than a foolish error of false generosity on the part of the donor nation, for which read the naively virtuous United States. Proper distance, mutual respect, non-interference, above all the avoidance of war—these were the pillars on which Kennan thought foreign policy ought to stand.

The Kennan Diaries is a generous selection from the 8,000 pages of diaries that George Kennan kept, with inconstant regularity, from the age of eleven. Edited by Frank Costigliola, a historian at the University of Connecticut, with helpful footnotes and a minimum of scholarly barbed wire placed between the reader and the text, the book affords a more intimate view of George Kennan than any biography is likely to provide. The emphasis in the diary's entries, naturally enough, is on international relations, but the reigning principle behind Costigliola's selections has been to favor Kennan's "most vivid prose while including representative examples of his various experiences, moods, concerns, and ideas." Professor Costigliola admires George Kennan for his political consistency, his unflagging energy and endurance, and his literary skill. But he doesn't allow his admiration to prevent his including diary material that, in an age of political correctness, might disqualify him in the eyes of the great virtucrats of our day, or subject him to two-penny psychoanalysis.

THE KENNAN DIARIES reveal the inner struggles of the man who fought for his ideas on foreign policy without success and the dark views that came in the wake of his failure. They correct the view of George Kennan as the ultimate State Department insider. Neither there nor anywhere else was Kennan ever among the inner circle of the select and the privileged. He refers to himself as a WASP, but, in the strict sense of the term, he wasn't. Scottish and English in his lineage, from a family that first arrived in America in the eighteenth century, he grew up not on the eastern seaboard but in Milwaukee. His family had none of the standard WASP connections, social or financial. He did not attend prep schools but public schools until, at thirteen, he was sent off to military school in Delafield, Wisconsin. His father was a tax attorney, upstanding and well-regarded but, owing to ineptitude in business, not wealthy; his mother died, of peritonitis from a ruptured appendix, when George was two months old. The Kennans were not among the social elite, not even in blue-collar Milwaukee.

Kennan went to Princeton but his admission there was far from assured. His biographer John Lewis Gaddis reports that he was "the last student admitted," and no one else from his military school found acceptance in an eastern college. At Princeton he was neither a dazzling student nor entirely at ease socially. Aboard ship on his first trip to Europe, he speaks of cutting fellow passengers who try to communicate with him with "true Princeton snobbery," which suggests that he knew what it was like to have this snobbery turned on him. His diary records his planning an essay on "Princeton and Democracy," which is to be both a defense against the charge of endemic snobbery at Princeton and an attack on those "who make social prestige during undergraduate years the sole aim in life." Money was a problem for him at Princeton. He did clerical work at his eating club, the undistinguished Key and Seal, to help reduce his bills there.

After deciding not to go to law school, Kennan ended up in the foreign service. Despite his successes, even here he was something of an outsider. "Like a character out of Dostoyevsky," Walter Isaacson and Evan Thomas write in *The Wise Men: Six Friends and the World They Made*, "Kennan enjoyed the alienation that came from being a detached observer." As a young foreign service officer, he was earnest but awkward; among colleagues at the State Department he was often the odd man out. As early as twenty-eight, he wrote in his diary that he was "condemned to a rare intellectual isolation . . . my mental processes will never be understood by anyone else." He was never part of the Georgetown set of Joseph Alsop, Alice Roosevelt Longworth, and Dean Acheson. At a State Department outing, he played baseball in a three-piece suit.

Kennan's talents suited him for foreign service. He acquired foreign languages fairly easily, and was said to have spoken a pure and aristocratic Russian. His scholarly instincts drove him to read up on a subject with thoroughness and in depth. He was an effective lecturer. So brilliant a prose writer was he that many of his colleagues in the State Department did not always take his reports quite seriously. Eugene Rostow, according to Isaacson and Thomas, put Kennan down as "an impressionist, a poet, not an earthling."

The Kennan Diaries are sometimes used to set out ideas, sometimes to record historical events or meetings, often to fight his depression. He claimed his diary was useful to him in sorting out his confusions and aiding him in gaining perspective on his defeats: "If this writing will help me to gather and order my spiritual forces again (and writing sometimes does) it will be worth the time," he notes. "He kept the diary as a way of keeping himself together," Frank Costigliola notes.

When under the lash of depression Kennan wrote copiously in his diary, and what depressed him above all was the want of influence of his ideas on those in power. Other reasons for his depression are what he refers to as his "weaknesses": his garrulity, his philandering impulses, his unsteady temperament. Anger works its way into the diary at what he takes to be steady decline of America's manners and mores, the nation's heedless technological advance, its coarse politics, and a great deal else.

THE ONLY PEOPLE for whom Kennan expresses affection are the Russians, not the Soviet leaders but the people forced to live under their systematically brutal regime. "I sometimes feel that I would rather be sent to Siberia among them (which is certainly what would happen to me if I were a Soviet citizen) than to live on Park Avenue among our own stuffy folk," he wrote. He remarks on his mystical link with St. Petersburg, then called Leningrad, that

> I know that in this city, where I have never lived, there has nevertheless, by some strange quirk of fate—a previous life, perhaps?—been deposited a portion of my own capacity to feel and to love, a portion, in other words of my own life;

and that this is something which no American will ever understand and no Russian ever believe.

Alone again, as the song has it, naturally.

"I suppose I am a literary person myself, slightly manqué," Kennan noted in his diary. At one point he planned to write a biography of Chekhov. With the exception of Dostoyevsky—"there is not one reasonably normal, decent soul among all his characters"—he was enamored of the great Russian writers of the nineteenth century. Gibbon's *Decline and Fall of the Roman Empire* was a key book for him. Difficult to think of anyone other than Kennan in the State Department or in government generally who could have read and appreciated Leon Edel's five-volume biography of Henry James. More than once in his diaries he expresses the wish to write fiction. His prose, always fluent and confidently cadenced, is notable for succinct formulation.

THE DARKNESS IN GEORGE KENNAN, which grew and deepened with age, was there from the beginning. Kennan was a misanthrope. One of the chapters of *Around the Cragged Hill* is titled "Man, the Cracked Vessel." The cracks come from man's impulses and urges, his vanity and egotism. Kennan saw these cracks in his countrymen as if through a microscope. Returning from a trip to Mount Vernon, he notes the "shapeless, droopy people," and remarks that "it was never clearer that man is a skin-disease of the earth." All technology was to him malevolent unless proven otherwise. He saw the world filled with "people drugged and debilitated by automobiles and advertisements and radios and moving pictures"; and in later life he allowed that he would trade in the American space program for a decent national telegraph system and efficient railway. Visiting southern California, he found there "that tendency of American life which it typifies . . . childhood without the promise of maturity." In California, generally he finds "an immanent sterility for which no cure is apparent." Later he will note that "the white man" made a mistake settling the place.

In 1942, writing in the third person, Kennan asked whether "the conviction that when in a depression he was nearer to reality, to a certain tragic and melancholy reality, than at other times. It was, in other words, not the depression which was abnormal, but the irrational hopefulness, which prevailed at other times." In his case, depression was lightly admixed with megalomania. He quotes from Shakespeare's *Henry VIII* on his own fall from power:

> I have touched the highest point of all my greatness;
> And from that full meridian of my glory,
> I haste not to my setting; I shall fall
> Like a bright exhalation in the evening,
> And no man see me more.

He claims to have had "no real successes, and I dare not hope for any." Later he adds: "I must regard my role in the public life of this country as played out. My future is purely private life." Private life meant a life of scholarship, and he did turn out a few works of diplomatic history: *The Decline of Bismarck's European Order: Franco-Russian Relations, 1875–1890* (1979) and *The Fateful Alliance: France, Russia, and the Coming of the First World War* (1984). But it wasn't enough for a man who had known the heightened glories of public success. "Life," he writes in 1963, "consists principally of waiting to die." Departing the planet at 101, George Kennan had a long time to await that event.

IRONY OF IRONIES, the further out of power he was, the greater his popularity seemed to grow. He claimed to receive more than five hundred invitations to give lectures and talks every year, and he accepted a fair number of them. "My reputation follows me around like a shadow or like a mask I am obliged to wear." When he came out against American participation in the Vietnam War, his popularity grew even greater. He campaigned for Eugene McCarthy against Lyndon Johnson. He was the go-to guy when the *New York Review of Books* needed a strong piece against the errancy of American foreign policy. During the years of the Vietnam War, he was a heroic figure for the American left.

Yet no one more loathed hippie culture and war protesters than he. "They say we are both Americans," he writes in his diary when encountering hippies abroad, "but you are stranger to me than the Hottentots.

Benevolently, and with no reaction more negative than a slight shudder, I consign you to your various delights, thankful only that no one compels me to share them with you." At one point he thinks perhaps of writing about domestic affairs, but finds himself unable to do so "when one of the greatest of the problems is the deterioration of life in the great cities and when one of the major components of the problem this presents is the Negro problem, which is taboo." He detests the standard left-wing thinking that equates poverty with virtue, affluence with wickedness. He remarks on the tawdriness of the media and the deep humorlessness of the universities. He lambasts the entertainment industry and the dreadful use it

> makes of its near monopoly, not merely the low intellectual level but the shameless pornography, the pathological preoccupation with sex and violence, the weird efforts to claim for homosexuality the status of a proud, noble, and promising way of life. . .

Were its author alive when *The Kennan Diaries* was published, the Political Correctness Police would soon enough have knocked on his door.

Instead the world rained prizes down upon him: Pulitzers, National Books Awards, the Albert Einstein Peace Prize, the Reith and the Jefferson Lectures, honorary degrees, the Medal of Freedom, everything but the Nobel. He felt his fate was to be a prophet, but he was perhaps a prophet too much honored. As he wrote, he was "probably the most honored [person] outside the entertainment industry and the political establishment in this country. How could this have happened? And how to put it in its proper place?" Part of the reason, he believed, was that "there is not much competition." Another part, surely, was that he was too careful a caretaker of his career to go public with his dark views on America and the world, confining them chiefly to his diary.

None of his prizes and awards brought him the least contentment. He never relinquished the hope for power and influence. "I have the curious experience," he wrote, "of being probably the most extensively honored private person in the country and, at the same time, the person least heeded when he speaks."

Nor did he ever have any doubt about the correctness of his views on foreign policy. He is confident that the views expressed in *Around the Cragged Hill* "have been major contributions to the development of political philosophy in our age, and to have this go wholly unrecognized is a bitter disappointment." At the age of eighty-seven he asks: "Is there not a grotesque anomaly between the esteem bestowed on the person and the scant regard for his views?" When in 1989 Soviet Communism crumbles, owing chiefly to a policy of heating up the arms race in direct opposition to his own views, his diary is silent, expressing little pleasure in the eradication of the most humanly wasteful regime in the history of the world.

I N HIS CHAPTER ON GOVERNMENT in *Around the Cragged Hill,* Kennan writes of the human thirst for authority and power, and of the distortions in character that attaining them can cause. He cites Henry Adams on this point:

> The effect of power and publicity on all men is the aggravation of self, a sort of tumor that ends in killing the victim's sympathies; a diseased appetite, like a passion for drink or perverted tastes; one can scarcely use expressions too strong to describe the violence of egotism it stimulates.

Quoting Adams, poor George Kennan might have been describing himself.

Isaiah Berlin

(2016)

"What are you? You call yourself a thinker, I suppose."
—R. H. S. CROSSMAN TO ISAIAH BERLIN

PROLIXITY, THY NAME IS ISAIAH, last name Berlin. So one feels on coming to the last letter in the four-volume collection of the letters of Isaiah Berlin, edited with sedulousness and unstinting devotion by Henry Hardy. A former editor at Oxford University Press, Hardy, not long after meeting Berlin in 1972, took it upon himself to gather together Berlin's various writings, which today, nearly two decades after his death, fill up no fewer than 17 books, including 10 reissues of his older books. He has now come to the end of editing these letters. No writer or scholar has ever been better served by an editor than Isaiah Berlin by Henry Hardy.

I write "writer or scholar," but it is less than clear whether Berlin was one or the other, or for that matter if he were either. Berlin began his university life as a philosopher, in the age of British analytic philosophy, which, though he recognized its usefulness, he found too arid for his tastes, altogether too dead-ended. He gradually came to the conclusion that he wanted a subject "in which one could hope to know more at the end of one's life than when one had begun." He turned to traditional political philosophy, which led him to his ultimate general subject, his passion: the history of ideas.

As FOR HIS OWN CONTRIBUTION to this history, Berlin is credited with formulating the useful distinction between negative and
positive liberty. Negative liberty covers that part of life—private life,
chiefly—not covered by coercion or interference by the state, allowing
freedom to act upon one's desires so long as they don't encroach upon the
freedom of others. Positive liberty is that entailed in choosing one's government, which in turn determines in what parts of life interference and
coercion ought to be applied to the lives of citizens in pursuit of what is
deemed the common good. Much has been written about this distinction by contemporary philosophers, not a little of it disputatious.

The other idea associated with Berlin's political thought is pluralism,
sometimes denoted "value pluralism," holding that useful values can be,
and often are, in conflict. Berlin was opposed to the notion that the central questions of human life can have one answer. Wallace Stevens's "luna-
tic of one idea" was not for him. In a talk called "Message to the Twenty-
First Century," read on his behalf at the University of Toronto in 1994,
three years before his death, Berlin wrote:

> if these ultimate human values by which we live are to be
> pursued, then compromises, trade-offs, arrangements have
> to be made if the worst is not to happen. . . . My point is that
> some values clash: the ends pursued by human beings are all
> generated by our common nature, but their pursuit has to be
> to some degree controlled—liberty and the pursuit of hap-
> piness . . . may not be fully compatible with each other, nor
> are liberty, equality, and fraternity.

"The Hedgehog and the Fox" is Berlin's most famous essay, taking off
from an epigraph supplied by the 7th-century BCE Greek poet Archi-
lochus: "The fox knows many things, but the hedgehog knows one big
thing." The essay is on the intellectual travail of Leo Tolstoy—a natural fox in Berlin's reading, who, in his search for the unifying principle
controlling the multiplicity of human actions, longed to be a hedgehog. The temptation of hedgehoggery was never one to which Berlin
himself succumbed.

Fructifying as these ideas have been, it is not as a political philosopher that Berlin is chiefly of interest. He was instead that less easily defined phenomenon, a *flâneur* of the mind, an intellectual celebrity in three different nations, England, America, and Israel, a personage, no less—yet perhaps not all that much more. As for his reputation in England, the 27-year-old Berlin, anticipating his own career, recounts telling Maurice Bowra "that in Oxford & Cambridge only personalities counted, & not posts, & that striking and original figures always overshadowed dim professors etc." He was himself nothing if not striking; it is only his originality that is in question.

In many ways Berlin, as he would have been the first to say, led a charmed life. Born in 1909 in Riga, Latvia, the only surviving child of a successful Jewish lumber merchant, he and his family, after a brief stay in the Soviet Union, departed in 1921 for England. A tubby boy, with a lame arm caused at birth by an obstetrician's ineptitude, a foreigner in a land not without its strong strain of xenophobia and anti-Semitism, the young Isaiah Berlin carefully negotiated his way up the slippery slope to eminence. He gained entrance to St. Paul's School in London, thence to Corpus Christi, Oxford, and thence to an early fellowship at All Souls, the first Jewish fellow in the history of that college. He waited until his mid-forties to marry Aline Halban, *née* Gunzbourg, a woman whose substantial wealth allowed him to live out his days in great comfort, amidst costly paintings and servants, and putting him permanently out of the financial wars.

Gregarious and charming, Berlin met everyone: Sigmund Freud, Chaim Weizmann, Winston Churchill, David Ben-Gurion, Felix Frankfurter, Igor Stravinsky, Jacqueline Kennedy, Anna Akhmatova, Boris Pasternak ... the list goes on. Less a Casanova than a Mercurio, he found his way into the select circles of such women as Marietta Tree, Sibyl Colefax, and Emerald Cunard. Before long, Berlin himself became a name others wished to add to their own lists of social and intellectual collectibles.

Awards and honors rained down upon him: the presidency of the British Academy, honorary degrees, festschrifts, doctoral dissertations written about his works, an Order of Merit, international prizes, headship of Wolfson (a new Oxford college), all this and more—and yet none of it was sufficient to convince Berlin that he was a figure of the first quality. Self-deprecation is a *leitmotif* that plays throughout his letters over nearly 70 years. "I am quite clear that such career as I have had was securely founded on being overestimated," he wrote to the archeologist John Hilton toward the end of his life.

One might suspect this to be false humility on Berlin's part. From the evidence abundantly supplied by his letters, however, he genuinely felt himself, as a thinker, a scholar, a writer, and a Jew in England, a nowhere man. Berlin kept no diary; he wrote neither autobiography nor memoirs, though he produced a book, *Personal Impressions* (1980), of portraits of friends and famous men he had known. His letters are the closest thing of his we shall have in the line of introspection. They are a gallimaufry, a jumble, an extraordinary mixture of attack, sycophancy, resentment, confessions of weakness, gossip, exaggeration, generosity, kindliness, superior intellectual penetration, and character analysis.

ALTHOUGH THE FOUR VOLUMES of Berlin's letters run to more than 2,000 pages, these published letters, Mr. Hardy informs us, are a selection merely and scarcely all of his letters. These letters give us insight into Berlin's character that Michael Ignatieff's biography, *Isaiah Berlin* (1998)—researched while its subject was alive and published at his request posthumously—fails to give. The letters emphasize Berlin's doubts and failings and are far removed from Ignatieff's hero worship.

The letters make plain why Berlin never wrote the great book every serious intellectual with scholarly pretensions hopes to write. "I really must try and achieve one solid work—say a study of [Vissarion] Belinsky [the 19th century Russian literary critic]—and not scatter myself in all these directions all over the place," he wrote. In 1981 to Joseph Alsop he confesses: "Occasionally I wonder how many years I have left," and "will I be able to write a big book in the years left to me, and does it matter whether I can or not?" He never did.

Other impressive intellectual figures in Berlin's generation failed to write the masterwork everyone thought was in them, Hugh Trevor-Roper, Maurice Bowra, Arnaldo Momigliano, and Edward Shils among them. Why these extraordinary men failed to do so remains a mystery, but in Berlin's case it is clear that he talked and dawdled and scribbled it away in correspondence. Even his prodigious letter writing, he claimed, was a form of stalling. "Answering letters, in fact, is a kind of drug," he wrote to one of his stepsons, "great relief from real work."

The letters themselves tend to be vast rambles. To a lifelong correspondent named Rowland Burdon-Muller, Berlin writes: "Forgive me if I do not write you a long letter," and then proceeds to write him a long letter. To Margaret Paul, an economics tutor at St. Hilda's College, he writes: "By nature I like to say too much, to exaggerate, embellish, inflate." In this same letter he goes on to do just that. To the novelist Elizabeth Bowen he writes: "Please forgive me. I write on & on as I talk, & how tiresome that must often be. . . . I really must not go on and on." To Felix Frankfurter: "God knows why I go on—maundering like this."

Everyone who ever met Isaiah Berlin remarked on his rapid-fire, glittering, torrential talk. Edmund Wilson, in his journal, writes that Berlin showed up at his, Wilson's, London hotel and talked uninterruptedly for nearly two hours.

> He won't, where the competition is easily overpowered and he can get the bit between his teeth, allow anyone else to talk; you have to cut down through his continuous flow determinedly, loudly and emphatically, and he will soon snatch the ball away from you by not waiting for you to finish but seizing on some new association of ideas to go off on some new line of thought.

Later in his journal Wilson added: "His desire to know about everybody and everything seems to become more and more compulsive." Coming from Edmund Wilson, himself a famous monologist, this is strong criticism.

Berlin's loquacity was transformed into verbosity in his writing. Had the government ever declared a tax on adjectives, he would have had to declare bankruptcy. Triplets in adjectives, nouns, clauses was his speciality. Here is a sample sentence from "The Hedgehog and the Fox," a splendid essay that would nonetheless gain from being cut by at least a third:

> With it [Tolstoy's attitude toward history] went an incurable love of the concrete, the empirical, the verifiable, and

an instinctive distrust of the abstract, the impalpable, the supernatural—in short an early tendency to a scientific and positivist approach, unfriendly to romanticism, abstract formulations, metaphysics.

Berlin was a man to whom it was not unnatural to append a postscript three times the length of the letter itself. From Harvard he writes to his wife about his being asked at a dinner party to say "a few words" about the current political situation, to which he responded: "'No, no, I cannot make a short statement. Are you asking me to say a few words?' Everyone laughed, I hope happily."

T S. ELIOT SOMEWHERE NOTES that every good letter should contain an indiscretion. Berlin's letters score high on this criterion. "*Plauderei* [chatty gossip] is my natural medium," Berlin writes in one of them. A sideline interest in these letters is Berlin's take-downs of people to whom he writes with great intimacy in other letters. Of the aforementioned Rowland Burdon-Muller, a wealthy homosexual with radical political views, he writes to Alice James, daughter-in-law of William James, that he "gets me down no less than you," and that he is, though "genuinely civilised, not a little snobbish and talks too much." To this same Burdon-Muller, he writes of the philosopher Stuart Hampshire, whom he genuinely liked, that he is about to deliver a lecture "suitably enough on 'Emotion and Expression,' or something of the kind, which sounds more like his own personality than like philosophy." Of Noel Annan, one of his intimates, he writes to Marion Frankfurter, "I am glad you like Annan—who hasn't much substance but a certain amount of sensibility & is the Bloomsbury (official) dauphin &, they hope, commentator." Of the Schlesingers, Arthur and his first wife, Marian, he writes: "She is much more intelligent & a better man in all ways."

Several of the figures in *Personal Impressions* whom he elevates in his high panegyrical style are taken down in his letters. Aldous Huxley, for example, is "enormously unsympathetic, I think." The saintly Albert Einstein of *Personal Impressions* is in the letters "a genius but surely a foolish one with the inhumanity of a child." Maurice Bowra, whom he elsewhere lauds for his nonconformist spirit and role as "a tremendous liberator in our youth," is in the letters this "pathetic, oppressive, demanding, guilt-inducing, conversation-killing, embarrassing, gross, maddening, at once touching and violently repellent, paranoiac, deaf, blind, thick skinned, easily offended presence." He thanks Felix Frankfurter for sending him a copy of his memoirs, and tells him how much he looks forward to reading it—then writes to Rowland Burdon-Muller that "the vulgarity of the whole thing is exceedingly depressing . . . the book has given me nothing but acute embarrassment." F. Scott Fitzgerald wrote that it was the sign of high intelligence to be able to keep two contradictory ideas in one's mind at the same time; but to keep two contradictory ideas of the same person is, one should think, rather a different order of business.

Henry Hardy, perpetual counsel for Isaiah Berlin's defense, contradicts the notion that Berlin was a logorrheic, social climbing time-waster, reminding readers of his letters that he published some hundred and fifty essays and gave a great many lectures. But, as Berlin himself acknowledges, he was able to produce written work chiefly under deadline pressure; he likened himself to a taxi, "useless until summoned I stay still." Lecturing was torture for him, only relieved when he lost the use of a vocal cord and had a proper excuse for turning down invitations to give further lectures.

BERLIN WAS ONE OF NATURE'S TRUE EXTROVERTS, who flourished on committees, in common rooms, at dinner parties. "I am utterly miserable if alone," he wrote to Stuart Hampshire, "and avoid it now by every possible means." As for his need to please, he allowed toward the end of his life that its source was to be found in his efforts to adapt to a new environment when, as a 10-year-old boy, he emigrated with his family from Riga. Might it also have sprung from his precarious position as a Jew in English intellectual life? In his letters, Berlin is always on the *qui vive* for anti-Semitism, which in England could be found in the highest places. "The upper classes of England, and indeed, in all countries," he wrote to Alistair Cooke, "have a large dose of anti-Semitism circulating in their veins." In England he felt it was to be found in Bloomsbury, in the form of a "club anti-Semitism," not least in Bertrand Russell, E. M. Forster, and Maynard Keynes in whom "it was at once genuine and superficial." (One recalls here Virginia Woolf, in her diary, writing about first meeting Berlin, noting, "a Portuguese Jew, by the look of him.") In government, Ernest Bevin, the trade unionist who became Secretary of State in the Labour government, was no friend of the Jews. Even Winston Churchill was not without his touches of anti-Semitism: "And Winston, too," Berlin writes, again to Alistair Cooke,

> who was a stout Zionist, did not particularly like Jews. He may have liked Baruch . . . but . . . quite definitely thought of them as foreigners of some kind, *metiques*, resident aliens, some of them perfectly nice, but still not Englishmen, not Scotsmen, not Welshmen, not Irishmen—Jews.

Berlin never expressed shame at his Jewishness, nor attempted to hide it in the manner of Proust's character Bloch, who removed all evidence in himself of the "sweet vale of Hebron" and broke the "chains of Israel," and in later life sported a monocle. Berlin was not synagogue-going, except on high holy days; he wanted to but finally could not believe in an afterlife, though to comfort his aged father he claimed that he did. "As for my Jewish roots," he wrote, "they are so deep, so native to me, that it is idle of me to try to identify them." Another time he claimed that Jewishness "was not a burden I ever carried, and not an attribute I ever felt made a difference to my philosophical opinions, to my friendships, to any form of life that I lived."

One wonders if being Jewish didn't confer a permanent insecurity on Berlin. Touchier than a fresh burn, he seems never to have forgotten a bad review of any of his books. He held on to grudges more firmly than an Irishman (in Irish Alzheimer's, the joke goes, one forgets everything but one's grudges). He threatened to sue Robert Craft unless he removed a paragraph on Berlin's loquacity from one of his Stravinsky books, *Dialogues and a Diary* (1963). He sometimes found insult where it is unclear any was intended. When Michael Oakeshott introduced him before a lecture at the London School of Economics by saying, "Listening to him you may be tempted to think you are in the presence of one of the great intellectual *virtuosos* of our time, a Paganini of ideas," Berlin found this to be "ironic disparagement."

Oakeshott remained on Berlin's permanent enemies list. The pro-Soviet historian E. H. Carr was on it; so, too, were Harold Laski, Lillian Hellman, A. L. Rowse, C. P. Snow, and George Steiner, whom he regarded as "having too professional an interest in the Holocaust, and [to] glory in being obsessed by it." He disliked above all Hannah Arendt. "I see nothing in her writings of the slightest interest, and never have." To Derwent May he writes that "she had become conceited, fanatical, and talked terrible nonsense both about Jews and about history in general; and what a strange thing it was that all those intellectuals in New York should be taken in by all this cultural rhetoric." Arendt's *Eichmann in Jerusalem* (1963) he thought both "heartless and wrong."

B ERLIN'S JEWISHNESS may also have had to do with his never finding it easy to take strong positions, at least public ones, especially if it might make him enemies. "For reasons that must have been deep in his personality," writes David Pryce-Jones in his memoir *Fault Lines* (2015), "he wanted influence without the attendant publicity. In the absence of civil courage, that necessary virtue, he preferred a strategy of backing into the limelight." In his letters he called the student rebels of the 1960s "barbarians" of little intellectual quality, stirred into action by ennui. He felt much the same about the university campaign for egalitarianism, which in intellectual matters he knew could be fatal. But he wrote or publicly said nothing about this outside his letters. "I am temperamentally liable to compromises," he writes, when what he really means is that he wavers.

Where possible, he did his best to lend respectability to his tergiversations on subjects upon which some might think it impossible to remain neutral. To Morton White, who taught philosophy at Harvard, he writes in 1966:

> You and I and Arthur [Schlesinger]—I feel we are all there, stuck together in some curious middle-of-the-road patch of territory—no clear answers about Vietnam, about Berkeley

U., about any of the questions upon which it is so easy and
delightful to have clear black or white positions, doomed
to be condemned by both sides, accused of vices which we
half acknowledge because of general skepticism and doubt
about our position, or positions in general, and not because
we think them just or fair.

In his eighties, he writes to Henry Hardy that his propensity to please
"probably does spring from unconscious efforts to fit myself into a totally
new environment in 1919. As it is successful, the need for it evaporates, I
suppose, but its traces cannot but remain in all kinds of subconscious,
unexpected and perhaps rather central ways." Elsewhere he writes: "I
wish I had not inherited my father's timorous, rabbity nature! I *can*
be brave, but oh after what appalling superhuman struggles with cowardice!" The question is whether Berlin's floundering on most of the
key issues of the day was the result of genuine perplexities or of fear of
displeasing.

In one of his letters, Berlin allows that in writing about other people he was often guilty of writing about himself. Nowhere does this
come through more strongly than in his Romanes Lectures on Russian
novelist Ivan Turgenev. Berlin suffered from what I think of as Turgenev Syndrome. Or perhaps Turgenev suffered, *avant la lettre*, from
Isaiah Berlin Syndrome. Each man found himself locked in the middle between radicals and rebels, bureaucrats and tsars (crowned and
uncrowned). Both were chary of offending the young. Writing of Turgenev, Berlin might be writing about himself: "audacity was not among
his attributes"; he was "by nature cautious, judicious, frightened of all
extremes, liable at critical moments to take evasive action"; and "all that
was general, abstract, absolute repelled him."

At the center of Berlin's lecture on Turgenev is the reaction aroused
against the novelist by the publication of *Fathers and Sons* in 1862, and
especially by his portrait of the character Bazarov, the new man of 19th-
century Russia, the nihilist, who in his ruthless scientism some claimed
to be the first Bolshevik. Those on the right thought Turgenev was glo-
rifying Bazarov; those on the left, that he was ridiculing him. Berlin, in
what might again be autobiography, writes:

It was his irony, his tolerant scepticism, his lack of passion, his "velvet touch," above all his determination to avoid too definite a social or political commitment that, in the end, alienated both sides. . . . But, in the end, he could not bring himself to accept their [the radicals'] brutal contempt for art, civilized behavior, for everything that he held dear in European culture.

Berlin closes his Romanes lecture by defending those, like Turgenev and like himself, who are caught in the middle, arguing that wishing "to speak to both sides is often interpreted as softness, trimming, opportunism, cowardice." He enlists in defense of Turgenev admirable middle-of-the-roaders of whom this accusation was untrue: it "was not true of Erasmus; it was not true of Montaigne; it was not true of Spinoza . . . ; it was not true of the best representatives of the Gironde." He neglects only to say that it is also not true of himself.

I N HIS ANTI-COMMUNISM, Berlin was stalwart. The Communist question was never troubling, for as a young boy he had experienced the levelling brutality of Russian Communism at firsthand. Explaining his anti-Communism to Arthur Schlesinger, Jr., he writes: "No doubt inoculation by the 1917 Revolution was in my case a dominant fact." He considered Stalin's murderousness not a departure but a natural continuation of the policies of Lenin. He considered Stalin even more monstrous than Hitler. To his friend Shirley Anglesey he wrote that the fall of the Soviet Union "is much the best thing that has happened in our lifetime."

About Zionism Berlin had few doubts, and in one of his letters to Marion Frankfurter he writes about Chaim Wiezmann wanting him to join the Israeli government "and abandon all the ludicrous efforts to teach little English boys unnecessary subjects." He was never seriously tempted, and late in life wrote to the Polish historian of ideas Andrzej Walicki that "I know it was no good my going there, that I would sooner or later, and probably sooner, be torn to pieces by contending parties and would be completely frustrated and made totally impotent."

In defense of Israel, he wrote to Karl Miller, then editor of the *London Review of Books*, calling him out for the strong anti-Zionist pieces he was publishing (and which the journal, under its new editor, continues to publish). He gave advice to Teddy Kollek, then mayor of Jerusalem, on how best to handle visiting American and English intellectual eminences, Robert Lowell among them, showing them the best of Israel in the hope of turning them into Israel's defenders.

Berlin wrote strong letters to Noam Chomsky and I. F. Stone arguing with their views on Israel published in the *New York Review of Books*. As he wrote to Mark Bonham Carter about Chomsky, "hatred of all American establishments governs him, I think, much more than thoughts about Israel as such, or fear of a world war triggered off by Israel." Then he adds: "Besides, despite his often shocking actions, I wish to preserve my remote friendship with him." Why?, one wonders.

I used to think that Berlin's relationship with Robert Silvers, the editor of the New York Review of Books, resembled that of a cardinal now lost to history who was asked how he could serve under so miserable a figure as Pope Pius XII, and who answered, "You don't know what I have prevented." In 1970, as Berlin wrote to Arnaldo Momigliano, he conducted Silvers on a carefully planned tour of Israel, including a lengthy meeting with Golda Meir. As with Lowell, it didn't take, and did nothing to alter the anti-Israel line of the New York Review of Books, which remains firmly in place in our day. Toward the end of his life, Berlin seemed wobbly even on Israel, for he loathed the conservative Likud government of Menachem Begin and contemned the occupation of the West Bank. "Now of course," he wrote to Kyril Fitzlyon, the British diplomat, "[Israel] has an appalling government of religious bigots and nationalist fanatics, and God knows what will happen." The old Jewish leftist in Berlin, even in regard to Israel, never quite died.

To JUDGE BERLIN SOLELY, or even chiefly, by his opinions would be reductive. His letters reveal him to be a deeply cultivated man. Music meant a great deal to him, and his knowledge of it was considerable. Like most serious historians and social scientists of any quality, he was steeped in literature, and sophisticated and subtle in his judgment of it. At another time he might have been a first-rate literary critic. He preferred Tolstoy over Dostoyevsky, remarking, "Tolstoy is always sunlight even in his most severe and tragic passages—Dostoyevsky is always night. . . . It is with relief that I stop reading him, and return to ordinary life." He notes the want of poetry in Balzac. He prefers Proust over James, adding that the former is braver, "and indeed one has to be in French which does not allow emotional timorousness to be translated into such indeterminate vagueness as English." To his friend Jean Floud he writes: "I cannot take more of the Bellow-Kazin-Malamud-Roth regional culture; it is too claustrophobic, sticky, hideously self-indulgent."

The four volumes of letters are also filled with lovely tidbits. Berlin reports Patrick Shaw-Stewart saying of Lady Diana Cooper that "she has no heart but her head was in the right place." About A. L. Rowse, he writes:

> The thing about Rowse which is not so often noticed is that underneath the nonsense, the vanity, the ludicrous and dotty and boring egotistical layers, he is quite a nasty man—very cruel to those who do not recognize his genius if they are weak and defenceless, and filled with hatred if they are in any degree formidable: a man who, I think, has some of the temperament of genius without a spark of genius, which is quite difficult to live with.

In a brilliant *aperçu*, he sets out the sonata form that after-dinner speeches take:

> First light matter, allegro; then grave things which you really wish to impart, if any; then, allegro again, jokes, light matter, desire to please the audience; and in some awful cases a rondo, i.e. you go back to the beginning and start again.

In a letter to Arthur Schlesinger, he offers the best short definition of democracy I know: "the government, or those in power, have systematically to curry favor with the citizens for fear of being thrown out."

It is difficult to determine how, precisely, Isaiah Berlin judged his own life. He did not have a high opinion of his writing. In a letter to Noel Annan, he remarks that after his retirement from the presidency of Wolfson College

> I shall spend some time on some very obscure topics in the
> field of history of ideas—at once obscure and difficult with-
> out scholarly training, pedantic without being precise, gen-
> eral without being of interest to anyone outside a very nar-
> row circle.

Elsewhere he notes that what he has written will be little more than the
stuff of other people's footnotes.

The fate of England saddened him. In one of his letters he likens the
Englishmen visiting America to Greeks visiting Rome. "Ex-empires are
curious places in which to live," he writes to Shirley Anglesey, "or indeed
flourish." In his sixties, he complained he had no one to look up to; in
his early eighties he asks, "Why must the end of my life be covered in
this growing darkness?" His was a remarkable generation of writers and
scholars, included among them Hugh Trevor-Roper, A. J. Ayer, Evelyn
Waugh, A. J. P. Taylor, Stuart Hampshire, Lewis Namier, and Elizabeth
Bowen—the last gasp, really, of an English aristocratic intellectual tradition that would be replaced, dismally, by Margaret Drabble and Christopher Hitchens, A. S. Byatt and Terry Eagleton. He wrote to Stalin's
daughter that "the *vieille Angleterre*, the civilised aristocrats, the marvel-
lous novelists and poets, the urbane, cultivated statesmen—that England, believe me, is no more." Berlin was lucky not to have lived on to our
day, when England appears to have become the country of Sir Elton John
and Sir Mick Jagger.

To the end of his life Berlin received honorary degrees—evidence, he
felt, "that I am harmless." Not yet 87, he wrote to Ruth Chang, a young
American philosophy professor, that he could not care less how he is
remembered: "I do not mind in the least if I am completely forgotten—I
really mean that." Poor Isaiah Berlin, all his life he played it safe, gave pleasure to his friends, took care to make no enemies in important quarters,
and would seem to have won all the world's rewards, except the feeling of
self-satisfaction that comes with accomplishment and courageous action.

Michael Oakeshott

(2015)

HILOSOPHERS, HELD MICHAEL OAKESHOTT (1901–1990), are of two kinds: didactic and contemplative. The former tend to have minds that gravitate to the formation of bold and graspable ideas, the latter to thoughts less readily summarized. Aristotle's golden mean, Descartes's *cogito*, Kant's categorical imperative, Hegel's dialectic, and Marx's economic determinism are examples of the first kind of philosopher. Schopenhauer, Santayana, and William James, figures without a reigning idea associated with their names, are examples of the second. The first group risks being too quickly understood; the second risks being easily misunderstood. Michael Oakeshott himself was among the second kind of philosopher.

In his essay "America's 'Exceptional' Conservatism," Irving Kristol tells of arriving at his desk one morning during his time as editor of *Encounter* in London to discover the mail had brought, unbidden—or over the transom, as the phrase then was—a lengthy essay titled "On Being Conservative" by Michael Oakeshott, whom Kristol much admired. Kristol read the essay, he notes, "with pleasure and appreciation." He reports that "it was beautifully written, subtle in its argument, delicate in its perceptions, and full of sentences and paragraphs that merit the attention of anthologists for decades, perhaps even centuries, to come." Having finished reading the essay, Kristol turned to his typewriter and tapped out a letter of rejection.

Greatly admiring the essay though he did, Irving Kristol disagreed with it, and in fundamental ways. Kristol was, as he put it, "then in the early stages of intellectual pregnancy with those attitudes and dispositions that later emerged as 'neoconservatism,'" and he found his own thoughts on a distinctly different track than Oakeshott's. Kristol's thinking had a religious bent; Oakeshott's seemed ineluctably secular. Kristol was future-minded; Oakeshott locked firmly into the present. Finally and decisively, Oakeshott's conservatism, in Kristol's reading, offered no "guidance in coping with all those necessary evils, and destroyed whatever philosophical equanimity we have received as a result of reading the writers of philosophy."

Part of Irving Kristol's disagreement with Michael Oakeshott had to do with the radical differences between English and American conservatism. England is (or at least was) a society aristocratic in spirit and based heavily on tradition. America is based on revolution. Americans, even ultra-conservative ones, have not given up on the idea of progress; English conservatives wish (or used to wish) to retard, even stop, progress. Evelyn Waugh once remarked that he would never again vote for the Tories: They had been in power for more than eight years and hadn't turned back the clock one minute. American conservatism, Kristol recognizes, is "a populist conservatism," which "dismays the conservative elites of Britain and Western Europe, who prefer a more orderly and dignified kind of conservatism—which in actuality always turns out to be a defensive and therefore enfeebled conservativism."

Contemporary American conservatives look to the Founders and *The Federalist* as the sources of their political philosophy. Yet, according to Oakeshott in "Rationalism in Politics," the Founders themselves were men who had no need of "persuasion that knowledge begins with a *tabula rasa*." The Declaration of Independence, in this reading, is not a conservative document, but rather one closer to the ideas behind the French Revolution and "many later adventures in the rationalist reconstruction of society."

At the heart of Irving Kristol's disagreement with Michael Oakeshott, though Kristol doesn't mention it, is the fact that Kristol was an intellectual, an immensely well-read and highly thoughtful intellectual, to be sure, and an activist; Oakeshott was a philosopher, one without the least interest in changing the world. As a philosopher, Oakeshott was labeled an idealist in the tradition of such English philosophers as J. M. E. McTaggart, R. G. Collingwood, and F. H. Bradley. Oakeshott's systemic philosophy, as found in his *Experience and Its Modes* (1933), can be technical and, hence, formidable (or so I found) and not for amateurs, of whom I am one. Yet his view of the role of philosophy is limited, modest, skeptical even.

Oakeshott's philosophy isn't about "persuading others, but making our minds clear." For him, philosophy was in no wise a privileged form of knowledge but, instead, a manner of thinking, a machinery for making distinctions, a continuing act of clarification—one especially useful for investigating and waylaying presuppositions. Too often, he felt, philosophy was devoted to "making riddles out of solutions," and philosophers were people who spent their lives "imagining where the candle flame went when it was blown out."

Although he declared himself a conservative, Oakeshott suggested no programs, advocated no policies, and worked with no specific ends in mind. He held that the best we can do is attend to those "thinkers and statesmen who knew which way to turn their feet without knowing anything about a final destination." Scientists, historians, politicians, economists, and poets all perceived the world through what he termed their separate "mode of experience." And each of these modes, in the nature of the case, was partial, incomplete, only part of the story. Experience was, for various reasons, so richly complicated that the whole story might not be available: Certainly it was not to be encompassed through any discrete mode. Nor was there a mode encompassing all other modes; no one mode, not even the philosophical, is architechtonic.

What there is, Oakeshott believed, is conversation—unending conversation about the complexities of life and life's proper ends. This conversation, he held, ought never to lapse into argument. Nor is it hierarchical. Every thoughtful person can participate. In "The Voice of Poetry in the Conversation of Mankind," he wrote that "conversation is not an enterprise designed to yield an extrinsic profit, a contest where a winner gets a prize, nor is it an activity of exegesis; it is an unrehearsed intellectual adventure." Life, for Oakeshott, as he put it in "A Place of Learning," is "a predicament, not a journey." The predicament is how to make the best of it and get the best out of it.

The answer for Oakeshott, as he set out most emphatically in "On Being Conservative," is to cultivate

> the propensity to use and to enjoy what is present rather than to wish or look for something else; to delight in what is present rather than what was or what may be. To be conservative, then, is to prefer the familiar to the unknown, to prefer the tried to the untried, fact to mystery, the actual to the possible, the limited to the unbounded, the near to the distant, the sufficient to the superabundant, the convenient to the perfect, present laughter to utopian bliss.

For Oakeshott, conservatism was a disposition rather than a doctrine. From this disposition certain political positions followed, views of change and innovation key among them:

> Whenever stability is more profitable than improvement, whenever certainty is more valuable than speculation, whenever familiarity is more desirable than perfection, whenever agreed error is superior to controversial truth, whenever the disease is more sufferable than the cure, whenever the satisfaction of expectations is more important than the "justice" of the expectations themselves, whenever a rule of some sort is better than the risk of having no rule at all, a disposition to be conservative will be more appropriate than any other; and on any reading of human conduct these cover a not negligible range of circumstances.

Oakeshott found more reinforcement for these views in Montaigne and Pascal and Hume than in Burke or Bentham.

Politics did not hold out much promise for Oakeshott. He held that government

> is a specific and limited activity, namely, the provision and custody of general rules of conduct, which are understood,

not as plans for imposing substantive activities, but as instruments enabling people to pursue the activities of their own choice with the minimum frustration, and therefore something which it is appropriate to be conservative about.

Oakeshott had his own religious sentiments and complex morality, but he felt that neither religion nor morals had to do with politics, and politics had nothing whatsoever to do "with making men good or even better." Dreams of perfect justice or perfect freedom ought to be excluded from politics, for "the conjunction of dreaming and ruling generates tyranny."

The role of government should be much simpler: "to keep its subjects at peace with one another in the activities in which they have chosen to seek their happiness." Ideally, politics, Oakeshott believed, should not be (as it has been in recent years in the United States) about dueling virtues, with one side intent on crushing the other. Nor, for those of conservative disposition, ought politics

to inflame passion and give it new objects to feed upon, but to inject into the activities of already too passionate men an ingredient of moderation; to restrain, to deflate, to pacify and to reconcile; not to stoke the fires of desire, but to damp them down.

Oakeshott's strong antipathy was for what he terms "rationalism" in politics. Rationalism is the reign of confident reason expended on a subject that cannot readily be reasoned upon. Politics, "always so deeply veined with both the traditional, the circumstantial, and the transitory," will not obey the kind of technical expertise under whose banner rationalism travels. For the rationalist, no problem evades solution, and perfection will arrive promptly when, one by one, all problems are solved.

"Political activity," Oakeshott writes, "is recognized [by rationalist thinkers] as the imposition of a uniform condition of perfection upon human conduct." His book, *On History* (1983), concludes with a dazzling essay, "The Tower of Babel," about the greatest utopian planning project of all time: that of erecting a building that would reach to heaven. The essay ends on a scrap of verse left by a poet of the day that reads:

> Those who in fields Elysian would dwell
> Do but extend the boundaries of hell.

The villainous thinkers for Oakeshott are those who claim to have all the answers. Thus, he condemns Francis Bacon, Descartes, Machiavelli, Locke, Bentham, Godwin, and, of course, Marx and Engels, "authors of our most stupendous rationalisms." The rationalist thinkers can only breathe in an atmosphere of pure abstraction: "Like Midas, the Rationalist is always in the unfortunate position of not being able to touch anything, without transforming it into an abstraction; he can never get a square meal of experience."

The thinkers Oakeshott most admired are Montaigne, Pascal, Hobbes, and Hume. They understood that, in political activity,

> men sail a boundless and bottomless sea; there is neither harbor for shelter nor floor for anchorage, neither starting place nor appointed destination. The enterprise is to keep afloat on an even keel; the sea is both friend and enemy; and seamanship consists in using the resources of a traditional manner of behavior in order to make a friend of every hostile occasion.

Elsewhere in the same vein, he wrote: "If we are looking for something that is difficult to understand—this life supplies the need, we require to invent no others."

Unlike most modern philosophers, Oakeshott was steeped in literature. When he writes of the rationalist's knowledge never being more "than half knowledge, and consequently he will never be more than half-right," he cites a character in a less-than-well-known Henry James story, "The Private Life," who is in the same condition. Oakeshott's writing is rife with literary references and allusions: He read Cervantes, La Rochefoucauld, Goethe, Austen, Keats, Landor, Valéry, Proust, D. H. Lawrence, A. J. Symons, and T. S. Eliot. He dabbled in Chinese literature. He planned, though it never got underway, a biography of Lord Nelson. He was a philosopher with a literary sensibility.

This shows up in Oakeshott's prose style, which, from the outset, was impressively aphoristic. In the first 20 pages of his *Notebooks 1922–86*, begun when he was 21, one finds the following sentences:

> The first act of a democratic state would be to form an aris-
> tocracy. . . . Religion is the poetry of morality. . . . Thought
> is always spasmodic. There is no such thing as an unbroken
> chain of thought. . . . The quest for God is the whole mean-
> ing of human life. . . . Present society is pretty well calculated
> to demoralize a great character.

All these, be it noted, were written before he was 25.

Oakeshott's *Notebooks* are partly precisely that: notes made from observations from his reading of Plato, Aristotle, Spinoza, and others; insights
from his experience; adumbrations of works he would like to compose.
Other material can be intensely personal, some of it confessional. It can
go from the most arresting general thought to a searing *cri de coeur*. Many
of his entries are about what used to be called "love life," for Oakeshott at
several points states that love is the ultimate meaning of life. Chunks of the
Notebooks are given over to a woman he refers to as *La Belle Dame Sans
Merci*, whom he pursued for decades without consummation.

As Edward Gibbon wrote of Charlemagne, so might one write of Oakeshott: "Of all his moral virtues, chastity was not the most conspicuous."
Although thrice married, Oakeshott was a sedulous seducer, and often
had two or three love affairs going on simultaneously.

The *Notebooks*, along with giving a more comprehensive of Oakeshott's
general views than do any of his other books, give us a stronger sense of the
man. The ample subjects of Love, Death, and Religion dominate its pages,
though they are not necessarily the most interesting, if only because they
are not subjects upon which originality is readily adduced. Politics come
in chiefly for contempt: "Politics are an inferior form of human activity,"
he writes. Later: "Politics seen as a struggle for power—is it any more than
this?" He longed for a modern Voltaire "who would take the superstition
out of politics."

The two things that qualify a person for being a conservative, he held,
were having a passionate interest outside politics and a strong sense of
mortality. And, dare one indite this in so political a time as the present:
"A general interest and preoccupation with politics is the surest sign of a
general decay in a society." Still, politics is necessary to life lived among
"people whom chance or choice has brought together."

The problem, Oakeshott felt, was not only that "politics is an uninteresting form of activity to anyone who has no desire to rule others" but that those it attracts are, too often, unimpressive human beings. At one point he calls them "scoundrels." What isn't required, but is too often evident, in politics is "manufacturing curable grievances." What is needed is the assurance of "those little things: to go where we like & when; having paid my taxes to spend my money on what I wish." His final word is this: "Politics is the art of living together & of being 'just' to one another—not of imposing a way of life, but of organizing a common life."

So much of Oakeshott's views on politics are propelled by his unshakeable belief in the imperfectability of human beings. Montaigne is his intellectual hero here, the Montaigne who understood that all human judgment and wisdom is fallible. In "A Place of Learning," Oakeshott disavows a belief in human nature, asserting that "there are only men, women and children responding gaily or reluctantly, reflectively or not so reflectively, to the ordeal of consciousness, who exist only in terms of their self-understandings." Self-understanding, though, is a rarity. "The intellectual life of the majority of men and women," he writes, "is cankered by indiscriminate knowledge."

He underscored the wretched condition of "people who have no selves other than those created by 'experts' who tell them what they are." Others walk about with heads "so full of ideas that there is no room for sense." In a world of boundless distractions, serious education—not "education that is merely instruction in the current vulgarities"—is the only (if somewhat dim) hope: "To be educated is to know how much one wishes to know & to have the courage not to be tempted beyond that limit." Genuine culture, he held, teaches that "there is much one does not want to know."

For Oakeshott the trick was somehow to be above the humdrum world and yet also be in it. "One is under an obligation to be happy with the here and now," he writes, a sentiment he expresses more than once. Yet he also notes that "it is certain that most who concentrate upon achievement miss life." On his gravestone, he wanted this bit of verse from the Scottish poet William Dunbar:

> Man, please thy Maker, and be merry,
> And give not for this world a cherry.

While still a young man, Oakeshott set out to achieve a life that dispensed with everything doctrinaire: "Whenever I have become conscious of a presupposition," he writes, "I have questioned it." And so he does, relentlessly and impressively, in the pages of the *Notebooks*. He even questions whether curiosity is a good thing, noting that neither Aristotle nor Aquinas thought it was. He deflates the importance of the study of mathematics beyond basic arithmetic. Even the sacred subject of science falls under his blade. He calls the scientist a blackmailer who

> trades upon the stupidity of mankind. First he whets our appetites & flatters our hopes, then he lets loose a civilization more horrible than we could have imagined, & then he says "you can't do without me." But he does nothing to rescue us.

Michael Oakeshott may not have produced a systematic philosophy of the kind that supplies persuasive answers to life's most pressing questions. As often as not, he chipped away at what he deemed the hollowness of many of those answers, showing, persuasively, how unpersuasive they really were. Along the way, he provided in his teaching and writing a model of a clear mind operating at the highest power. On one occasion, he called himself a mere "interested spectator," on another, "a wanderer, that is, one with no destination, or only interim destinations." His own life's work, a brilliant ramble, resembled nothing so much as the glorious never-ending conversation he revered and to which he made so many notable, even unforgettable, contributions.

John O'Hara

(2016)

J OHN O'HARA WAS WONT TO COMPLAIN publicly about the state of his reputation, thereby joining the majority of writers, most of whom keep this standard complaint to themselves. What, exactly, apart from being insufficiently grand to please him, was his reputation?

I should say it was—and remains today—that of a writer a substantial notch below Ernest Hemingway, F. Scott Fitzgerald, and William Faulkner, about all of whom he spoke and wrote reverently. Five or so years younger than these three novelists, O'Hara labored in their long shadows. He had the additional problem of being thought stronger as a writer of short stories than of novels, though he wrote no fewer than 17 novels. He is credited as a master of dialogue, a practitioner if not the progenitor of the *New Yorker* story, a never-less-than-interesting commentator on American manners.

To give some notion of his self-evaluation, O'Hara was disappointed that he never won the Nobel Prize. He planned to use part of the money to buy a Rolls-Royce. He bought the Rolls anyhow, but died, in 1970, at the age of 65, with a still unsettled reputation. Although many of the big critical guns of the time had fired off their opinions of his work, no true consensus emerged. Nor has it even now.

In a review for the *New York Times Book Review* of O'Hara's third collection of stories, *Pipe Night* (1945), Lionel Trilling wrote: "More than anyone else now writing, O'Hara understands the complex, contradictory, asymmetrical society in which we live." He added,

> No other American writer tells us so precisely, and with such a sense of the importance of the communication, how people look and how they want to look, where they buy their clothes and where they wish they could buy their clothes, how they speak and how they think they ought to speak.

Trilling went on to place O'Hara in the distinguished line of American novelists that includes William Dean Howells and Edith Wharton.

Irving Howe, in a 1966 *Saturday Review,* held that there was, finally, something thin and disappointing in the piling up of O'Hara's social observations, remarking of his gift for dialogue that "were mimicry the soul of art, O'Hara would be our greatest master." Contra Trilling, Howe held that O'Hara lacked the "deep personal culture" of Edith Wharton that allowed her "to bring to bear upon her material an enlarging standard of humane tradition and civilized reflection." Alfred Kazin and Arthur Mizener wrote disparagingly about O'Hara; Guy Davenport and John Cheever praised him. If literary criticism were a prizefight, the decision on O'Hara would be a draw.

John O'Hara was born in 1905 in Pottsville, Pennsylvania, the seat of Schuylkill County, anthracite coal country, near Philadelphia, the son of a physician. Perhaps the most crucial fact about him is that he was Irish. Hard now to remember that the Irish in America were once a despised group: The term paddy wagon, used by policemen rounding up drunks and other rowdies and still in use today, gives a strong notion of the social standing of the Irish in the early decades of the 20th century. To rise out of the working class, and even the middle classes up into the upper reaches of American life, could be a bumpy run for the Irish, shanty or lace-curtain.

Themselves victims of snobbery, the Irish, in F. Scott Fitzgerald, John O'Hara, and (somewhat lower down the social scale) James T. Farrell, became the great 20th-century chroniclers of American snobbery The goal for the wealthier and more ambitious Irish was to achieve the status of WASPs, with the Roman Catholic church added on. One thinks here of Joseph Kennedy, of his compound at Hyannis Port, his children at Harvard, pushing, pushing, pushing until one of his sons arrived at the best American address of all, 1600 Pennsylvania Avenue NW, Washington, DC.

The barriers for the Irish were fewer in smaller towns like Pottsville. Dr. Patrick Henry O'Hara had a flourishing practice and his family lived on exclusive Mahantongo Street in Pottsville, renamed Lantenengo Street in many of his son's stories and novels. Dr. O'Hara wanted his oldest son to succeed him in his medical practice, and when John chose not to do so, a chill, never to be entirely shaken off, arose between father and son. In a number of O'Hara stories, the O'Hara character, rechristened James Malloy, is in a never-fully-explained strained relationship with his physician-father.

A wild kid, John O'Hara was smoking and already drinking in his early adolescence. He got tossed out of various prep and private schools for disorderly conduct. His great dream of going to Yale was shattered when his father, at the age of 57, died of Bright's disease, leaving heavy debts in his wake. No Dink Stover, no boola-boola for O'Hara, who seems never quite to have got over missing out on Yale. A story—O'Hara tells it himself—has it that Hemingway, Vincent Sheean, and James Lardner pooled their money to go off to Spain but had an odd two francs left over, causing Hemingway to say: "Let's take the bloody money and start a bloody fund to send John O'Hara to Yale."

Not getting to go to Yale may have been the best thing that ever happened to him. Had he done so, he might have lost that sense of outsider status that can be so important to a writer. Besides, colleges have never been in the least helpful to any serious writer.

For a number of years, O'Hara wandered in the jungles of journalism. Between 1925 and 1932 he worked for various newspapers and magazines, ranging from the *Pottsville Journal* to Henry Luce's *Time*. A drinking man, easily angered, he was fired from one publication after another for the usual sins: arguing, unexplained absences, unreliability generally.

In 1928, he published his first piece in the three-year-old *New Yorker*, then edited by its founder Harold Ross. Over the years, as a freelancer, O'Hara would publish more than 400 stories and reportorial pieces in that magazine. He would have three marriages, put in a not-especially-successful stint as a Hollywood screenwriter, have a great financial success with

Pal Joey (1940), the musical based on his stories and for which he wrote the book for its long-running stage performance. Other of his stories and novels *Butterfield 8* (1935), *Ten North Frederick* (1955)—would also be made into movies. He had a good run, John O'Hara; but for a man of boundless literary ambition, a good run is nowhere near good enough.

The epitaph on O'Hara's gravestone reads:

BETTER
THAN ANYONE ELSE
HE TOLD THE TRUTH
ABOUT HIS TIME
HE WAS
A PROFESSIONAL
HE WROTE
HONESTLY AND WELL

It's important to point out that O'Hara composed that epitaph himself. What is its truth quotient? He was indubitably a professional; he did write honestly; he may he even have told the truth about his time better than anyone else. The question is: Does that truth matter, today, in our time?

Although O'Hara wrote about bootleggers, faded movie stars, cab drivers, farmers, big shots, and others, his real subject was life lived at what H. L Mencken called "the country club stage of culture." Many of his characters have the center of their social lives anchored in their country clubs. The country club of O'Hara's day offered golf, bridge, evenings of dinner and dancing and boozing. At Gibbsville's Lantenengo Country Club, adultery was also on offer. So many of the stories in this new Library of America edition of John O'Hara's stories, expertly and unobtrusively edited by Charles McGrath, have extramarital affairs at their center that the entire volume would not have been mistitled *Adultery*. But then, when one thinks about it, what drama does life at the country-club stage of culture—otherwise so boring—offer other than sleeping with one's best friend's husband or wife? While sex is at the heart of so many of O'Hara's stories, in these stories, it must be said, he treats it in the best adult fashion, which is to say that he rarely descends to the naming of parts or describing these parts at play.

In *Appointment in Samarra* (1934), O'Hara's first novel, there is also the prospect of drunkenness and insulting people. Just such an act on the part of the novel's main character, Julian English—who, in his drunkenness, throws his drink in the face of a rich country-club bore whose financial support he needs—propels the novel into motion. Julian runs the Cadillac agency in Gibbsville, a town of roughly 25,000, a mixture of English, Welsh, Irish, and Pennsylvania Dutch that O'Hara named after Wolcott Gibbs, his friend at the *New Yorker,* and that appears in several of his stories. He is part of the town's *gratin,* or top crust, but he has a drinking problem. He loves his wife, Caroline, but does not let this stand in the way, when drunk, of bonking in the backseat of his car, the mistress of Ed Chantey, the town's bootlegger-gangster. Later in the novel he will get into a fight with two other members, also while boozed up, that will force him out of his club.

As for Caroline English, in a characteristic passage, O'Hara fills us in on her by comparing her with her 10-years-younger cousin Constance:

> The cousins were pretty good types of their respective colleges: Caroline had gone to Bryn Mawr, Constance was at Smith—the plain girl who goes to Smith and competes with the smart Jewesses for Phi Beta Kappa, distinguished from the pretty girls who go to Smith and write to Yale. Caroline was the perfect small-town girl at Bryn Mawr; from private school in her home town, to a good prep school, to Bryn Mawr and the Bryn Mawr manner, which means quick maturity and an everlasting tendency to enthusiasms.

All his days, John O'Hara would be preoccupied with status and its outward symbols. Colleges, fraternities, addresses, cars, Liberty scarves, Dunhill lighters, Herbert Johnson hats from Brooks Brothers—in O'Hara's novels and stories, these are meant to place and lock in his characters' social position. He prided himself on knowing how speech reflects social class and character. No woman who graduated from high school, he once claimed, would ever say "half a buck," which sounds right to me. In *Appointment in Samarra*, a lower-class nightclub singer confuses the word "eunuch" with "unique" and a working-class boy mistakes the word "instigated" for "implicated." He believed one could tell a lot about a person who calls the evening meal "dinner" and another who calls it "supper," about someone who plays squash and someone who plays handball.

The danger of such a delicate radar for status is that it can devolve into stereotypes, which in O'Hara's fiction it sometimes does. In *Appointment in Samarra* he mentions "a handsome young Harvard Jew." Later in the novel he has Julian think that "he did not like to see men driving hatless in closed cars; it was too much like the Jews in New York who ride in their town cars with the dome lights lit." Believing that you are what you drive, O'Hara names enough different cars by make—Pierce-Arrows, Cunninghams, Franklins, Garfords, Duesenbergs, Packards, Mercers, Stutz Bearcats, et alia—to stock a large used-car lot. Membership in one or another college fraternity, in an O'Hara story, can pin a character down as firmly as an exotic butterfly on a lepidopterist's velvet pad. "Probably out of spite," O'Hara writes, "Julian did not accept the invitation to join Phi Delta Theta, his father's fraternity, but had joined Delta Kappa Epsilon." Dekes, Betas, Tau Beta Pis, Psi Upsilons, the Porcellian Club at Harvard, the Ivy Club at Princeton—all these have great significance in O'Hara stories. One such story, "Graven Image" (1943), is about a man who bears the lifelong scars of not being invited to join Porcellian.

The narrative of *Appointment in Samarra* leaves enough loose threads for a man to hang himself. Toward the end of the novel, Julian English does not do this but, sensing his life shattered, a bottle of Scotch and a pack of cigarettes in hand, he goes out to his closed garage, sits in his car, locks the doors and windows, turns on the motor and lets his life leach away in suicide from the carbon dioxide. Julian English is not John O'Hara, yet one gets the feeling that, in him, O'Hara is describing a life of the kind he himself might have led had he not found salvation in writing.

This Library of America edition contains 60 of John O'Hara's short stories. They vary greatly in length and in quality. A number of them end disappointingly, but satisfactory endings are the great problem in short stories. So many writers of them know how to soar, but too few how to land the plane. None of these O'Hara stories is dull, none boring. One is improbable, "A Man to Be Trusted," about a woman having a love affair with a 13-year-old boy. The three best stories in the collection are "Imagine Kissing Pete," "Pat Collins," and "Natica Jackson," which also happen to be its three longest stories; another lengthy story, "Mrs. Stratton of Oak Knoll," peters out sadly over its final 20 or so pages. O'Hara's novels sometimes give one more than is required, his shorter stories less. The novella, that form of indeterminate length between the story and novel, shows him atop his game.

Storytelling in itself, this volume leads one to think, may not have been O'Hara's chief talent; portraiture and social observation are where his strengths lay. Often he will present a brilliant character but be unable to find a plot in which that character might play out his destiny. For good or ill, O'Hara was the least moral-minded of writers. On the one hand, the strong hand, he was not in the least tendentious, he set things down as he saw them; on the other, the shaky hand, moral questions, generally at the center of what gives fiction both its drama and its staying power, are often sorely missing from his work.

One encounters in these stories some of the characters from *Appointment in Samarra*: Julian and Caroline English and Julian's father Dr. English, Whit Hofman, Ed Chaney, and others put in cameo appearances. A character named James Malloy, a writer, narrates a number of these stories, rather like the usually unnamed narrator of Somerset Maugham stories but with less of a cosmopolitan tone than the more sophisticated Maugham commanded. O'Hara may have been the American Maugham, although Maugham was better able to shape a story than O'Hara and who was a more pure storyteller.

Later in life, O'Hara became a great grump, bemoaning critics, literary coteries, the want of prizes and praise for his writing, leaving the *New Yorker* for 11 years owing to a deflationary review by Brendan Gill of his novel *A Rage to Live* (1949). He was a man who never forgot unfavorable reviews, even in the *Trenton Sunday Advertiser.*

In earlier days, John O'Hara had been a patient listener and acute observer, which went to make him so impressive an impersonator in his fiction. "He do the police in different voices," as T. S. Eliot had it in *The Waste Land.* O'Hara could do female nightclub singers, thugs, rich old women, savvy Hollywood agents, Pennsylvania Dutch. His skill at dialogue was such that he could float an entire story along its stream. So smoothly convincing is his dialogue that one feels a sense of low gotcha triumph catching him out in the rare miscue: The misuse of "put me on" in "The Assistant." The error in "I Can't Thank You Enough" of the character who says, "Hurry back, as they say down South," when what they actually say is "Hurry on back." The jarring "You make me sick" in "How Old, How Young."

What entices more than anything else in O'Hara's stories is his knowingness. This comes through sometimes in subtle observation, sometimes in risky generalization. In "Pat Collins," he remarks of a character named Dick Boylan, who runs a speakeasy in Gibbsville, that "possibly as an Irishman, *he was immune* to what the non-Irish call Irish charm." In "Natica Jackson," he notes that "stingy women are apt to be insatiable in bed," an observation as interesting as it is difficult to test. Of a character in "The Assistant," he writes: "There was thought behind everything he had on, and behind the thought no taste." Another character, this one in "Fatimas and Kisses," has "the special look of dignity offended, the look of small people who do not feel entitled to anger." A now-retired Hollywood female star in "The Sun Room," thinking no doubt about Judy Garland, remarks, "If you want to be popular with the queers, you'd better have a weakness." Rich stuff; this, and it abounds in O'Hara's writing.

For all its richness, for all John O'Hara's skill as a mimic and sharpness as an observer of the life of his time, his writing fails the memory test. Having read 60 of his stories within the past month or so, I find that, with the exception of only three or four, I cannot recall anything of their content. Lucid, smart, never less than interesting, these stories nonetheless leave no strong impress because they are devoid of conflict, specifically moral conflict, of the struggle over difficult decisions that gives a larger meaning to literature and to life itself.

John O'Hara was a good and honest writer, always worth reading, but owing to this marked absence in his work, a less-than-great one.

F. Scott Fitzgerald,
A Most Successful Failure

(2017)

66 **T**HE TRUE PARADISES," wrote Proust, "are the paradises that we have lost." F. Scott Fitzgerald would have enthusiastically seconded the motion. In his short life (1896–1940), Fitzgerald had come rather to specialize in lost paradises. His first novel, published when he was 23, was *This Side of Paradise*. The first major biography of Fitzgerald, written by Arthur Mizener, was titled *The Far Side of Paradise*. Now David S. Brown, a historian by training and trade, has written *Paradise Lost*, an excellent study of Fitzgerald that summarizes past scholarship on the novelist and sets out the argument that, in his fiction, he was both a moralist and a social critic working the same vein as Thorstein Veblen, Randolph Bourne, and H. L. Mencken—that he was, in other words, a chronicler of the depredations of capitalism gone haywire on American life. Mr. Brown argues that Fitzgerald also joined "Freud, Conrad, Adams, Spengler, [Frederick Jackson] Turner, and Eliot in trying to make sense of the modern age."

F. Scott Fitzgerald is perhaps best known as the chief representative, if not the leading exemplar, of the Jazz Age, that period in American life between the end of World War I and the onset of the Depression in 1929.

The tendency has been to think of him as a romantic, a bit of a snob, and a boozer. He was all three, of course, but he was also much more—a vastly talented writer with a gift for imbuing what he wrote with a charm that, when he was at his best, seemed quite magical. His specialty was endowing the wishes and dreams of his characters with an aura of poetry.

The critic Edmund Wilson, Fitzgerald's friend acquired at Princeton, did him no service when, as early as 1922, he wrote that Fitzgerald had "been given imagination without intellectual control of it . . . the desire for beauty without an aesthetic ideal and . . . a gift for expression without very many ideas to express." Wilson did concede that, for all his faults, Fitzgerald's fiction "does not commit the unpardonable sin: it does not fail to live." (The same cannot be said of Wilson's own attempts at fiction, *I Thought of Daisy* and *Memoirs of Hecate County*.) That much of Fitzgerald's fiction continues to live, now nearly a century after he wrote it, guarantees his place in American literature, the Nathaniel Hawthorne, as Mr. Brown nicely proposes, of the 20th century.

"I didn't have the two top things: great animal magnetism or money," Fitzgerald wrote. "I had the two second things, though: good looks and intelligence." Neither of the latter conduced to grant him his two youthful wishes, which were to play football for Princeton and to prove his courage in World War I. Nature denied him the physique for the first (he was 5-foot-6 and weighed 130 pounds); history denied him the second (soon after he received his commission, the war ended). A second set of wishes—success as a young novelist and marriage to a beautiful and ebullient Southern girl—did come true, though this seems to be a case of the gods first acceding to the wishes of those whom they would destroy.

Fitzgerald wrote about his own youthful triumph with his novel *This Side of Paradise* (1920) and about what a mixed blessing it was. "The compensation of a very early success is a conviction that life is a romantic matter," he noted in *The Crack-Up* (1936), adding that in his case early success meant "the fulfilled future and the wistful past were mingled in a single gorgeous moment—when life was literally a dream." Whatever its joys, an early success does not supply the best training for the harder days ahead in later life.

As for winning the Southern belle, Zelda Sayre, of Montgomery, Alabama, she agreed to marry Fitzgerald only if he could make money from his writing; after his first novel was accepted and proved a commercial success, they married. A writer with more than a proclivity for dissipation and a strong case of Irish flu (also known as alcoholism), Fitzgerald could not have found a worse partner than Zelda. She suffered her first breakdown in 1930 and, though thought neurasthenic, was evidently what is now labeled bipolar.

Mr. Brown devotes several judicious pages to the toll that the Fitzgerald marriage, with its infidelities and rivalrousness, took on both parties. "What is our marriage anyway?" Zelda wrote to Scott. "It has been nothing but a long battle ever since I can remember." Fitzgerald told a friend that "I don't know whether Zelda and I are real or whether we are characters in one of my novels." Poor Zelda, in and out of sanitariums, lived on eight years after her husband, only to die of asphyxiation in a fire.

Mr. Brown's book is a useful corrective to the figure of F. Scott Fitzgerald as a hopeless drunk and unrestrained reveler—diving into the fountain at the Plaza and all that—which has been vastly overdone. Fitzgerald had, after all, published three novels before he was 30. He was never less than stalwart in fulfilling his duty. He worked hard to pay off his wife's costly medical bills and sent their daughter, Scottie, to the best private schools. In the middle 1930s, he set aside his artistic plans to work in Hollywood for the kind of money that allowed him to close the books on his debts.

Weak, wavering though Fitzgerald often was, strong character was one of his ideals. "He believed in character," he wrote about Charlie Wales, the hero of his story "Babylon Revisited." "He wanted to jump back a whole generation and trust in character again as the eternally valuable element. Everything wore out." A central aspect of the novelist's criticism of the 1920s, in which he came to full maturity, is that its gaudy opulence took its toll on character.

Fitzgerald also believed in his art, at which he worked with the ardor of the true professional. In his introduction to *The Stories of F. Scott Fitzgerald* (1951), Malcolm Cowley recounts the multiple revisions that Fitzgerald put his novel *Tender Is the Night* through, discarding great chunks of it as he went along. He kept notebooks in which he recorded observations, descriptions and overheard bits of conversation that might one day be useful for his fiction. His artistic ideal was Joseph Conrad, and he aspired to be the American Conrad. He was more cavalier with his short stories, claiming that a moderate-length story shouldn't take more than a day to write, a lengthier one three days. He published many of his stories in the *Saturday Evening Post*, where the fees were impressively high. Between 1920 and 1937, Mr. Brown reports, he published 65 stories there.

The regnant American figures of the 1920s were its songwriters: Cole Porter, the Gershwins, Irving Berlin, Jerome Kern, Rodgers and Hart. Fitzgerald thought he might well have become a songwriter himself, "but I guess I am too much a moralist at heart and really want to preach at people in some acceptable form, rather than to entertain them." He was able to get away with his preaching only because he could do so in his fiction subtly, charmingly, and, yes, entertainingly. What Fitzgerald preached was, as Mr. Brown puts it, the "ongoing saga—the one about the man, the generation, and the country that had fallen short." Notes harking back to a better time play throughout his fiction. One recalls here Nick Carraway's admiration for his father in *The Great Gatsby*.

Fitzgerald remarked that there can never be a good biography of a good novelist because a novelist is so many of the characters he has created. Yet his own most interesting characters turn out to have been portraits or partial projections of himself. Amory Blaine of *This Side of Paradise*, the literary dilettante at Princeton, is fairly closely modeled on the novel's author. Jay Gatsby's love for Daisy Buchanan resembles Fitzgerald's own hopeless youthful love for Ginevra King, the daughter of a vastly wealthy Chicago banker whose money put her well out of his league. At the beginning of *Tender Is the Night*, Dick and Nicole Diver would appear to be loosely based on Gerald and Sara Murphy, the swank couple who made the Riviera fashionable for Americans, but the book ends with the Divers more resembling the Fitzgeralds as their marriage caves in owing to Nicole's mental illness and Dick's drinking. In the unfinished novel *The Last Tycoon*, the Hollywood producer Monroe Stahr, is meant to resemble MGM's Irving Thalberg, the only man said to have understood the "full equation" required for successful movies. The novel turns on a doomed affair, suggesting Fitzgerald, who in his last years carried on a love affair with the gossip columnist Sheilah Graham.

What ties these fictional heroes together is that all are failures. Fitzgerald, as is well known, died thinking himself a failure. (His writing was out of fashion, and his final royalty check, as Mr. Brown notes, was for the humiliating sum of $13.13.) Yet Fitzgerald had a way, in his writing, of making failure seem not only fascinating but noble. All his heroes, like their author, were romantic dreamers: Gatsby's dream was to recapture the past, Dick Diver's to bring the luster of charm to everyone he loved and befriended, Monroe Stahr's to make art in a Hollywood world where it was held in contempt. Each is doomed to failure; each in his own way is admirable. Success would only have robbed them of their allure.

The background to Fitzgerald's fiction, Mr. Brown avers, is "social breakdown." By this he means that "the collapse of once dominant classes, values, and taboos had given his work an immediacy that worked on two levels, most obviously as ruminations on topical issues and, more important, as deeper meditations on historical change." This gives Fitzgerald's best fiction a weight, a gravity, that it might otherwise not possess. "In Fitzgerald's writings, rather, we encounter an America unusually thick with fallen heroes, martyrs to a powerful social-mobility mythology," writes Mr. Brown. "Embedded in these offerings is the disquieting notion that we have drifted far from our inheritance as the children of pioneers to fashion a culture that teaches its young to love too much the privileges and protections of wealth."

Early in his career, Fitzgerald set out the following program as a goal for writers: "An author ought to write for the youth of his own generation, the critics of the next, and the schoolmasters of ever afterward." Given the unceasing flow of books by and about him and the fact that, excepting perhaps only J. D. Salinger's *The Catcher in the Rye*, *The Great Gatsby* must be the most taught book in American classrooms, Fitzgerald accomplished this goal, though at his death in 1940 he could not have known it.

Mr. Brown shares with Fitzgerald himself the view that *Tender Is the Night* was his best novel, *Gatsby* his second best. The latter Fitzgerald thought "a kind of tour de force and the other a confession of faith" and went on to compare *Gatsby* to a sonnet and *Tender* to an epic. Having recently reread both novels, I would agree that *Tender Is the Night* is a work on a larger canvas, with many more characters and touching on more themes. Yet it also contains a larger than fair share of longueurs, patches of egregious overwriting and a less than compelling plot, if plot it may be said to have at all. *The Great Gatsby*, on the other hand, is without a false note, on a grand theme, penetrating in its observations and exquisitely plotted—in all as nearly perfect a novel as American literature provides.

Before his death, bemoaning the unjust neglect of his writing, Fitzgerald noted that "even now there is little published in American fiction that doesn't slightly bear my stamp—in a small way I was an original." An original he indubitably was, and one of the splendid services rendered by Mr. Brown is to have convincingly made the case that F. Scott Fitzgerald was an original in a way much grander than he himself realized.

Wolcott Gibbs

(2011)

THE *NEW YORKER*, like New York itself, is always better in the past. In the present, it seems always to be slipping, never quite as good as it once was. Did the magazine, founded in 1925, have a true heyday? People differ about when this might be. The *New Yorker's* heyday, it frequently turns out, was often their own.

I began reading the magazine in 1956, at the age of nineteen—not my heyday, which, near as I can tell, has yet to arrive—drawn to it originally because someone told me that the then-current issue had a story by J. D. Salinger. Harold Ross, the magazine's founder and tutelary spirit, had died four years earlier. William Shawn was on the first stretch of his thirty-five-year tour (1952–1987) as editor-in-chief. The writers Harold Ross had hired remained in place—the big four among them were James Thurber and E. B. White, Joseph Mitchell, and A. J. Liebling—and the ethos of the magazine was still that which Ross had imprinted on the magazine.

Ethos is a word that Harold Ross, even if he knew it, probably wouldn't have permitted in the pages of his magazine. Urban sophistication, emphasizing life's eccentricities (and often featuring its eccentrics), with an amused view of human ambition, was the spirit with which Ross imbued the *New Yorker*. The magazine was apolitical, serious without being heavy-handedly so. During World War II, its war reporting was first-class, and it gave over an entire issue, in 1946, to John Hersey's account of the devastation caused by the atomic bombing of Hiroshima. Yet when I came to the magazine, there were still columns devoted to horse-racing, Ivy League football, jazz, and night-club entertainment. The general tone of the proceedings was casual, playful, and yet, somehow, withal adult.

An impressive roster of contributors, in those days their names printed not under the titles of their articles and stories but at the conclusion, popped in and out of the *New Yorker's* pages each week. S. J. Perelman, Mary McCarthy, Janet Flanner, Edmund Wilson, Dorothy Parker, Robert Benchley were part of the magazine's literary vaudeville. Many *New Yorker* writers began their professional lives as newspapermen, lending them an anchor in reality, if not cynicism, before turning to the unpretentious belles-lettristic journalism practiced at the magazine.

If in those years there were a representative *New Yorker* writer, his name was Wolcott Gibbs. Gibbs, too, began writing for newspapers. A man of all work, he contributed Talk of the Town pieces, Notes & Comments, profiles, light verse, short stories, drama and movie and book criticism, and delicious parodies. (The most famous of his parodies—a parody-profile, actually—was "Backward Ran Sentences," which was about the rise of Time, Inc., written in *Time Magazine* style.) In the Foreword to a collection of his pieces called *More in Sorrow*, Gibbs claimed to have contributed more words to the magazine over its first thirty years than any other writer. In *Here at the New Yorker*, Brendan Gill notes that Gibbs was also the magazine's best editor of other people's copy. As an editor, deletion was his speciality; he was a cut man in the corner of lesser writers.

Wolcott Gibbs is not a name any kid taking next year's SATs need be concerned about. A few collections of his journalism appeared during his lifetime, he had a play with a modestly respectable run on Broadway, he published a book of stories. Today, he seems a man of another era, unlikely to arouse interest in a world clamorous with so many other demands on our attention.

Gibbs might have passed into oblivion but for the fact that an editor and journalist named Thomas Vinciguerra, much taken with Gibbs's writing, has gone to the work of assembling an impressive, and substantial, collection of his prose, the preponderance of it from the *New Yorker*.

Reading through Mr. Vinciguerra's book sets off many observations, notions, insights into the world of smart journalism, criticism, and the writing life, both now in our day and then at the *New Yorker*.

As we Americans reckon such matters, Wolcott Gibbs was well-born. One of his paternal forebears, Mr. Vinciguerra informs us, signed the Declaration of Independence; another was Secretary of the Treasury under John Adams; yet another a governor of Connecticut. On his mother's side, he was descended from Martin Van Buren. Yet the family was tapped out financially before Gibbs was born, in 1902, owing to a bad investment, a bungled land purchase in New Jersey.

Sent to the Hill School, in Pennsylvania, where Edmund Wilson also went to prep school, Gibbs took a pass on college, as did many of the good writers of his and the preceding generation. Brendan Gill remarks that Gibbs suffered feelings of inferiority for not have gone to university, though this seems unlikely. H. L. Mencken, who similarly didn't bother with college, claimed that between listening to boring German professors and working as a journalist covering fires, executions, and bordello raids, there really wasn't any choice. Mr. Vinciguerra reprints a mock commencement address to non-college-graduates Gibbs wrote that establishes his awareness of the inanity of much college education.

Wolcott Gibbs died at fifty-six, in 1958, in bed, cigarette in hand, a batch of galley proof of a collection of his writings on his lap. In his introduction, Thomas Vinciguerra leaves open the question of whether he was a suicide, which was what Gibbs's third wife suspected. He was a dedicated drinking man, a serious boozer, as were many of the staff assembled by Harold Ross. The *New Yorker* of those days was not a place where in the mornings it wouldn't at all do to tell people to have a great day.

While he could cause laughter in others, Wolcott Gibbs was not himself a notably cheerful man. ("I suppose he was the unhappiest man I have known," wrote his friend, the playwright S. N. Behrman.) When a newly arrived writer at the *New Yorker* asked him if he had had a pleasant New Year's, Gibbs instructed him to practice an anatomically impossible act on himself. As a drama critic, this same want of conviviality found its way into his prose, but with winning effect. He came across as the very opposite of the enthusiast, a man much put upon, giving the clear impression that he wished he could have departed most plays after the first act; or, better still, never left his apartment and gone to the theatre in the first place.

All this might result in mere glumness if Gibbs didn't write so well. Of the great and gaudy snob Lucius Beebe's early days in journalism—Beebe later made his mark as the chronicler of café society—Gibbs wrote: "He had an apathy about facts which verged closely on actual dislike, and the tangled wildwood of his prose was poorly adapted to describing small fires and negligible thefts." Gibbs described the mustache of Thomas E. Dewey, the man who lost the 1948 presidential election to Harry S. Truman, as "bushy, dramatic, an italicized swearword in a dull sentence." He referred to posterity as "the silly bitch," to Eugene O'Neill's "involved and cosmic posturings," to the liberal newspaper *PM* as "a journal of salvation," to the "genial condescension of an Irish cop to a Fifth Avenue doorman."

Gibbs claimed "to be comparatively accomplished only in the construction of English sentences," but he also had a nicely angled point of view and the courage of his opinions. Intellectually, he was hostage to no one, not even Shakespeare. He thought *Romeo and Juliet* an ill-made play: "There are too many innocent misunderstandings and staggering coincidences, too many potions and poisons; in the end, far too many bodies cluttering up the Capulets' not so very quiet tomb." Sacred cows, he felt, made good hamburger. Paul Robeson, he wrote, over-acted in the part of Othello.

To the gods of modernism, he brought no sacrifices, but instead a heavy dose of useful philistinism. Of *Waiting for Godot*, he wrote: "All I can say in a critical sense, is that I have seldom seen such meagre moonshine stated with such inordinate fuss." Jean-Paul Sartre's *No Exit* he called "little more than a one-act drama of unusual monotony and often quite remarkable foolishness."

On lighter matters, writing about Maurice Chevalier's stagey pursuit of women, he compared French seduction to women's basketball: "There is a lot of squealing and jumping up and down, but certainly not much in the scoring department." In explaining the breakup of the old Algonquin Round Table group, he wrote:

Those who did not move away [to Hollywood, to Connecticut or Bucks County] were by now temperamentally unfit
for the old close association, since there is nothing more en-
ervating to the artist than the daily society of a lot of people
who are just as famous as he is.

One of Gibbs's few idols was Max Beerbohm, also a literary man of all
work, with great skill as a caricaturist added. Gibbs and Beerbohm shared
the quality of sublime detachment. No man of his day was less *parti pris*
than Wolcott Gibbs. After reading the more than six hundred pages of
his writing in *Backward the Sentences*, I cannot characterize his politics.
A. J. Liebling, his colleague on the *New Yorker*, claimed that his own politics were "let Paris be gay," which turned out not to be true in the case
of Liebling (who was a fairly standard liberal), but was, I believe, true of
Gibbs, though gaiety, clearly, was scarcely his speciality.

In a fine formulation, Mr. Vinciguerra writes that Gibbs "embodied
[the *New Yorker's*] archetypal combination of blunt honesty, acid wit,
exacting standards, and elegant condescension." The *New Yorker* of those
days seemed mildly aristocratic, making everything seem easily within
the grasp of its writers and, perhaps as important, of its readers. Hilton Kramer, in an essay-review of James Thurber's *The Years with Ross*,
recounts that a *New Yorker* fact-checker called him countless times to get
straight the positions of various French art critics for a piece the magazine's then art critic, Robert Coates, was writing about the European art
scene. When the piece appeared, Kramer was struck "at the absurdity of
the feigned ease" with which it was presented in Coates's published copy.

I marveled at the discrepancy between the pains taken to get
the facts of the matter as accurate as possible, and the quite
different effort that had gone into making the subject seem
easy and almost inconsequential to the reader.

What was going on? "For myself," Kramer wrote,

I don't see how we can avoid concluding that the principal reason for the *New Yorker's* method is ignorance: the ignorance of writers first of all, and ultimately the ignorance

of readers. In a society which could assume a certain level of education and sophistication in its writers and journalists—which could make the assumption because it shared in that education and sophistication—there would be more of a public faith that writers knew more or less what they are talking about.

The magazine has never been without its critics. Robert Warshow, in 1947, wrote:

> The *New Yorker* has always dealt with experience not by trying to understand it but by prescribing the attitude to be adopted toward it. This makes it possible to feel intelligent without thinking, and it is a way of making everything tolerable, for the assumption of a suitable attitude toward experience can give one the illusion of having dealt with it adequately.

The charge here on the part of Hilton Kramer and Robert Warshow, of course, is middlebrowism—the pretense of culture when the efforts behind attaining true culture have been efficiently eliminated for the reader.

The charge of middlebrowism became more difficult to prove as the *New Yorker* began, under William Shawn, to load up on certified intellectual contributors. Edmund Wilson was the first of these, writing regularly for the magazine's book section. Dwight Macdonald soon joined Wilson, and his assignment was, precisely, to attack such middlebrow cultural artifacts as Mortimer Adler and Robert Hutchins's *Great Books of the Western World*, the *New Revised Standard Version of the Bible*, and *Webster's Third International Dictionary*. Harold Rosenberg signed on as the magazine's regular art critic; Susan Sontag wrote for the magazine. Vladimir Nabokov, Isaac Bashevis Singer, Saul Bellow, and other highbrow novelists regularly published stories in the *New Yorker*. Two of the great controversial intellectual publishing events—Hannah Arendt's *Eichmann in Jerusalem* and James Baldwin's essay "The Fire Next Time"—first appeared in the magazine's pages.

The reason so many intellectuals, in effect, went over to the *New Yorker* is no more complicated than that they were asked. The money the magazine paid was much greater than that paid by any other even semi-serious magazine. Quite as important, the *New Yorker* had the best of all American audiences. Anything published in its pages was certain to be read by everyone a writer cared about. Even people who didn't much like the magazine felt obliged at least to glimpse it. Writing for the magazine, one discovered an America one could not be sure existed until one heard from its readers: the cardiologist from Tacoma, Washington, who kept up his ancient Greek, the lady from Tyler, Texas, who read Proust in French and with intellectual penetration.

A writer's editor, William Shawn's regular contributors not merely appreciated but adulated him. Two of my friends who were staff writers under his reign never referred to him as other than Mr. Shawn. Editorially, Shawn was immensely tolerant, allowing writers to take years to complete assignments (he could also hold back pieces for decades and not run them at all). He permitted his writers to run on at great, sometimes stupefying, length: long John McPhee pieces on geology or E. J. Kahn pieces on corn were notable winners in the eye-glazing boredom category. A man who does not press a writer about deadlines, never suggests that length might be a problem, and pays him handsomely—that, from a writer's point of view, is an immortal editor.

William Shawn was the editor responsible for changing the *New Yorker*, taking it from the realm of smart into that of intellectual journalism. Was it a happy change? Under it, Wolcott Gibbs was replaced as a drama critic after his death by Kenneth Tynan, a man much more attuned—some would say too well attuned—to the avant-garde. Arlene Croce, along with Edwin Denby, the best dance critic America has known, covered ballet. Movies, which had hitherto been treated as best trivial entertainment, became under Pauline Kael, quite literally, the talk of the town, with Miss Kael's opinion on the latest movie weighing more heavily among the so-called educated classes than the opinions of the chairman of the Federal Reserve.

The magazine also became more political. Earlier, E. B. White would occasionally print Notes & Comments editorials urging the need for world government, an idea always up there among the top ten dopiest political ideas of all time. Under Shawn, political ideas became more specific. He ran Rachel Carson on pollution, Lewis Mumford on city planning, and several pieces highly critical of the conduct of the American involvement

in Vietnam. The magazine's politics was liberal, but—an important qualification—liberal without being hostage to any political party, professing to
speak on behalf of the greater good of the nation.

During his long editorship, William Shawn held to an unvarying policy
of no profane words or descriptions of sex in the *New Yorker*. (Whenever
one saw a John Cheever or John Updike story in *Harper's* or *Esquire*, one
could be fairly certain that it contained bits of fancy fornication.) Harold Ross's advice upon hiring editors for the magazine was "Don't f--- the
contributors," which Wolcott Gibbs claimed was the closest Ross came to
enunciating an editorial policy. This was a policy violated by of all people
Shawn himself; after his death it was revealed by Lillian Ross, one of the
magazine's long-time reporters, that she and the married Shawn had had a
love affair of many years standing.

Much to the consternation of the *New Yorker*'s staff, in 1987 William
Shawn's retirement was forced, at the age of 82, by S. I. Newhouse, who
had bought the magazine for his Conde Nast publishing empire. Robert
Gottlieb, a successful publisher's editor, replaced Shawn. His major contribution to the magazine was to allow profane language and sexy stories
in its pages. He departed five years later, to be replaced by Tina Brown,
who set out to make the magazine genuinely with-it. She had a taste for
*epate*ing the genteel with gaudy covers and photographs, and also made
it seem, through her selection of articles, as if the most important things
in the world were Hollywood, designer culture, and royalty.

After Tina Brown left the *New Yorker* in 1998 to begin a short-lived
magazine called *Talk*, the magazine was taken over by David Remnick,
an earnest journalist who had written well on the Soviet Union and other
matters. *New Yorker* staff members, feeing this a return to seriousness, were
pleased. Remnick's ascension also meant a turn toward a more specific politics. The politics were liberalism now distinctly aligned with the Democratic Party; both in a large number of its general articles that make American foreign policy seem what the left calls "the imperialist project," and
in its "Comment" editorials written most weeks by Hendrik Hertzberg,
which read with all the complexity of old western movies: good guys wear
Democratic hats, villains Republican ones, and that isn't the Lone Ranger
but Barack Obama riding to the rescue.

Relevance has its costs. In its covers, its coverage of events, its need to seem *au courant,* its insistent politics, the *New Yorker* has begun to seem more and more like a weekly news or opinion journal ("of salvation") than the magazine once adored by earlier generations of readers. The *New Yorker* Wolcott Gibbs's wrote for, elegant, literary, ironic, laced with a bracing skepticism, was the spiritual house organ for people looking for relief from the clang of rivaling opinions, the barkering of each week's Next New Thing, the knowingness of haughty punditry, the maelstrom of the world's unrelenting noise. The *New Yorker* of the current day flourishes financially, its circulation in the ascendant. The *New Yorker* of Wolcott Gibbs's time, published in the world we now live in, would probably not last out the year.

Evelyn Waugh

(2017)

WHEN THE FINAL REVIEWS—that is, the obituaries—came in, Evelyn Waugh's were mixed. His literary accomplishments were noted, so too his Catholic apologetics, but heavy emphasis was put upon his reactionary views and his snobbery. Waugh's son Auberon, responding to these obituaries, noted that they were wrong about his father's snobbery (he scarcely cared about pedigree) and his politics ("politics bored him"), and missed the main point about him: "it is simply that he was the funniest man of his generation."

Quite so, though it needs to be added that in the case of Evelyn Waugh funny was not always the same as amusing. Amusing suggests light, whimsical, charming. P. G. Wodehouse is amusing. Waugh's humor tended to the dark, and, given his often gratuitous pugnacity, usually had a victim, or at least an edge. When the favorite of his five children, his daughter Margaret, wished to live on her own, he told her "you are no more ready for independence than the Congo." After Randolph Churchill had what turned out to be a benign tumor removed through surgery, Waugh remarked that it was the only thing about Randolph that was wasn't malignant and they removed it. When someone called his attention to a typographical error in one of his books, he replied: "Now that they no longer defrock priests one cannot get any decent proofreading."

Waugh's humor was also strong in the line of mischief. While serving in the British Army in Yugoslavia during World War II, he spread the rumor that Marshal Tito was a woman, a lesbian into the bargain. Of his teaching at a boys school in Wales he claimed to "take a certain pleasure in making all that I teach as dreary to the boys as it is to myself." When his friend Ronald Knox asked him if he, Knox, seemed to nod off while giving a lecture, Waugh replied that indeed he did, but only for "twenty minutes." He described travel to Mexico as "like sitting in a cinema, seeing the travel film of a country one has no intention of visiting." Of the reception of his novel *Brideshead Revisited* in America, he wrote: "My book has been a great success in the United States which is upsetting because I thought it in good taste before and now I know it can't be."

Waugh soon enough acquired a reputation for social ruthlessness, a ruthlessness nicely abetted by his heavy drinking. "Even his close friends were not spared," Nancy Mitford wrote, "he criticized everyone fiercely and was a terrible tease, but he set about it in such an amusing way that his teasing was easily forgiven." Not everywhere, not by everyone. Martha Gellhorn, a friend of Waugh's friend Diana Cooper, called him "a small and ugly turd." Duff Cooper, Diana's husband, reacting to a malicious comment Waugh made about Lord Mountbatten at a dinner party, lashed out: "How dare a common little man like you, who happens to have written one or two mildly amusing novels, criticize that great patriot and gentleman. Leave my house at once." On his own social combativeness, Waugh has Gilbert Pinfold, his autobiographically-based, eponymous character in *The Ordeal of Gilbert Pinfold*, ask, "Why does everyone except me find it so easy to be nice?"

Philip Eade's recent biography of Waugh goes a fair way to answering that question. Eade's book is subtitled, with some precision, *A Life Revisited*, for it is Evelyn Waugh's life and only glancingly his work to which he devotes his attention. His biography is a chronicle of Waugh's recent ancestry and early childhood, his education, two marriages, and career on to his death in 1966 at the age of sixty-three. Waugh's books and their reception are mentioned in due course, but it is his career and the formation of his character that holds chief interest for Philip Eade.

Rightly so, I should say, for Evelyn Waugh's novels, travel writings, and biographies (of Edmund Campion and Ronald Knox) do not really require elaborate critical exploration. All Waugh's writing requires is attentive readers, alive to his elegant prose, sense of his craftsmanship at plotting, and the manifold comical touches that bedizen his pages. "Germans," a character in *Brideshead Revisited* remarks, "sometimes seem to discover a sense of decency when they get to a classical country." In *A Handful of DustI,* a secondary character, Mrs. Rattery, reveals that she has children, two sons: "I don't see them often. They're at school somewhere. I took them to the cinema last summer. They're getting quite big. One's going to be good-looking, I think. Their father is." Rather a different angle on parenting, this, one might say.

Philip Eade recounts Evelyn Waugh's life in an admirably economic and straightforward manner, with a nice sense of measure and in a prose style free of jargon and cliché. He neither Freudianizes him nor condemns his lapses into social savagery. Without a trace of tendentiousness, free of all doctrine, Eade the biographer seeks to understand the strange behavior of Evelyn Waugh through telling the story of his life without commenting censoriously on it. The task is far from a simple one. Waugh's friend Freddy Smith, the second Earl of Birkenhead, in a memoir of his war days with him, wrote: "Evelyn, like Max Beerbohm, but probably for different reasons, had decided to drop an iron visor over all his intimate feelings and serious beliefs and by doing so excluded one from any understanding of his true character. . .This deep reticence detracted in a sense from his conversation, which was of the highest order, because however brilliant and witty, one always felt that he was playing some elaborate charade which demanded from him constant vigilance and wariness."

Early in the pages of *The Ordeal of Gilbert Pinfold*, a novel recounting the nervous breakdown of its hero, Waugh stages an interview for Pinfold with a journalist from the BBC. (Waugh himself underwent such a breakdown owing to his overdosing on bromide and choral combined with his heavy alcohol intake, a potion he hoped would help him attain sleep.) Of this interview Pinfold notes that the interviewer

> seemed to believe that anyone sufficiently eminent to be interviewed by him must have something to hide, must be an impostor whom it was his business to trap and expose, and

to direct his questions from some basic, previous knowledge
of something discreditable.

When during an actual interview by John Freeman of the BBC, Waugh
was asked why he lived in the country, he answered that it was not because
of a love of sport or rural life, but "to get away from people like you."

In *The Ordeal of Gilbert Pinfold*, from behind the screen of Pinfold,
Waugh describes his own menacing social profile with a nice exactitude.
Pinfold observes that "his habits of life were self-indulgent and his utter-
ances lacked prudence." As for his tastes, the strongest of them were negative. "He looked at the world *sub species aeternitatis* and he found it flat
as a map; except when, rather often, personal annoyance intruded." The
part he decided to play "was a combination of eccentric don and testy
colonel . . . it came to dominate his whole outward personality" as "he
offered the world a front of pomposity mitigated by indiscretion that
was as hard, bright and antiquated as a cuirass."

Soon after he came to consciousness Evelyn Waugh was made aware
that he was not his father's favorite child. His old brother Alec—later a
popular, now a largely forgotten novelist—was. A five-year difference in
age separated the two brothers, just the right distance to prevent close-
ness and make intimacy difficult. Evelyn did not so much hate his father
as hold him in contempt. His father was a reviewer (of more than 6,000
books), essayist, publisher (with the firm of Chapman & Hall). Evelyn
would later say that he "did everything at deleterious speed." He also early
noted his father's pomposity, which, combined with his gross sentimentality, precluded all possibility for admiration on the part of his younger
son. The older he grew the more dismissive, not to say derisive, of his
father he became. Waugh found succor as a child with his mother and his
nanny. He would always find intimacy easier with women—Diana Cooper, Nancy Mitford, Anne Fleming—than with men.

"The Golden Boy" is the title that Alexander Waugh, grandson of Evelyn and son of Auberon, in *Fathers and Sons,* his family history, gives to
the chapter on Alec Waugh. Golden he may have seemed to his father
but rather a zinc dud he must have seemed to his younger brother. While
at Sherbourne, the public school of choice for the males in the Waugh
family, Alec was caught in a homosexual scandal that made it impossible

for Evelyn to attend the same school, and so he had to attend Lancing, a public school a step down on the status ladder.

The young Waugh was also less than enamored of his first name, with its sexual ambiguity. His first book, *Rossetti: His Life and Works*, published in 1928 when he was twenty-five, was reviewed in the *Times Literary Supplement* under the assumption that its author was female, the reviewer referring throughout to its author as Miss Waugh. This was another annoyance in a life that seemed to be filled with annoyances. He was early and perennially a victim of boredom; in his uncompleted novel *Work Suspended* he speaks of "ruthless boredom." His friend Douglas Woodruff noted: "He was constantly suffering from *ennui*, which ought to be recognized as a major affliction more wearing and painful than most physical disabilities." One ready-to-hand weapon in the combat against boredom, according to Woodruff, was to be found in his readiness "to say the disconcerting thing in the hopes of making something happen or getting a rise, or in some other way breaking the monotony of all too easily predictable social exchanges." In Yugoslavia, for a notable example, Waugh put it about that Birkenhead was having a homosexual affair with an Istrian intellectual and had also become a drug addict through the use of morphia. And, one must understand, he rather liked Birkenhead. Such free-floating malice evidently helped him get through the day.

As early as his school days, Evelyn Waugh's terror of boredom and taste for the ridiculous days combined to make him a figure of subversion. Max Mallowan, later an archeologist and husband to Agatha Christie, remembered him at Lancing as "popular among the boys for he was amusing and always ready to lead us into mischief, but had a way of getting others into trouble and himself invariably escaping." Mallowan adds that "he was courageous and witty and clever, but also an exhibitionist with a cruel nature that cared nothing about humiliating his companions as long as he could expose them to ridicule." Philip Eade tells of a fellow student who made the mistake of using the word "preternatural," for which he paid the price of being known as for ever after as "Preters." Cecil Beaton, who first encountered Waugh at Lancing, remained terrified of him all his life.

Waugh won a scholarship to Hertford College, Oxford, where he continued his hijinks, with heavy drinking and homosexuality added. He spoke of the "aesthetic pleasure of being drunk," by which one gathers he meant the glow of giving way without hesitation to his social effrontery and inherent outrageousness. As for homosexuality, "everyone was queer at Oxford in those days," the poet John Betjeman remarked. Waugh's great homosexual flame was a young man named Alistair Graham, one of the figures upon whom he partially modelled his *Brideshead Revisited* character Sebastian Flyte, and through whom he gained his first entrée into the upper-class English world he later portrayed in *Brideshead*. Harold Acton, who read Eliot's *The Wasteland* out of a megaphone from the window of his rooms at Oxford, was another university connection. Never at all serious about study, Waugh finished Oxford with a disappointing third-class degree.

His first ambition was to become a draughtsman, and so after Oxford he went off to the Heatherly School of Fine Art in London. He also briefly tried his hand at cabinet making, until he realized, as he put it, "that there was nothing for it but to write books; an occupation which I regarded as exacting but in which I felt fairly confident of my skill." In the meanwhile he spent his nights drinking and bonking about town among the Bright Young Things, gathering material, though he may not have known it at the time, for *Vile Bodies*, his novel about the young dissolutes of the day.

Having shed his homosexuality in the way public-school Englishman of the era seemed to do, Waugh played a wide field of women, and, when it came to marriage, chose Evelyn Gardner, perhaps the ditiest of them all, who had been previously engaged no fewer than nine times, sometimes, it was said, simultaneously to more than one man. He was twenty-four, she twenty-three, and in the spirit of the times he proposed marriage by saying, "Let's get married and see how it goes."

"I saw a young man," Evelyn Gardner noted of her first impression of Waugh, "short, sturdy, good-looking, given to little gestures, the shrugging of a hand which held a drink, the tossing of a head as he made some witty, somewhat malicious remark. He was easy to talk to and amusing." Diana Cooper described Gardner as "though very pretty not much else." A friend of Evelyn Gardner—now, to distinguish her from her husband, called Shevelyn—noted that "I don't think she is wildly in love with E. W., but I doubt if she is capable of sustained passion." The friend was correct. The marriage lasted less than two years, broken off when Shevelyn began an affair with a man of negligible significance named John Heygate, whom she later claimed never to have loved. At the breakup of his marriage, Waugh was twenty-six. His own comment on the marriage was that "fortune is the least capricious of deities, and arranges things on the just and rigid system that no one should be happy for long."

Not long after his marriage ended, Waugh underwent what his father called his "perversion to Rome." Much evidence exists that the breakup of his marriage was not the sole cause of his religious conversion, though it must have weighed in heavily on the decision. In his autobiographical volume *A Little Learning*, Waugh notes that he had much earlier attempted suicide by drowning, and was only stopped from completing the job by the incessant biting of jellyfish. In *Vile Bodies*, a novel he felt he had botched, Waugh more than suggests the emptiness of life among the higher bohemia of Bright Young Things, his social milieu of choice, that was decadent London society between the wars. Modernity itself became an affront to him. Catholicism was the spar he chose to grasp against its choppy seas.

The Jesuit Father Martin D'Arcy, who oversaw Waugh's religious instruction, remarked that he came to Catholicism through his revulsion with the modern world and its faithlessness, hoping, as D'Arcy wrote, that through it he could regain "a recrudescence of hope and even gaiety." T. S. Eliot, in *The Wasteland*, claimed to show "fear in a handful of dust." Evelyn Waugh, before his conversion, already knew that fear. *A Handful of Dust* is of course the title of what many find Waugh's most perfect novel.

On September 29, 1930, Evelyn Waugh was received into the Roman Catholic Church. Why Romanism? Because he felt it was the oldest, and hence most fundamental version of Christianity. Philip Eade quotes Waugh as saying that "Catholicism was Christianity, that all other forms of Christianity were only good insofar as they chipped little bits off the main block." In an essay titled "Conversion to Rome," Waugh wrote that he saw the world as essentially a struggle "between Christianity and Chaos," and Christianity represented order. Did his conversion alter his behavior? Not, apparently, outwardly. Hilaire Belloc told Mary Herber, the mother of Waugh's second wife Laura, that "he has the devil in him." Waugh himself told John Betjeman that he was "by nature a bully and a scold." After witnessing his rudeness to a French intellectual she introduced him to, Nancy Mitford asked him if it weren't a contradiction that he was so rude a man and yet he claimed to be a practicing Catholic. "You have no idea," he replied, "how much nastier I would be if I was not a Catholic. Without supernatural aid I would hardly be a human being." He might have added, as he wrote in his essay on his conversion, that "the Protestant attitude seems often to be, 'I am good; therefore I go to church'; while the Catholics is, 'I am far from good; therefore I go to church.'"

Evelyn Waugh didn't like being labelled a Catholic writer, in the way that Graham Greene, Francois Mauriac, and J. F. Powers were. Saul Bellow and Philip Roth similarly chafed at being called Jewish writers. Such labels do not make a writer seem minor so much as parochial. Yet Waugh led a very Catholic life. His closest friends—Greene, Christopher Sykes, Ronald Knox—were Catholics, and he was himself Mass-going, confession-giving, legalistic on theological matters, observing of all ritual, deeply disappointed by the loosening of Church doctrine and practice proposed by Vatican II. Catholicism ultimately changed the kind of novelist he was, taking him beyond comedy while never really abandoning it.

Comical all Waugh's novels indubitably are, often riotously so. He may be the only modern novelist in whom one remembers secondary characters and comic bits as vividly as anything else in his books. Who can forget the vicar in *A Handful of Dust* who continues to give sermons originally written during his time in India, citing tropical conditions and colonial distance, to his congregation gathered in wintry England. Or in the same novel the bit in which the friends of Tony Last's adulterous wife search out a mistress for Tony to divert his attention from his wife's betrayal, and one suggests "Souki Foucault-Esterhazy," to which another responds: "He [Tony] isn't his best with Americans." Or the prostitute with her out-of-wedlock child who, despite her lowly station, is not above a touch of anti-Semitism. Or, in *Brideshead Revisited*, Charles Ryder's quite balmy father; or Anthony Blanche "ageless as a lizard, as foreign as a Martian"; or the voice of a London hotel receptionist that sounded the note of "hermaphroditic gaiety." Or Major Athorpe in *Sword of Honor* who never travels without his own portable water closet; or, in *Scoop*, the definition of "the news" as "what a chap who doesn't care much about anything wants to read. And it's only news until he's read it. After that it's dead."

Evelyn Waugh's was the comedy of detachment, both in his fiction and in his life. His grandson Alexander claimed this detachment came as a reaction to his father's sentimentality. Who else but he could write of his first-born child, his daughter Teresa: "I foresee that she will be a problem—too noisy for a nun, too plain for a wife. Well standards of beauty may change in the next 18 years." In Yugoslavia, his reaction to a German *stukas* bombing raid was to compare it to German opera—"too loud and too long." He did deadpan in prose, no easy literary maneuver. He could nab a character in a single sentence, or phrase, such as the younger sister Cordelia in *Brideshead Revisited*, who "moved in the manner of one who has no interest in pleasing."

In a *Paris Review* interview three years before his death, Waugh remarked:

> I regard writing not as an investigation of character, but as an exercise in the use of language, and with this I am obsessed. I have no technical psychological interest. It is drama, speech, and events that interest me.

Precise, pellucid, flawless in usage and deployment of syntax, confidently cadenced, Waugh's was perhaps the purest English prose written in the past century.

Evelyn Waugh has been viewed as chiefly a comic writer. V. S. Pritchett noted that Waugh was always comic for serious reasons, and he distinguished his earlier from his later books by making the distinction that the former "spring from the liberating notion that human beings are mad," while his later ones, especially his war trilogy *Sword of Honour*, "draws on the meatier notion that the horrible thing about human beings is that they are sane." Even these earlier books, though, spoke to a yearning for a steadier, more stable world.

After his conversion to Catholicism, Evelyn Waugh found a theme—the emptiness of life without faith. For some this theme diminished him and deprived his writing of interest. Of *Brideshead Revisited*, Waugh's most unremittingly Catholic novel, Isaiah Berlin noted that it "seems to start so well and peter out in such vulgarity," and referred to Waugh as "a kind of [Charles] Maurras—a fanatical, angry, neurotic, violent writer, thoroughly un-English in most ways." In his diary, Noel Coward lamented the infusion into Waugh's novel *Unconditional Surrender* of "long tracts of well-written boredom. The whole book is shadowed by a dark cloud of Catholicism, which suffocates humor and interferes with the story." Edmund Wilson, who in 1944 considered Waugh "the only first-rate comic genius that has appeared in English since Bernard Shaw," two years later, on the occasion of the American publication of *Brides-head,* found himself "cruelly disappointed," the novel "more or less disastrous," the work a failure of taste, "mere romantic fantasy," its author's snobbery "shameless and rampant," with Waugh's hitherto laudable style gone "to seed." Wilson would later sketchily review Waugh's *The Loved One*, his satire on American funerary rites, and exclaim that "to the non-religious reader, however, the patrons and proprietors of Whispering Glades [the posh California cemetery mocked in the novel] seem more sensible and less absurd than the priest-guided Evelyn Waugh."

Edmund Wilson, always a bit of a village atheist, a man readier to believe in revolution than in God, suffered a want of sympathy for writers—Conrad and Kafka among them—given to spirituality. Myself a bit of a village agnostic, I find Evelyn Waugh's delving into questions of faith elevated his fiction. One doesn't have to be Catholic, or consider conversion to Catholicism, to be interested in the theme of faith—understanding it, finding it, retaining it under difficult conditions. The drama of faith, Waugh's ultimate subject, went directly against the grain of a secular age, but in taking it up in his novels Evelyn Waugh, the brilliant humorist, became a major writer.

J. F. Powers

(2013)

WHEN JAMES FARL POWERS died in 1999, the *New York Times* headline on his rather brief obituary read, "J. F. Powers, 81, Dies; Wrote about Priests." His Wikipedia entry describes Powers as "a Roman Catholic American novelist and short story writer who often drew his inspiration from developments in the Catholic Church and was known for his studies of Midwestern Catholic priests."

Sounds narrow, provincial, claustral, unpromising. Not, it turns out, so. In the American priesthood J. F. Powers found a subject that, through his talent for telling detail, irony, and humor, he mined to produce some of the most striking fiction of his day, fiction that holds up well in ours.

That day—the 1940s through the early 1960s—was for American Catholics very different from today. Catholic life in those years provided a distinct culture within America. For Catholics, the Church, capital and small letter C, was both the center and periphery of life. Catholicism had an authority and hold on American Catholics that has long been leaching away and now seems much less firm, if not tenuous.

In the very Catholic city of Chicago, where I grew up, Catholicism was a natural part of the cityscape. Priests in clerical collars, nuns in full habit walked the streets, rode public transportation, bustled about in libraries, were in evidence everywhere. If one were a Catholic, one sent one's children to Catholic primary and secondary school—parochial schools, they were then called—where they learned Latin, took courses in theology, and studied under the lash of unremitting discipline. The likelihood of children going to Catholic schools mixing with public school children was slight. Voluntary segregation by religion was the order of the day.

An impressive group of Catholic intellectuals and artists was active, men and women for whom Catholic theology was at the center of their thought. Its international roster included Evelyn Waugh, Father Brian D'Arcy, Graham Greene, Father Ronald Knox, Jacques Maritain, Flannery O'Connor, Anne Fremantle, Thomas Merton, Padraic and Mary Colum, and many more. The conversion of Protestant artists and intellectuals was not uncommon. Robert Lowell became Catholic, though did not remain so for long; so did Allen Tate and other of the writers and critics known as the Fugitives. *The Catholic Worker, Commonweal,* and *America,* and others provided a serious Catholic intellectual press.

This rich Catholic culture provided both background and foreground for J. F. Powers's life and career. Powers was a devout but never pious Catholic, allowing himself a certain latitude for criticizing those things in the Church he felt coarse, such as the *Index Liborum Prohibitorum,* or list of books and movies the Church censored. So serious was his Catholicism that on Christian grounds he was a conscientious objector during World War II, for which he served thirteen months in prison and another eighteen months on parole working at drudgery jobs in hospitals.

Powers wrote two novels and three books of stories. Each of the novels, *Morte D'Urban* (1962) and *Wheat That Springeth Green* (1988), is about a remarkable priest, Father Urban Roche and Father Joe Hackett, respectively, neither of whom is devoted to the saving of souls or the work of aiding the poor but rather to the humdrum everyday business of keeping the Church running. His short stories, thirty of which are in *The Stories of J. F. Powers* (New York Review Books), are preponderantly about priests, certainly the best ones are.

Powers tells a straight story, usually in an enclosed space. Often his priests never leave the parish, or even the rectory. They do their jobs, deal as best they can with bishops, curates, housekeepers, pets, occasionally whacky parishioners, and, later, radical changes in the Church. They are fond of food and sometimes too fond of a drink or perhaps three. Crises of conscience sometimes arise, but it is the quotidian detail, the daily rhythm of priestly life, that absorbs and fascinates in Powers's fiction. As Father Joe Hackett tells his young curate:

> This [the Catholic Church] is a big old ship, Bill. She creaks, she rocks, she rolls, and at times she makes you want to throw up. But she gets where she's going. Always has, always will, until the end of time.

When first published, Powers's fiction met with criticism from Catholics who preferred their priests less worldly and more saintly. The priests in Powers's fiction are flawed, utterly believable, and most of them somehow, flaws and all, admirable. Here is Father Hackett on the priesthood:

> … it was still a job—a marrying, burying, sacrificing job, plus whatever good could be done on the side. It was *not* a crusade. Turn it into one, as some guys were trying to do, and you asked too much of it, of yourself, and of ordinary people, invited nervous breakdowns all around.

Powers had planned a novel about family life, but never got round to writing it. His own family life was richly complicated. In *Suitable Accommodations: An Autobiographical Story of Family Life*, Katherine A. Powers, the novelist's eldest daughter, has assembled those of her father's letters touching on the subject of his family in the hope of suggesting the kind of novel he might have written. The book is excellent on many counts, not least for Powers's unrelenting charm, even in adversity.

J. F. Powers grew up in a family in which he felt that his father was made to sacrifice his art—he was a talented pianist—to "the secondary things" that marriage and family required of a father and husband: a job that will put food upon the table, home-ownership, settling down in the evening with *Time Magazine* after yet another dullish day. "The American Tragedy," he calls it. In a letter to his future wife, he writes: "I am determined that it will not happen to me. Help me."

Suitable Accommodations is a fit title, for suitable accommodations is what the Powers family, having moved more than twenty times, including two lengthy stays in Ireland, never found. Powers believed that artists shouldn't have to take regular jobs. On this subject he was intransigent. He was a man of inflexible integrity. The questions these letters pose is that of the cost of integrity, and who is asked to pay the bill?

The unspoken hero of *Suitable Accommodations*, as its editor points out in an afterword to the book, was Betty Wahl Powers, her mother and Powers's wife. Betty Wahl Powers not only herself wrote every day—she published an occasional story in the *New Yorker* and a novel called *Rafferty & Co.*—but, her daughter writes, "cooked every meal from scratch and sewed most of our clothes; she went to her parents for aid; she scrimped, rationed, and cobbled together the wherewithal for our survival."

Life *chez* Powers was no delight for the children. "Growing up in this family is not something I would care to do again," Katherine Powers writes. "There was so much uncertainty, so much desperation about money, and so very little restraint on my parents' part in letting their children know how precarious was our existence." She calls her parents' marriage a *folie a deux*, which seems an accurate description.

Getting down to work wasn't always easy for Powers. Given the chaos of his child-ridden household, he required a separate office, off the premises, in which to write. He would take an occasional teaching job—at St. John's, Marquette, Michigan—but turned down many others, including an editorship at *Commonweal*. "And the truth about me is that I just don't qualify as an ideal husband," he wrote to Katherine Anne Porter. "Ah, well," he wrote to Robert Lowell, "let me be a lesson to you. Stay single. That way you can afford to be yourself." Meanwhile the Powers children—a second, a third, a fourth, a fifth—kept coming.

Powers made a decent score when the *New Yorker* accepted one or another of his stories. He frequently borrowed money from Father Harvey Egan, a priest to whom some of the most amusing letters in this volume were written. His wife's parents from time to time allowed him and his large family to move in with them. He received Guggenheim and Rockefeller grants and was made something called a *Kenyon Review* Fiction Fellow. He put up at various points at Yaddo, the writers colony near Sarasota, which has the added attraction for him, a modest player of the ponies, of a nearby racetrack. But whatever he earned, it was never enough.

"I can't believe I'll ever make much on my work," Powers wrote to Father Egan, to whom he earlier wrote that "whatever else old JF may be, he's never dealt in sex. But, no, there's no one saying it, and America's cleanest writer goes his lonely way." Reviews of his books tended to be praising. The English critic Walter Allen compared him to Chaucer, which, if one discounts the bawdiness in Chaucer, isn't bad.

Powers's fiction was too subtle to acquire a large readership. Yet *Morte D'Urban* won the National Book Award in 1963, against competing novels by Vladimire Nabokov, Katherine Anne Porter, John Updike, and Dawn Powell. *Morte D'Urban* is his best book, and, in its quiet way, a great book. As the ad used to say you didn't have to be Jewish to love Rosen's Rye Bread, neither, allow me testify, do you have to be Catholic to love the fiction of J. F. Powers.

These letters reveal Powers's literary tastes as chaste. He did not much care for the writing of Faulkner, nor did he think much of Hemingway. As a Catholic, he was supposed to like the novels of Graham Greene, but did not. Norman Mailer and James Baldwin, he wrote to the novelist Jack Conroy, "make my arse tired." To the critic Michael Millgate he wrote that he has "just finished not finishing Iris Murdoch's *The Flight from the Enchanter* . . . Such books, and Nancy Mitford's, serve only to impress me with the genius of Evelyn Waugh."

One should come away from *Suitable Accommodations* disliking J. F. Powers for what ostensibly was his selfishness in putting his own art ahead of the comfort and welfare of his wife and of the children he brought into the world. In later years, he had his own doubts about the wisdom of doing so, but his wife seems not to have fundamentally disagreed with this decision. He may have been unreliable but he was never unfaithful. "It's a sad state of affairs," he writes to her, "when a man's most carnal thoughts are all about his wife."

In these letters, Powers shows a winning modesty, neither playing the whining, unappreciated artist nor the man the fates have treated unfairly. Drollery abounds: If an American is ever made Pope, he writes to a friend, he should take the name Bingo. After writing one of the few awkward sentences in the book, in a letter to Charles Shattuck, then the editor of *Accent*, he writes, "Take that sentence to the cleaners next time you go."

The letters in *Suitable Accommodations* end at 1963. Powers went on to live thirty-six more years. He finally settled into a job teaching creative writing and English literature at St. John's Abbey in Collegeville, Minnesota, after which his literary production seems to have slowed. Although he called himself "non-political," Katherine Powers notes that her father viewed the 1960s with "appalled incredulity." Fortunately, he died before the pedophile scandal among the Catholic priesthood, which would have sickened and enraged him. Changes in the Church could not have pleased him. After all, the older American Catholicism, which he understood so well and captured so vividly in his fiction, helped make J. F. Powers the superb artist he was.

Edward Gibbon

(2015)

We must consider how little history there is; I mean real
authentick history. That certain Kings reigned, and certain battles
were fought, we can depend upon as true; but all the colouring,
all the philosophy, of history is conjecture.

—SAMUEL JOHNSON,
from JAMES BOSWELL'S *Life of Johnson*

A PUDGY MAN with a big head, double chin, and pursing mouth,
under five feet tall, foppishly overdressed, stilted in conversation, Edward Gibbon was easily the greatest English historian
and quite possibly the greatest historian the world has known. How did
this preposterous little man—a snob with often ludicrous opinions who
was known as he grew older and fatter as Monsieur Pomme de Terre—produce *The History of the Decline and Fall of the Roman Empire*, a panoramic
work of roughly a million and a half words with some 8,000 footnotes,
covering 1,300 years of history? More than two centuries after Gibbon
wrote it, the entertainment value of his history is as great as it was when
it appeared in three volumes between 1776 and 1788, its standing in literature as firmly fixed.

Psychotic tyrants, savvy eunuchs, cunning courtesans; brutal barbarian tribal chiefs; battlefields bedewed with blood and strewn with the
white bones of human corpses; Byzantine luxuriance; Saracen leaders
"never seen to smile except on a day of battle"; ragtag Roman crusaders
no less fanatical than the forces they were recruited to fight; Russians,

Hungarians, Persians, Moors all engaging in tortures of a rare exquisivity—cutting off noses, ears, tongues, hands; putting out eyes with needles; poisoning husbands; the rope, the rack, the axe all finding full employment—in Gibbon's pages it all goes whirring by, leaving one in a state of nearly perpetual dazzlement.

Through it all there are the emperors, the central figures of the history—and what a rogue's gallery they are! Caracalla "was the common enemy of mankind," a "monster whose life disgraced human nature"; Elagabalus was no "rational voluptuary," also a transvestite; Maximin, "though a stranger to real wisdom . . . was not devoid of a selfish cunning"; the reigns of Valerian and his son Gallienus provided a 15-year period that "was one uninterrupted series of confusion and calamity"; Maxentius was "a tyrant as contemptible as he was odious"; Valens "was rude without vigor, and feeble without mildness"; Theophilus was "a bold, bad man . . . whose hands were alternately polluted with gold, and blood." Gibbon writes: "Such was the unhappy condition of the Roman emperor . . . almost every reign is closed by the same repetition of treason and murder."

One can't really hope to take it all in; one follows instead the plangent tale over centuries in its broader lineaments. "The flow of his narrative, the clarity of his prose and the edge of his irony," wrote C. V. Wedgwood, "still have the power to delight and, although seven generations of scholars have added to or modified our knowledge of the epoch, most of what Gibbon wrote is still valid as history."

Scholars have noted the shortfalls of Gibbon's scholarship. François Furet commented that in his history Gibbon "deprived the German people of their basic dignity." Bernard Lewis contended that Gibbon's portrait of Muhammad "is still much affected by myths" and "gives expression to his own prejudices and purposes and those of the circles in which he moved." Steven Runciman claimed that Gibbon's Greek was weak and that "the spirit of Byzantium eluded him," while "the splendor of his style and the wit of his satire killed Byzantium studies for nearly a century." Gibbon himself had second thoughts about beginning his story of Rome's decline with the Emperor Commodus, son of Marcus Aurelius, when well before that time Rome had such intemperate and vice-ridden emperors as Tiberius, Caligula, and Nero. But in the end all this seems negligible next to his monumental accomplishment.

Is genius possible in the realm of scholarship? It can be if aligned to art. If the historian has the instinct of an artist, he will not confine himself to accurate recounting of facts, causes, and consequences, but will widen his view to personalities, the play of character on the outcome of events, and what all this conveys about human nature. In an early unpublished work, Gibbon wrote: "Every man of genius who writes history infuses into it, perhaps unconsciously, the character of his own spirit."

Gibbon's spirit was one of supremely detached skepticism, reinforced by common sense to a high power, with a masterly command of the rich irony that gave forcible expression to both. This spirit derived from the time in which he lived and the peculiar circumstances of his own life.

In his *Memoirs of My Life*, Gibbon noted, "I *know* by experience that from my early youth I aspired to the character of an historian." Aspiration is one thing, achievement quite another. What were the accidental determinants that made Edward Gibbon the majestic historian he turned out to be?

Edward Gibbon was a bachelor. He may have been one of nature's true bachelors, though not at first by choice. Gibbon spent his late adolescence and early adulthood in Lausanne, in French-speaking Switzerland. At the age of 21, he met, courted, and proposed to Suzanne Cuchord, the charming daughter of a Swiss clergyman, but a woman without a dowry. His father forbade the marriage. "I sighed as a lover," Gibbon wrote in his *Memoirs,* "I obeyed as a son."*

Nietzsche said that a married philosopher is a joke. A married historian, productive in the way Gibbon was, is not so much a joke but perhaps an impossibility. One can be the author of a vast historical work of the kind of *The History of the Decline and Fall of the Roman Empire,*

---

* Suzanne Cuchord went on to marry Jacques Necker, the chief financial minister of Louis XVI; and later, pleased by her husband's wealth and position, lightly lorded it over Gibbon, who had earlier rejected her for want of her money and the ultimate courage of his ardor. If asked, Gibbon would doubtless have considered it a fair exchange: She found a rich husband who, until the French Revolution, wielded great power; he, Gibbon, ended up composing a masterwork. With Necker, Suzanne also gave birth to a daughter, Germaine, later Madame de Stael, the famous bellettrist.

which was 20 years in the composing, or be happily married, but one is unlikely to bring off both.

Gibbon found himself in Lausanne not by choice but under the lash of his father's anger. While at Oxford, at 16, he converted to Catholicism. The conversion put paid to his career as a student, for the university did not allow Catholics; nor, at that time, could Catholics hold public employment or sit in Parliament. Gibbon's father sent him off for reconversion—de-programming, we might call it today—to Switzerland and the successful if tepid recultivation of his Protestantism under a Calvinist clergyman.

He remained in Lausanne for five years, and those years turned him from an Englishman into a European. When he first arrived, he spoke no French. Soon he was translating Latin works into French and French ones into Latin, and keeping a French journal. He met Voltaire, who was not much impressed by him, went to plays, and corresponded with scholars on ancient history and literature. "I had ceased to be an Englishman," he wrote.

> At the flexible period of youth, from the age of sixteen to twenty-one, my opinions, habits, and sentiments were cast in a foreign mold; the faint and distant remembrance of England was almost obliterated; my native language had grown less familiar; and I should cheerfully have accepted the offer of a moderate independent fortune on the terms of perpetual exile.

Money, or rather the want of it, was another crucial ingredient in Gibbon's life's work. His grandfather had been a successful merchant, in textiles, who acquired a fortune, then lost it in the South Sea Company bubble, then recouped much of it. His father had neither the business sense nor the resilience of his grandfather, and through social ambitions, pretensions, and mismanagement, squandered much of what had been a considerable fortune. "His gay character and mode of life," Gibbon, in mild understatement, wrote, "were less adapted to the acquisition than to the expenditure of wealth." Gibbon was set free financially only after his father died in 1770 when Edward was 33 and came into a diminished inheritance. This short financial leash was his unexpected good fortune. As he wrote in his *Memoirs*, "I am persuaded that had I been more indigent or more wealthy, I should not have possessed the leisure or the perseverance to prepare and execute my voluminous history."

Gibbon's determination to undertake his great work came six years before his father's death. He had first planned a life of Walter Raleigh, then a history of the liberty of the Swiss, then an account of the Republic of Florence under the Medicis. In 1763, he set out on the classic Englishman's Grand Tour of Europe. In Rome on the evening of October 15, 1764, he later wrote, "as I sat musing in the Church of the Zoccolanti or Franciscan friars, while they were singing Vespers in the Temple of Jupiter* on the ruins of the Capitol," he decided to dedicate himself to a study of such ruins. Only later did he widen his compass and take on the fall of the entire Roman Empire. The first of his history's six volumes appeared in 1776, the last in 1788.

Outwardly an account of the defeat of the Roman ideal, the true subject of *The History of the Decline and Fall of the Roman Empire* is human nature, and, in Gibbon's recounting, it's a far from pretty picture. He writes that the study of history proper is "little more than the register of the crimes, follies, and misfortunes of mankind." It was ever thus, and part of Gibbon's project is to convince his readers of that. "There exists in human nature," he writes, "a strong propensity to depreciate the advantages, and to magnify the evils, of the present time." *The History of the Decline and Fall of the Roman Empire* shows us just how wearily constant human nature has been through time. Gibbon makes his case for this through a series of aphoristic statements, among them:

> Avarice is an insatiate and universal passion.
> Fear had been the original parent of superstition.
>
> How much swifter is the progress of corruption than its cure.
>
> The most glorious or humble prospects are alike, and soon bounded by the sepulchre.

---

* It was in fact in the Temple of Juno, an odd mistake for a historian to make.

Of an earthquake:

> The historian may content himself with an observation, which
> seems to be justified by experience, that man has much more
> to fear from the passions of his fellow-creatures, than from
> the convulsions of the elements.

Of the invention of gunpowder:

> If we contrast the rapid progress of this mischievous discov-
> ery with the slow and laborious advances of reason, science,
> and the arts of peace, a philosopher, according to his tem-
> per, will laugh or weep at the folly of mankind.

The reigning tone of *The History of the Decline and Fall of the Roman
Empire* is Olympian. The book is written as if by a god looking down on
and recording the ambitions, grand or squalid, of human beings in their
attempts, virtuous or vice-ridden, to achieve mastery over their destiny.

How today is one to read *The Decline and Fall of the Roman Empire*? I
recently did so at the rate of roughly 20 pages a day, early in the morning,
over a five-month period. The greatest compliment I can pay it is to say
that I regretted finishing it.

EARLY IN HIS THIRD VOLUME, Gibbon writes:

> There are few observers who possess a clear and comprehen-
> sive view of the revolutions of society; and who are capable
> of discovering the nice and secret springs of action, which
> impel, in the same uniform direction, the blind and capri-
> cious passions of a multitude of individuals.

Gibbon was one of those few. He describes military campaigns and
discrete battles with impressive concision. (He himself served two
years as an officer in the Hampshire militia, chiefly guarding French
prisoners of war, which gave him a feeling for the military spirit; to a
true writer, no experience is wasted.) No one who has read it will forget his capping sentence after describing the battle of Salice toward
the close of the fourth century, where dead soldiers were left on the

ground without burial: "Their flesh was greedily devoured by the birds of prey, who, in that age, enjoyed very frequent and delicious feasts . . . " His hatred of war was genuine. "Military discipline and tactics," he reminds us, "are about nothing more than the art of destroying the human species."

Yet Gibbon admired military valor, just as he admired civic virtue, freedom ("the first step to curiosity and knowledge"), honor, and rationality. The decline of Rome in his pages is marked by the falling away from these virtues through avarice, indulgent luxury, laxity, tyranny, barbarity, and religious intolerance. His otherwise dark history is relieved only occasionally by such admirable figures as Boethius (480–524 CE), author of *The Consolation of Philosophy* and "the last of the Romans whom Cato or Tully could have acknowledged as their countryman," or the Emperor Majorian, who ascended to the eastern emperorship in 457 CE and "who presents the welcome discovery of a great and heroic character, such as sometimes arise in a degenerate age, to vindicate the honor of the human species."

In his essay, "Gibbon's Historical Imagination," Glen Bowersock notes that Gibbon "treated the raw materials of ancient and medieval history much as a novelist treated the plot line." Gibbon was a regular reader of novels. His admiration for Henry Fielding was unbounded. In *Memoirs of My Life* he refers to "the romance of *Tom Jones*, that exquisite picture of human manners [that] will outlive the palace of the Escurial and the imperial eagle of the house of Austria." Gibbon never thought of writing fiction himself, yet, as Bowersock notes, he "shaped his truth as if it were fiction, preserving thereby the animation of human history and the art of the novelist." As Simon Leys noted: "The novelist is the historian of the present and the historian the novelist of the past."

The loss of Roman literature was in itself for Gibbon one of the signs of the degradation of Rome. After the 42-year reign of the Antonine emperors in the second century CE, he writes:

> The name of Poet was almost forgotten; that of Orator was usurped by the sophists. A cloud of critics, of compilers, of commentators, darkened the face of learning, and the decline of genius was soon followed by the corruption of taste.

There is one towering exception in the almost unending horror of the imperial stream that followed, and that is Julian the Apostate, who lived for 32 years (331–363 CE) and ruled for eight (355–363 CE). Educated in Greece, philosophic by training and temperament, Julian

> had an inflexible regard for justice, tempered by a disposition to clemency; [and possessed] the knowledge of the general principles of equity and evidence, and the faculty of patiently investigating the most intricate and tedious questions which could be posed for discussion.

Courageous in battle yet "prudent in his intrepidity," he led and won decisive battles against the relentlessly encroaching barbarians. Quite as impressive as a governor, he ruled with "a tender regard for the peace and happiness of his subjects," and staved off corruption whenever he discovered it. Gibbon quotes Julian on his own virtue as a ruler: "Was it possible for a disciple of Plato and Aristotle to act otherwise than I have done?" Julian could not stay the fall of Rome, though Gibbon applauds him for delaying it, however briefly.

Julian's actual apostasy was not, for Gibbon, the least of his virtues. This apostasy was of course from Christianity, which, along with the unending onslaught of barbarians from both the east and west and the internecine quarrels among the Romans themselves, was, in Gibbons's view, the chief force that brought the Roman Empire to ruin. As the historiographer Arnaldo Momigliano notes, Gibbon's great distinction resides in his setting center stage the central truth that "late antiquity meant the replacement of paganism by Christianity," which was not something he celebrated.

Owing to the infamous 15th and 16th chapters of his first volume, Gibbon became notorious for his anti-religious views. These chapters describe the conversion to Christianity of the Emperor Constantine (272– 337 CE) and all that followed from it. Constantine began by tolerating the Roman Empire's oppressed Christians and ended, through his own conversion, by bringing the religion to the seat of the Roman Empire itself. As to the kind of Christian Constantine was, Gibbon notes that his conversion hadn't the least effect on his cruel conduct; on matters of religious doctrine, "his incapacity and his ignorance were equal to his presumption."

Christianity *per se* was not Gibbon's problem. Religious faith that brought intolerance or empty asceticism among its adherents was. Gibbon's artful malice was set aflame by what he took to be ignorant superstition. The polytheism of pagan Rome, tolerant of other religions, was more to his taste, though he mocked this, too. The oracles at Delphi, he concluded, were wiser about lining their pockets than about the future. He was no more merciful on the subject of the Jews: "That singular people seems to have yielded stronger and more ready assent to the traditions of their remote ancestors, than to the evidence of their own senses." He argued that Jews did not proselytize because they,

> the descendants of Abraham, were flattered by the opinion, that they alone were the heirs of the covenant, and they were apprehensive of diminishing their inheritance, by sharing it too easily with the strangers of the earth.

Religious rites were to him merely comic: "Many a sober Christian would rather admit that a wafer is God, than that God is a cruel and capricious tyrant." Priests and monks above all were to be distrusted. To a philosophic eye, Gibbon wrote, "the vices of the clergy are far less dangerous than their virtues."

Gibbon mocked "those minds which nature or grace had disposed for the easy reception of religious truth." He satirized that truth as it was set forth in "the science, or rather the language, of Metaphysics" in its Christian version regarding the immortality of the soul. The intolerance of the Christians, once in power, an intolerance of others and of deviationists among their own ranks, aroused his ire: "In the course of their intestine dissensions, [Christians] have inflicted far greater severities on each other, than they experienced from the zeal of the infidels."

The obscurity of arcane Christian doctrine and the hypocrisy of popes and priests stimulated Gibbon's irony, an irony he claimed to have learned from Pascal's *Provincial Letters*. He mentions the monk Antiochus, "whose one hundred and twenty homilies are still extant if what no one reads may be said to be extant." Of the trial of John XXIII (1370–1419 CE), the so-called anti-pope, Gibbon writes: "The most scandalous charges were suppressed; the Vicar of Christ was only accused of piracy, murder, rape, sodomy, and incest." He attributes to Pope Innocent III "the two most signal triumphs over sense and humanity, the establishment of transubstantiation, and the origin of the inquisition." G. M. Young, the 20th-century historian of Victorianism, claimed for Gibbon a victory over religion—for after Gibbon's eviscerations, "no institution could ever again profess to be outside the empire of history and not subject to its laws."

ODD THOUGH IT MIGHT SEEM to say of a book running to more than 3,000 pages, *The History of the Decline and Fall of the Roman Empire* is a work of great economy. Gibbon's work is the reverse of that of the medieval historian Gregory of Tours, about whom he wrote: "In a prolix work (the last five books contain ten years) he has omitted almost everything that posterity desires to learn." Gibbon notes that, to avoid tedium, which will result in neither amusement nor instruction, he is going to pass over discussion of documents (the "Eighteen Creeds," for example) or years of uneventful rule ("later Turkish dynasties may sleep in oblivion since they have no relation to the decline and fall of the Roman Empire"). Remarking in a footnote on the tedious negotiations that succeeded the synod of Ephesus, he writes: "The most patient reader will thank me for compressing so much nonsense and falsehood in a few lines." His method is to highlight only the significant. "When any extraordinary scene presents itself," he writes, "we shall spare no pains nor paper to open it at large to our reader but if whole years should pass without producing anything worthy of his notice we shall not be afraid of a chasm in our history but shall hasten on to matters of consequence and leave such periods of time totally unobserved." The book's only longueurs are found in those pages given to descriptions of ecclesiastical controversy over Christian doctrine.

"In human life," Gibbon announces, "the most important scenes will depend on the character of a single actor." Perhaps the best thing in *The History of the Decline and Fall of the Roman Empire* are Gibbon's "characters," or short biographies—ranging from a single sentence to a lengthy paragraph to three or four pages—of the great figures who pass through his pages. Augustus, Constantine, Justinian, John Chrysostom, Attila, Belisarius, Athanasius, Procopius, Theodora, Mohamet, Tamberlane, Charlemagne, Saladin, Petrarch, comprise but a small portion of an enormous roster of the most significant actors in history upon whom Gibbon descants. He produced such biographies through his erudition but did so concisely through his unparalleled powers of formulation. Pope Boniface VIII "entered [his holy office] like a fox, reigned like a lion, and died like a dog." Of the Emperor Hadrian, he writes:

> The ruling passions of his soul were curiosity and vanity. As they prevailed, and as they were attracted by different objects, Hadrian was, by turns, an excellent prince, a ridiculous sophist, and a jealous tyrant.

Above all, there is the pleasure of Gibbon's prose. As a stylist, he was unsurpassed in all of 18th-century English literature. Striking off sentences of high formality, often structured round powerful parallelisms, laced with innuendo-like irony—Byron called Gibbon "the lord of irony"—he composed with an easy mastery of epithet and a pungent sense of the dramatic. No one had a finer feeling for the architecture of a sentence. Set out in confident cadences, many of these sentences end on a high note of drama, others in comical surprise. Consider the following:

> Julian was convinced that he had seen the menacing countenance of war; the council which he summoned, of Tuscan Haruspices, unanimously pronounced that he should abstain from action; but on this occasion, necessity and reason were more prevalent than superstition; and the trumpets sounded at the break of day.

Or this, of the Emperor Gordian the younger:

> Twenty-two concubines, and a library of sixty-two thousand volumes, attested the variety of his inclinations; and from the productions which he left behind him, it appears that the latter as well as the former were designed for use rather than for ostentation.

Gibbon is said to have composed while walking about his study, limning a full paragraph in his mind before sitting down to write it out. This is all the more remarkable considering that some of these paragraphs run 600 or 700 words or more. His diction was flawless and often charming; the music of his paragraphs came from his alternation of long and short sentences. Where he paraphrased others—Herodotus, St. Augustine—he often improved them by adding the luster of his own polished prose. A work of the length and breadth of *The History of the Decline and Fall of the Roman Empire* would not be thinkable—or readable—if less handsomely written.

"Some fame, some profit, and the assurance of daily amusement" are the motives Gibbon gave for writing his history. He received £4,000 for the first three volumes of his history (about $750,000 in today's money), and the same sum for the last three. He spent five drab years in Parliament, where he spoke rarely and never with distinction. He returned to Lausanne in 1783, where he completed his last two volumes. The history's final sentence reads:

> It was among the ruins of the Capitol that I first conceived the idea of a work which has amused and exercised near twenty years of my life, and which, however inadequate to my own wishes, I finally deliver to the curiosity and candour of the Public.

Upon inscribing that splendid sentence, which he did on the night of June 27, 1787, between the hours of 11 and 12, Gibbon, after laying down his pen,

> took several turns in a berceau, or covered walk of acacias, which commands a prospect of the country, the lake, and the mountains. The air was temperate, the sky was serene, the silver orb of the moon was reflected from the waves, and all nature was silent.

He was 47 years old. His immense satisfaction in the accomplishment is beyond imagining.

Although he received enough criticism for his chapters on religion to feel the need to publish a *Vindication*, or defense, of his methods and position, *The History of the Decline and Fall of the Roman Empire* was quickly recognized as a masterpiece, and Gibbon's reputation was permanently established. His contemporary Horace Walpole wrote to a friend:

Lo, there is just appeared a truly classic work: a history, not majestic like Livy, nor compressed like Tacitus; not stamped with character like Clarendon; perhaps not so deep as Robertson's *Scotland*, but a thousand degrees above his *Charles*; not pointed like Voltaire, but as accurate as he is inexact; modest as he is *tranchant* and sly as Montesquieu without being so *recherché*. The style is smooth as a Flemish picture, and the muscles are concealed and only for natural uses, not exaggerated like Michelangelo's to show the painter's skill in anatomy; nor composed of the limbs of clowns of different nations, like Dr. Johnson's heterogeneous monsters. The book is Mr. Gibbon's *History of the Decline and Fall of the Roman Empire*.

Even better was a letter to Gibbon from David Hume, one of his intellectual heroes, who would not live to read the last five volumes:

Whether I consider the dignity of your style, the depth of your matter, or the extensiveness of your learning, I must regard the work as equally the object of esteem, and I own that if I had not previously had the happiness of your personal acquaintance, such a performance from an Englishman in our age would have given me some surprise.

Gibbon's response to the reaction of the Duke of Gloucester—"Another d-mn'd thick, square book! Always, scribble, scribble, scribble! Eh! Mr. Gibbon?"—is not known.

Gibbon next worked on his autobiography, which he never completed to satisfaction (and which was posthumously stitched together by his friend Lord Sheffield). With the aid of a younger historian named John Pinkerton, Gibbon had also planned to publish a chronicle of England from the fifth century to the beginning of the House of Tudor. But his health gave way. He had long suffered from gout in both legs, and he had an embarrassingly large hydrocele, or sac of serous fluid around the testicle, that badly disfigured him. He had three operations on it, and the third put him out of the game. He died in the winter of 1794, at the age of 57.

Thomas Carlyle, who published his history of the French Revolution in 1837, an even hundred years after the birth of Edward Gibbon, wrote of his predecessor: "Gibbon is a kind of bridge that connects the antique with the modern ages. And how gorgeously does it swing across that gloomy and tumultuous chasm of those barbarous centuries." Through 20 years of solitary labor, this chubby little man also proved that the first, if not the sole, criterion for a great historian is to be a great writer.

Herodotus

(2014)

HERODOTUS, the first Greek and thereby the first Western historian, had bad press long before there was anything resembling a press. Aristotle referred to him as a "story-teller," which was no honorific. What he meant was that Herodotus made things up, another word for which is "liar." Thucydides had little good to say about Herodotus and thought his attempt to recapture the long-gone past foolhardy. History, for Thucydides, meant contemporary, or near-contemporary, history, with an emphasis on politics and warfare. In his *Histories*, Herodotus went well outside these bounds, writing about Egypt, Scythia, Persia, and other countries; he took up the study of customs and *moeurs* among them, as might a modern anthropologist.

More than 400 years later, the attacks on Herodotus's reputation continued. In an essay titled "The Malice of Herodotus," Plutarch criticized him for undue sympathy for the Persians and other barbarians, a want of respect for facts coupled with a lack of balanced judgment, and a partiality for Athens. Worse attacks were to come from other commentators over the succeeding centuries, some of whom held that Herodotus relied too heavily on oral evidence, others that he was plain dishonest.

Herodotus (ca. 484–425 BCE) was a Carian, born in Halicarnassus in Asia Minor, in what would now be western Turkey. He was, in other words, from the periphery of the Greek world, and his book is the result of a sort of intellectual tourism. He traveled, collected stories, consulted documents where they existed, and wrote down his findings. No one knows for certain whether he visited all the countries he wrote about or how he came into his extensive knowledge. In the opening sentence of the *Histories*, he states his purpose:

> Herodotus, from Halicarnassus, here displays his enquiries, that human achievement may be spared the ravages of time, and that everything great and astounding, and all the glory of those exploits which served to display Greeks and barbarians alike to such effect, be kept alive—and additionally, and most importantly, to give the reason they went to war.

Cicero called Herodotus the "father of history." Yet Arnaldo Momigliano, the great 20th-century historiographer of the ancient world, ends his brilliant essay on Herodotus by noting, "It is a strange truth that Herodotus has really become the father of history only in modern times." History, or, more precisely, historical methods, Momigliano explains, finally caught up with Herodotus. Ethnographic research brought a new respect for Herodotus's own early interest in ethnography. Those who did archeological exploration in Egypt and Mesopotamia found Herodotus's writings on these subjects useful. His writings also became valuable to biblical scholars in their study of Oriental history. Oral history, on which he drew heavily, became a standard tool of modern social science and history. Herodotus was also the first serious historian to give due attention to women. In his *Histories*, he devotes several pages to Artemisia, the queen of Halicarnassus, who commanded the Asian Dorian fleet during Xerxes's attack on Greece. As for his accuracy, Momigliano writes, "We have now collected enough evidence to be able to say that he can be trusted."

About Herodotus's style there has never been any doubt. "The power of his tragic vision of history," wrote Hugh Lloyd-Jones, then-Regius professor of Greek at Oxford, "is enhanced by his possession of literary gifts of the highest order." Lloyd-Jones holds that, apart from Plato and, on occasion, Demosthenes, no prose stylist among the Greeks compares to Herodotus:

> His prose is clear, rapid, euphonious, marvelously varied according to variations of his subject matter; he can write in a plain and simple manner, with short sentences loosely strung together, but he can also build up elaborate periodic structures making effective use of many poetical words.

Charm and style, the two great preservatives for historical and every other kind of literature, Herodotus had in abundance.

Temperamentally, literarily, and methodologically, Herodotus and Thucydides could scarcely have been further apart. Thucydides's strength was in analysis, Herodotus's in description. Concision, dazzling formulation, and intellectual penetration were where Thucydides's power lay, while expansion and sympathy for human difference was Herodotus's forte. Herodotus appears to have been a man of wider tolerance, with a more generous nature and disinterested outlook than Thucydides. Herodotus's motive was pure knowledge; Thucydides, meanwhile, wrote under the cloud of having been exiled for 20 years from Athens because of his failure to arrive in time to rescue the Athenian forces at the Battle of Amphilipolis early in the Peloponnesian War.

Thucydides gained greatly on Herodotus in popularity during the Cold War, as his *History of the Peloponnesian War*, which chronicles the conflict between Athens and Sparta, found a ready analogy in the clash between the United States and the Soviet Union—at least among people who read history for lessons about the present. Now that that war is over, the analogy is of lessened cogency, and Herodotus's star is rising. Evidence for this is the appearance of three recent translations of the *Histories*, with a fourth—by the English classicist Peter Green—in the works.

Of the two historians, Herodotus had the happier story to recount. Thucydides's was the story of the decline of Greece owing to the internal disputes that brought on the Peloponnesian War; Herodotus's was the rise of Greece through the victory of the greatly outnumbered Greeks over the Persians during the Greco-Persian Wars (ca. 490–479 BCE). The *Histories* covers roughly 150 years, ending with the Persian defeat at the Battle of Plataea, in Boetia, when the alliance of Greek city-states dealt the *coup de grâce* to the more than two-million-man army of Xerxes.

Herodotus takes more than 300 or so pages to get around to the Greco-Persian conflict that is the true subject of his work. "But if I may digress here," he writes in the middle of commenting on the hornless cattle of Scythia, "as I have sought opportunities to do from the moment I started this account of my enquiries. . ." These digressions might be irksome were they not so interesting: Herodotus provides portraits of Cyrus, Croesus, Darius, and Xerxes, and recounts the battles of Marathon and Thermopylae, Salamis and Plataea. "Marvelous deeds," as he puts it, are his subject matter.

Strange deeds, too—and odd facts. Herodotus tells of flying snakes in Arabia, mummification and necrophilia in Egypt, the Scythians' use of cannabis, cauterization bringing good health to Libyan nomads, the Persian custom of burying people alive. He reports on gold-hunting ants in India, why the skulls of the Persians are thicker than those of the Egyptians, the black semen of the Indians and Ethiopians, horses eating snakes, a mare giving birth to a hare, a woman's urine returning to a king his eyesight, the singer Arion being rescued by a dolphin. Was he making these things up, or was he just unable to resist a good story?

Often he will append to a supposed fact or a story that its origin is in hearsay. At times, he expresses incredulity: "I am obliged to tell the things that are said," he writes, "but I am under no obligation to be persuaded by them." He also holds that his "own responsibility, however, as it has been throughout my writing this entire narrative, is simply to record whatever may be told by my sources."

If a story amuses or edifies Herodotus, he stops his narrative to take as many pages as are necessary to tell it. An example is the tale of the Lydian king Candaules's obsession with the beauty of his wife. So obsessed is he that he regularly tells Gyges, favorite among his bodyguards, how devastatingly beautiful she is, and he insists that Gyges, to see that he is not exaggerating, look upon her naked. Despite the bodyguard's reluctance to do so, Candaules positions him so that he may watch her disrobe for bed without being seen. She does see Gyges, however, and the next day she offers him two alternatives: be executed for his trespass or gain possession of her and ascendance to the throne by killing Candaules. Gyges chooses the latter. The plot to kill the king is successful, and Gyges rules for 38 years. Fully four generations later, the Lydian empire, then under the reign of Gyges's descendant Croesus, is destroyed in revenge for the murder of Candaules. The gods in Herodotus tend to have long memories.

Croesus is another figure who captures Herodotus's imagination. In reward for services rendered, Croesus offers Alcmaeon, the founder of the line of Pericles, all the gold he can carry on his person. Wearing a large tunic and loose boots, Herodotus reports, Alcmaeon

> stuffed his legs with as much gold as his boots could hold, and then, after he had filled the fold in his tunic brim-full with gold, he sprinkled gold-dust over the hair on his scalp, shoved some more into his mouth and left the treasury barely able to drag his boots along as he went.

So amused was Croesus at the spectacle that he provided Alcmaeon with double the amount of gold he had taken.

Herodotus, like Jimmy Durante, had a million of 'em. When the Athenian lawmaker Solon visits Lydia, Croesus, after displaying his immense wealth, asks Solon who is the happiest man he knows, fully expecting the answer to be him, Croesus. Instead, Solon cites an Athenian named Tellus: He "lived at a time when his city was particularly well off, he had handsome, upstanding sons, and he ended up a grandfather with all his grandchildren making it to adulthood." Tellus also died well—in battle—and was honored in death by his fellow citizens. Croesus then asks who is the second happiest man. Solon cites two brothers, young men of Argos, prizewinning athletes who brought honor to their mother and died in full knowledge of their own glory.

Solon's point is that one can never say that a man is happy, no matter his wealth and other attainments, until one knows that he died content. The fates are full of strange tricks, and "the heavens will often grant men a glimpse of happiness, only to snatch it away so that not a trace of it remains." Unimpressed, Croesus dismisses Solon; yet the Athenian's wisdom is confirmed in the sadness of Croesus's later life, for he would lose a favored son in a hunting accident, and his empire would eventually be crushed by the Persians.

"There was never a mortal," Herodotus writes, "who did not, right from birth, have misfortune woven into the very fabric of his life—nor will there ever be. Indeed the greater the man the greater the misfortune." Of Cyrus's son Cambyses, the mad king of Persia who murdered his brother and married his sister, and whose own dagger accidentally pierced his thigh causing his death by gangrene, Herodotus writes, "No man has it within himself to turn destiny aside." In the *Histories*, when a ruler laughs at the misfortunes or presumptions of others, it is only a matter of time before fate wipes the smile off his face and his own—usually horrendous—fall arrives. The only hope for men is to see things as they truly are and not to lapse into negligence, over-confidence, or madness through possession of power. Few political leaders in the *Histories* are able to do so. Herodotus writes:

> I shall . . . proceed with the rest of my story recounting cities both lesser and greater, since many of those that were great long ago have become inferior, and some that are great in my own time were inferior before. And so, resting on my knowledge that human prosperity never remains constant, I shall make mention of both without discrimination.

Herodotus believed that divine agency entered into the affairs of men. Oracles play a strong role in the *Histories*. "I would never presume to challenge the veracity of oracles," he writes, "nor would I accept anyone else doing it, either." For Herodotus there was a higher order, a providence whose wisdom often surpassed the understanding of mere mortals and whose power did not always work for the benefit of men.

In Book Three of the *Histories*, seven Persians meet to decide on the best form for their government to take. Arguments are made for and against democracy, oligarchy, and monarchy. Although Herodotus was himself anti-despotic in his politics, Darius, who argues for monarchy and will presently become king, wins out. This, though, is quietly subverted in Book Seven, when the deposed Spartan king Demaratus informs the Persian king Xerxes that, whatever the numbers of his men and ships, the Greeks will not desist from fighting, even if the forces against them are a thousand men to one. The best fighters, Demaratus argues, are free men;

when they are imbued with a *nomos*, or inbred law, they are compelled to fight on, no matter the odds or conditions. They never surrender. Persian soldiers flee when their leaders go down, but Greeks, and especially Spartans, never do. They fight not for their leaders but out of their hatred of slavery and love of their *polis*. Demartus proved correct, of course, as the battles of Thermopylae and Plataea demonstrated.

In Herodotus's view, the Persian plan of continuous expansion doomed their empire from the outset. The Greeks, owing to their belief in honor and civic pride, their love of freedom and independence, and their distrust of too-great opulence, were wary of empire—at any rate, empire on the scale that the Persian kings craved. Later, in a period not covered by the *Histories*, the plans of expansion on the part of the Athenians, when they acquired their maritime empire, would in turn doom them, the debacle in Syracuse putting *fini* to all hopes of further expansion. For Herodotus, instability is the rule of life; the fortunes of countries, like those of men, go up and down. "Human happiness," he writes, "never continues long in one place."

The subject of the *Histories* is the richness of human nature in action. Herodotus's philosophy arises out of the plentitude of his details. This philosophy holds men to be perpetually in peril of overstepping their bounds—bounds set by good sense and reinforced by the gods. Those who do not understand this go under. But even those who understand may not necessarily come to a good end. Herodotus provides story after story proving that human justice is not the first order of the gods. He also demonstrates that superior storytelling is not only the most captivating form of history but also the most entrancing mode of philosophizing.

Tom Holland's new translation of the *Histories* is fluent, readable, nicely paced, and lively. Some would say too lively. Peter Green, in the *London Review of Books*, calls it "uncomfortably chatty." By this he is referring to the sometimes-jarring intrusion of contemporary idiom into the text. So, in the King Candaules story, the king's wife "rumbled" that her husband had planted his bodyguard in her room. When the Lydian king Ardys's attack on a nearby city fails, we read that he is "given a bloody nose." Arion, the man carried to safety by the dolphin, is in his music a "trend-setter" who "raked in a fortune" through his singing. King

Croesus, never wanting a justification for warring against others, could always "manage to rustle up some flimsy pretext."

These examples all come from the first 13 pages of the Holland translation. More egregious ones appear throughout the text, as when Xerxes convenes a meeting of Persian noblemen in order "to pick their brains" and then warns his counselors against "bad-mouthing" his guest-friend Demaratus.

This note of contemporaneity, even vulgar contemporaneity, in the Holland translation can be, as I say, jarring; but it is not, finally, marring. Randall Jarrell once said that "a novel is a prose narrative that has something wrong with it." The same may be said of nearly all translations. None exists, no matter how elevated and meticulous the effort, with which one cannot find fault. A small number of great writers cannot be well translated at all; one thinks here of Henry James, and perhaps also Wallace Stevens. An even smaller number are so great that not even a poor translation can spoil them. Herodotus is of this select company.

Tacitus

(2016)

FOR A MAN WHO DELVED into the lives of others, not all that much is known about the life of Cornelius Tacitus, historian of Rome under the empire. He was born in 56 or 57 CE and is thought to have died around 125 CE. His family came from Narbonensis (the modern Provence), or possibly from Northern Italy, and so he was not Roman by birth. He was what the Romans called a *novus homo*, or new man. He married the daughter of Gnaeus Julius Agricola, the Roman general, a man of the provincial nobility who conquered and brought under Roman suzerainty large swathes of Britain. Apart from birth, skillful oratory was one of the main avenues to advancement in Rome, and Tacitus's brilliance as an orator, attested in a number of letters by his contemporary Pliny the Younger, was of the highest order.

Tacitus was made *quaestor* (one of the lower magistrates), *aedile* (concerned with the care of the city, its corn supply, water, and games), and *praetor* (young men put in charge of important administrative tasks). He may have led a Roman legion and governed a province, possibly in Germany, and was later suffect consul, and then proconsul, in Asia. He sat for many years in the Roman senate, an institution much reduced in importance by Augustus, subsequently shredded of its dignity by later emperors—"Men ready to be slaves," Tiberius called Roman senators of his time—and all but emasculated in Tacitus's day by the emperor Domitian. He was close to 45 before he turned to the writing of history.

In an infrequent insertion of himself into his historical work, Tacitus, in his *Histories*, wrote: "I must not deny that my public career was launched by Vespasian, promoted by Titus, and advanced by Domitian." The odd locution—"I must not deny"—is owing to the fact that his rise under these men, especially under the vicious Domitian, was not something of which a man could be unequivocally proud. The disclaimer was also meant to imply that this would in no way render him intellectually hostage to those who had promoted his career.

In the *Agricola*, his panegyrical monograph on the career of his father-in-law, Tacitus wrote:

> There can be great men even under bad emperors, and that duty and discretion, if coupled with energy and a career of action, will bring a man to no less glorious summits than are obtained by perilous paths and ostentatious deaths that do not benefit the Commonwealth.

True, this, of Agricola; less true, probably, of his son-in-law. Only the rule of the benevolent emperor Trajan allowed Tacitus the freedom to speak and write as he wished. "Modern times are indeed happy, as few others have been," Tacitus wrote of life under Trajan, "for we can think as we please, and speak as we think." As Pliny the Younger put it of the reign of Trajan, under which he had himself flourished: "Now at last men's merits bring them official recognition instead of the danger of the past."

Tacitus has had his critics, among them Voltaire and Napoleon; the latter saw nothing wrong with imperial rule in which the emperor answers to no one. Racine, though, called Tacitus "the finest painter of antiquity." Edward Gibbon, known to slay fellow historians in acidulous footnotes, spoke with unremitting praise of Tacitus, referring to "the discerning eye" and "masterly pencil," calling him "the first of historians who applied the science of philosophy to the study of facts." Gibbon added that "the expressive conciseness of his descriptions has deserved to exercise the diligence of innumerable antiquarians, and to excite the genius and penetration of the philosophic historians of our own times." High marks, these, from the toughest of all historical graders.

Great swathes of Tacitus's writing have gone missing. What parts of his two major works have been lost is a subject of scholarly speculation. Donald R. Dudley, author of *The World of Tacitus*, has asserted that Tacitus's original plan was to cover the years between the principate of Augustus (begun in 27 BCE) to the last year of Domitian (96 CE). This would have accounted for both the Julio-Claudian and the Flavian dynasties.

As things stand, central subjects and events in the Tacitean oeuvre are lost. These include the pages devoted to the maniacal Emperor Gaius, or Caligula. The first six years of the reign of Claudius are absent. The fate of fascinating figures that Tacitus promises to take up later never return because of missing portions of his manuscripts. Of the destruction of Pompeii, all we get is this: "An earthquake also demolished the populous Campanian city town of Pompeii." Gone, too, is the suicide of Nero and the murder, earlier, of Tiberius's cruel henchman Sejanus. Apart from some excoriating paragraphs at the conclusion of the *Agricola*, the immitigably cruel Domitian escapes Tacitus's deft literary scalpel.

Tacitus's two main works are the *Histories* and the *Annals*. The first dealt chiefly with the Roman civil wars of 69 CE, the Year of the Four Emperors, Galba, Otho, Vitellius, and Vespasian; the second is a yearly account, beginning in 14 CE (the year of the death of Augustus) and ending in 68 CE, which takes up the leading Roman events, domestic and foreign, as they occurred. Tacitus remarks that he hoped to go on to recount the reigns of Nerva and Trajan, but whether he did or not, we shall never know. He had earlier published his *Agricola* and his *Germania*, the latter a geographical and ethnological study of the German tribes to the west of Rome; "Germany" at that time included what are today the Czech Republic, Slovakia, Poland, the Baltic countries, and Scandinavia. In part a paean to the barbaric tribes of Germany as noble savages, the *Germania* was used by the Nazis to glorify the German warrior tradition. Finally, one of his first surviving compositions, the *Dialogus*, is a treatise, in dialogue form, on the rudiments and principles of oratory and on its value for intellectual development and personal advancement.

Modern scholars have found in Tacitus inaccuracies, biases, deep stretches of ignorance—see, especially, his few pages on the Jews—but none of this ultimately has diminished the grandeur of what he wrote. The reason is that Tacitus was as fully a literary artist as he was a historian. His was a style that abandoned the periodic sentence, eschewed the flowery, commanded devastating metaphors, lanced pretensions with exquisite irony, selected the perfect details—a style that meted out the just literary punishment for the multiplicity of egregious crimes of which he was chief chronicler. Sir Ronald Syme, his best biographer, calls Tacitus "the crown and summit of imperial literature," and there is no reason to dispute the claim.

About his own motives as a historian, Tacitus was unambiguous. "It seems to me," he wrote in the *Annals*, "a historian's foremost duty is to ensure that merit is recorded, and to confront evil words and deeds with the fear of posterity's denunciations." Tacitus was, in other words, a moralist, with a pessimist's view of human nature and a talent for describing human nature outraged, which, under the rule of the Roman emperors, it frequently was.

"I shall write without indignation or partisanship," he claimed, "in my case the customary incentives to these are lacking." Tacitus felt no personal disappointments, bore no grudges, took no partisan positions. Yet he was a man of pitiless insight with a strong sense of honor and distaste for hypocrisy. Montaigne, who claimed to have read the *Histories* in a single sitting, held that "Tacitus was a great man, upright and courageous, not of a superstitious but of a philosophical and high-minded virtue." This, *ipso facto*, rendered him a relentless critic of Rome under the emperors.

Tacitus understood (as Syme has it) that, since Augustus, "the Roman constitution was a screen and a sham." He never took seriously the pretensions of Augustus, Tiberius, and other emperors that the Roman Republic was still intact. Under the principate, all power rested with one man, the emperor, and the lure of power and its subsequent attainment, with only rare exceptions, brought its own corruptions. In Tacitus, some emperors are better than others; but most soon leave the path of virtue, and all die unhappily.

Describing life under the Caesars restricted Tacitus chiefly to recording cowardly betrayals, petty rivalries of courtesans and freedmen and slaves, acts of vengeance, and horrific cruelty. Assassination, execution, enforced suicide, regicide, patricide, matricide, siblicide—in the Roman Empire, during the first century CE, enormity was business as usual. Recounting the relentless executions and suicides demanded by Nero, Tacitus writes that "this slavish passivity, this torrent of wasted bloodshed far from active service, wearies, depresses, and paralyzes the mind."

Tacitus claimed to envy the historians of the Roman Republic. They

> told of great wars, of the storming of cities, of kings van-
> quished and taken captive; and in home affairs, of the con-
> tentions of tribunes and consuls, of the land laws and corn
> laws, of the struggles of the people with the Senate; it was a
> wide and spacious theme in which they could move with ease.

Montaigne disagreed, arguing that in tracing "the lives of the emperors of his time, so strange and extreme in every way, and the many notable actions that their cruelty in particular produced in their subjects, he had a stronger and more attractive matter to treat and narrate than if he had to tell of battles and universal commotions." Most readers would agree with Montaigne.

Not that Tacitus was entirely condemnatory. To quote Syme again, he knew that "an evil man may be a sagacious ruler; an autocrat is not omnip-otent; a tyrant or a fool may be guided by wise counselors." Good men crop up in his pages, but they are few. Thrasea Paetus, the Stoic philosopher and senator condemned by Nero, was among those Tacitus seems genuinely to have admired; Germanicus, grandson-in-law of Augustus and the adop-tive son of Tiberius, and Corbulo, Nero's successful general, are two others. More than once he apologizes for the grim events he is under obligation to record, but such was life in Roman society, "where to corrupt and to yield to corruption is called living in the fashion of the day."

The degradation of the senate and other political institutions since the time of the republic is a theme that plays through Tacitus. The cause of this degradation was the enlarged powers of the emperors. "From time imme-morial, man has had an instinctive love of power," he wrote in *Histories*.

With the growth of our empire, this instinct has become a dominant and uncontrollable force. It was easy to maintain equality when Rome was weak. Worldwide conquest and the destruction of all rival communities or potentates opened the way to the secure enjoyment of wealth and an overriding appetite for it.

Grand themes interest Tacitus less than shoddy behavior. As a moralist, he is less concerned with economic development or the conditions of the populace than in the drama of human nature as played out by people in power, the men (and sometimes the women) who led Rome during the dark years covered by his histories. The personalities of princes, their wives, consorts, counselors, and enemies dominate his pages.

During the conga line of emperors in 69 CE, one finds one's antipathies nicely divided by the comparative wretchedness of each of Rome's rulers. The line begins with Galba, old and feeble, rumored to be brutal and miserly, dominated by counselors whose crimes further tarnished his legacy. Otho ascended the throne after the assassination of the disappointing Galba, who "by common consent possessed the making of a ruler—had he never ruled." Vitellius next contested Otho for the emperorship. Each shamelessly sucked up to the army, which now, in effect, selected Rome's emperors and for whom money was more important than character.

"Here then," Tacitus writes of Otho and Vitellius, "were the two most despicable men in the whole world by reason of their unclean, idle and pleasure-loving lives, apparently appointed by fate for the task of destroying the empire." In any struggle between the two, he notes, "the only certainty was that the winner would turn out to be worse." Not that the populace was likely to notice: So debased had Roman society become that "few Romans had any capacity to judge or real desire for the public good."

Otho ruled for four months and then, when defeated in battle by Vitellius's troops, took his life by stabbing himself. Not long after, Vitellius was stabbed by one of his own soldiers. His final view was of his jeering troops and the sight of his statues being pulled down from the very spot where Galba was murdered. "Thereupon," writes Tacitus, "he fell lifeless beneath a rain of blows. And still the mob reviled him in death as viciously as they had flattered him while he lived."

Character sketches drawn with masterly concision supply some of the most brilliant passages in Tacitus. "In the delineation of character," Macaulay wrote,

> Tacitus is unrivaled among historians, and has very few superiors among dramatists and novelists. By the delineation of character we do not mean the practice of drawing up epigrammatic catalogues of good and bad qualities, and appending them to the names of eminent men. No writer, indeed, has done this more skillfully than Tacitus; but this is not his peculiar glory. All the persons who occupy a large space in his works have an individuality of character which seems to pervade all their words and actions. We know them as if we lived with them.

"Of audacious character and untiring physique, secretive about himself and ever ready to incriminate others, a blend of arrogance and servility," Tacitus writes of Sejanus, to whom Tiberius entrusted the running of Rome while he was off in Caprae, "he concealed behind a carefully modest exterior an unbounded lust for power." Tacitus calls Sejanus a "small-town adulterer" and notes that the cause of this vicious man's rise to power "was rather heaven's anger against Rome— to which the triumph of Sejanus and his downfall, too, were catastrophic." As for heaven's anger, Tacitus's theodicy was encapsulated in his belief that "Rome's unparalleled suffering supplied ample proof that the gods are indifferent to our tranquility, but eager for our punishment."

Under the empire, women came to wield greater power than under the republic—not, usually, for the better. Livia, the two Agrippinas (older and younger), Messalina, Poppaea, the empowered Roman women are often subtler, but no less cruel, than the men, and equally shorn of virtue. Men used swords, the women's weapons of choice were seduction and poison. Poppaea, who replaced Octavia as Nero's wife and later plotted her murder, is described by Tacitus as having

> every womanly asset except goodness. . . . To her, married or bachelor bedfellows were alike. She was indifferent to her reputation—insensible to men's love and unloving herself. Advantage dictated the bestowal of her favors.

Poppaea died, pregnant, when, in a fit of anger, Nero kicked her in the stomach.

Women in Tacitus are also capable of acts of great courage. A woman named Epicharis, indirectly in on the Pisonian conspiracy against Nero, after a day of excruciating torture strangled herself lest under further torture she betray others. Tacitus writes:

> What admirable courage in a freed slave, in a woman who, doomed to so awful an ordeal, screened by her fidelity people who were strangers, almost unknown to her, while free-born men of a stronger sex, Roman knights and senators, waited not for tortures to betray in mutual emulation their nearest and dearest.

The violence, the sheer bloodiness, of Roman life Tacitus conveys almost by the way. If a company of Roman troops showed cowardice or other dereliction in battle, they risked decimation, in which 1 of every 10 among them was arbitrarily put to death. If a slave killed his master, under Roman law, all the slaves in the household were executed. Such was his rage against Sejanus that Tiberius ordered his friends and all his family executed, including his son and young daughter. Of the daughter, Tacitus reports: "Because capital punishment of a virgin was unprecedented, she was violated by the executioner with the noose beside her."

Tiberius is Tacitus's greatest portrait—a "classic," as Donald R. Dudley calls it, "of denigration." Tiberius is the major figure in the *Annals*, for he reigned for 22 years, longer than any emperor in the Julio-Claudian line except Augustus, who ruled for 40 years. Tacitus's skill at balancing the emperor's cruelty is nicely set off against his deceptive subtlety. Tiberius's paranoia is at the forefront of Tacitus's portrait. Yet he is given credit for his accomplishments: He kept Rome prosperous and at peace. In the portrait provided by Suetonius in his *Lives of the Caesars*, Tiberius is a relatively modest ruler who, once he deserts Rome for Caprae, becomes a monstrous pervert. "Some aspects of his criminal obscenity are almost too vile to discuss," Suetonius writes—and then, of course, discusses them: "Imagine training little boys, whom he called his 'minnows,' to chase him while he went swimming and get between his legs to lick and nibble him." Such, according to Suetonius, was "the filthy old man [Tiberius] had become."

Tacitus reports it was in the year 23 CE that Tiberius, then 65, "turned tyrannical—or gave tyrannical men power." On his perversions, Tacitus omits details, noting only that

> his criminal lusts shamed him. Their uncontrollable activity was worthy of an oriental tyrant. Free-born children were his victims. He was fascinated by beauty, youthful innocence, and aristocratic birth. New names for types of perversion were invented.

These perversions, as Tacitus the literary artist knew, were better imagined than described. The brief obituary of Tiberius in the *Annals* is crushing:

> While he was a private citizen or holding commands under Augustus, his life was blameless. . . . [H]e concealed his real self, cunningly affecting virtuous qualities. However, until his mother [Livia, wife of Augustus] died, there was good in Tiberius as well as evil. Again, as long as he favored (or feared) Sejanus, the cruelty of Tiberius was detested, but his perversions unrevealed. Then fear vanished, and with it shame. Thereafter he expressed his own character by unrestrained crime and infamy.

Attempts have been made by modern historians to rehabilitate the reputation of Tiberius, but Tacitus's portrait lives on, persuasive both as history and as great literature.

"A degenerate ruler," wrote the historian Sallust (86–35 BCE), "is always supplanted by better men than himself." Sallust did not live long enough to see his maxim refuted under the principate. Of the emperors who followed Tiberius, Caligula and Claudius had much blood on their hands. Nero, who took up rule at the age of 17 at the death of his adoptive father Claudius, brought Roman decadence to new heights. He was the first Roman emperor to live on borrowed eloquence, for his former tutor, the Stoic philosopher Seneca, was his speechwriter. Nero would eventually order Seneca's suicide. No great crime, this, for an emperor who had earlier arranged for the deaths of his stepbrother Britannicus and his mother Agrippina.

Tacitus writes of Nero's reign: "Even in good surroundings people find it difficult to behave well. Here every form of immorality competed for attention, and no chastity, modesty, or vestige of decency could survive." For those who like to discover past history foreshadowing the present, Nero, toward the end of his reign, staged a wedding in which, Tacitus writes, "the emperor, in the presence of witnesses, put on the bridal veil. Dowry, marriage bed, marriage torches, all were there. Indeed everything was public which even in a natural union is veiled by night."

Everywhere Tacitus saw "striking proofs of the nature of fortune, whose treacherous surface combines the peak and the abyss." He held that "the more I think about history, ancient or modern, the more ironical all human affairs seem." The Roman notion of the afterlife, murky at best, held that men lived on only in the memory of their accomplishments or of their evil deeds. Recording those accomplishments and deeds in memorable language has also allowed Tacitus to live on, unsurpassed among Roman historians and, alongside Herodotus and Thucydides, one of the three great historians of antiquity.

Encyclopaedia Britannica— The Eleventh

(2016)

NCYCLOPEDIA, in its root definition, means circle of knowledge. Pliny the Elder (23–79 CE), perhaps the world's first encyclopedist, used the word to describe his "Natural History." The circle implies all-round education, which in turn suggests everything worth knowing, hence omniscience. In 1751, under Denis Diderot and Jean d'Alembert, the famous French *Encylopédie* began publication with roughly this ambitious intention. Seventeen years later, in Edinburgh, a printer and antiquary named William Smellie brought out the first of a three-volume set of books under the title *Encyclopaedia Britannica*, a work that would see its final print version—32,640 pages in 32 volumes—published in 2010. We all live now of course with that useful, if not always reliable, hodgepodge called Wikipedia.

Self-improvement is at the heart of the encyclopedic enterprise. People certified with degrees from what the world considers the best universities and colleges sometimes forget that we are all autodidacts, on our own in the endless attempt to patch over the extraordinary gaps in our knowledge. Doing so in an efficient way is the promise held out by an encyclopedia, which claims to provide all the world's pertinent knowledge, right there in 24, 29, 32 volumes, usually with a bookcase thrown in at no extra charge.

Encyclopedias, and by extension encyclopedists, can and have had their not especially hidden agendas. The French Encyclopédie was, in effect, a house organ for the Enlightenment; its editors wished to change the way people thought, which meant that they wanted to secularize learning, thereby striking a blow against the educational dominance of the Jesuits. The program of many lesser encyclopedias was more straightforward: to make a profit. The one encyclopedia that set out to do both, show a profit while embodying the spirit of its age, was the Eleventh Edition of the *Encyclopaedia Britannica* (1910–1911).

The Eleventh was the last great encyclopedia. Its greatness derived not alone from its contributors or its organization but from the spirit infusing it. This spirit was one of confidence in progress—material, scientific, artistic, if not religious then spiritual. The society in which the Eleventh was composed and published considered itself, as Denis Boyles notes in *Everything Explained That Is Explainable*, to be "the Rome to the long nineteenth-century's Greece, an era in which engineers spoke the language of visionaries. And it was English."

English the Eleventh Edition indubitably was, in its principal editors, in the vast majority of its contributors, in its imperialist confidence. Behind the scenes, though, the work was the inspiration of an American huckster named Horace Everett Hooper. A huckster with a difference, Hooper was also an idealist: He was wily for the public good, or at least that portion of the public intent on its own educational betterment.

In American publishing, the decades preceding the appearance of the Eleventh were marked by highbinders and sidewinders. Pirating English books was all but standard practice. (Charles Dickens, much aggrieved by these offenses when practiced upon his own books, demonstrated his grievance in his novel *Martin Chuzzlewit*, a chronicle of American operators and charlatans.) In this freewheeling publishing atmosphere, Mr. Boyles reports, the English *Encyclopaedia Britannica* was "a very lucrative target." The encyclopedia had better sales in the United States than in England. The hunger for self-improvement among Americans made *Britannica* fine game for publishing poachers, who served it up to their readers in revised and bogus versions. "Entries," Mr. Boyles writes, "were edited, omitted, and added at will, and sometimes without much regard for quality."

Over the years, the cachet of the *Encyclopaedia Britannica* never waned; only its profits did. "The *Britannica*," Mr. Boyles writes, "had brought prestige, but not much profit, to every proprietor and publisher who had touched it since its first appearance in 1768." As *Britannica* increased in size over the years, selling it became all the more difficult. Horace Everett Hooper had ideas about how to change this. One of the poachers would soon become the gamekeeper.

Among the books Hooper sold in America were various versions of the Ninth Edition of *Britannica*. He not only sold it but was immensely impressed by it. Much therein was worthy of admiration. The Ninth Edition of *Britannica*, brought out in 25 volumes between 1875 and 1889, represented a dazzling anthology of English writing. Articles ran to 40,000 words and some to the length of small books. Among its contributors were James Bryce, Matthew Arnold, William Morris, John Stuart Mill, and Robert Louis Stevenson. (Contributors to the Seventh Edition had included William Hazlitt, Thomas Malthus, Walter Scott, and Mill.) The Ninth Edition was one of the splendid achievements of the Victorian Age.

Horace Hooper, Mr. Boyles writes, "understood that his business wasn't just selling books. It was monetizing authority." An Anglophile, Hooper took it upon himself to improve the sales of *Britannica* in England by leashing it to that other grand English editorial institution, the *Times*. Such was the authoritativeness of the *Times* that in some foreign countries its correspondents were thought more powerful than the English ambassador. "The *Times*," Mr. Boyles writes, "was as imperishable a part of national life as the Church of England, though more widely believed." Despite its towering prestige, the *Times* was a financial loser. Hooper intervened with a plan by which the two, newspaper and encyclopedia, could each profit.

On the business side, the fortunes of the *Times* began to change when a man named Charles Moberly Bell, who had earlier been a cotton merchant and a *Times* correspondent in Egypt, became the paper's business manager and began to put its financial house in order. The idea of rescuing the *Times* through its sponsoring of a revised version of the Ninth

Edition was Hooper's. If the *Times* would permit him to sell the old Ninth Edition of *Britannica* under its auspices—in what would be called a *Times* edition—it would gain serious sums in royalties while *Britannica* would gain allure and sales leads through its association with the *Times*.

Britannica soon thereafter moved its editorial offices to the top floor of the *Times* building at London's Printing House Square. Hooper brought aboard an advertising adept named Henry R. Haxton, a Hearst journalist of bohemian spirit who counted among his friends Ambrose Bierce, James Whistler, and Stephen Crane and who didn't mind pushing the pedal all the way down on his advertising copy. In effusive, highly colored prose, Haxton's ads suggested that people must acquire the *Encyclopaedia Britannica* or remain forever benighted. As Mr. Boyles puts it, Haxton made it seem "that the *Britannica* was not just a book, it was a cure."

In 1903, Hooper and Haxton devised a contest called "The *Times* Competition," whereby readers of the newspaper were asked to answer, in essay form, questions on subjects of general information. Prizes amounting to £3,585 were offered, first among them a full four-year scholarship to Oxford or Cambridge. Haxton claimed in advertisements that those who entered the competition would acquire "Closer concentration of mind, Practice in ready reasoning, Quickness in finding facts, A new form of recreation, An invaluable fund of general information." One could not pick up the questions at the *Times* offices but had to mail in one's request. Readers wise in the ways of salesmanship will grasp that this provided an astonishing list of leads for selling the Ninth Edition. These were used, in the best full-court-press salesmanship, to inundate possible customers for *Britannica* with mail and even telegrams. "From my bath, I curse you" was the reply of one such recipient of these sales tactics. But the general public response was, in Mr. Boyles's words, "immediate and overwhelming."

Some might view this as commercial genius, but to many Englishmen of the day it was American vulgarity let loose and a besmirching of the dignity of the *Times*. By such heavy-breathing advertising and promotions, Hooper and Charles Moberly Bell, both victims of English upper-class xenophobia, withstood insults and resistance, but their methods eventually brought the *Times* out of the red. The Hooper innovation of selling *Britannica* on the installment plan was no small help. Mr. Boyles estimates that Hooper and a business partner named Walter Montgomery Jackson cleared more than a million dollars between them and the *Times*—measured by today's exchange rate, something like £6.5 million.

The editor of the revised Ninth Edition and later of the Eleventh—the edition called the Tenth was actually the Ninth with nine supplemental volumes added—was a literary journalist named Hugh Chisholm. Sharing Hooper's idealism, Chisholm felt that *Britannica* was "the best way of democratizing self-education." He coordinated the gargantuan project of the Ninth Edition, whose immensity entailed 1,507 contributors, a staff of 64 assistant editors, some 40,000 articles and an index of roughly 500,000 entries, the whole weighing in at 250 pounds. Along with being a brilliant editorial manager, Chisholm was a trenchant writer. Mr. Boyles quotes him from his *Britannica* entry on Lord Acton:

> Lord Acton has left too little completed original work to rank among the great historians; his very learning seems to have stood in his way; he knew too much and his literary conscience was too acute for him to write easily, and his copiousness of information overloads his literary style. But he was one of the most deeply learned men of his time, and he will certainly be remembered for his influence on others.

In a highly readable style, nicely seasoned with occasional ironic touches, Denis Boyles limns the intricate business negotiations that went into the creation of the Eleventh Edition. He chronicles *Britannica*'s departure from the *Times* after Lord Northcliffe acquired the newspaper in 1908; its being taken up by Cambridge University, until that university's Syndics found its marketing measures too garish; and its sale, in 1920, to Sears, Roebuck in the United States, which sold it chiefly through its catalog.

Mr. Boyles provides excellent portraits of the key figures responsible for the 19th- and early-20th-century editions of *Britannica*. His last chapter is given over to the Eleventh's mishandling, owing to its having been a work of its time, of such key, and in our day super-sensitive, subjects as Women, African-Americans, Native Americans, Asians, Arabs, and its difficulties with Catholic and Protestant readers. None of this finally diminishes the overall accomplishment that is *Encyclopaedia Britannica*'s

Eleventh Edition. Mr. Boyles ends by asserting that the ethos of progress that undergirded the Eleventh was put paid to by World War I:

> Even the most visionary Edwardians would never have ventured to guess that a deeply held belief in the ideology of Progress would lead eventually to the first twenty-four hours of the Battle of the Somme.

The élan of the Eleventh Edition would never be regained. In the United States the set was marketed differently, chiefly by door-to-door salesman, whose pitch was less to self-education than to the guilt of parents concerned about the social mobility of their children. Prestige, though, still clung to the encyclopedia: Well into the 20th century, the person who wrote the *Britannica* article on any given subject was thought to be the world's leading authority on that subject.

In 1943, Sears wished to unload the *Encyclopaedia Britannica* and donated it to the University of Chicago. Robert Hutchins, then president of the university, didn't see how an intellectual institution could also run and sell such a work, so he offered it for a derisive sum to William Benton, a former advertising man who was then his vice president for public affairs, with the university to receive a handsome royalty. At Benton's death in 1973, these royalties had amounted to $47.8 million.

Business was carried on as usual until 1968, when Benton hired Sir William Haley as the editor in chief of *Britannica*. Haley had been a director of the *Manchester Guardian*, the director-general of the BBC and editor-in-chief of the *Times*—a résumé that could have been completed in its perfection only by his having also been editor of the *Oxford English Dictionary*. I was one of Sir William's senior editors and held him in the highest esteem. A cultivated man of gravity and wide knowledge, he planned to expand *Britannica*'s coverage and raise its literary and intellectual quality through his connections with Isaiah Berlin, Hugh Trevor-Roper, and other members of a remarkable generation of English philosophers, historians, and scientists.

The *Encyclopaedia Britannica* under Sir William Haley figured to be a splendid set of books, a rival, perhaps, to the great Eleventh Edition. Alas, it was not to be. Corporate politics worked against Haley, who departed the company. (When I left not long after, he wrote to me: "I am glad you have departed the *Britannica*; they worship different gods than we.") Robert Hutchins, the one man with influence over Benton, contrived to elevate his old sidekick Mortimer Adler to the directorship of a vastly revised *Britannica*. Once in charge Adler, a man whose high IQ was matched only by his low sensibility, twisted the set into separate volumes of longer and shorter entries, called respectively the Macropaedia and the Micropaedia, with a vast index volume called the Propaedia. The result was an intellectually tidy and not especially readable work. The great day of *Britannica*'s distinction was done and, after the advent of the Internet, would never return. You can look it up.

Grammar

(2014)

GRAMMAR IS NOT EVERYBODY'S IDEA of a good time. Thanks to the remarkable inefficiencies of the Chicago public school system, I was able to steer happily clear of the subject until college. Until then, the entirety of my grammatical knowledge included beginning a sentence with a capital letter and ending it with a period and never using the word "ain't." Commas to me were so many gnats strewn upon sheets of printed paper, a colon was an internal organ, and a dash a synonym for just a touch of ketchup or mustard. As for the semicolon, my understanding of it was equal to my understanding of Mandarin Chinese, in which, for all I knew, it might have passed as a letter.

Part of the problem here is youth, which is often unprepared to receive knowledge that does not immediately excite. How, after all, could a male adolescent, hormones churning, care about a dangling participle when his own participle so seldom dangled? I could scarcely have told you what a split infinitive was because I had no notion of what an infinitive might be. If a sentence wished to run on, hey, that was fine by me. Ask me the meaning of the genitive, the ablative or the gerundive and I would probably reply that it is not nice to mix with Mr. Inbetween. Grammar, fair to say, was not my long suit.

I first learned grammar through instruction in French by a modest man named Philip Kolb, who I subsequently learned was the editor, in French, of the letters of Marcel Proust. Only later, gradually, did I pick up the rudiments of English grammar. When I was a university teacher in a department of English, I corrected my students' obvious lapses in grammar, but I should certainly never correct anyone else's grammar, in public or private, nor do I deign to correct that of the contemporary authors whose books I occasionally review. The critic John Simon has made rather a speciality of this. I once met a man who told me that John corrected a toast he gave at a wedding.

I used the word "speciality" in the penultimate sentence of my last paragraph, and not the word "specialty," and straightaway became a touch nervous. H. W. Fowler, whose magisterial *Modern English Usage* I keep near my desk, informs me that it is all right to do so. The two words, he reports, seem to call out for differentiation, though little progress has been made in achieving it, and "writers use either form for any of the senses according as they prefer its sound in general or find it suits the rhythm of a sentence." The wrestle with language, like that with conscience, is unending.

Not the least notable thing about *Gwynne's Grammar*, the work of Neville Martin Gwynne, an English businessman and earlier an Etonian who went on to Oxford, is that it spent some time on best-seller lists in Britain. What makes this all the more extraordinary is that the book is a textbook, one with no pictures—"pictures in textbooks," Mr. Gwynne writes, "actually interfere with the learning process"—and with not the least wisp of dumbing-down in its composition.

Mr. Gwynne does not deny that grammar can be hellishly complicated. "Rather," he writes,

> the encouragement that I offer is that whatever work is involved is overwhelmingly worth it and also that this work gradually becomes progressively easier as the skills involved become more habitual and indeed as making the necessary effort becomes more habitual.

If any criticism might be made of *Gwynne's Grammar*, it might be about the extravagance of its author's promises. Mr. Gwynne holds that grammar is crucial to clear thinking, which may well be right. He also claims that "the rules [of grammar] always have a logic underpinning them," which, alas, isn't always the case. In a five-step syllogism, he contends that "grammar is the science of using words rightly, leading to thinking rightly, leading to deciding rightly, without which—as both common sense and experience show—happiness is impossible." Improvement in grammar, he also argues, unfailingly affects "both mind and character." All of which, as the English say, sounds like overegging the pudding.

On the underegging side, Mr. Gwynne writes that there is "virtually nothing original in [his book] except its manner of presentation." This manner is simple enough. Mr. Gwynne defines the parts of speech, the elements of punctuation, and the grammar of writing verse (once considered a standard practice of the cultivated). He then follows up in each instance with examples of these things both properly and improperly used. His definitions—terse, logical, precise—are among the best things in the book. He defines a definition—not an easy thing to do—as "a statement of the exact meaning of a word or phrase that sufficiently distinguishes it from any other word or phrase, preferably in the fewest possible words." A sentence "is most comprehensively defined as a word or group of words expressing a complete statement, wish, command or question, whether as a thought or in speech or in writing." He defines grammar as "being simply the correct use of words."

As Mr. Gwynne moves into the subtler elements of grammar, he sets out the range and use of verbs and their tenses, the basic rules of syntax, the mechanics of punctuation. With his customary precision, he guides his readers through the arcana of the subjunctive and introduces the notion of modal verbs. He makes the clean distinction between a clause and phrase by noting that a clause is a phrase with a verb in it, a phrase a clause without a verb. He takes up the active and passive and those troublesome fraternal twins, transitive and intransitive.

Something quite new to me is Mr. Gwynne's dictum on the placement of multiple adjectives, according to which adjectives of opinion come before those of size, which come before those of age, which come before those of shape, which come before those of color, which come before those of origin, which come before those of material purpose.

His illustrative sentence on this point runs: "The book you are holding is therefore a nice little just-published oblong-shaped attractively colored much needed hardcover grammar textbook."

Memorization is a strong element in the Gwynne pedagogical method. He insists on the importance of readers memorizing his definitions and rules. He believes the rote method of learning, currently much despised, essential to acquiring grammar. Returning to that ordering of adjectives, I had myself thought to memorize it but found I could not. But, then, my little gray cells, unlike those of Inspector Poirot, may not be in top condition.

The personality of its author is not the least attraction of *Gwynne's Grammar*. Mr. Gwynne is unflinchingly, unapologetically rear-guard. Straight out of the gate he announces that "the word to indicate whether anyone is male or female is 'sex,' not 'gender,' which is purely a grammatical term," an assertion that, if taken up, would wipe out every Gender Studies program in American universities. Excepting the need for new words for new things, he is against any changes in language that "are not in the direction of greater richness, clarity, and precision." His position on splitting infinitives is to note that "Shakespeare never needed to split an infinitive," with the implication that therefore neither should we. Case closed.

Mr. Gwynne's literary opinions are no less firmly held. He attacks Ezra Pound and T. S. Eliot for setting verse free. Late in the book he remarks, though by this point he need scarcely do so, "I am not an innovator. On the contrary, my position throughout this book is that of defender and promoter of what has been shown to work over long periods of time and what is real."

N. M. Gwynne and Steven Pinker, the author of *The Sense of Style*, would not, fair to say, be ideal cabin mates on a lengthy cruise along the Mediterranean. For Mr. Pinker, Mr. Gwynne would qualify supremely for what in his book he calls a "language grump," or "pedant," or "anal retentive," or "Miss Thistlebottom," his term for the type of old-fashioned school marm. For Mr. Gwynne, Mr. Pinker would be written off as a man with no literary standard, a mere psycholinguist and cognitive scientist, which at Harvard is what Mr. Pinker is. As teachers, Mr. Gwynne is a suit-and-tie man, Mr. Pinker, I should imagine, an open-collar guy. Mr. Gwynne makes no effort to charm; Mr. Pinker perhaps overestimates his own charm. Mr. Pinker is at ease using such words and phrases as "feedback," "fun facts," "case-selection circuitry"; he advises his readers to think of grammar as "the original sharing app." Mr. Pinker is a man who goes with the flow, Mr. Gwynne a man who wishes to stop that flow, dead, in midstream.

A psycholinguist, I take it, is someone who investigates the psychological uses and implications of language; a cognitive scientist someone who studies all that has to do with the mechanics of thought, from within the brain and beyond. In "The Sense of Style" Mr. Pinker brings both these endeavors to bear on a book that sets out to improve writing style chiefly through considering the capacity and needs of readers. How much confusion can a reader accommodate is the central question in his book, and how best to eliminate that confusion is his goal. "The curse of knowledge," he writes, in a chapter devoted to the needless complexity of much academic and scientific prose, "is the single best explanation I know of why good people write bad prose."

Unlike Mr. Gwynne, Mr. Pinker does not blame the Internet for the barbarization of the young and the encouragement of slovenly writing habits. He believes there are many occasions in which one not only may but is well advised to split infinitives. He holds, with Calvin Trillin, that the person who invented the word "whom" had little more in mind than to have those who use it sound like butlers. Mr. Pinker thinks, contra Mr. Gwynne, that it is not always true that "good prose always leads to good thinking." In his book, he occasionally uses cartoons and tells old jokes to reinforce and underscore points. He does not feel that sloppy writing bodes the end of civilization and suggests, if he does not come right out and say it, that those who do may require psychotherapy.

Many of the long-standing rules about grammar and usage that Mr. Pinker's language grumps get worked up about—ending a sentence with a preposition, using "decimate" to mean anything other than wiping out a tenth, and many others—he considers little more than *bubbe mieses*, Yiddish for grandmother's tales. Where Mr. Gwynne stresses the importance of etymology, Mr. Pinker highlights the fallacy of etymology, pointing out that "*deprecate* used to mean 'ward off by prayer,' *meticulous* once meant 'timid,' and silly went from 'blessed' to 'pious' to 'innocent' to 'pitiable' to 'feeble' to today's 'foolish.'" Etymology in defense of restricted meanings, in other words, is for him no defense.

All this makes Messrs. Gwynne and Pinker sound like stalwart opponents in the old battle between the Prescriptivists and the Descriptivists, or between those who believe the rules of grammar and usage ought to be rigidly prescribed and enforced and those who believe that common use dictates regular changes in the rules and in the meanings of words. But Mr. Pinker argues that this battle is ultimately phony, a myth. Few rules in the realms of grammar and usage hold up as true rules; they are instead, in his view, "tacit conventions." The last third of *The Sense of Style* is devoted to demolishing the most cherished of putative rules of grammar and usage; he does this by coming up with exceptional cases that do not prove but blow up the rules. Of the age-old distinction between the words "can" and "may," he holds that "the distinction is usually moot, and the two words may (or can) be used more or less interchangeably."

Such quotations are made all the more compelling because of Mr. Pinker's linguistical learning, which is considerable. His knowledge of grammar is extensive and runs deep. He also takes a scarcely hidden delight in exploding tradition. He describes his own temperament as "both logical and rebellious." Few things give him more pleasure than popping the buttons off what he takes to be stuffed shirts.

Mr. Pinker makes a useful distinction between formal and informal writing and speech, and claims—who could dispute him?—that ours is an age of informality. He seeks to have academics write less woodenly, and especially less obscurely. Not inflexible in his rebellion, he often sensibly suggests staying with conventional usage lest one offend the easily enraged "gotcha" crowd by departing from it. He does not argue that anything goes but instead fills his readers in on the fact that they are already freer in their use of language than they might have thought. He wants them unfettered by hollow dicta. All this should be liberating.

Why, I wonder, isn't it, at least not for me? I would find making use of Mr. Pinker's loosening of the rules, as Robert Frost said of the writing of free verse, like playing tennis without a net. I feel a certain elegance in what I have been taught and still take to be correct English, and so, except when doing so results in a barbarous construction, I choose never to split an infinitive. I prefer not to end my sentences with prepositions because I have learned that the best-made sentences tend to close on strong words. "Disinterested" for me will always mean "impartial"; "literate" will mean "able to read and write," not "reasonably well-read." I plan to continue to observe the old distinction between the words "can" and "may," to use "each other" when referring to two people and "one another" when referring to more than two, and I'm sticking with "directly" or "soon" as the only meanings of the word "presently." As for the reader, that figure with whom Mr. Pinker is most concerned—I've never met the guy and therefore feel no obligation to make things all that much easier for him. All I owe him is clarity and such relief as I can provide him from boredom. In the end I write for myself and for anyone who cares to eavesdrop on my conversations in prose with myself.

Rather than align myself with the Gwynnians or the Pinkertons, I say a blessing on both their houses, and I would add: Let the language battles between them rage on—except that to do so would expose me to the charge of ending this composition on a preposition, which I cannot allow.

Clichés

(2015)

"**M**OTHER,**"** asks 10-year-old Johnny upon returning from school, "do I have a cliché on my face?"

"A cliché on your face? Whatever do you mean, Johnny?"

"A cliché," he answers, "you know, a tired expression."

Johnny nailed it: Clichés are tired expressions. Their fatigue comes from their having been overused, and often badly used. They are words and phrases that no longer carry much meaning and have even less force. They reveal mental laziness on the part of those who use them. They are despoilers of style. Using clichés is like dressing out of the dirty-laundry bag—someone else's dirty-laundry bag.

Who is to say what is a cliché? Some clichés are obvious, of course, like throwing that baby out with the bathwater or watching someone like a hawk. But others are in doubt. Has "boots on the ground" now achieved cliché status? Has "go-to guy" arrived there? And what about "take," as in "what's your take on the subject?" Until recently, a cliché was what arbiters of language claimed it was, and, being arbiters, they could sometimes be arbitrary.

This has now changed, owing to modern computational lexicography, which allows linguists to gather statistical evidence on how frequently words and phrases are used, and in what combinations, and by whom, and in what settings. Overuse alone does not always mark a cliché. According to Orin Hargraves, a lecturer in linguistics who works on computational analysis of language at the University of Colorado, "It is often misapplication, rather than frequency of application, that leads to the perception of a phrase as a cliché." In *It's Been Said Before*, Hargraves sets out as his criteria for clichés that

> they are frequent, often used without regard to their appropriateness, and they may give a general or inaccurate impression of an idea that could often benefit by being stated more succinctly, clearly, or specifically—or in some cases, by not being stated at all.

Clichés can, of course, be clever, and some contain a fairly high truth quotient. Many clichés began life as dazzling metaphors or scintillating similes. The Bible and Shakespeare, an old joke has it, are magnificent, but contain way too many clichés. Clichés can also be useful for spinning off, reversing, and doubling back on, for comic results. Maurice Bowra once remarked that an overly friendly Oxford don had given him "the warm shoulder." Philip Larkin, after leaving his first librarian job in the provincial town of Wellington, which he described as "a hole of toads' turds," wrote, "I'd have missed it for anything." I have been known sometimes to introduce my wife as my "better three quarters."

As Hargraves acknowledges, clichés are long-lived. They offer ready refuge to the unoriginal. Speakers find them useful in connecting with audiences. He notes:

> Many, perhaps most, writers must resort to cliché from time to time in order to connect with their readers in a way that formal language, often barren of cliché, does not allow them to do.

Is it a cliché to say that clichés are always ready to hand? Whether it is or not, they are.

Orin Hargraves is, by self-designation, a "cliché-killer," out to divest the English language of as many clichés as possible by highlighting their illogic and ridiculing their stupidity. Excellent cliché hit-man though he is, he realizes that the job cannot be done with anything like thoroughness and that most clichés will live on; he even believes that some clichés deserve to do so, if only because they can put people at ease by their informality and familiarity. "None of these judicious uses of cliché," he writes, "if kept in check, is objectionable." He distinguishes between clichés and proverbs, and he does not regard as clichés those idioms that do the job of precise expression more economically than lengthier phrasing, among them "shed light," "leaps and bounds," and "part and parcel." His larger intention here is to bring about a greater awareness of the inanity of most clichés and to point out "the detriment that they typically represent to effective communication."

The great swamp in which clichés nest, it will surprise no one to learn, is journalism, which, Hargraves writes, "has been historically and continues to be the true home of the cliché." As such, journalists are also the great vectors, or spreaders, of cliché. If anything, more clichés show up in contemporary journalism than ever before because of the increased absence at budget-restricted newspapers of that necessary drudge, the copy editor. Hargraves also finds the blogosphere to be "particularly rich in cliché today," and for the same reason: want of editing. He doesn't mention the Twitterverse, but given its need for quick and clipped communication, clichés to the tweeter are, as one might have said before reading Hargraves's book, as meat and drink.

After its introductory chapters, *It's Been Said Before* is organized into seven chapters, four by grammatical function (nominal, adverbial, adjectival, and predicate clichés) and three by semantic function (as framing devices, modifiers, and collocations). Within each of these chapters, clichés are listed in alphabetical order, followed by a core meaning of the cliché, usually three examples of it in use, and a brief paragraph about the cost of using the cliché. A chapter of afterthoughts closes out the book, beginning with its author's acknowledgement that it would be a peculiar kind of reader who had read all that precedes it. I, as a reviewer, am, by duty, that peculiar reader; but Hargraves's point here is to underscore that he has produced a volume best used as a work of reference. If a writer thinks he is striding into cliché country in his own work, he can consult this book's index to see if a particular phrase is listed there, then turn to the appropriate page to determine why it has gained its shabby status as a cliché.

The first thing a reading of *It's Been Said Before* conveys is how pervasive are clichés. In the mine-filled field of language—where grammatical error, semantic imprecision, and misusage abound—clichés are buried everywhere. In the work of some fearless writers, cliché explosions go off in every paragraph, though these scribblers seem neither to notice nor to mind.

Although Hargraves has looked into thousands of clichés over the two years he spent studying them, he has assembled and dispatched (by my rough count) 517 notable clichés for this book. A few were new to me: "jump the shark," for one; "shift the dynamic," for another. A small handful of my own favorites are missing: "a teachable moment," "a paradigm shift," "totally awesome," "a window of opportunity," and the single word "fraught," which, whenever I come upon it, makes me think of Fraughty the Snowman.

Harvgraves is neither a belletrist nor a language curmudgeon. Not the least wisp of snobbery clings to his pages. He does not set out to reform the English language and its use. What he intends, he tells us in his final chapter, is to call to the attention of interested readers and writers the need to excise from prose those deposits of stale language that come in the form of clichés and that block, if they do not sometimes befuddle, clear communication. He wants his readers to "write mindfully"—mindful, that is, of when their own language is precise and lively and when wobbly and deadening.

> The best way to ensure that your writing is as good as you can make it . . . is simply to consult your imagination and judgment as you write and take note of whether you are using an expression that has found its way into the stream simply because it's always there, swirling lifelessly in an eddy, where it was recently deposited by some other writer you have read.

Orin Hargraves also happens to be an amusing man, never more so than when he is in sarcastic mode, slashing away at clichés. Some clichés, for Hargraves, are "swayback workhorses"; others come from "the fetid stew of clichédom." In response to the cliché "the elephant in the room," he writes: "Elephants in rooms outnumber elephants in Africa by nearly twenty to one." Let us forget that "800-pound gorilla," which, if found in the same room with one of those elephants, can make for a densely packed room and provide serious housekeeping problems. Of "meteoric rise," he notes, with astronomy on his side, that meteors usually fall. "Slippery slope" he allows has the appeal of alliteration but not much else. He excoriates "bright eyed and bushy tailed" by remarking that it contains "a lot of syllables for a small idea." Using the phrase "a whole host" is "a sure sign that you are running to the nearest exit from the theater of engaged thought."

The cliché "for all intents and purposes" suffers from the people who use it not being able "to separate *intents* from *purposes*." He notes that "totally overcome" is the "absolutely fantastic" of a younger generation. Of "sound the death knell," he notes that the "poor little knell" is much overworked and that the cliché, if used at all, ought perhaps only to be used in the past tense. On "time to think outside the box" he writes that it is "time to think outside the box about 'think outside the box.'"

Because Hargraves organizes his catalogues of clichés by function and not subject, there is no separate listing of the preponderance of clichés in certain fields. Sports clichés are one such field, though "sports clichés" might itself be a redundancy, for, deprived of their clichés, broadcasters and sportswriters would be out of work. Five prominent clichés that have their origins in sports that Harvgraves notes are "game changer," "on steroids," "the whole nine yards," "take it to the next level," and "touch base." A sixth is "ballpark figure," which Hargraves doesn't include. "Going forward" is not a cliché exclusive to sports—Hargraves cites it as "now irresistible to politicians, business spokespersons, and even sports journalists, all of whom use it in preference to a number of plainer expressions such as *now, in the future,* and *from now on*"—but athletes who have been caught doping, beating up wives or girlfriends, or toting guns all do seem to have one thing in common: the wish to put it all behind them and "just go forward."

The only directly political cliché that occurs in *It's Been Said Before* is "staunch conservative/Republican." If Orin Hargraves has a politics, he has kept his book free of them. Regarding this cliché, he notes that

> instances of *staunch conservative/Republican* outnumber
> *staunch liberals/Democrats* by nearly four to one, suggesting

that the users of these phrases are speaking or writing for-
mulaically—or alternatively and not very persuasively, that
liberals and Democrats are less steadfast in their principles
and so do not merit the *staunch* label.

Another possibility—one I favor—is that the word "staunch" here really
stands for unbending, if not fanatic. In this reading, conservatives and
Republicans are staunch, while liberals and Democrats, more reasonably,
are merely steady and flexible.

Which brings to mind a pair of linked clichés from the years of the Ronald Reagan presidency, during which so many of Reagan's budget items
were "savage cuts" that had "chilling effects." In those days, one couldn't
pick up the *New York Times* without finding those "savage cuts" causing
yet more and more "chilling effects." So many chilling effects were in the
air that it seemed a mistake to read the *Times* without wearing gloves and a
muffler lest one catch cold.

The attraction to clichés is akin to what H. W. Fowler called "vogue
words," which he defined as words that emerge "from obscurity, or even
from nothingness or a merely potential and not actual existence, into
sudden popularity." Vogue words soon enough morph—is "morph"
itself such a word?—into clichés. "Tipping point" is an example. Hargraves writes that "tipping points first came to light in considerable
numbers in the 1960s and today people and situations reach them all
the time," adding that before the phrase came into vogue, "there were
more straws breaking camels' backs." The word "outliers" is another
vogue word headed on its way to the unhappy hunting ground of cliché
country. Many such vogue words—which are really little more than
new clichés—have been loosed upon the world through the books of
the journalist-sociologist Malcolm Gladwell.

Outside the ken of *It's Been Said Before* is the role that clichés play
beyond the written or spoken word. Clichés directly affecting life also
exist, exerting genuine pressure on people and often determining crucial
decisions for them. For years, the term "middle class" had this kind of
cliché standing, and what it stood for was dullness, safe-playing, a com-
fortable but empty existence, selling out. The reigning impulse for many

people under the sway of the tyranny of this cliché was to avoid being, or even seeming, middle class, no matter how truly middle class they were. As we now know, without a solid middle class, and without large sections of the populace regularly ascending into it, the country is in jeopardy.

"Midlife crisis" is another such cliché, fading perhaps a bit by now, but once explaining, and thereby half justifying, all sorts of stupid behavior, chiefly on the part of men, from buying red convertibles to taking up with women 30 years younger than themselves. "Reinventing oneself" is yet another, more contemporary, cliché, suggesting that one's life can fairly easily be changed, quickly rendering one a new and happier person, as if human character were so plastic, so malleable.

The only way to ward off clichés in speech and writing, as Hargraves suggests, is to use your imagination and judgment. The same applies to clichés in life, with the added and sometimes painful necessity of consulting reality before being taken in by any of them.

Literary Rivals

(2015)

IF THE REASON academic arguments are waged at a pitch of such high intensity is that the stakes are so low, the reason writers are so disputatious with other writers is that they cannot abide rivals. The famously ill-tempered Evelyn Waugh set out some of the reasons for this when he wrote:

> Humility is not a virtue propitious to the artist. It is often pride, emulation, avarice, malice—all the odious qualities— which drive a man to compete . . . until he has made something that gratifies his pride and envy and greed.

In the realm of reputation, no writer feels justice has been done him, while he is equally certain many of his contemporaries have been unjustly praised and rewarded. A black day it is for most writers when prizes, grants, awards are announced and they are not among the recipients. "Don't call Saul [Bellow] this morning," my friend Edward Shils said to me one day. "The Nobel Prize for Literature has been announced this morning, and he didn't win it a second time." Clive James's most memorable poem, "The Book of My Enemy Has Been Remaindered," nicely captures the spirit of *Schadenfreude* prevalent among writers.

Physicians, scientists, lawyers, businessmen may be as rivalrous as writers—classical musicians, I'm told, are even more so—but they usually do not possess the particular skills that make malice memorable. Writers have at their disposal the resources of language, which, when on the attack against rivals, lends an added sharp aftertaste to their innuendos, imprecations, invective, rancor, animosity, and simple viciousness.

Free-floating hostility is the ether in which most writers cavort. Often, though, this hostility neither floats nor is free, but is anchored and nicely aimed at a particular rival. Sometimes the rival is located across centuries, causing bad feeling to run one way only. Vladimir Nabokov never passed up a chance to speak ill of Fyodor Dostoyevsky, on the grounds of both his style and his ideas. Leo Tolstoy failed to understand what the fuss was about William Shakespeare, whose writing, unlike his own, had no unified vision nor sought any. Henri Troyat, one of Tolstoy's biographers, recounts an afternoon when the grand old man was strolling on his estate Yasnaya Polyana with Anton Chekhov. He turned to the younger writer and said:

> Anton Pavlovich, I admire your stories. No one admires your stories more than I. Write more stories, wonderful stories, imperishable stories. But your plays, Anton Pavlovich, really, your plays are worse even than Shakespeare.

The malice of writers divides between that which takes place in everyday life, in conversation and direct confrontation, and that which is embedded in their novels, plays, poems, reviews, and literary criticism. The novel in its roman à clef version has long been a useful weapon for one writer to attack another. No one who has read *The Devils* is likely to forget Dostoyevsky's acid portrait of Ivan Turgenev as the pretentious, dandiacal, mincing, whoring-after-youth character he named Semyon Yegorovich Karmazinov. Mary McCarthy blasted Philip Rahv, a former lover, in her novel *The Company She Keeps*, causing him to threaten a lawsuit. Randall Jarrell later did a similar job on Miss McCarthy in his novel *Pictures from an Institution*, remarking that for all her powers of intelligence, wit, and observation, the character he modeled on McCarthy was deficient "in most human qualities" and "had not yet arrived even at that elementary forbearance upon which human society is based." Lillian Hellman inaugurated a lawsuit in 1980 against Mary McCarthy for calling her a liar on the *Dick Cavett Show* that continued until Hellmann's death in 1984. Litigious beasts, scribblers, touchy, easy to take offense.

For some writers, vengeance is a dish best served not cold but in print. Phillip Roth wrote an entire novel, *The Anatomy Lesson*, to repay a withering criticism of him in *Commentary* by Irving Howe; in the novel Howe is called Milton Appel, and is described as "President of the Rabbinical Society for the Suppression of Laughter in the Interest of Loftier Values." In yet another novel, *I Married a Communist*, Roth attempted to repay, with interest added, his former wife Claire Bloom for a memoir the actress wrote in which she accused him of hitting on her adolescent daughter's girlfriends. W. Somerset Maugham took time out to trash his ex-wife, Syrie, and his step-daughter, in a memoir called *Looking Back*.

Saul Bellow never attacked fellow writers in his novels, saving his contumely for ex-wives—he was a veritable literary Bluebeard—and old friends he felt had let him down. Bellow was keenly aware of literary rivals and once, in the late 1970s, told me he thought he was winning the literary public-relations derby over Norman Mailer and Robert Lowell by steering clear of political pronunciamentos and keeping his own counsel. But he neither forgot nor forgave anyone who wrote critically about his novels.

In 1959 in *Esquire*, Mailer published an essay called "The Talent in the Room," a catalogue of his fellow contemporary novelists. The gist of the essay is that there wasn't much talent in that room. William Styron had "compromised himself." Bellow wrote "in a style I find self-willed. . . . I cannot take him seriously." Jack Kerouac lacked "discipline, intelligence, honesty." James Baldwin was "incapable of saying 'F___ you' to the reader." Mailer's chief charge was that none of these writers had the literary panache of, yes, you will have guessed it, Norman Mailer. Many years later, Mailer told an interviewer that novelists were "as competitive as star athletes. Particularly the ones who break through into public renown."

Richard Bradford, previously the author of a biography of Martin Amis, has taken up the subject of writerly combat in its various ramifications in a new book called *Literary Rivals*. Bradford holds that the difference between British and American literary rivalries is

> the former often involved skulking and latent motives implied in writing, while, from behind the books, the author

fomented politely in the real world. The vociferous nature
of American writing, meanwhile, was reflected in the unrestrained virulence of its authors' feuds.

The British Bradford turns out to be better—more knowledgeable,
subtler, smarter generally—on English than American literary rivalries.
His book begins with several misbegotten pages on the post-World War
II generation of American novelists, chiefly Mailer, Gore Vidal, and Truman Capote. Bradford believes that what put the pepper in their personalities was the failure of any of them to achieve that elusive holy grail, the
Great American Novel. "No one," he writes, "is agreed on what this epic
behemoth involves, but it can best be regarded as an avenue for collective
narcissism." That all failed at this endeavor, he feels, bred an "all-pervasive
spirit of rancor and animosity."

Closer to the truth, I believe, to say that this generation of writers had
men of belligerence and maliciousness who had the first access to television, and hence to celebrity. Mailer's bumptiousness, with a slight threat
of violence behind it, often made for good television; Capote, frequently
appearing half in the tank on late-night television talk shows, was expert
at attracting attention through scandalous gossip; and Vidal was sheer
poison, with outdated snobbery added, and, given the chance, would
have devised a put-down for a blind orphan. Immodest and ungener-
ous, none of these writers required failure at writing the Great American
Novel to stoke his malice.

Bradford's book contains chapters, some quite brief, on the bad feeling between Coleridge and Wordsworth, Theodore Dreiser and Sinclair
Lewis, F. R. Leavis and C. P. Snow, and (descending downward) the biographer Bevis Hillier and the novelist and critic A. N. Wilson, McCarthy
and Hellman. A chapter on Hemingway's betrayals in print of Gertrude
Stein and Sherwood Anderson provide a portrait of poisoned feeling
on the part of a writer who had achieved greater acclaim than those he
attacked. In fact, in *A Moveable Feast*, Hemingway betrayed nearly everyone who ever helped him as a young man (Ezra Pound only excepted)—
most cruelly F. Scott Fitzgerald, whose virility he mocked.

Not whole chapters but pages, sometimes a few paragraphs, are given
over to the attacks of Mark Twain on Bret Harte, Tom Wolfe on John

Irving, Norman Mailer on John Updike, Anthony Burgess on Somerset Maugham, Paul Theroux on V. S. Naipaul, and others. The book ends on a nugatory chapter on the row in the Islamic world over Salman Rushdie's novel *Satanic Verses*.

Between chapters, Bradford supplies examples, some famous, of writers casting aspersions—or asparagus, as I once heard a politician in Chicago's City Council say—on one another. "Remarks are not literature," Gertrude Stein once told Hemingway, though she neglected to add that they can be devastating nonetheless. Truman Capote said of Jack Kerouac's *On the Road*, "that's not writing, that's typing." Cyril Connolly remarked of Vita Sackville-West that "she looked like Lady Chatterley above the waist and the gamekeeper below." Ruth Rendell commented that "to say that Agatha Christie's characters are cardboard cut-outs is an insult to cardboard cut-outs." In response to a harsh review by Tibor Fischer of his memoir *Experience*, Martin Amis said: "Tibor Fischer is a creep and a wretch. Oh yeah, and a fat arse."

Bradford's chapter on dueling among writers is centered on English figures, and thus misses what would have been the most consequential duel in all of literary history: the one that almost took place between Turgenev and Tolstoy. Their falling out began with Tolstoy's falling asleep while Turgenev read the manuscript pages of *Fathers and Sons* to him. Things heated up when Tolstoy insulted Turgenev's method of raising his illegitimate daughter. They proceeded further when Turgenev, a large man, threatened to punch Tolstoy in the face. Tolstoy challenged Turgenev to a duel to the death, with pistols, which was only averted when days later both men calmed down. These events occurred in 1861, which means that if the duel had in fact taken place and Tolstoy were killed, the world would have been deprived of both *War and Peace* (1869) and *Anna Karenina* (1877).

The strongest chapters in *Literary Rivals* are on the rivalries between Samuel Richardson and Henry Fielding, Charles Dickens and William Makepeace Thackeray, Edmund Wilson and Vladimir Nabokov, and the secret (one-way) rivalrousness Philip Larkin felt for Kingsley Amis.

Between Richardson and Fielding, personal rivalry was not at stake; they quarreled instead over the question of how best to depict human nature in literature. For Richardson, as set out in such novels as *Pamela; or Virtue Rewarded* (1740–1741) and *Clarissa* (1747–1748), moral instruction ought to be the primary concern of the novelist. For Fielding, as set out in *Shamela* (his novel-length parody of Richardson), *Joseph Andrews* (1742), *Tom Jones* (1749), and *Amelia* (1752), the rich variety, contradictoriness, and comedy of human emotions and motives ought to be the novel's primary concern. Literary men divided on the question. Samuel Johnson was in the Richardson camp, James Boswell in Fielding's. Fielding and Richardson, Bradford notes, never met. But Richardson harbored malevolent feelings toward Fielding, claiming that his portraits of whoremongerers and scenes of low life were purely autobiographical. Fielding, a cooler hand, wrote to congratulate Richardson on the artistic success of *Clarissa* and even recommended the book in the *Jacobite's Journal*.

A more intense, because more personal, rivalry was the one between Charles Dickens and William Makepeace Thackeray. Here, Bradford reports, rivalrousness was less the cause than simple bad feeling, on Dickens's part for Thackeray. The feeling was generated by Dickens's not entirely well-founded belief that Thackeray was helping to spread gossip about Dickens's love affair with the young actress Ellen Ternan. Decades earlier, in 1836, Dickens had turned down Thackeray as an illustrator for *The Pickwick Papers*. Added to this, the two writers operated under the same differences of literary worldview separating Samuel Richardson and Henry Fielding. Dickens, for all his dazzling brilliance, his comic genius, was a writer intent on reform. Thackeray was a writer more in the tradition of Fielding, one who, in Richard Bradford's words, held that "the world in which we exist and apprehend can never be explained in terms of abstractions or ideals." Bradford quotes a striking letter from Thackeray that in part reads: "He [Dickens] doesn't like me—He knows that my books are a protest against his—that if the one set are true, the other must be false." Thackeray himself, in a lecture, quoted his then 10-year-old daughter saying, "I like Mr. Dickens books much better than your books, Papa." The kid had it right, of course, and poor Thackeray, alas, knew it.

Richard Bradford's most interesting chapter is devoted to the public falling-out of Edmund Wilson and Vladimir Nabokov, ostensibly the result of

Wilson's 1965 attack in the *New York Review of Books* on Nabokov's translation from the Russian of Alexander Pushkin's 1825 novel-poem *Eugene Onegin*. Wilson's friendship-ending sentence in that review read thus:

> Since Mr. Nabokov is in the habit of introducing any job of this kind which he undertakes by an announcement that he is unique and incomparable and that everybody else who has attempted it is an oaf and an ignoramus, incompetent as a linguist and scholar, usually with the implication that he is also a low-class person and ridiculous personality, Nabokov ought not to complain if the reviewer, though trying not to imitate his bad literary manners, does not hesitate to underline his weaknesses.

The argument between the two was presumably over Russian prosody, but the falling out, as Bradford recounts it, ran much deeper. "There was, I believe," he writes, "another reason for the feud, one that neither of them referred to explicitly, but which lurks beneath the surface of their otherwise apparently trivial disagreements." It was a fundamental disagreement between Wilson and Nabokov about Communism. Wilson wrote approvingly of Communism in *To the Finland Station*, his history of socialism with its happy ending provided by Lenin's arriving at the Finland Station to lead the Bolshevik revolution. Nabokov suffered from Communism, personally and drastically, its cruelties having forced him, a Russian aristocrat, into permanent exile. Nabokov wasn't above lecturing Wilson on the hollowness of Marxism and demeaning his portrait of Lenin ("No not even the magic of your style has made me like him . . . ") and pointing out the dangers of inflating the monstrous Lenin and his murderous career.

Seven years later, Wilson came back with an excoriating criticism of Nabokov's political novel *Bend Sinister*. "You aren't good at this kind of subject," he wrote, "because you are totally uninterested in these matters and have never taken the trouble to understand them." Wilson, who praised Leon Trotsky's literary acumen, seems to have overlooked Trotsky's cavalier denunciation of Nabokov's beloved father in his *History of the Russian Revolution*, where he refers to the elder Nabokov (a liberal democrat in pre-revolutionary Russia) as "almost symbolic in his self-satisfied correctness and dry egotism." The other possibility is that

Wilson, who knew about this, was seeking revenge for Nabokov's own animadversions about his politics.

Nabokov returned this volley with the high condescension of explaining to Wilson the difference between the tsars' unjust and inept government and the utterly crushing tactics of totalitarianism under the Bolsheviks. Difficult to imagine, as Bradford notes, that Edmund Wilson took kindly to being lectured to by a recent immigrant, especially one he had aided substantially when he first arrived in America by finding publishers and making other literary connections for him.

More than politics was entailed in the breakdown of this friendship. Wilson and Nabokov also had fundamental literary differences. A crucial element in this disagreement Bradford finds in one of the stories in Wilson's *Memoirs of Hecate County*, "The Princess with the Golden Hair," which has some of the most cringe-inducing writing about sex on record. The story also has a narrator of extravagant cultural pretensions. Nabokov called Wilson's descriptions of sex anti-aphrodisiacal: "I should as soon have tried to open a sardine can with my penis." However perverse its theme, in *Lolita* Nabokov, Bradford reminds us, never describes the sex between Humbert Humbert and the nymphet who is the name of his desire. As for Humbert himself, he is, by dint of his cosmopolitan elegance, the reverse of the klunky narrator of Wilson's story. Wilson, meanwhile, criticized *Lolita*, not in print but in a letter to its author, in which he referred to the novel's "nasty subject," adding that "I don't feel you have got away with it."

Resentment fed on resentment, and friendship dissolved into enmity between the most powerful critic and subtlest novelist of their time. "From the moment Nabokov and Wilson first began to see in each other the apotheosis of everything they privately despised," Bradford writes, "it was clear that civilized tolerance would not be a limitless resource." Correspondence between the two writers began to sputter, and they met only once more, in Switzerland, at Nabokov's home in Montreux, with neither expressing regret over their lost friendship. Another rainy day, one might say, in the Republic of Letters.

Bradford is especially good in his portrayal of the ultimately false friendship between Kingsley Amis and Philip Larkin. Amis was a lady killer, in more than the usual sense. He was movie-star handsome as a young man, and women fell into his bed as readily as smelt into fishing nets. He also killed them in his novels. Among his victims was Monica Jones, who (off and mostly on) was Philip Larkin's friend and lover, and on whom Amis modeled the wretched character Margaret Peel in his career-making satirical novel *Lucky Jim*, portraying her as a deeply neurotic woman very much in business for herself. Bradford claims that Amis did this out of jealousy of her intimate friendship with Larkin, thinking it would break up the relationship.

For his part, Larkin felt envy toward Amis for his easy success with women. He also harbored a secret grudge on the ingratitude side of the ledger, for it was he who suggested and worked on some of the funniest parts of *Lucky Jim*, including the famous lecture, delivered drunk, on Merrie England. In letters to Monica Jones, Larkin makes plain how much of the novel was owed to him. He also grew tired of playing confessor to Amis, and of the one-sided relationship that, in their meetings, seemed to have Amis doing most of the talking. Larkin ceased to answer Amis's letters. As with Edmund Wilson and Vladimir Nabokov, years went by without the two supposedly best friends meeting. At Larkin's funeral, one learns from James Booth's recent biography of the poet, Amis remarked, "I sometimes wonder if I really knew him." Turns out, Bradford persuades us, that Amis was right. The man he viewed as his dearest friend was nearly an enemy.

The general effect of *Literary Rivals* is to detract not from the grandeur of literature but from the people who compose it. Writers, one comes away from this book feeling, often operate under the same low motives, feel the same unpleasant emotions, as everyone else. Their literary struggles with truth and beauty seem not to have done much to improve their characters.

Lest my attempt at a magisterial tone here has fooled anyone into believing I am myself above all this, let me assure him that I have felt many of the same unpleasantly contentious authorial emotions described in Bradford's book. I have felt anger and puzzlement at what I take to be the unearned success of fellow writers, enjoyed holding on to grudges against some among them, delighted in learning of the personal failures of others. After a career as a writer of more than 50 years, it could scarcely be otherwise. Examples abound. Allow me to present merely a few.

As a writer of short stories, I do not understand the vaunting of Alice Munro, who in 2013 won the Nobel Prize. Her stories all seem to me one and the same: A woman of middle years in provincial Ontario is having a love affair, or has recently had a love affair, or long ago had a love affair, with a man not worthy of her, and has been, or soon will be, plunged back into the doldrums of provincial life. Neither dazzling in the telling, nor satisfying in their endings, Munro's stories, all washing into one, are not in the least memorable. Yet they command attention and respect that is beyond my comprehension—the kind of attention and respect, not to put too fine a point on it, I should like to have for my own stories.

Some years ago, in the 1990s, Joyce Carol Oates wrote a letter to the *New York Times* insisting that I be fired, for reasons of political incorrectness, from my job as editor of the *American Scholar*. Since that time I have kept a cold spot in my heart for Miss Oates, whose dark and unrewarding novels I gave up reading long before that letter appeared. So imagine my pleasure when not long ago I read that Gore Vidal said that the three most depressing words in the English language are *Joyce Carol Oates*. Little as I normally care for Vidal's toad-tongued wit, this time the old scold, our cut-rate Voltaire, scored heavily with me.

A critic I much disliked, though he never criticized any of my writing, was Alfred Kazin. One day I learned that he had had a heart attack. I remember telling my wife that I genuinely detested Kazin, his schmaltziness, his phony virtuousness, the meanness that was the other side of his literary and political sentimentality, but that, nevertheless, I didn't want him to die. My wife replied that she quite understood. "You merely want him to have more stress in his life," she said. Yes, I thought, exactly, I hoped that Kazin had had painful divorces, children who despised him, a plethora of professional and personal disappointments. When *Alfred Kazin's Journal* was posthumously published, it turned out all my hopes had come true. Kazin's life was a one-man domestic dystopia: he paid heavy alimony, was charged with wife-beating, had children who found him impossible—the full catastrophe. I read his *Journal* with a little marimba band gaily playing in my heart.

Competitiveness, envy, *Schadenfreude*—you and me, I fear, will never be quits. Why should we? I am, after all, a writer.

Why Read Biography?

(2016)

WHEN I COME UPON artists, philosophers, scientists, statesmen, athletes I admire, I find myself interested in their backgrounds, which is to say in their biographies, in the hope of discovering what in their past made possible their future eminence. I find it more than a touch difficult to understand anyone so incurious as not to have a similar interest.

I have myself written scores of biographical essays, but never a full-blown biography. I once took a publisher's advance to write the biography of the American novelist John Dos Passos, a figure now slowly slipping into the vast limbo inhabited by the once famous but now nearly forgotten. I was thirty-two, John Dos Passos was then seventy-three, and would die a year later. After I had signed my publishers contract, I wrote to inform Dos Passos that I hoped to write his life, and sent him some samples of my own published writing. He wrote back to say that he would be pleased to help me in any way he could, though he would prefer I put my liberal politics in moth balls and promise never again to use the word "explicate."

Three great facts, or so I thought, dominated John Dos Passos's life. The first is that he was born a bastard—but, an interesting twist here, an upper-class bastard, the son of a man who was a successful American lawyer and of a mother who was a Virginian of high social standing. He, John Dos

Passos, went to Choate under the name John Madison, and thence to Harvard. The second fact is that he wrote a, if not *the,* Great American novel, *USA* by title, a work using modernist techniques to explore the pressures that society puts on men and women of all social classes; it is a book that, when I first read it at the age of nineteen, greatly moved me. The third fact is that Dos Passos underwent a strong political conversion, from a man who in 1932 voted for William Z. Foster, the Communist Party candidate for President, to a man of deeply conservative principles and views. The work of the Stalinists in the Spanish Civil War, prepared to kill the innocent to gain their ends, not only changed Dos Passos's politics forever but turned such old friends as Ernest Hemingway against him.

A splendid biography of John Dos Passos was there to be written, but, alas, I never wrote it. Life, in the form of demands too elaborate and dull to go into here, intervened, and I was forced to that most odious act known to the professional writer: having to return my publisher's advance. Others have since written biographies of John Dos Passos, but none, to my mind, altogether successfully. Dos Passos's own fame is perhaps now too far faded for anyone of high literary power to take on the task of writing a first-class biography of him. Not that, let me add, at thirty-two I was myself likely to have been up to the job. I have come to believe that at the heart of any fully realized literary work, apart perhaps from satire and parody and lyrical poetry, is honoring the complexity of the subject, and in the case of John Dos Passos I am fairly certain that I could not have done so at that relatively early age.

A successful biography is at a minimum one that conveys what the world thinks of its subject, what his closest family and friends think of him, and, finally, crucially, and sometimes most difficult to obtain, what he thinks of himself. I have lately read two excellent biographies of Cicero (106–43 BCE), one by the German classicist Manfred Fuhrman, the other by the nineteenth-century French classicist Gaston Boissier, and what makes both biographies especially good is the large cache of 900 or so of Cicero's letters that have survived along with another hundred or so letters from his correspondents. These letters reveal Cicero in all the pride, fear, hope, disappointment, vanity, and grandeur of a man playing Roman politics at the highest level. Cicero's letters, marshalled into pertinent order by brilliant biographers, bring him to life in a far more intimate way than any other figure in classical antiquity.

I read these biographies of Cicero, along with some among his voluminous writings, because Cicero is one of the hundred or so key figures in western history, and my ignorance of the details of his life is one of the many thousand gaps in my own knowledge of that history. I read them because one of the pleasures of biography is reading about men and women who played the game of life for higher and more dramatic stakes than one has oneself, or is ever likely to do. I read them also because they reveal Cicero to be perhaps the first example of the intellectual in politics—he is the political intellectual *par excellence*—a subject of long fascination to me, an intellectual not in politics.

Cicero was a human type of the highest interest: the man riven by the division between his ideals and his personal ambition. He felt himself drawn to the Roman aristocracy yet put off by its insolence, felt the natural conflict between the temperament of the man of letters and the politician (for he was both). He was alternately fascinated and disgusted by politics, regularly retreating from them to his library at his villa at Tusculum, then drawn back to the fray at Rome. He was a man who knew disappointment in a mistaken marriage, and tragedy in the loss of a beloved daughter when she was thirty. He left a bibulous son, in whom his family line petered out. Attempting always to avoid extremes, longing for a return to the glories of the Roman Republic, about which he may have been guilty of fantasizing, Cicero ended up being killed by Marcus Antonius's men, who nailed his severed head and the hands that wrote attacks upon Antonius up in the Forum for all to see.

In Gaston Boissier's brilliant biography, *Cicero and His Friends*, one is offered dazzling portraits of such figures as the financier Pomponius Atticus, of whom Boissier writes: "... he was the most adroit man of that time, but we know that there are other forms of praise that are of greater value than this." Of Cicero's protégé Marcus Caelius Rufus, Boissier writes:

> Those cautious and clear-eyed persons, who are entirely taken
> up with the fear of being dupes, and who always see the faults
> of others so plainly, are never anything but lukewarm friends
> and useless allies.

Boissier describes Cicero's brother Quintus playing the "ungrateful and difficult part of younger brother of a great man." He provides portraits of leading female figures of the day, including Clodia, the Lesbia of Catullus love poems, of whom it was said that "she danced better than it was proper for an honest woman to do." These observations on women are capped off by the remark of Cato "that the day that they [women] become your equals they will be your superiors."

I hope you find some of these remarks about Cicero's friends and contemporaries as interesting as do I. If you do, I trust the reason is that you share my interest in human character, and in that still, that probably perpetually, mysterious force behind it, human nature. "The proper study of mankind," as Alexander Pope had it, "is man." If there is a more interesting subject than human character, I do not know it. Part of its interest derives from its bottomlessness, its inexhaustible variety. Why does one person, despite all the disadvantages dealt him by the lottery of birth, survive, surmount, and go on to achieve greatness, while another, with every advantage allotted to him, stumbles, falls, goes down? Biography is the most promising place to seek out the answers.

Some people read biography to compare the subject's life with their own. In the cant term, they "identify." One wonders, though, if this isn't a crude way of reading biography. I read Peter Green's biography of Alexander the Great, I promise you, without once thinking of weeping because I had no more worlds to conqueror. Nor did I identify when I read E. F. Benson's *The Life of Alcibiades*; instead I marveled at the hijinks of a man who may been the world's greatest seducer and con artist. I should have to be a fantast of the first water to imagine myself as in any way comparable to such men.

Identifying with historical figures is reminiscent of Vladimir Nabokov's remarking on the coarseness of identifying with characters in fiction. The best readers, he felt, identified with the artist. By this I take it Nabokov meant that when a character in fiction gets in a tight spot, don't worry about that character, worry instead about how the artist will get him out of it. One ought to read biographies in roughly the same spirit, with a certain sophisticated detachment, if worrying, then expending that worry not on the life of the subject but on the skill of his chronicler, the biographer, whose task it is to take the measure of the person he is writing about with reasonable exactitude and penetrating judgment, all going to form a persuasive portrait.

Many years ago I read through the five volumes of Leon Edel's biography of Henry James. As a writer, I cannot say that I identified with James, a man infinitely more subtle than I. But I did, I like to think, take a few lessons from Henry James. James, some of you will recall, wrote a story called "The Lesson of the Master," in which a famous novelist advises a young writer not to marry because it will impede his art. When the wife of the famous novelist dies, he turns round and marries the woman the young writer loves. Might the lesson here be that the best advice is *not* to take advice, at least in matters of the heart?

Edel's biography provides the best account I know of the quotidian life of the professional writer. The biographer recounts James's dealings with editors and publishers, his hopes for popularity and commercial success ("I can stand lots of gold," James once remarked, though little enough of it came his way through his writing), above all his loneliness and the almost certain loneliness of anyone who chooses, as James did, the spectatorial, as opposed to the active, life.

Henry James was both fascinated and repelled by biography. He himself wrote a biography of the American sculptor William Wetmore Story. The biographical question plays out in many of James's own stories, and in none more than in the story called "The Figure in the Carpet." The narrator of that story seeks to discover the animating force behind the work of an older novelist he admires named Hugh Vereker. Verker allows that there is such a force—"It's the very string that my pearls are strung on," he tells the narrator—but he isn't about to reveal what it is. Another literary critic, a man named George Corvick, claims after long effort to have discovered it, this repeated theme that turns up ever so subtly in Vereker's work, "something like the figure in a Persian carpet." Before revealing it in a book he is writing, Corvick dies in a carriage accident. He had revealed the great secret to his wife, but she, too, is not telling. Vereker himself dies, and the great underlying force propelling his work is never discovered, which, one senses, is fine with Henry James.

The metaphor of the figure in the carpet is wonderfully suggestive, causing us to look into our own lives to discover if there is some repeated pattern or theme that has guided our destiny, made us succeed or fail, brought us contentment or depression. Galen Strawson, the English philosopher, in a chapter of a recent book called *Life-Writing,* thinks otherwise, holding that life is what we make of it, free fall, essentially patternless, leaving us all in the condition not of Persian but of shag rugs. Is this so? If it is, does this not leave us little more than mere bugs in a vast rug of a design beyond all possible fathoming?

About Henry James's strange story one thing is clear: James sides not with his narrator but with his invented novelist Hugh Vereker. In another, more widely known story, "The Aspern Papers," James writes with contempt about the prying biographer ready to do anything to acquire the letters of a long-dead famous poet—by some thought to be Lord Byron—from his now elderly lover. Such is the want of scrupulosity on the part of the biographer that James has one of the other characters in the story call him a "publishing scoundrel."

Late in life Henry James burned a vast quantity of his letters, an act meant to discourage any possible biographers of his own life. An empty gesture, as it turned out, for so charming were James's letters that everyone else saved those he sent to them, with the consequence that the University of Nebraska, which is publishing all his extant letters, is this year to bring out its tenth volume of Henry James letters, and this volume goes up only to 1880. James lived on to 1916.

Leon Edel, who much admired Henry James, nonetheless could not resist Freudianizing him. Edel's rather orthodox Freudianism mars but does not destroy his five-volume work. He does not lock James into an Oedipus Complex. ("Greek myths covering private parts" was Vladimir Nabokov's characterization of Freud's thought.) But he does make great hay out of what he takes to be the sibling rivalry between Henry James and his equally brilliant if utterly different older brother William, even hinting at homoerotic feeling for William on the part of Henry. Was the rivalry truly there? My own view is that the two brothers were so different in their mental makeup—the intellectual note sounding most strikingly in William, the aesthetic in Henry—that rivalry wasn't really at issue. They played different games, philosophy for William, literature for Henry. Comparing the two is rather like asking who was the better athlete, Michael Jordan or Roger Federer.

Leon Edel does show remarkable restraint—for a Freudian, that is—in not prying into Henry James's sex life. So far as is known James never had physical relations with anyone, male or female. Anticipating those later biographers and critics who would write in a less decorous time, Edel, considering the possibility that James was homosexual, noted that there is no firm evidence to suggest that Henry James ever engaged in acts of homosexuality, and lets it go at that.

Biographers who came after Leon Edel, alas, have not. For some among them Henry James's homosexuality is presumed; his active pursuit of his true sexual nature is assumed to have been restrained only by his timidity. ("The art of the biographer," James wrote, "that devilish art, is somehow practically *thinning*; it simplifies while seeking to enrich.") *The Master*, a biographical novel by the Irish writer Colm Toibin portrays homosexuality as at the center of James's life, and has him ogling handsome male servants. The problem here is not just a case of mistaken identification, but the effect this figures to have on skewering the interpretation of James's novels and stories in a homosexual direction. Henry James, were he alive, would have been appalled.

Biography is of course subject to other skewerings, in our time the political not least among them. The politics of the biographer, if he allows them into his work, can have fatal effect. I first noted this some years ago in Andrew Motion's biography of the poet Philip Larkin. Humorlessly picking his way through the Philip Larkin-Kingsley Amis correspondence and other of Larkin's letters, Motion, with a great display of self-virtue, convicts Larkin of misogyny, racism, and the other standard charges leveled in the court of political correctness. This has since been set right by a recent biography of Larkin by a man named James Booth, who has shown Philip Larkin to be a more than decent man in his relations with women, the people who worked for him at Hull University Library, and everyone else who ever encountered him.

Years before this, something similar befell H. L. Mencken, who was also brought in by the political correctness police, anti-Defamation League division. In Mencken's case, to the usual complaints of racism and sexism, anti-Semitism was added. These charges, too, turned out to be unjust. Mencken, such was the largeness of his heart, married a woman knowing she was dying; he did so principally to bring comfort to her. Mencken's best friends were, in fact, Jews. Dim-witted biographers seem unable to decipher the difference, as in the cases of Larkin and Mencken both, between comically expressed reactionary opinions and lives marked by gracious actions.

A flagrant case of politics ruining biography is that of a Stanford professor named Arnold Rampersad in his biography of the novelist Ralph Ellison. I came to the Rampersad biography, published in 2007, with a special interest, hoping he might solve a minor but genuine mystery for me. Many years ago Ralph Ellison invited me to join him for lunch at the Century Club in New York. I met him there on a sunny winter's day at noon, and departed in the dusk at 4:30 p.m., with the same happy glow as a boy I departed double-feature movie matinees. We talked about serious things, gossiped, told each other jokes, laughed a great deal. I enjoyed myself hugely, believed Ellison did too, and departed the Century Club confident I had made a new friend of a writer I much admired.

Soon afterward I wrote to Ralph (as he now was to me) to thank him for the lunch and an immensely enjoyable afternoon. No answer. A week or so later, I wrote to him again, inviting him to write for *The American Scholar*, of which I was then the editor. No answer. After an interval of another three or four weeks, I wrote yet again to inquire if he had received my earlier letters. Nothing. Puzzled, I wrote to him no more. Had I so misperceived what I thought the reciprocal pleasure of that lunch at the Century Club?

A few years after this, I had a letter from a reader of mine asking if I knew Ralph Ellison. He went on to say that he and his wife had met Ellison and his wife at the Newport Jazz Festival, and the four of them spent the most pleasing weekend together. Afterwards, though, Ellison had answered none of his letters. What, he wondered, as I earlier had wondered, might have gone wrong?

On the strangeness of Ralph Ellison's behavior in these instances, Professor Rampersad, his biographer, sheds no light. Instead much of his attention is taken up by finding Ralph Ellison nowhere near so virtuous a man as he, Arnold Rampersad, apparently is. Rampersad's charge against Ralph Ellison, adding on to his being a bad brother and a poor husband, is that, in Rampersad's words, Ellison's "life is a cautionary tale to be told against the dangers of elitism and alienation, especially alienation from other blacks."

What Ralph Ellison turns out to have been guilty of is not having, so to say, got on the bus. He was and remained an integrationist, and thought the black power movement a grave mistake. He insisted on the complexity of black experience in America, and refused to play the victimhood game, refraining from the rhetoric of public rage and demagoguery. He was an artist before he was a politician, and in the realm of art was an unapologetic elitist, believing in pursuing the best in western high culture and African-American folk culture to the exclusion of all else. He did not line up to praise young black writers simply because they were black. Art, he held, was color-blind. Nor did he praise established black writers—James Baldwin, Toni Morrison—if he did not think them truly praiseworthy. Rampersad's charge finally comes down to what he takes to be Ralph Ellison's pernicious opinions, and the way one knows they are pernicious is that they do not comport with his biographer's opinions.

Left to speculate upon what was behind Ralph Ellison's odd behavior toward me and, I gather, others he had charmed, I have concluded that Ellison was a gracious and gregarious man who later came to regret his own natural sociability. In 1952 at the age of 39 he wrote *Invisible Man*, a novel that won all the prizes and worthy acclaim of its day. Although he lived on for another forty-two years and produced two excellent collections of essays, Ralph Ellison never wrote another novel. How this must have worn on him psychologically one cannot hope fully to know. He would go out into the world, his natural charm easily making him friends, and afterwards return to his desk, the scene of decades-long defeat, determined not to waste further time on these newly made friends. Or so I have conjectured.

In his biography of Ralph Ellison, Professor Rampersad not merely wrongly degraded a good man, but, in his biography's pretense to definitiveness—the work runs to 672 pages—the book is likely to scare away other Ellison biographers for decades, which is a sadness and an injustice. To be definitive has increasingly become the goal for contemporary biographers. A definitive biography, by current standards, leaves nothing out. Straightaway one sees the impossibility of the goal. Unless one does a day-by-day, hour-by-hour, minute-by-minute account of a life, definitiveness, defined as utter thoroughness, cannot be achieved.

The greatest biography ever written, James Boswell's *Life of Johnson*, which I reread within the past year, is not definitive. For one thing, the book largely shirks Samuel Johnson's early life, and concentrates on the twenty-one years during which Boswell knew Johnson, roughly from 1763 to 1784, beginning when he was twenty-two and Johnson fifty-four. Nor has any biographer ever intruded himself, in a biography, so completely as Boswell did in his book about Johnson. So much is this the case that some have claimed that the *Life of Johnson* is, two for the price of one here, both a biography and an autobiography.

The making of the *Life of Johnson* is of course Boswell's emphases on Samuel Johnson's habits, his "inflexible dignity of character," his ponderous physical presence, above all his brilliant conversation, into which Boswell often all but goaded him. Samuel Johnson was an extraordinary writer. The essays from *The Rambler* are among the finest we have. As a biographer, his *The Life of Richard Savage* and *The Lives of the Poets* hold up splendidly. In "The Vanity of Human Wishes," he composed a poem that still lives. His *Dictionary* is one of the most impressive one-man intellectual performances of all time. Along with Matthew Arnold and T. S. Eliot, Samuel Johnson is one of the three indispensable literary critics in all of English Literature.

Yet it took James Boswell to bring him to life. Boswell held that in his biography Johnson "will be seen as he really was; for I profess to write neither panegyric, which must be all praise, but his Life; which, great and good as he was, must not be supposed to be entirely perfect." Boswell claimed that in his book Johnson was seen "more completely than any man who has ever yet lived," and he made good, I believe, on the claim. With all his gruffness, his blunderbuss conversation in which he "often talked for victory," his intellectual bullying, his acts of extraordinary Christian charity, Samuel Johnson emerges in Boswell's *Life*, flaws and all, a moral hero. Without Boswell, Johnson would perhaps not have found his prominent place in the pantheon of English Literature. No biographer has ever rendered his subject a greater service than James Boswell did Samuel Johnson.

The tendency of modern biographies, under the tyranny of definitude, has been for them to grow longer and longer. This may have begun with Mark Schorers's 869-page biography of Sinclair Lewis (published in 1961). A recent biography of Bob Hope runs to 565 pages, the first volume of Gary Giddins's biography of Bing Crosby to 768 pages, James Kaplan's recent biography of Frank Sinatra to 992 pages, J. Michael Lennon's biography of Norman Mailer to 960 pages, and the first volume of Zachary Leader's biography of Saul Bellow to 812 pages. Why are these biographies so lengthy? They are so because of their authors' mistaken ambition for biographical definitiveness. They not only want every word redeemable about, but the last word on, their respective subjects.

Along with being longer, contemporary biographies are less interested in moral heroism (Samuel Johnson) or simple greatness (Alexander of Macedon, Thomas Edison) of the kind that aroused the interests of earlier readers. Modern biographers labor in search of secrets, often ones linked to sexual behavior. Owing to Lytton Strachey's biographical essays in *Eminent Victorians* (1918), modern biographers are as frequently eager to demean as to exalt their subjects. Strachey undertook to deflate the Victorians, who, with such figures among them as John Stuart Mill, Charles Darwin, Benjamin Disraeli, and George Eliot, constitute perhaps the greatest intellectual efflorescence of any period in history. The book made great waves at the time of its appearance, and had a strong if not necessarily salubrious influence in changing the nature of biographical writing toward the iconoclastic.

Perhaps the best vantage for a biographer is to admire his subject without being chary of recounting his weaknesses. A model of such a book, in my own recent reading, is the Russian-born Henri Troyat's *Turgenev*. Troyat, who also wrote biographies of Tolstoy, Pushkin, and Chekhov, brought his *Turgenev* in at a mere 162 pages. The biography conveys a literary artist's life and character in a lucid and illuminating way. When one has come to its end one feels that one knows Ivan Turgenev well and has a clearer view of his novels than formerly. If anything is left out, one feels it cannot have been essential.

"The history of the world," wrote Thomas Carlyle, "is but the biography of great men." Not everyone would agree. Sir Ronald Syme, who wrote impressive biographies of Sallust and Tacitus, is among those who would not. "At its worst," wrote Syme in his *The Roman Revolution*, "biography is flat and schematic; at its best it is often baffled by the hidden discords of human nature. Moreover, undue emphasis upon the character of a single person invests history with dramatic unity at the expense of truth."

Biography and history are of course not the same, and yet biography is what many among us find most enticing in history: as when Tacitus writes about Poppaea, Nero's second wife, that she possessed

> every womanly asset except goodness. . . . To her married or bachelor bedfellows were alike. She was indifferent to her reputation—insensible to men's love and unloving herself. Advantage dictated the bestowal of her favors.

Ronald Syme himself greatly enlivens his history of *The Roman Revolution* with dab biographical touches, as when of a secondary figure named L. Munatius Plancus he writes: "A nice calculation of his own interests and an assiduous care for his own safety carried him through well-timed treacheries to a peaceful old age."

In the end, biography is one of the best safeguards against the conceptualizing of history— "Create a concept," wrote Ortega, "and reality leaves the room"—and of the belief that human beings are invariably defeated by the overwhelming forces of history. Biography counters determinism, the notion of history being made chiefly, or even exclusively, by irresistible tendencies, trends, and movements; it reinforces the idea that fortune, accident, above all strong character can rise above the impersonal forces of politics, economics, and even culture, to forge human destiny and change the flow of history itself. For this reason, and many more, I say, long live biography.

Part Three

Jewish

Sholem Aleichem

(2014)

"Let's talk about something more cheerful.
Have you any news of the cholera in Odessa?"

—SHOLEM ALEICHEM

ON HIS FIRST TRIP TO AMERICA in 1906, Sholem Aleichem was introduced to Mark Twain by a New York judge named Samuel Greenbaum. Sholem Aleichem, Greenbaum remarked by way of introduction, was "the Jewish Mark Twain." Twain graciously responded, "Tell him I am the American Sholem Aleichem." Whether Mark Twain and Sholem Aleichem read each other is unclear, but they had a fair amount in common. Both had wide public recognition, each was beloved by his readers.

Mark Twain and Sholem Aleichem also had in common that they were money writers. They were both in constant need of funds to finance their rather grand styles of living. Twain married the daughter of a wealthy coal dealer from Elmira, New York, and forever after struggled to keep her in the manner to which she had been brought up. In the effort to do so, he made several bad investments and fell into deep enough debt to have his financial life taken over by Henry Flagler, a Rockefeller partner, who sent him off to Europe while he sorted out and paid off his debts. *Life on the Mississippi,* one of Twain's best books, is ruined by a padded-out second half, required to make it long enough to qualify as a work that could be sold by subscription, which would bring in greater royalties. Money was never for long out of Mark Twain's mind.

Nor was it out of Sholem Aleichem's. He was born Sholem Rabinovich in 1859, son of a moderately successful trader and shopkeeper. His
father, Nochem Rabinovich was traditionalist in his religion yet modern in his intellectual outlook. Cheated by a partner, he went bust; and
not long after, his wife died of cholera when her son, the future writer,
was thirteen.

After three years in a Russian secular school, Sholem Aleichem, at seventeen, left home to go out on his own. He worked briefly as an assistant
to a lawyer, then as a tutor in Russian to the children of well-to-do Jewish families. He would later be employed as a "crown rabbi," a job that
entailed gathering statistics on the births, deaths, and conscriptions of
small-town Jews for the Russian government.

The great turning point in Sholem Aleichem's life came in 1883 when
at the age of twenty-four he married, much against her father's will, a girl
he had earlier tutored named Olga Loyeff, the daughter of a successful
estate manager. Two years later, his father-in-law, Elimelekh Loyeff died,
leaving his daughter, his only remaining child, the equivalent in current
dollars of $2.6 million. Under Russian law, the money belonged to her
husband. At twenty-six, Sholem Aleichem found himself a wealthy man.

Sholem Aleichem and his wife Olga, with the first two of what would
eventually be their six children, moved into a plush apartment in the city
of Kiev (the Yehupetz of so many of his stories). Technically, they lived
there illegally, for the Jewish populations of Russian cities, under the laws
of the Pale of Settlement, were held to strict quotas.

In these, his newly rich days, Sholem Aleichem devoted quite as much
time to business as to writing. He founded a company speculating in
commodities; he played heavily on the Jewish version of the bourse in
Kiev. He never had a seat on the Kiev exchange, but was a kind of day-
trader *avant le lettre*. Like his fictional character Menakhem Mendl, the
ever hopeful loser, Sholem Aleichem, too, tapped out, and before long
dissipated his father-in-law's inheritance. His mother-in-law paid off his
debts; and though she lived with him, never spoke to him again.

While still flush, Sholem Aleichem published a large anthology of
Yididsh writing. He paid his contributors handsomely, and put considerable energy into the editing of their work. He felt that he had a stake

in Yiddish as a literary language, and wanted a hand in helping to direct its future. Yiddish literature may have been his only sound investment.

All this and a great deal more I learned from Jeremy Dauber's excellent new biography of Sholem Aleichem. Dauber's is chiefly a biography of the day-to-day life of a writer and an examination of the meaning of his works. He recounts Sholem Aleichem's complicated relations with editors and publishers, his travels, his literary ambitions, the origins and meaning and fate of his writing. *The Worlds of Sholem Aleichem* expends little space on tracing out its subject's neuroses or delving into scandalous behavior. Sholem Aleichem devoted so much of his relatively short life to work that there was scarcely time for either.

"Sholem Aleichem's rueful realism provided ironic counterbalance to his rampant optimism," Dauber writes. The optimism is less easily explained than the realism, which came from his having been brought up and lived as a Jew in Russia. From czars to commissars, the Russians have always treated their people as if they were a conquered nation. But they seemed to take especial pleasure in making life hard for the Jews.

One of the dirty little secrets of art is that sometimes the worst social and political conditions prove the most fertile ground for its growth. Think of the Italian Renaissance, with its many despots, its taste for *vendette* and other manifold cruelties, out of which derived the greatest visual art the western world has known. Think of nineteenth-century Russia, until 1862 still a slave-holding country, barbarous in so many other ways, which in Tolstoy, Dostoyevsky, Turgenev, and Chekhov produced the greatest writers of fiction in all of literature.

Sholem Aleichem came of age at a time when the Jews in Russia and Eastern Europe generally were oppressed from without and riven from within. Yet these conditions were richly promising for the right artist. Sholem Aleichem, the right artist, was a man who loved his fellow Jews, experienced firsthand the despotism tormenting them, and strongly felt the conflicts dividing them.

Life was pure hell for the Jews in Russia under Czar Nicholas, then eased up a bit under Czar Alexander, whose assassination in 1881 brought the government fist down even more heavily on the five million Jews living within the Russian Pale of Settlement. Everything possible was done

to stop Jews from maintaining lives of dignity and calm. From the early
1880s on, the Russian government incited pogroms in Kiev, Rostov-on-
Don, Nizhni-Novgorod, Kishinev, Odessa, and elsewhere. Strict Jewish
quotas were set for Jews entering secular Russian schools. Many towns in
the Pale of Settlement were reclassified as villages, forcing Jews to evacu-
ate them, while at the same time Jews were expelled from Moscow and
St. Petersburg. The Black Hundreds, with the complicity of the Czarist police, incited peasants to maraud Jewish neighborhoods and towns
without fear of punishment. In 1905, with the outbreak of the Russo-
Japanese war, Jews were conscripted into the Russian army in vastly dis-
proportionate numbers. Earlier, under Czar Nicholas, Jewish boys, when
they turned eighteen, were drafted into the Russian Army for twenty-five
years, during which time they generally either died or gave up their religion; most lost all connection with their families.

In "Eighteen from Pereshchepena," one of Sholem Aleichem's railroad
stories, a character asks:

> How can anyone expect us to survive so many troubles, so
> many quotas, so much discrimination? Every day, every blessed
> day, there's some new regulation against us. Why, there must
> be a regulation per Jew already!

Maurice Samuel, the chronicler of Eastern European Jewry, writes that
"it was a principle of Russian law that everything was forbidden to Jews
unless specifically permitted."

Jews in Russia were shaken from within by great cultural changes
underway during these years. The most emphatic of these changes was
found in the conflict between conventionally religious Jews and those
Jews who, under the banner of the Haskalah, or Jewish Enlightenment, wished to modernize traditional Judaism by broadening Jewish education. Although the Haskalah was never about assimilation,
but about widening the boundaries of Jewish ghetto and shtetl life,
it nonetheless stirred strong emotions among Jews, often within the
same families. As Sholem Aleichem notes in his autobiography, during the era of the Haskalah, "to show piety was humiliating," and to
be "a fanatic was worse than a libertine." Many younger Jews became

political, revolutionary even, abandoning Jewish worship, which they viewed as mired in retrograde superstition.

The first question facing the young Sholem Aleichem was whether to write in Yiddish or Hebrew. The Haskalah favored Hebrew, and the *maskilim*, as intellectual advocates of Haskalah were called, looked down on Yiddish as the Jargon, even though it was the language of 98 percent of the Jews living in the Pale of Settlement. Sholem Aleichem's father, though pious in his religion, nonetheless reflected this split; favoring Hebrew over Yiddish as proper language for Jewish literature, he wanted his son to write in Hebrew, which he did at the beginning of his career.

Sholem Aleichem came to recognize that the Yiddish-speaking Jews who were his subject were best written about in their own language. "For Sholem Aleichem," Ruth Wisse wrote in her introduction to the collection of his stories called *The Best of Sholem Aleichem*, "the unfixed nature of Yiddish was its greatest attraction, and its infinite range of dialects and oral styles the best literary means of capturing the dynamic changes—or the resistance to change—in the culture." Writing in Hebrew, when he thought in Yiddish, as Jeremy Dauber notes, meant for Sholem Aleichem essentially translating himself from one language to another.

Yiddish at that time also gave Sholem Aleichem much the larger potential audience. Scholem Aleichem was never interested in being a small-public writer. His stories were published not in quarterlies, or what the Russians used to call the "thick" magazines, but in Yiddish-language newspapers, where they were read by Jews all over the world. He wanted the largest possible audience for his writing, and through his dazzling stories won it at a relatively early age.

In *From the Fair*, his autobiography, written toward the end of his life, Sholem Aleichem remarks on his early gift for mimicry. Skill at mimicry may be the first sign of the verbal artist in the making. For Sholem Aleichem, it would prove indispensable. His speciality in fiction was the monologue, as in the Tevye stories, or epistolary fiction, as in the exchange of letters between Menakhem Mendl letters and his properly complaining wife Sheineh-Sheindl. In his railroad stories, it is rarely the author speaking; instead he records the stories Jews packed into third-class recount on long rail trips. Sholem Aleichem's literary ventriloquism was flawless.

A Jew without irony is probably not fully a Jew, but Sholem Aleichem's irony was never contentious, never superior to its subject, never malignant. The Yiddish poet Itzik Fefer described it as "lyrical irony." Sholem Aleichem found what was extraordinary in the most ordinary Jews, highlighting their oddity, comedy, sadness, and endurance. The standard cliché about Sholem Aleichem's writing is that he provokes laughter through tears. In *No Joke*, her recent book on Jewish jokes, Ruth Wisse comes closer to capturing it where she characterizes Sholem Aleichem's irony as "more accurately understood as laughter through fears."

If one is searching for influences on Sholem Aleichem, one thinks first of his fellow Ukrainian, Nikolai Gogol, the only authentic comic genius among Russian writers, and an artist who, like Sholem Aleichem, was always playful but never shallow. Cervantes and Laurence Sterne were two other novelists he delighted in. He admired Tolstoy above all the Russian novelists, crediting him with being the only Russian writer who understood Jews. He thought well of Maxim Gorky, for both his socialism and his philo-Semitism, and for a time, in imitation of Gorky, he grew his hair long and went about in a loose tunic.

Like Dickens, whose writing he loved, Sholem Aleichem had the copiousness, the unending flow, the inexhaustible inventiveness of the natural writer. He rewrote, cut, polished his prose, but ideas for stories seem never to have been in short supply. He produced a story a week for the Yiddish press for roughly twenty-five years. At various times in his later years, physicians had to ask him to cease writing as part of their plan for his recuperation, but he found himself unable to do so. He was writing the stories that went into *Mottel, the Cantor's Son* up to a few days before his death.

"I feel a kind of bond exists between me and the people, that is, between all the people who read *jargon*," Sholem Aleichem wrote. "It seems to me like I need them and they need me." Through his stories, he showed the pressures under which they lived, the rich complicatedness of their lives, and through the force of his art he authenticated them. "What kind of extraordinary, yet plausible, Jewish work of literature could be created that would ironically juxtapose the past and the changing present," Jeremy Dauber writes, "and, for good measure, include doses of playfulness, disruption, along with the occasional self-referential or autobiographical excursion?" This was precisely the kind that Sholem Aleichem created, over and over again.

He do the Jews in different voices, to wring a change on T. S. Eliot's famous line from *The Waste Land*. In his various stories, Sholem Aleichem did *schnorrers, hondlers, yentes, luftmensches, ganevs, nudniks,* petty tyrants, children, and dreamers, above all dreamers. Sholem Aleichem describes himself in his autobiography as "the constant dreamer," and so he remained all his days; to the very end of his life he was hoping for a big score on the stage of the New York Yiddish theatre. Only the women in Sholem Aleichem are landed, grounded, anchored in reality, burdened with the unpleasant task of bringing their husbands, sons-in-laws, children back down to earth. Their chief weapon in doing so is the combined curse and aphorism: "As mother says, God bless her," Menakhem-Mendl's wife Sheineh-Sheindel says, "the worm within the radish thinks there's no sweeter place."

Sholem Aleichem was able to create characters who are garrulous without becoming tiresome. Part of the pleasure of the performance is in his picking up the different tics that repeat themselves in his characters' speech; the character who fastens on the phrase "in plain Yiddish," as we today should say "the bottom line is"; the character who is always making "a long story short," but doesn't, not really; the character who in recounting his own troubles says over and over that they should only be visited on "Purishkevich," a right-wing anti-Semite of the day; the character who cannot get through four or five sentences without falling back on "etcetera, etcetera, etcetera." His stories can begin at the beginning, the end, or *in media res.* "'Speaking of the Drozhne fire'..." one story begins, when of course no one was speaking of it.

In *From the Fair*, Sholem Aleichem repeats a story that his grandfather told him. The story is about a Jew who approaches his nobleman landlord for the renewal of his lease on an inn he runs that brings him a minimal profit but is his sole income. He finds the nobleman drunk among friends. When he makes his request, the nobleman says that he will accede to the request if the Jew will climb up to the roof of his house and allow him to shoot at him as if he were a bird. The Jew, with great trepidation, does so, reciting the *Shema Yisroel* as he climbs the ladder to the roof. "Jews of the old school," Sholem Aleichem writes. One might think the prayer will save him; one might think the nobleman, even in his drunkenness cannot be so brutish as actually to shoot the poor Jew. Once the Jew attains the roof, the nobleman asks him to spread his arms, bird-like, and he fires and hits the Jews in the forehead, killing him. Afterward the nobleman, a man of his word, renews the lease for ten years, at the same rent, despite his having had higher offers. "Noblemen of the old school," writes Sholem Aleichem. Nothing about this story is as one might have expected. Everything about it is believable. The two capping comments— "Jews of the old school," " Noblemen of the old school"— couldn't be more perfectly placed. "I, loving my people with *warm* heart and *cold* reason," Sholem Aleichem wrote, ". . . tell the truth."

Sholem Aleichem dedicated his first novel, *Stempenyu*, to S. M. Abramovich, better known under the penname Mendele Mocher Sforim, and considered "the grandfather of Yiddish Literature"; Sholem Aleichem addressed him as *zeide*. Abramovich told him that the novel was not his form; that, as a writer of great comic gifts, he did best to work in shorter literary forms. Sholem Aleichem continued to turn out the occasional novel, and he also attempted with great financial hope, to write for the stage, but Abromovich was correct. The 1,500 to 5,000-word sketch or story was where he shone.

More skillful with character than plot, Sholem Aleichem, when his writing centered on the same character in different stories, produced what in effect were the equivalent of novels. Such is the case with the stories about Menakhem-Mendl, the so-called Railroad stories, the stories about Motl the Cantor's son, and of course the stories about Tevye the Diaryman. Religion forms the background but culture is the true subject of these various works – the culture of Jewish life at a time of constant change and perpetual peril.

As for his religion, Sholem Aleichem lived the Jewish life of the *miskilim*. He wore no yarmulke, did not observe the laws of *kossruth*. He was sentimental about Jewish holidays, and always wanted his family around him at holiday times. In his own household, he spoke not

Yiddish but Russian. Yet in his will he beseeches his descendants not "to guard their Jewish descent" and specifies that those who fail to do so "have thus erased themselves from my will, 'and they shall have no portion and inheritance among their brethren.'"

Jewish stories are without happy endings. The standard Jewish story, it has been said, is about disaster avoided. The closest to hope these stories come is in the recognition that things could have been worse. Critics have noted that Sholem Aleichem's stories do not have true endings; they merely conclude. ". . . The stories move toward a climax," Irving Howe wrote, "and then, just when you expect the writer to drive toward resolution they seem deliberately to remain hanging in the air. They stop rather than end." Howe, who took Sholem Aleichem to be a highly self-conscious literary artist, posits various reasons for this, all tenable. Jeremy Dauber's view is that by doing away with endings that explain "what it all means" Sholem Aleichem "yanks away our security blanket as readers." I would only add that the want of conventional endings in so many of these stories feels aesthetically right.

Sholem Aleichem left Russia in 1905, when, from the window of his hotel room, he witnessed a pogrom in the streets of Kiev. (The Mendel Beilis trial for ritual murder in 1911 convinced him he could never live in Russia again.) He would be a permanent transient for the remainder of his life: living in Lemberg, London, Geneva and Montreux in Switzerland, the Italian Riviera, New York, and other places.

Dandaical in dress, expensive in his tastes, Sholem Aleichem was, as Dauber has it, "a spendthrift." He was the sadness kind of spendthrift, one with a worried conscience. However much money he earned, he always needed more. Living in permanent transience with his large family on the road was costly. Dauber recounts his unending negotiations and disputes with Yiddish newspaper and book publishers over fees, advances, and copyrights; his attempts at a theatrical bonanza. (He had two plays mounted on the same night in New York—one under the direction of Boris Thomashevsky, the other by Jacob Adler, the great figures in the New York Yiddish theater—and both flopped.) When S. M. Abramovitch accused him of extending his series of Menakhem-Mendil stories merely for the money, Sholem Aleichem was much offended. His pen, he argued, was never for sale. He claimed he "*always* writes for writing's sake." But the money was nice—and needed.

He gave readings throughout Eastern Europe at which thousands attended. An authentic hero of culture to his Yiddish readers, he was met at train stations by admiring crowds. The large Eastern European Jewish emigration to America, begun in 1881. When Sholem Aleichem first arrived in New York, in 1906, a crowd awaited him at the dock, including editors of the leading Yiddish press and theater, academics, readers who adored his writing. Even the *yekkes*, the German Jews well settled and financially successful in America, the Warburgs and the Schiffs, invited him into their homes. But it was all downhill from there. Along with his theatrical failures, he made the wrong newspaper contracts for his writing, his readings were not always well attended. He would later refer to America as "the land of cultural servitude and senseless humiliation," where an "author is a *schlimazl*." He returned to Europe the following year.

On one of his reading tours, in 1908 in the town of Baranovitch, in Ukraine, Sholem Aleichem's health broke down. He was found to have acute pulmonary tuberculosis. The last eight years of his life would be spent in expensive convalescence undergoing ultimately unsuccessful recuperation. He continued working, even tried turning some of his stories into scripts for silent films. (He was a great admirer of Charlie Chaplin.) World War I drained much of the hope left in him. He returned to America in 1914, to much less acclaim than on his first voyage, and here he remained, living in the Bronx. He now seemed, as Jeremy Dauber puts it, less a visiting celebrity than a refugee. He died in 1916 at the age of fifty-seven. Estimates of the number of people who attended his funeral vary between 30,000 and a quarter of a million.

If Sholem Aleichem is remembered today he is so generally as a figure through whose stories the nostalgia for a long lost way of shetl life is reflected. Of his writing, very little of which had appeared in English while he was still alive, today only the Tevye stories are known, and these through the adaptations of the Broadway musical and movie versions of *Fiddler on the Roof*. To be remembered, appreciated, world famous for something one didn't quite do would have been an irony not lost on that great ironist Sholem Aleichem.

The Tevye stories represent Sholem Aleichem at his best. David Roskies, a professor of Yiddish at the Jewish Theological Seminary, calls Tevye himself "the greatest storyteller in Jewish fiction." Another critic, Itzik Manger, has called Tevye "a comic Job." He is one of the half dozen or so great comic characters in western literature—with Don Quixote, Falstaff, and Mr. Wilkins Micawber. Tevye is a great comic character because, like these others, he is not comic merely. He is in fact fully as tragic as he is comic, perhaps more so.

In Tevye, Sholem Alcheim found the perfect character—the vivid objective correlative—to describe the plight of the Jew in Russia in the last decades of the nineteenth century. Tevye is the poor Jew who does not let his poverty detract from his dignity. He is also a fine vessel for purveying Sholem Aleichem's ironic vision. "'We've heard, Tevye,' they [some peasants] tell him, 'that you're an honest man, even if you're a rat-Jew.' I ask you, do you ever get such compliments from Jews?"

When we first encounter him, Tevye is a laborer, married, with seven daughters. He is given to endless quotations from the Pentateuch and the rabbinical literature known as the *Mishnah*. ("'You Bible a person half to death,' he wife Golde tells him, 'and think you have solved the problem.'") He prides himself on his erudition; he is, he says, a man "who reads the fine print." With his aged horse and cart he drags logs and lumber between his village of Anatevke and Boiberik, the rich Jewish suburb of Yehupetz (Kiev). One day in the forest he picks up two lost women and returns them to their opulent dachas in Boiberik, for which he is rewarded with food, a cow, and thirty-seven rubles. With this money he buys more livestock, and, with the aid of his wife Golde, becomes the moderately successful Tevye the Dairyman.

Tevye talks chiefly to three others: himself, as he makes his rounds between Anatevke and Boiberik, where he sells his milk, butter, and cheese; the scribbler Sholem Aleichem, to whom he recounts his troubles; and God, with whom he for the most part argues. The story of Tevye is the story of his daughters, who are all comely and, in differing ways, fiercely independent. In the stories of each of the five older daughters one is meant to discover the departures from Jewish tradition that confronts Tevye but also Russian Jewry generally. Each is a love story but told from the point of view of the girls' father, Tevye.

The first of his daughters, Tsaytl, goes against his wishes, and turning away from a marriage with a wealthy widower butcher, marries Motl Komoyl, a poor tailor without prospects, whom she loves. "What do you have against my daughter," Tevye asks Motl, "that you want to marry her?" In the end Tevye relents, deciding that his future son-in-law may only be a tailor, but he is honest and of his love for Tsaytl there can be no doubt. He concludes that "if everyone acted sensibly, there wouldn't be a Jewish wedding in the world." He determines to reconcile himself to the marriage. "Tevye, I said to myself, stop hemming and hawing and sign on the dotted line." There remains only to convince his wife Golde, who, in a nice touch of Jewish snobbery even among the poor, laments that until now there has never been a tailor or shoemaker in the family.

Tevye's daughter Hodl takes up with a tutor, one Pertchik, who turns out to be a political radical. They plan to marry, and it becomes clear that Tevye's permission means little to them. Pertchik's secret political work will take him away from her for a good while, but Hodl is ready patiently to stand by him. Eventually Pertchik will be sent off to Siberia, where Hodl will join him. The night before her departure to meet her husband, she and her father spend alone, saying little, feeling everything.

"What a mistake it was," says Tevye, "to go and have such daughters." What makes the mistake complicated is his fathomless love for them. They might very well, indeed, have taken their strong independent strain from him. As Tevye says in another of his monologues with Pani Sholem Aleichem, "Trust no one but God. Just leave it to Him. He'll see that the worms are exiting you like fresh bagels and you'll thank him for it, too." Still, he adds, "there's a great God above and . . . a man must never lose heart while he lives."

Tevye's problems are not alone with God, with whom he claims somehow to have made his peace. "My problem," he says, "was with men. Why did they have to be so bad when they could as well have been good?" Which is of course another question for God, who seems to be deficient, as Tevye sees it, in a sense of justice.

A Jew must have confidence and faith. He must believe, first, that there is a God, and second, that if there is, and if it's all the same to Him, and if it isn't putting Him to too much trouble, He can makes things a little better for the likes of you.

Another of Tevye's daughter's will marry a temporarily wealthy four-flusher named Podhotzur, with whom she will eventually run off to America. Yet another has her affections trifled with by the son of a rich family who eventually deserts her, causing her, in her heartbreak, to drown herself.

Most drastic of all, Tevye's daughter Chava marries a Gentile, a Russian from a peasant family, causing him to think, "Was I really the world's greatest sinner, that I deserved to be its most punished Jew," and "was it for this that I had been such a good Jew all my life?" Easily the most poignant moment in the Tevye stories occurs when the apostate Chava appears out of the forest to cry out that she needs a word with her father, and he, with so much love in his heart for her, but already having declared her dead, drives off in his cart without deigning to recognize her.

The Tevye stories recapitulate the chronicle of the Jews in late nineteenth century Russia: the break with tradition, the politicization of the young, intermarriage, and finally, in the last Tevye story, their dispossession from their shtetl homes, to depart for . . . Odessa, America, Israel, who knew? Tevye is a widower at the close, and he reminds Pani Sholem Alecheim that he used to tell his wife that the *mishna* holds that life is no different with or without children. "Either way," he says, "there's a great kind merciful God above. I only wish I had a ruble for every dirty trick he's played on me. . . ."

Although he wrote many brilliant stories—"Drefuss in Kasrilevke," "On Account of a Hat," "A Yom Kippur Scandal," and others—Sholem Aleichem's right to a posthumous reputation is based upon, and justified by, the Tevye stories. The nature of that reputation, it turns out, has varied wildly. For a while in the Soviet Union, Sholem Aleichem was valued as an anti-Tsarist writer. In Israel, where the old shtetl life was viewed more with revulsion than nostalgia, he was regarded chiefly as the author of children's stories. In America, Sholem Aleichem's reputation was most complicated of all.

The complication set in and quickly thickened with the production, first on stage and then on film, of *Fiddler on the Roof*. The great Yiddish actor Maurice Schwartz earlier had a success playing Tevye on stage. But the musical, with music by Jerry Block and Sheldon Harnick, choreography and direction by Jerome Robbins, produced by Hal Prince, swept the boards. By 1971 *Fidder on the Roof*, Dauber notes,

> approaching its eighth year [on Broadway], . . . blew by *Hello, Dolly!* to become the longest-running musical in Broadway history to date . . . by that time an estimated 35 million people had seen the show.

Eventually the musical ran for 3,242 performances, setting the record for the longest running stage production in the history of Broadway.

On the question of what the play and film did to the American sense of Sholem Aleichem's art, Dauber concludes that the musical rendered Sholem Aleichem, at least in the public mind, that vague entity a folk artist, and a writer who kindled a nostalgia for old world shtetl life. (Nostalgia, the sociologist Robert Nisbet wrote "is the rust of memory.") Despite its high quality as entertainment, despite its many charming songs—"If I were a Rich Man," "Tradition," "Sunrise, Sunset," "Miracle of Miracles"— *Fiddler on the Roof* softened and sentimentalized Sholem Aleichem. In a review of the play that appeared in *Commentary* in 1964, a review predicting its enormous box-office success, Irving Howe made plain the difference between the musical and the literary work from which it was made.

Marianne Moore once spoke of Ireland as the greenest land she'd never seen; Anatevka in *Fiddler on the Roof* is the cutest *shtetl* we've never had. Irresistible bait for the nostalgia-smitten audience, this charming little *shtetl* is first shown in the style of Chagall—itself a softened and sweetened version, sharply different from Sholem Aleichem—and then prettified still more. It all bursts with quaintness and local color, and the condescension that usually goes along with them. The condescension is affectionate, though not innocent, for while the creators of this play clearly want to do right by their subject, they must pause now and again, as [the drama critic] Walter Kerr has remarked, "to give their regards to Broadway, with remembrances to Herald Square." For they too work in a tradition, and it is a fatal one: the pressure to twist everything into the gross, the sentimental, the mammoth, and the blatant. And since everyone connected with this play is very sophisticated, they make allowance in advance for all the obvious points of danger: there are quarrels among the Jews, not everything in Anatevka is idyllic, and there even occurs a *papier-mâché* pogrom. Yet none of these "touches of realism" matters very much, for the spirit of Broadway proves invincible.

The movie, which I recently watched for the second time and which has the magnificent Israeli actor Topol in the part of Tevye (Zero Mostel played him—and I have no doubt over-played him—on Broadway) suffers the same want of reality. As Jeremy Dauber writes: "It would have been—and has been—difficult for any filmmaker to shoulder the enormous moral and aesthetic responsibilities of representing a vanished Eastern European Jewry." The movie suggests an order and grandeur to shtetl life that it could scarcely in reality have possessed. The director, Norman Jewison (who despite his name isn't Jewish) also clarified what in the Tevye stories was properly left ambiguous: He had Tevye and his family, after being expelled from Anatevke, headed for New York; he allows Tevye to give his daughter Chava his final blessing, which in the story he doesn't. He has him demand of the Russian military officer in charge of the village that he leave his land, when in the story Tevye merely relates how he ironically expressed his anger to the officer, and in his own account is probably exaggerating. Finally, neither the stage nor the movie version allows Tevye to grow older, as he does in the stories. At one point, upon reporting his having to depart his home, he tells Sholem Aleichem,

> Had I been twenty years younger, and still had my Golde—had I been, that is, the Tevye I was—oho, I wouldn't have taken it lying down: why, I would have settled his [the Russian officer's] hash in a moment.

Fiddler on the Roof won seven Tonys and three Oscars. But it won for the long dead Sholem Aleichem an even grander prize—the recognition among people who know the Tevye stories that the highest literary art can never be altogether successfully transferred either to the stage or to the screen without losing the full quality that makes it truly great. And the highest literary art, indubitably, is what Sholem Aleichem produced.

Jokes: A Genre of Thought

(2017)

EPICURUS (341–270 BCE), the Greek philosopher and founder of the school of Epicureanism, may also have been the world's first shrink. Along with a cosmology and an ethics, Epicurus had a program for stemming anxiety, a four-step method for achieving serenity. Here are the steps:

1. Do not believe in God or the gods. Most likely they do not exist, and even if they did, it is preposterous to believe that they are watching over you and keeping a strict accounting of your behavior.

2. Do not worry about death. Death is oblivion, a condition not different from that of your life before you were born: an utter blank. Not to worry either about heaven or hell; neither exists—after death there is nothing, nada, zilch.

3. As best you are able, forget about pain. Two possibilities here: Either it will diminish and go away, or it will get worse and you will die. Should you die, *hakuna matata*, for death, as we know, presents no problem, being nothing more than eternal dark, dreamless sleep.

4. Do not waste your time attempting to acquire luxuries, whose pleasures are certain to be incommensurate with the effort required to obtain them. From this it follows that ambition generally—for things, money, fame, power—should also be foresworn. The game, quite simply, isn't worth the candle.

To summarize: Forget about God, death, pain, and acquisition—and your worries are over. I've not kitchen-tested this program myself, but my guess is that, if one could bring it off, it might just work. "Live the unnoticed life," as Epicurus advises, and serenity will be yours—unless, that is, you happen to be Jewish.

I have known brilliant, stupid, flashy, dull, savvy, foolish, sensible, neurotic, refined, vulgar, wise, nutty Jews, but I have yet to meet a serene Jew, and I'm inclined to think there may never have been one. Marcus Aurelius, on visiting Palestine in 176 CE, remarked: "O Marcomanni, Quadi, and Sarmatae, at last I have found people more excitable than you."

Jewish habits of thought, featuring irony, skepticism, and criticism, taken together, further preclude serenity. These habits derive from Jewish history and personal experience. An Irish friend then in his nineties once asked me if there were any Yiddish words that weren't critical. I told him there must be some, though I did not know them. Even words that might seem approbative, like *chachem* for wise man, with the slightest turn take on an ironic twist. "No great *chachemess*, Hannah Arendt," my friend Edward Shils used to say when Ms. Arendt's name came up.

The quest to grasp Jewish character, both on the part of Jews and on that of others, has been endless, and is probably unending. What is it about the kind of jokes Jews tell and appreciate, and about jokes featuring Jews as well as their appetite for humor, that is notably, ineluctably Jewish?

Great though the Jewish penchant for jokes is, Jews are of course not alone in joke telling. In one of her essays, the classicist Mary Beard cites the joke anthology *Philogelos* (Laughter Lover), a fourth-century work written in Greek but widely promulgated in Rome. Included in the *Philogelos*, according to Professor Beard, are "jokes about doctors, men with bad breath, eunuchs, barbers, men with hernias, bald men, cuckolds, shady fortune tellers, scholars and intellectuals and more of the colorful (mostly male) characters of Roman life." Keith Thomas, in a lecture titled "The Place of Laughter in Tudor and Stuart England," notes that "jokes are a pointer to joking situations, areas of structural ambiguity in society itself; and their subject matter can be a revealing guide to past tensions and anxieties." About past—also present—tensions and anxieties, Jews know a thing or two.

The English philosopher Simon Critchley, in his book *On Humour*, writes that jokes help us to see our lives "as if we had just landed from another planet." Critchley adds that "the comedian is the anthropologist of our humdrum everyday lives," who helps us to see them in effect from the outside. He calls every joke "a little anthropological essay." I have myself long thought of jokes, at least the more elaborate and better ones, as short stories.

Here is a joke told me by Saul Bellow:

> Yankel Dombrovsky, of the shtetl of Frampol, is 42 years old, unmarried, shy generally, frightened of women in particular. Recently arrived from the neighboring shetl of Blumfvets is Miriam Schneider, a young widow. A Jewish bachelor being a *shandeh*, or disgrace, a meeting is arranged between Yankel and Miriam Schneider. Terrified, Yankel turns to his mother beforehand for advice.
>
> "Yankel, darling son, please not to worry. All women like to talk about three things. They like to talk about family, about food, and about philosophy. Bring these up and I'm sure your meeting will go well."

Miriam Schneider turns out to be 4'8", weighs perhaps 230 pounds, and has an expressionless face.

> Oy, thinks Yankel, oy and oy. What was it Mama said women like to talk about? Oh, yes, food. "Miriam," he asks in a quavering voice, "Miriam, do you like noodles?"
>
> "No," says Miriam, in a gruff voice, "I don't like noodles."
>
> *Veh es meer*. What did Mama say? Family, that's right, family.
>
> "Miriam," he asks, "do you have a brother?"
>
> "Don't got no brother," Miriam replies. Worse and worse. What was the third thing Mama said? Philosophy. Oh, yes, philosophy. "Miriam," Yankel asks, "if you had a brother, would he like noodles?"

Three people are required to perfect a joke: one to tell it, one to get it, and a third not to get it. For those who might have missed it, the object of this joke, of course, is philosophy, especially contemporary academic philosophy. Saul Bellow told me this joke when we were discussing the career of an Oxford philosopher. Bellow had a strong taste for jokes, but, unlike me, he had the patience to hold back telling them until the occasion arose when they made or underscored a point. His wit was generally more free range, sparked by the occasion. Once, walking together through the Art Institute of Chicago we passed Felice Ficherelli's painting *Judith with the Head of Holofernes*, about which Bellow remarked, "That's what you get for fooling with a Jewish girl." I, upon hearing what I take to be a good joke, am more like the yeshiva boy running through the village exclaiming, "I have an answer. I have an answer. Does anyone have a question?" I need to tell the jokes to friends as soon as possible. Freud, about whose thought there cannot be too many jokes—the best is Vladimir Nabokov's characterization of it as "Greek myths hiding private parts"—once said that a fresh joke is good news. The good news is that someone is thinking. Jokes, superior ones, are a genre of thought.

As such the genre is best maintained in the oral tradition. When I tell the "if you had a brother, would he like noodles?" joke, I do so, when speaking in Yankel's voice, in a tremulous greenhorn English accent, and, when speaking in Miriam's voice, in a tone of gruff insensitivity. I like to think performance improves the joke by perhaps 20 percent. Without voice and gesture to accompany them, jokes on paper, or as is now more common on a computer or cell phone screen, are a distant second best.

The first joke in S. Felix Mendelsohn's *The Jew Laughs: Humorous Stories and Anecdotes* (1935) is about the result of telling a joke to a muzhik, a baron, an army officer, and a Jew. In different ways the first three fail to understand the joke, and the Jew, who alone gets it, replies that "the joke is as old as the hills and besides, you don't know how to tell it." Michael Krasny, early in his *Let There Be Laughter: A Treasury of Great Jewish Humor and What It All Means*, notes that "there is an old saw about how every Jew thinks he can tell a Jewish joke better than the one who is telling the joke." Old saw it might be, but one with a high truth quotient. Alongside several of the jokes in Krasny's collection, I noted, "my version is better."

I made similar markings in the margins of William Novak's *Die Laughing: Killer Jokes for Newly Old Folks*, a collection of jokes about aging and about being older generally. Many of these, in the nature of the case, are variants of gallows humor. They touch on too lengthy marriage, what the French call the *désolation générale* of the body, sexual diminishment, physicians, the afterlife, and more. In 1981 Novak had produced, along with Moshe Waldoks, a collection called *The Big Book of Jewish Humor*. The jokes in *Die Laughing* have, perhaps out of fear of redundancy with his earlier book, been de-Judenized, some to less than good effect. The punchline of the joke about the fanatical golfer who returns home late from his regular golf date because his partner and dearest friend died on the golf course early in the round is a case in point. In his explanation to his wife for his tardiness in returning home he explains that for several holes after his friend's death "it was hit the ball, drag Bob, hit the ball, drag Bob." The joke is much improved if Bob is named, as in the version in which I originally heard the joke, Irving. Novak tells the joke about the parsimonious widow who, learning that the charge for newspaper obituaries is by the word, instructs the man on the obit desk to print "O'Malley is dead. Boat for sale." The joke is better, though, in the Jewish version, as "Schwartz dead. Cadillac for sale," and is even one word shorter, thereby saving Mrs. Schwartz a few bucks.

Michael Krasny has a popular radio interview show on the NPR affiliate in San Francisco and is a university professor of English and American literature. Out flogging books of my own, I have twice been on his show and know him to be highly intelligent, cultivated, and good at his job. I've also met William Novak, who, along with being a collector of jokes, is, if an oxymoron be allowed, a well-known ghostwriter. He wrote the autobiographies of, among others, Lee Iacocca, Nancy Reagan, Oliver North, and Magic Johnson. Around the time I met William Novak I mentioned to my editor Carol Houck Smith that he was working on the autobiographies of Tip O'Neill and the Mayflower Madame. "Dear me," she said, "I hope he doesn't get his galleys mixed up."

Both Messrs. Krasny and Novak's books are filled with excellent jokes. I might wince slightly at the rare oral sex joke in *Die Laughing*, but, as Novak remarks after telling one such joke, "Too crass? You should see the ones I left out." Michael Krasny has a weakness for name-dropping. He mentions, among several other drops: "Steve Jobs was someone I liked"; "my sweet friend Rita Moreno"; "my friend the novelist Isabel Allende"; and recounts an afternoon on which he kept Dustin Hoffman in stitches with Jewish jokes at a meeting with him and the director Barry Levinson. Myself the author of a book on snobbery, perhaps I am unduly sensitive to name-dropping, as I remarked over lunch the other day to my good friend the Pope.

Yet Michael Krasny and William Novak are men of good sense who wish only to bring pleasure to their readers, and both do. Novak doubtless shares with Krasny the latter's wholly commendatory conservatory hope that the jokes and humor he loves "will remain an ongoing part of many lives for, well, at least the next few thousand years."

The problem is in the nature of their enterprise: the recounting of one joke after another. Krasny, to be sure, interlards his jokes with anecdotes from his personal experience and offers occasional interpretations of his jokes. Novak introduces his separate joke categories with brief and unfailingly amusing essays. Still, as a character in an Isaac Bashevis Singer story says, "You can have too much even of kreplach."

In our meetings, I have no recollection of exchanging jokes with Michael Krasny or William Novak, and I'm glad of it, for as Jokey Jakeys, as I think of habitual Jewish joke-tellers, things might have gotten competitive, and hence mildly abrasive. Jokey Jakeys like to hear a swell joke, but not as much as they love to tell one.

Here is a joke that appears in neither Michael Krasny's nor William Novak's book:

> Sam Milstein is told his wife, now in the hospital, is dying. When he arrives, she asks him, in the faintest whisper, if he will make love to her one last time. He mentions the unseemliness, not to mention the awkwardness of his doing so—the wires, the tubes, and the rest—but she insists, and so he goes ahead. Lo, that same evening, *mirabile dictu*, Sylvia Milstein's vital signs rise; the next day she is taken off her respirator; and three days later she returns home in full health. Her family throws a party to mark her

miraculous return to normal life. Everyone is delighted and immensely cheerful, except her husband Sam, who is clearly depressed.

"Sam," a friend says, "your beloved wife has returned from near death. Why so glum?"

"You'd be glum too," Sam replies, "if you could have saved the life of Eleanor Roosevelt and you never even lifted a finger."

That joke is immitigably, irreducibly, entirely Jewish. Sam cannot be Bob, nor the Milsteins the O'Malleys. As for what is so Jewish about it, I should answer, in a word, everything: the politics, the depression, even the sex.

A question Michael Krasny asks but doesn't quite fully answer is, Why are Jews so funny? They have what Henry James called "the imagination of disaster." Optimism is foreign to them. They find clouds in silver linings. If they do not court suffering, neither are they surprised when it arrives. They sense that life itself can be a joke, and one too often played upon them. They fear that God Himself loves a joke.

Adam, alone in the Garden of Eden, brings up his loneliness to God.

"Adam," the Lord says, "I can stem your loneliness with a companion who will be forever a comfort and a consolation to you. She, this companion—woman, I call her—will be your friend and lover, helpmeet and guide, selfless and faithful, devoted to your happiness throughout life.

"But Adam," says the Lord, "there is going to be a price for this companion."

When Adam asks the price, the Lord tells him he will have to pay by the loss of his nose, his right foot, and his left hand."

"That's very steep," says Adam, "but tell me, Lord, what can I get for a rib?"

That joke is of course entirely unacceptable today; it is anti-woman, misogynist, politically incorrect. Michael Krasny brings up political

correctness in passing, but in our day political correctness, in its per-
vasiveness, is the great enemy of joke-telling and of humor in general.
Consider a simple joke Henny Youngman used to tell: "A bum came up
and asked me for 50 cents for a cup of coffee. 'But coffee's only a quarter,' I said. 'Won't you join me?' he answered." Today there are no bums,
only homeless people. As soon as one sanitizes the joke by beginning,
"A homeless person came up to me . . ." the joke is over and humor has
departed the room.

Pervasive though political correctness has become, it, like affirmative
action, does not apply to the Jews or to Jewish jokes. Anti-Semitic jokes
abound, not a few told by Jews. All play off Jewish stereotypes, some milder
than others. The four reasons we know Jesus was Jewish, for example, are
that he lived at home till he was past 30, he went into his father's business,
he thought his mother was a virgin, and she (his mother) treated him as if
he were God. Fairly harmless. But then there are the world's four shortest
books: *Irish Haute Cuisine, Great Stand-Up German Comics, Famous Italian Naval Victories*, and—oops!—*Jewish Business Ethics*.

What we need is not more anti-Semitic jokes, but more jokes about
anti-Semites:

> A Jew is sitting in a bar, when a man at the other end, three
> sheets fully to the wind, offers to buy drinks for everyone at
> the bar, "except my Israelite friend at the other end of the bar."
> Twenty minutes later, the same man instructs the bartender to
> pour another round for the house, excluding, of course, "the
> gentleman of the Hebrew persuasion at the end of the bar." A
> further fifteen minutes on, the man asks for one more round
> for everyone, "not counting, of course, the follower of Moses
> who's still here, I see." Finally exasperated, the Jew calls down
> to the drunk, "What is it you have against me anyway?" "I'll
> tell you what I have against you. You sunk the *Titanic*."
>
> "I didn't sink the *Titanic*," the Jew says, "an iceberg sunk the
> *Titanic*."
>
> "Iceberg, Greenberg, Goldberg," says the drunk, "you're all
> no damn good."

Michael Krasny remarks that the standard source ascribed to Jewish humor is "located in a kind of masochism but also in suffering. It is self-deprecatory and self-lacerating, and it sees Jews as outsiders, marginal people, victims." A good definition, that, of the comedy of Woody Allen, with psychoanalysis and jokes added. But Krasny also sees in these Jewish jokes "a strain of celebration," and cites Jewish American Princess, or JAP, jokes as an example. A brilliant JAP bit I know is that performed by the comedian Sarah Silverman, impersonating a faux Jewish American Princess, in which she invents a niece who claims to have learned in school that during the Holocaust, 60 million Jews were killed. In her best ditzy JAP voice, Silverman corrects the child, saying that not 60 but six million Jews were killed, adding, "60 million would be something to worry about."

A few categories of superior Jewish jokes failed to find their way into the Krasny or the de-Judenized Novak volume. Jewish waiter jokes are, for one, missing. Allow me to supply merely the punchlines of a few: "Vich of you gentlemen vanted the clean glass?" "You vanted the chicken soup, you should've ordered the mushroom barley." Another missing category is jokes about German Jews, or *yekkes*, as they are known, for the formality that did not allow them to remove their suit jackets in public. "What's the difference between a *yekke* and a virgin?" one such joke asks. The answer is, "A *yekke* remains a *yekke*." And in the category of out-of-control Jewish wifely extravagance the winner is Rodney Dangerfield's "A thief stole my wife's purse with all her credit cards. But I'm not going after him. He's spending less than she does."

Of the endless category of synagogue jokes, Michael Krasney tells the superior joke about the rabbi who rid his shul of mice by luring them onto the *bimah* with a wheel of cheese, and while there, bar mitzvahing them all, whereby they never returned. I wonder if he knows my friend Edward Shils's favorite joke in this, the synagogue category:

> A peddler, just before sundown, arrives at the study of the rabbi of the shtetl of Bobrinsk. Three men are in the study at the time. The peddler asks the rabbi if he will keep his receipts over Shabbat, when an observant Jew is prohibited from having money on his person. The rabbi readily agrees.

Next day, after sundown, the peddler appears in the rabbi's study to collect his money. The same three men are there.

"What money?" the rabbi asks.

"The money I gave you to hold for me last night," the peddler says. "These men were there. They will remind you."

The rabbi turns to the first man. "Mr. Schwartz, did this man leave any money with me yesterday?" "I have no recollection of his having done so, rebbe," Schwartz says.

"Mr. Ginsberg," the rabbi asks, turning to the second man, "do you recognize this man?" "Never saw him before in my life," Ginsberg says. "Mr. Silverstein, what do you think about this?" "The man's a liar, rebbe," says Silverstein." "Thank you, gentlemen," says the rabbi. "Now if you will excuse me I shall deal with this man alone."

After the three men depart, the rabbi goes to his safe, removes the peddler's money, and hands it to him.

"Rebbe," says the peddler, "why did you put me through all that?"

"Oh," answers the rebbe, "I just wanted to show you the kind of people I have in my congregation."

When Edward told me this joke, which he much enjoyed, I assumed that he had in mind, as analogues to Messrs. Schwartz, Ginsberg, and Silverstein, his colleagues on the Committee on Social Thought at The University of Chicago.

In *Jokes and Their Relation to the Unconscious*, Freud wrote, "I do not know whether there are many other instances of a people making fun to such a degree of its own character [as do the Jews]." I myself cannot think of any. Who but the Jews joke about their mothers, their religious institutions ("Reform Judaism, isn't that the Democratic Party platform with holidays added?"), their own attitudes of compromise and resignation, their *nouveau riches*, their domineering wives, their uxorious husbands, the way their enemies think of them, and more? The Irish joke about themselves—an Irish friend not long ago told me that the famous Irish charm is inevitably lost only on the Irish themselves—but nowhere near so thoroughly as do the Jews, who find almost everything about themselves a source of humor.

"How odd of God to choose the Jews" runs a ditty composed by an English journalist named William Norman Ewer, to which various responses have been offered, perhaps the most amusing among them being "because the *goyim* annoy him." Chosen the Jews may have been, but the everlasting question remains: chosen for what? If pressed to come up with a single theme playing through the Old Testament, that theme would be testing, the relentless testing by God of the Jews from Abraham through Saul, David, and Solomon to Job and beyond. God submits the Jews to tests and trials of a kind that no other religion, so far as I know, puts its adherents through, including, some in our day might say, unrelenting anti-Semitism. Might it be, to revert to an earlier point, that a key reason there are no serene Jews is that every Jew somewhere in his heart knows that, no matter how well off he is or how righteously he has lived, further tests await.

Freud felt all jokes at bottom had for their purpose, however hidden, either hostility or exposure—all jokes, in other words, for him are ultimately acts of aggression or derision. I don't happen to believe that. Michael Krasny quotes Theodor Reik, in *Jewish Wit*, remarking that all Jewish jokes are about "merciless mockery of weakness and failing." I don't believe that, either. What I do believe is W. H. Auden saying that the motto of psychology ought to be "Have you heard this one?"

Jewish jokes are richer and more varied than any single theory can hope to accommodate. In *No Joke*, her excellent study of Jewish humor, Ruth Wisse notes that "Jewish humor at its best interprets the incongruities of the Jewish condition." That condition has imbued Jews with a style of thought when faced with received opinions and conventional wisdom. Among their grand thinkers, and their everyday ones, are, or ought to have been, those trained by life to think outside the box—or, as the Jew in me, having written out that cliché, needs to add, outside the lox. Jewish jokes are a victory over thoughtlessness.

Maury Skolnik tells his friend Mel Rosen, "Two Jews, each with a parrot on his shoulder, meet outside their synagogue, when . . ."

Rosen interrupts: "Maury, Maury, Maury, don't you know any but Jewish jokes?"

"Of course I do," Skolnik replies. "It's autumn in Kyoto, two samurai are standing in front of a Buddhist temple. The next day is Yom Kippur . . ."

Jews on the Loose

(2016)

FAME IS WHEN A CARICATURE OF YOU requires no caption. Fame is when everyone understands it is you when only your first name is mentioned: Marilyn, Frank, Hillary, Michael (Jordan and Jackson). Fame is also when a mad person imagines that he is you, though this criterion, granted, is more difficult to establish. Groucho Marx surely qualifies on the first two criteria, and, though I don't know of anyone who imagined that he was Groucho, more people have probably dressed up as him (it was George Gershwin's favorite outfit at costume parties) than any other comic. Still, even great fame has its limits. Not long ago, when I called Barnes & Noble to order a copy of *The Groucho Letters*, the sales clerk inquired, "How do you spell Groucho?"

A Gallup Poll taken in 1941 asking people to name their 15 favorite comedians found the Marx Brothers finishing 13th, behind Red Skelton, Danny Kaye, Jimmy Durante, Arthur Godfrey, and others. While these comedians have now fallen from public interest, the Marx Brothers have held on. If anything, they have stepped higher up the slippery ladder of renown, and are today firmly embedded in that charmed circle of movie comics granted immortality that includes Charlie Chaplin, Buster Keaton, W. C. Fields, and Laurel and Hardy.

At first glance, the attraction behind the Marx Brothers is not self-evident. They offer three rather homely men who specialize in the creation of havoc. One doesn't speak, but, honking a horn, wolfs after women, makes grotesque faces, drops silverware from his sleeve, extracts blow-torches, axes, and teacups from under his raincoat; he is a pit bull in a blond wig who does too lengthy solo numbers on a harp. Another speaks, but in a preposterous Italian accent, wears the clothes of an organ grinder's monkey, and plays a fast piano, occasionally shooting the keys with his index finger as if with a pistol. The third, the main man, wears grease-painted eyebrows and mustache, glasses, keeps a cigar going at all times, and walks like a caged gorilla with *shpilkes*. The speech of this third fellow is restricted to puns and put-downs, non sequiturs and sexual innuendos, all uttered in the tone of a relentless wise guy.

Antic, zany, madcap, anarchic, the Marx Brothers were successful first in vaudeville, then on the Broadway stage, and finally, most emphatically, in the movies. Their act resembled nothing so much as a comic strip brought to life. In fact, the names of the brothers were bestowed on them by a vaudeville comic named Art Fisher, who had been inspired by a popular series of comic strips by Gus Mager about monkey-like characters with names like Knocko, Sherlocko, and even Groucho. In order of birth, Leonard became Chico (originally Chicko) for his woman-chasing, Adolph became Harpo because he played the harp, and Julius became Groucho because of his innate glumness and cynicism. Milton, who played the straight man in the early days of the act, became Gummo, because of rubber-soled shoes he wore. Herbert, who replaced Gummo in 1925, became Zeppo, though it is not entirely clear why.

What the brothers did on stage and screen was far from adult and sometimes less adolescent than childish. Grown men in clownish costumes, they palavered and cavorted. Some of their humor was cruel, little of it victimless. If the Marx Brothers' movies have a collective underlying message, it is, surely, that respectable life is a sham, a scam, not to put too fine a point on it, bullshit. Why did people enjoy this coarse cavalcade of uproarious disruption and denigration?

That the Marx family was in its origins German-Jewish, given the image of German Jews as irretrievably formal, is a touch surprising.

The boys' father, Samuel, was from Alsace, and their mother, Minnie, was the daughter of an entertainer from Dornum, Germany. Sam Marx was handsome, an inept tailor, and devoted to the skirt chase, the only trait he seems to have passed on to his sons. Minnie was the brains and motor force of the family. (An old joke: When the boy told his mother he was to play the Jewish husband in a school play, she instructed him to return to school to tell the teacher that he wanted a speaking part.) Her brother was Al Shean, of Gallagher & Shean, a famous vaudeville comedy team that eventually appeared in *Ziegfeld Follies*. A stage mother to the highest power, she ran her home like a raucous vaudeville boarding house, and made sure show business was her sons' fate.

With the exception of Zeppo, none of the brothers completed high school. Only Groucho, who departed school in the seventh grade, seems to have found this troubling. He had literary aspirations, not to say pretensions. In the 1920s, he took an occasional seat at the famous Algonquin Round Table. (Harpo, befriended by the critic Alexander Woollcott, found himself more comfortably seated there.) In the 1950s, Groucho entered into a correspondence and distant friendship with T. S. Eliot. His occasional magazine pieces resembled minor Robert Benchley or James Thurber or sub-par S. J. Perelman, though it all came out sounding like a fellow named Groucho:

> A man in my position (horizontal at the moment) is likely to hear strange stories about himself. A few years ago they were saying I made a pig out of myself drinking champagne out of Miss Garbo's slipper. Actually it was nothing but very weak punch.

Off-screen, Chico was said to be the most charming of the brothers, Harpo the most likeable—charming and likeable are not the same—Groucho, slightly wall-eyed, easily the most rebarbative. (Minnie called her middle son *die Eifersüchtige*, the jealous one.) Chico was a hopeless gambler, and had often to call on his brothers to bail him out. Harpo was alone in having only one wife, and was an unambiguously good father to four adopted children.

As LEE SIEGEL'S *GROUCHO MARX: THE COMEDY OF EXISTENCE*, a book in Yale University Press's Jewish Lives series, makes plain, Groucho was a man who could find a cloud in every silver lining. As a souvenir of his first sex, with a prostitute in Montreal, he came away with the clap. The only careful saver among the brothers, he was wiped out in the market crash of 1929. He was hard on each of his three wives. Toward the end of his life, Groucho, looking rather pathetic in a beret, was led about by a starlet-caregiver named Erin Fleming, who his son Arthur ended up taking to court after his death, accusing her of stealing his father's money. Groucho died in 1977 and made the mistake of doing so the same week as Elvis Presley, who crowded Groucho's final exit off the front pages.

The Marx Brothers made 13 movies, *The Cocoanuts* (1929) the first, *Love Happy* (1949) the last. The later movies, after *A Night in Casablanca* (1946), did less well at the box office, though Groucho, sensing the brothers act was growing stale, began to talk of retirement as early as 1939. Although Harpo and Chico tried, only Groucho went on to further show business success, first in radio, then in television, with his comedy quiz show *You Bet Your Life*.

One need only write four or five perfect poems, it has been said, to live forever as a poet. Might the same be said of comedy? Will four or five perfect scenes or even jokes do it? Almost everyone has one or another Marx Brothers comic bit engraved in memory. For many it is that teeming stateroom scene aboard ship in *A Night at the Opera*. For some it is Groucho's rendition of "Hooray for Captain Spaulding, the African Explorer" (some people, you will recall, called him schnorrer). Or Groucho's remarking of Margaret Dumont, in *Duck Soup*, that he had been fighting for her honor; she won't. Others will remember one or another Groucho line: "One morning I shot an elephant in my pajamas. How he got in my pajamas, I don't know"; or, from *You Bet Your Life*, his asking a tree surgeon contestant if he ever fell out of a patient. Everyone, possibly even young clerks at Barnes & Noble, knows his, "I do not want to belong to any club that will accept me as a member."

The bits may loom larger than the movies themselves, a case of the parts being greater than the whole. Over the past three or so weeks I have watched all of the Marx Brothers' movies. The better ones have the participation of the comedy songwriters Harry Ruby and Bert Kalmar. Only one movie, *Duck Soup*, had the benefit of a superior director, Leo McCarey. *The Cocoanuts* and *Animal Crackers*, originally stage plays written by George S. Kaufman and Morrie Riskin ("No schmucks they," Groucho in a high accolade called them in an interview in the indispensable *The Marx Bros. Scrapbook*), seem the best written, not least because Kaufman shared something of Groucho's comic spirit. (A confirmed philanderer, Kaufman told Irving Berlin that he would have liked Berlin's song "Always" better if it were retitled "Thursdays.") Some prefer *Monkey Business* and *Horse Feathers*, the movies written by S. J. Perelman and Will Johnstone, though in later days Groucho denigrated Perelman, and vice versa. "They're mercurial, devious, and ungrateful," Perelman reports Herman Mankiewicz told him when Perelman took on the assignment of writing for the Marx Brothers. "I hate to depress you, but you'll rue the day you ever took the assignment. This is an ordeal by fire. Make sure you wear your asbestos pants."

Although aficionados tend to prefer the rougher cut movies made at Paramount over the smoother ones made at MGM under Irving Thalberg, the truth is that they all tend to wash into one another. Was *Monkey Business* the one about college football or was that *Animal Crackers*? (In fact it was *Horse Feathers*.) What is perhaps remarkable above all about the films is that in them the Marx Brothers are so utterly unsympathetic. One's sympathies go out to Chaplin's little tramp; to the sweet naivety of the hapless Buster Keaton; to the put-upon Oliver Hardy and the nonplussed Stan Laurel; even to W. C. Fields in his role as the besieged husband. Not so, not for a moment, does one feel the least sympathy with the Marx Brothers, whom one cannot imagine entertaining at one's home without first calling in the fire department. They could, even on the screen, seem menacing, and menacing is the very reverse of charming.

In 1939, the *New York Times* theater critic Brooks Atkinson, during an era when the *Times* still employed men with two last names, interviewed Groucho. At the close of the interview, Atkinson remarked that the Marx Brothers "have covered about as much comic ground as three fantastic characters with separate personalities are able to do without bogging down in formula." Tested for its truth quotient, that sentence scores in negative integers. The Marx Brothers' comedy was nothing if not formulaic. One begins with three characters whose personalities couldn't be more locked in, adds traditional dupes and stock villains and a minor love interest, and then lets loose the dogs. A pause in each movie occurs for a shoot-the-keys piano recital by Chico, and another for an unduly sensitive harp rendering by Harpo. (Groucho claimed to be bored blue by his brother's harp playing.). In a 1946 interview in *Photoplay*, Gummo, by then a successful Hollywood agent, mentioned that his brothers were looking for a new script. "The only trouble," he added, "is the stories all have plots."

In a book called *The Anatomy of Cinematic Humor*, Thomas H. Jordan remarks that the Marx Brothers' "films can be seen many times without losing their appeal, for there are so many gags and jokes that no one can possibly remember more than a small number." Nor would one want to, since a high percentage of Groucho's machine-gun-fire quips ("This man's a cad—a yellow cad") and Chico's immigrant malapropisms ("From now on you and me is gonna be insufferable") do not come off. Sometimes an amusing line will be followed by an empty pun, which undermines the earlier joke. In *The Cocoanuts*, for instance, Groucho shows Chico the map of a plot of land, noting the levies. "That's the Jewish neighborhood?" Chico replies. Funny. A few moments later, Groucho curses Chico by saying, "May all your teeth have cavities," to which to he adds, "And remember, abscess makes the heart grow fonder." Not funny. The slapstick changes—its most extravagant scene is the collapse of all the stage scenery in *A Night at The Opera*—but the chasing of blondes, the insulting of poor Margaret Dumont, the rat-a-tat-tat of Groucho embroidering clichés—"I am not hemmed to fit the touch of your skirt"—come to seem bits, mere *shtichlach*, little more.

This is, of course, a minority opinion. Opposed to it are numerous movie critics, celebrities, French surrealists, and most recently academics specializing in popular culture. Woody Allen thought what they did pure genius. (I myself much preferred Woody Allen's movies before he himself became a genius.) Salvador Dali, much taken with the Marx Brothers, called Harpo "the most fascinating and the most surrealistic character in Hollywood." No less portentous a figure than Antonin Artaud, in a

1932 article in *La Nouvelle Revue Française*, made the claim that the Marx Brothers' films were essentially surrealist poems, and chided American audiences of the movies for not going beyond laughter (never much of a problem for Artaud) to understand their deeper significance.

The significance imputed to the Marx Brothers' movies is primarily cultural but one wonders if it isn't ultimately political. The claim is that these movies constitute, in effect, an attack on the American establishment, root (its traditions and mores) and branches (its major institutions). The movies mock land speculation, first-class ocean travel, capital-S society, art collecting and connoisseurship, higher education, the opera, diplomacy and war mongering, corporate shenanigans, psychiatry and the medical profession, the legal profession, the myth of the American west, thoroughbred racing, and more. Today, though, for better and worse, there is no establishment, and many of their targets have long gone out of business. This hasn't stopped critics from pretending that the Marx Brothers' movies carry the same useful antinomian punch as at the time of their original production. The briefest dip into the criticism of the Marx Brothers' movies—Lee Siegel follows the academics in describing it straight-facedly as "Marxian" scholarship—leaves one, as Groucho might have said, reeling.

GROUCHO HIMSELF NEVER BOUGHT INTO the deeper significance of his and his brothers' act, and felt they were vastly over-analyzed. As for the attraction behind the movies, I wonder if Chico didn't capture it best in two short sentences, when he wrote, "The reason people like to see us doing any tomfool thing that comes into our heads is quite simple. It's because that's how a normal person would like to act, once in a while . . ." There may not be much more to say, really, unless you are writing a book on the Marx Brothers, and Lee Siegel has, in the nature of the case, a vast deal more to say. Siegel is what in our day is called a culture critic, which means someone who takes on not merely the arts, but all of the culture in its social ramifications. Whether he is writing about his refusal to repay his student loan, or about his admiration for Norman Mailer, Siegel's prose tends to overheat, and his normal penchant is to dramatize his subjects. He calls *Groucho Marx: The Comedy of Existence* "a biocommentary," in which he "weaves the outward facts of Groucho's life into and through a story about the inward facts of Groucho's life." Early in the book, Siegel makes the point that Groucho's brother Chico had a larger penis than he did. Hang on, in other words, to your couch, the psychoanalyst will be with us in a moment. No scene in any of the Marx Brothers' movies is, in Siegel's reading, without meaning. The lovely line "Did someone call me schnorrer?" is really an expression of Groucho's anxiety. Siegel is not even momentarily detained by the fact that this is a line in a song by Bert Kalmar and Harry Ruby.

"I do not want to belong to any club that will accept me as a member," Groucho's letter of resignation to the Friar's Club, was, at least, certainly written by Groucho. But in Siegel's microwaved prose, it becomes in "one of its countless dimensions . . . the obliteration not of the self who is making the joke, but of the existential convention, as it were, of having a self, an ego, to begin with." Never one to leave bad enough alone, Siegel goes on:

> If Groucho abolishes his own ego in one stroke with his fabled line—never mind, for a moment, that he also establishes his superior authenticity and power—then who is doing the abolishing? Who is Groucho Marx? He seems to exist in a totally negative space, in which his freedom is synonymous with the fact that he stands for nothing.

Bet you never thought of that.

Harpo's repeated bit of forcing others to hold his raised leg is for Siegel no mere comic touch but "the hidden need to use others for our gratification, and the ceaseless urge to use other people to 'get a leg up.' It is also, as so much of the Marx Brothers' comedy is, an act of self-emasculating aggression." Reading passages like this, I kept seeing the *You Bet Your Life* duck come down as Groucho announced, "Say the opaque phrase and collect a hundred dollars."

Without faulty parents, psychoanalytic interpretation is, of course, out of business. Siegel finds them easily enough in Groucho's family. Insufficient mother love is joined to a weak father to result in a son who "spent his career questioning just what manhood really is." The ineffectual Sam Marx, in Siegel's reading, "created sons who had a natural contempt for power, and sons who had a natural contempt for powerlessness." The brothers, as a result, set out to "discredit the concept of fatherhood itself." Siegel recounts Groucho's father telling him that if he didn't master pinochle he would never be a real man, which he reads as "an emasculating comment." Yet one of the sweetest, gentlest essays Groucho ever wrote was about his father. It tells the story of his comic business failures but emphasizes his love for a man who brought in paid boosters to the audience for his sons' vaudeville performances and became the family cook, specializing in kugels.

In his movie roles Groucho, for Lee Siegel, represents not an amusing attack on pretension but "the spirit of nihilism." Siegel disputes the view that Woody Allen is Groucho's descendant, for he feels that "Allen is simply too funny to be Groucho's direct descendant." Groucho is—and he is right about this—much darker. "No other comedians of the time," Siegel writes, "come close to the wraithlike sociopath Groucho portrays in the Marx Brothers' best films." A more compelling reason, I should have thought, is that, in their respective movie roles, Groucho plays a shtunk, Allen a nebbish with psychoanalytic tone and self-hating touches added at no extra cost. Groucho's heirs, I should have thought, are in the line of insult comedians, among them the unjustly forgotten Jack E. Leonard and Don Rickles.

For Lee Siegel, Groucho's true heir is Lenny Bruce. "In the work of Groucho and his two brothers," he writes, "the result is comedy sometimes so dark that it is not funny at all." He brings up Bruce's purported remark, shortly after the assassination of John F. Kennedy, that "Jackie hauled ass," apparently to avoid being shot herself, a remark in bad enough taste but one that scarcely captures Lenny Bruce's comedy.

As it happens, I was in the audience for Lenny Bruce's performance in a theater—he had earlier lost his cabaret license—on the Lower East Side of New York the weekend following the Kennedy assassination. Bruce appeared without fanfare or even introduction from behind the curtain, sighed, and said, "Oswald, it's a fucking rabbit's name. And who hasn't known a putz like Jack Ruby?" And then he did a bit about the reaction to the news of the assassination on the part of Vaughn Meader, a JFK impersonator, who understands that his career is now over (it was, in fact). Bruce went on from there to do a skit about a Jewish nightclub owner attempting to bribe a Puerto Rican busboy to service a putatively nymphomaniacal Sophie Tucker. ("I don't care how much money you offer, Mr. Rosenberg," the busboy says at the skit's close, "I will not *shtup* her!") All this is comedy of a very different order than the kind Groucho and his brothers ever performed or even thought of performing.

Groucho, as I mentioned earlier, exchanged letters and, when in London, had a dinner meeting with T. S. Eliot and his wife. The correspondence was light and, one gathers, was pleasing to both parties, allowing Groucho a connection with a hero of highbrow culture and Eliot one with a hero of popular culture. Lee Siegel sees it differently. He sees the relationship as, in the cant word of the day, fraught. He dissects a letter in which Eliot tells Groucho that he recently took his wife to see a rerun of *The Marx Brothers Go West*, and finds Eliot's letter at bottom "a triumph of genteel passive-aggression," another of the great cant words of the age. Siegel doesn't want to give Eliot credit for being a nice man who, late in life, came to like and admire Groucho, notwithstanding the infamous anti-Semitic lines in two of his poems, and his mention of undesirability of "free-thinking Jews," decades earlier in *After Strange Gods*. Eliot was also properly appalled, indeed horrified, by the Holocaust.

How Jewish was Groucho? Given the aggressiveness of the Marx Brothers' roles in the movies, there is, in the writing about them I have read, little in the way of anti-Semitism. Chico of course came on as a stagy Italian; Harpo was from another, thus far unidentified, planet. Despite his taking on such W. C. Fieldsian movie names as Rufus T. Firefly, Wolf J. Flywheel, and Dr. Hugo Z. Hackenbush, Groucho was recognizably, irretrievably, Jewish, a fact set in italics by his stage get-up of glasses, thick mustache, and fast, usually insulting talk. In its 1932 cover story on the Marx Brothers, *Time* magazine referred to him as a "prototypical Hebrew wiseguy." When Groucho consulted Herman Mankiewicz on how to play one of his movie roles, Mankiewicz replied: "You're a middle-aged Jew who picks up spit." Yet Broadway and Hollywood both, from the early decades of the last century through the 1960s, were themselves so thoroughly Jewish that anti-Semitism was never much of an intramural problem. Nor did it appear to be an extramural one, for the Marx Brothers everywhere found ready acceptance.

Lee Siegel never mentions anti-Semitism in connection with the Marx Brothers, but he does attempt to position them in the tradition of Jewish humor. Jewish humor, in his view, is entwined with Jewish wisdom, which it surely often is. He recognizes that it is also heavily imbued with irony. And he wonders to what extent self-hatred is the basis of Jewish humor, noting that Freud is responsible for the notion that Jewish humor is about self-disparagement. He speculates upon whether at its heart Jewish humor isn't the result of diaspora (no stand-up comics, true enough, in the Old Testament), alienation, and the condition generally of outsiderishness—a condition that breeds, simultaneously, an affinity for insult, a sense of self-debasement, and a feeling of superiority. "The status of the outsider," Siegel writes, "is one place to begin to construct a definition of Jewish humor." Yes, perhaps. Then again, Jewish humor is in the end probably no more than Jews being humorous, and they have found manifold ways of doing so, from subtle to slapstick, from the blatant to the philosophical, and, God willing, they will continue to do so.

In the end, Siegel is most interested in Groucho's psyche, which, he concludes, he purged on film. These performances are, he writes, his "fullest disclosure of who he really was. They are the biographical gold." I have been trying to think of how Groucho himself would reply to such a statement. I can imagine him riffing on the bit in *The Treasure of the Sierra Madre* where Walter Huston tells Humphrey Bogart and Tim Holt that what they've found is fool's gold, but he just might shoot a sidelong glance, and go into a version of his leering, loose-limbed, lovely Captain Spaulding dance. Did someone call him schnorrer?

Jewish Pugs

(2016)

IMPOSSIBLE, I SUSPECT, to convince anyone under 50 how central the sport of boxing was to American popular culture in the first five decades of the last century. No single event—not the Olympics, the World Series, Wimbledon, the Rose Bowl—held the attraction for Americans interested in sports that a heavyweight championship fight held. Nor did it even have to be a championship fight. At the age of 14, on the Friday night of October 26, 1951, I was sitting in the Nortown Theatre in Chicago when they stopped the movie—stopped the movie!—to announce that Rocky Marciano had just beaten Joe Louis in the eighth round of a scheduled 10-round fight at Madison Square Garden.

Prize fights, amateur and professional, were ubiquitous: staged in small clubs and at major stadiums, broadcast over the radio (the Friday Night Fights sponsored by Gillette Blue Blades—"for the quickest, slickest shave of all"), and, beginning in the late 1940s, on television, often several nights a week. A comic strip called *Joe Palooka*, about a heavyweight boxing champion, was widely syndicated during these years and was a favorite of boys. At the age of 12, I could name the champions and leading contenders in every weight division, from flyweight (108–112 pounds) to heavyweight (no limit), but then so could any normally sports-obsessed kid, and in my boyhood there were lots of us. When Joe Louis defeated Max Schmeling of Germany in a return-match first-round knockout in 1938—a fight, alas, before my time—Americans felt that it was a victory over the Nazis, and Louis became a national hero, even though the United States would not enter the war for another three and a half years. Boxing was immensely popular, international, a form of patriotism by other means, in a word, big.

A Canadian who had arrived in this country from Montreal at the age of 17, my father had no interest in baseball or football. Boxing, though, did interest him. He took me to Golden Gloves (amateur) fights at Rainbow Arena on Chicago's north side, and himself was lucky enough to have a ticket for the second of the three brutal Tony Zale-Rocky Graziano middleweight championship fights.

In Montreal my father had grown up with two brothers, Danny and Sammy Spunt, who owned a boxing gym, the Chicago equivalent of Stillman's in New York, called The Ringside. In the late 1940s, Chicago seemed safe enough for an 11-year-old boy to mount the El and travel alone downtown, which, for a brief period, I did, to hang out at their gym. Danny Spunt was especially kind to me. He directed me to a file cabinet filled with signed 8" x 10" glossy photographs of all the boxing champions and leading contenders of the day, and told me to take my pick: I took home a Willie Pep, a Gus Lesnevich, and a Sugar Ray Robinson. As long as I didn't get in the way, which I wasn't about to do, I could watch fighters spar, shadowbox, and work out on the light or heavy bags. The atmosphere couldn't have been more masculine, the smell of the joint a rich brew of liniment, leather, cigar smoke, and heavy sweat.

One day Danny Spunt took me into the locker room, where he introduced me to a seated fighter leaning against a locker after a workout, his fists taped, his only clothes a heavy leather Everlast protective jock.

"Kid," Danny said, "meet Tony Zale, the middleweight champion [he pronounced it "champeen"] of the world."

"Hi, champ," I managed to gurgle.

"Hi, kid," Zale replied. No meeting since in my life has impressed me half so much.

One of the leading younger fighters who trained at The Ringside in those days was a black welterweight named Johnny Bratton. His manager, a heavyset man in a green corduroy jacket and a coral-colored hat with a large feather in its band that he wore indoors, had flashing gold teeth. In 1951, at the age of 24, Johnny Bratton won the welterweight title by outpointing Charley Fusari. Less than two months later, he lost it to "Kid" Gavilan, a flashy Cuban whose arsenal included an uppercut that seemed to begin around the knees called the bolo punch. Afterwards it was revealed that Bratton fought Gavilan for some 10 rounds of their 15-round fight with a broken jaw. Tumbling downhill from there, Bratton was reduced to fighting bums until he himself was a bum other boxers fought on their way up. Years later, I read in the *Chicago Sun-Times* that he had been picked up by the cops around Chicago Stadium while attempting to sell a stolen fur coat. He spent much of the rest of his days in an insane asylum in Manteno, Illinois, and died in his mid-fifties. The other, not altogether uncommon, side of the boxing story, Johnny Bratton's.

By the time I became interested in boxing, Jewish boxers were no longer active. Such glory as Jews had derived from competing in the sport was long in the past. But even this past glory lived on. Across the courtyard in the building in which we lived on Sheridan Road in Chicago resided the Kaplans, Ida and Irv, Ida being the sister of Barney Ross, who in his day held the lightweight, light-welterweight, and welterweight championships. The father of a classmate, Billy Schoenwald, who later became a good friend, was Irv Schoenwald, a successful fight promoter. In the 1940s and early 1950s a former heavyweight, the slightly punchy "Kingfish" Levinsky (his name derived from his family's fish business on Maxwell Street, the city's permanent flea market), used to sell garish neckties out of a suitcase to Jewish businessmen who worked in the Loop. My father bought one off the old pug.

Mob corruption, of course, was always hovering on the edge of boxing, sometimes damnably close to the center. I had another friend whose father succeeded beyond all his imagining selling aluminum awnings, which allowed him to invest in boxers. His most famous fighter was a heavyweight named Ernie Terrell, who was WBA champion from 1965 to 1967, when he was beaten badly, humiliatingly, by Muhammad Ali. My friend's father got tied up with the Mob in Chicago—he had installed awnings for Tony "Big Tuna" Accardo, the head of the Chicago Syndicate and a frightening figure—whose thugs wanted to control his fighters. At one point, he was pursued by a hitman named Felix "Milwaukee Phil" Alderisio, had to go into hiding, and, after being rescued by the FBI, testified about Mob interests in boxing.

MIKE SILVER'S *STARS IN THE RING*, an excellent account of "Jewish Champions in the Golden Age of Boxing," is an elegant piece of bookmaking that is an outstanding specimen of a coffee-table book but also much more than that. The book contains photographs of the best 166 Jewish boxers (cauliflower ears are sometimes apparent; so, too, evidence of broken or flattened noses, rhinoplasty, one might say, by other means), along with biographical portraits of admirable concision tracing the trajectory of their careers.

Along with these biographies, *Stars in the Ring* provides essaylets on such items as the medical effects of boxing on the fighters; the grooming of future fighters who were newsboys defending their street-corner turfs; the Golden Gloves era; boxing in the Shanghai ghetto, in DP camps, and in Israel; and more. Silver chronicles the history of boxing from its bare-knuckles era, when the Sephardi boxer Daniel Mendoza "achieved something like superstar status," to the reign of the Marquis of Queensbury rules, and through its television heyday. He also sets out the sport's decline, both in popular appeal and in the quality of fighters; boxing, he regrettably allows, is the only sport in which the athletes haven't gotten better.

Jews had always been prominent middlemen in the sport of boxing. They were, Silver writes, "promoters, managers, trainers, corner men, gym owners, equipment manufacturers, and magazine publishers." He devotes a few pages to Nat Fleischer, editor and publisher of *The Ring* magazine and for decades the unacknowledged commissioner of boxing. Fleischer set up a rating system for boxers, argued for stringent medical examinations and rules, fought against the incursions of organized crime in the sport. "Sadly, after Fleischer's death in 1972," Silver writes, "*The Ring* began to deteriorate along with the sport," a view seconded by the boxing historian Harry Shaffer, who believed that Nat Fleischer "is what held it [boxing] together."

In the early decades of the last century, Jewish boxers were, if not preponderant, certainly commonplace. "The first four decades of the last century were a Golden Age for the sport of boxing in terms of status, the quantity and quality of talent, media coverage, and attendance figures," Silver writes, adding: "It was no less a Golden Age for Jewish boxers." He has discovered that there were more than 3,000 Jewish professional boxers active during this time, "or about 7 to 10 percent of the total number of professionals." More impressive yet: "Between 1901 and 1939 there were 29 Jewish world-champion boxers—about 16 percent of the total number of champions." In 12 different bouts for titles, both boxers were Jews. Silver continues:

> In the 1920s, 14 of the 66 world champions were Jewish, placing them second behind Italians, who had 19 world champions, but ahead of the Irish, who had 11. . . . By 1928 Jewish boxers comprised the single largest ethnic group among title contenders in the 10 weight divisions.

No other ethnic or religious group is likely to have been the subject of a work like *Stars in the Ring*. This is because no one exults like American Jews in the athletic prowess of their co-religionists. Who asks if Peyton Manning is a Lutheran, Tiger Woods a Catholic, Buster Posey a Presbyterian? For a superior athlete to be Jewish, though, is a high point of pride among Jewish men. I have myself sat in on countless conversations in which the question of whether one or another contemporary athlete is Jewish is discussed: Julian Edelman, wide receiver of the New England Patriots (yes), Stephen Strasburg, the pitcher for the Washington Nationals (alas, no). Is this because Jews, the "People of the Book," prefer not to be taken as altogether too bookish? A successful Jewish jock, demonstrating strength and physical courage, nicely rounds out Jews' sense of completeness as human beings.

Truly great Jewish athletes nonetheless have been less than abundant. Of those who qualify beyond question for hall of fame status, I can think of only five inarguable names: Benny Leonard, the lightweight boxing champion; Sid Luckman, the Chicago Bears quarterback; Hank Greenberg, the Detroit Tigers outfielder and first baseman; Sandy Koufax, the Los Angeles Dodgers pitcher; and Mark Spitz, the multiple gold-medal Olympic swimmer. Close but no cigar would be Barney Ross; Dolph Schayes, the elegant forward on the old Syracuse Nats professional basketball team; and Al Rosen, the Cleveland Indians third baseman. A small single room at the Holiday Inn might provide sufficient space for a Jewish Athletic Hall of Fame. The room would also require an ample walk-in closest to accommodate Jewish athletic oddities: for example, Moe Berg, major-league catcher and spy, who was said to speak six languages and was unable to hit above .240 in any of them; or Leach Cross (né Louis Wallach), known as the "Fighting Dentist," who one night loosened two of his opponents' teeth and the next day repaired them; and doubtless a few others.

Despite the Jewish masculine admiration for their own athletes, for years *The Jewish Daily Forward*, as Mike Silver notes, chose not to report anything about the large numbers of successful Jewish boxers. The paper relented only in 1923, when the lightweight championship bout between two Jews, Lew Tendler and Benny Leonard, known as the "Ghetto Wizard," was such hot news the paper couldn't leave it out. They ignored it until then in the belief that Jews should be interested in higher things, that boxing was, so to say, strictly for the *goyim*.

The various divisions between cerebral and physical, between sensitive and tough, between socialist and entrepreneurial, between neurotic and intensely commonsensical Jews have long been a source of endless wonderment, not to say immense amusement, to the *Judenkenner* among us, and reinforces the best definition I know of Jews, which is that they are just like everyone else, only more so. Still, the emphasis on braininess, as opposed to the physicality, of the Jews is a stereotype that hangs tough in public and indeed in Jewish consciousness. (In concert with this stereotype, the true religion of the modern Jew, it has been said, is diplomas.) This ignores the Maccabean precedent of the Jewish warrior and of the proven toughness and efficiency of the Israeli Defense Forces, perhaps the only large-scale institution left in the world that can, thank God, claim both.

Stereotypes, too, bear a truth quotient. In the case of the Jews, many immigrant Jewish parents would have been dismayed to discover their sons were professional boxers. A number of the boxers featured in *Stars in the Ring*—Frankie Callahan (né Samuel Holtzman), Eddie O'Keefe (né Morris Edward Paley), Harry Stone (né Henry Siegstein)—changed their names not to de-Judaize themselves but to hide their boxing careers from their old-world parents. No one, surely, could accuse a heavyweight called Abie Israel of doing the same.

The Jewish name-changing of boxers is a leitmotif that plays through Mr. Silver's pages. The lightweight contender Herman Gold became "Oakland" Jimmy Duffy. A junior welterweight named Morris Scheer became the second fighting Callahan, this one calling himself Mushy (after his Yiddish name of Moishe). A welterweight champion named Jackie Fields was originally Jacob Finkelstein. Perhaps the most elaborate nomenclatectomy was that done on John Dodick, a junior-lightweight champion in 1923, who began his career fighting under the name "Kid" Murphy, and then re-Judaized himself, once Jewish boxers became à la mode, as Jack Bernstein.

An epiphenomenon of boxing during its glory days was the battle of ethnics, chauvinism versus chauvinism. Jewish versus Irish, or Irish versus Italian, boxers gave an added flavor to a fight. Such must have been emphatically the case when Max "Slapsie Maxie" Rosenbloom fought the goyesquely named Joe "Hambone" Kelly. Jews, especially in New York, were among the leading fans of the sport, and fighters sometimes played to them by emphasizing their Jewishness. A Star of David on one's boxing trunks, such as that worn by the heavyweight Max Baer, who was only one quarter Jewish, was not uncommon. An English lightweight named Harry Mizler wore trunks with a Star of David on his left leg and a Union Jack on the right. Mike Silver mentions two Jewish fighters who entered the ring draped in *talleisim*, one of whom added a properly wound tefillin round his arm and forehead. One assumes he removed them when answering the bell for the first round.

THROUGH THE YEARS of intense Jewish emigration to America and on through the Depression, boxing was an alluring way to make a living for the sons of the lower classes. In the early decades of the 20th century no athletic events were better attended than prize fights, no financial rewards greater among athletes than those earned by boxers. Not every Jewish boy who went into the ring cashed in heavy chips at the close of his career. But if one fought regularly—and such was the popularity of the sport that many fighters had as many as two or three bouts a month—a serious income was available. A $20,000 payout for a night's work was not uncommon.

Some of Mike Silver's biographical entries are longer than others. The greater the fighter, the lengthier the biography: hence the longish biographies of Benny Leonard, "Slapsie Maxie" Rosenbloom (the sobriquet Slapsie derived from Rosenbloom's slapping rather than punching his opponents, lest he injure his hands and be out of work), and Barney Ross. Many are poignant in their details. When available, Silver accounts briefly for the lives led by these men after their boxing days are done. Post-ring careers range from driving cabs to working as bodyguards, from running gyms and spas to coaching actors about boxing and appearing in films, to salesmen and owners of small businesses, and in one notable case—that of a Scottish flyweight named Vic Herman—to portrait painting. "[T] he majority of Jewish fighters," Silver remarks, "were able to maintain a stable and productive life after their boxing careers ended." Sad are the closing passages in his book in which dementia pugilistica and other neurological disorders are reported. Early deaths are not infrequent. Saddest of all are the few instances of European Jewish boxers whose lives ended in Auschwitz.

Vast numbers of Jews were boxers, but how Jewish were they, really? When with the British comedy group Beyond the Fringe, Jonathan Miller was asked if he was a Jew, he answered, "I'm Jewish," by which I take him to have meant that he was born into Judaism but not, so to say, much of a practitioner. A notable exception among boxers was Barney Ross, whose father, like many an immigrant Jewish father, was devout in his Judaism; Silver describes him as "a Talmudic scholar." No life seems to have been so divided between glory and sadness as that of Barney Ross. His father, Isidore Rasofsky, was murdered by a robber in his small grocery shop, his mother had a nervous breakdown, and the children were dispersed among relatives and orphanages. A three-time champion, a decorated Marine, and a powerful money-earner, Ross also suffered from just about every addiction going: nicotine, booze, gambling (the ponies), heavy drugs. Silver mentions his $500-a-day heroin habit, acquired after he became hooked on morphine given him for the wounds he received at Guadalcanal. Whether

Ross turned to his father's religion because of his troubles or out of piety for family tradition, Silver does not say. But he took his Judaism seriously and even began wearing tzitzit under his bespoke suits. Good to be able to report, too, that Barney Ross was an early supporter of Israel, working with the American League for a Free Palestine, helping to smuggle weapons to the Jews, and raising hundreds of thousands of dollars for the new state. Barney Ross died, at 57, of lung cancer.

I have not made an exact count, but as one reads through the lineup of biographical subjects in *Stars in the Ring*, the great majority of Jewish boxers chronicled in its pages fought in the lighter weight divisions: bantam-, fly-, light-, junior-welter-, welter-, and middleweight. Of Mike Silver's list of "The Top 25 Jewish Boxers of All Time," only four were middleweights or above. One could of course be a hard hitter even at 112 pounds, and some of the Jewish boxers listed had high knockout ratios over their careers, but the lighter weight divisions required speed, savvy, and general prowess. Brains over brawn seems to have been the tendency in Jewish boxers.

The greatest Jewish boxer of all was Benny Leonard, who was 5' 5" and during his fighting days weighed between 130 and 153 pounds. Silver describes Leonard as a brilliant boxer with "the heart of a warrior," who had a "devastating right-hand counterpunch," and who left the sport unmarked after 219 bouts. He collapsed refereeing a bout at St. Nicholas Arena in 1947 and died soon thereafter of a heart attack at the age of 51.

Stars in the Ring ends on a doleful chapter on how boxing has become "a marginalized and debased fringe sport." The reasons are several. They begin at the top, or rather with the fact that there is no top. Boxing is a sport without a commissioner, which has allowed various rival organizations and federations to flourish, each creating its own titles and new weight divisions. The immediate result is that no one knows who is the champion of any particular weight or class—titles are spread out all over the joint. As Mike Silver puts it, by way of analogy with baseball, imagine the luster the game would lose if every year there were four different World Series winners.

Boxing went into a slump during and shortly after World War II, when so many young and some established fighters went off to war, though it looked to be resuscitated in the 1950s by television. Television, though, wrought its own complications. While it brought boxing to an audience of millions, it also helped kill the boxing clubs and small arenas. Why pay to witness a bout in person when one can see it for nothing on television? This had the effect of depriving novice fighters of work and, more important, of the experience necessary to acquire consummate skill at their trade.

The reigning complaint among the contributors to *The Arc of Boxing,* a book Mike Silver published a few years ago, is that the fighters who came up after the early 1950s simply were nowhere near the caliber of those who came before them. To take one example, Floyd Mayweather, Jr., who is generally regarded as the best contemporary pure boxer, is described by one of the book's contributors, Tony Arnold, as someone who uses his quickness "to overcome fighters with third-rate skills" but lacks real strategic intelligence and "ring guile." The reason is, as Silver explains, a dearth of qualified teacher-trainers and the lack of experience on the part of fighters, who in an age of television haven't fought enough to learn the manifold subtleties of their trade. "If you compare what boxing once was and what it has become," a neuroscientist named Ted Lidsky, himself once an amateur boxer, is quoted in *The Arc of Boxing* as saying, "this is checkers in comparison to chess."

As the skill among boxers diminished, the sport itself found new competitors for an audience in professional basketball and professional football. Mob interference, allowing only those fighters who were Mob-connected to get the best television bouts, didn't help. Worse, according to Silver, have been the exploitative promoters Bob Arum and Don King, who, by arranging mismatches and scheduling over-hyped televised title fights, contributed heavily to making boxing the shabby sport it seems today. (The major cultural contribution of Don King may be limited to his name being the answer to the riddle that asks, "What does one get by combining Viagra and Rogaine?")

Progress itself has worked against the future of boxing. With the long run of American prosperity that began after World War II, the old ethnic groups—Jews, Italians, Irish—ceased to need it to climb in status and prosperity. "The promise of America," Silver puts it, "did not [any longer] have to come with a broken nose or cauliflower ear." The vast majority of contemporary boxers are African Americans and Hispanics. With the current and quite legitimate alarm over head injuries in football, the future of the unforgiving sport of boxing, in which attacking the head of an opponent is usually a first priority, is further endangered.

The last major Jewish boxing champion was a man named Mike Rossman, a light-heavyweight and the first Jewish-American fighter to win a title in 40 years. (He won it in 1978 and lost it seven months later.) I confess to never having heard of Mike Rossman, and I wonder how many other similarly moderately obsessive sports fans like myself haven't heard of him either. Nor had I heard of two recent Russian Jewish boxers, Yuri Foreman and Dmitriy Salita, both as it turns out Orthodox in their religious practice. But, then, as Silver laments, most of the young today are probably entirely unaware that Jews ever played an important role in a once immensely popular sport that "was important enough to give every ethnic group their first American heroes." He adds that his reason for having written his book is that it is important to document the accomplishments of Jewish boxers,

> so that future generations can acknowledge and appreciate how a people with no athletic tradition, and with so many doors closed to them, used their intelligence and drive to open another door to opportunity and eventually dominate, both as athletes and as entrepreneurs, what was for several decades the most popular sport in America.

Mike Silver does not strike the autobiographical note until near the close of *Stars in the Ring*, when he mentions that on his fifth birthday his father bought him a pair of junior-size boxing gloves. When I was six years old, my father did the same for me. He also taught me the rudiments of the sport: jab, hook, right-cross, left-cross, uppercut, footwork, how to block blows. As for my own boxing career, my last fight, at age 10 outside Eugene Field Grammar School, was against a boy named Barry Pearlman. Stopped at the end of the first round by the school principal, it was pronounced a draw, and I retired soon after undefeated.

Harry Golden

(2015)

FAMOUS JOURNALISTS, LIKE FIREWORKS, pop, flare, ascend, and disappear. James Reston, Murray Kempton, Harrison Salisbury, Tim Russert and many lesser lights, after blazing vigorously in their day, soon after their deaths are extinguished, known only to fellow journalists, if even to them. Consider Harry Golden. Is there anyone around today under 60 who will remember that once famous name or what it stood for? Seems unlikely.

In his heyday—the 1950s and early '60s—Harry Golden had two books simultaneously on the *New York Times* best-seller list, was on the outer rim of the inner John F. Kennedy circle, and was mentioned in Martin Luther King Jr.'s "Letter From Birmingham Jail." Golden was invited to speak at universities, performed at the Concord Hotel in the Catskills, and was offered a reserved seat at Robert Kennedy's funeral. He appeared on the television talk shows of Dave Garroway, Steve Allen, Jack Paar and Johnny Carson; also on Edward R. Murrow. In 1961, *Life* magazine sent him to Jerusalem to cover the Adolf Eichmann trial. He was a celebrity in journalist's clothes.

Not that Harry Golden was a standard journalist. He never set out in life to write. He was a salesman, a self-starter, a main-chancer, an operator whose overestimation of his slickness landed him in the Atlanta Federal

Penitentiary in 1929 for running a bucket-shop stock operation, improperly investing—or failing to invest—clients' funds and keeping the profits for himself.

The son of Jewish immigrants, Golden had a fairly typical Lower East Side New York boyhood. Born Chaim Goldhirsch in 1903 in Galicia, he had a *luftmensch* father, a maven on all subjects but that of making a good living; an older and a younger brother; and two older sisters. As so often in Jewish immigrant families, the mother was the family's ballast and anchor, keeping the ship afloat. She died of cancer of the spine at 57 in 1924.

Harry Golden grew up holding the usual jobs: newspaper boy, delivery boy for a furrier with intellectual pretensions, desk clerk in a hotel owned by his brother Jake. He married an Irish Catholic woman, and, owing to the disgrace entailed, no member of his own family attended the wedding. He and his wife had four children and lived apart for decades. One of the children, Richard Goldhurst, would later serve as his father's unnamed collaborator and ghostwriter.

A small man, pudgy—"short of inseam and wide of waist," his biographer Kimberly Marlowe Hartnett notes in her biography *Carolina Israelite*—a cigar stuck in his mouth, bespectacled, with a chosen nose, Harry Golden bore a passing resemblance to a *Der Stürmer* caricature of a Jew. In his case, this wasn't a problem. He would later become an unwanted spokesman for his people, a man whose ingratiating style and schmaltziness were taken, mistakenly, for quintessentially Jewish.

After serving nearly four years in prison for his stock-market fraud, Golden moved, without his family, to Charlotte, North Carolina, a place where his disgrace was unknown. He was a drinking man, not a drunk but one requiring regular injections of booze early and refills through the day. Women found him attractive, and he did not avoid temptation in this line. If at this point in his life he had an occupation, it would be general hustler. His first job in the South was selling advertising space for local and regional newspapers; he later tried to get a mineral-water business under way. He was sloppy about money: He was frequently in trouble with the IRS; he bounced checks in Alabama. In a letter to a friend, Virginia Foster Durr, an early Southern white civil-rights advocate of great courage, called Golden "a phony, a sincere phony."

The sincerity was to be found in Golden's politics. As a boy in New York, he hung out at the Henry Street Settlement House, a great incubator of future socialists. He listened to his father schmooze away about Marxism. He read the little blue books put out by Haldeman-Julius, the Kansas City publisher. He had been 8 years old when the Triangle Shirtwaist Company fire of 1911 caused the deaths of 123 women and 23 men in the greatest industrial disaster of its time, and this left him a permanent labor sympathizer. Living in the South during the days of darkest segregation, he found a natural cause and subject in integration.

The debut issue of the *Carolina Israelite*, Harry Golden's essentially one-man paper—it came out, with great irregularity, monthly—appeared in February 1944. He was able to publish only with the financial help of local Jewish businessmen in Charlotte. The paper's motto, printed in large letters on its front page, was "To Break Down the Walls of Misunderstanding—and To Build Bridges of Good Will." A subscription cost $2; two years along, in 1946, it had a partly bogus subscription list of 3,481 subscribers. At the height of its editor's popularity in 1961, the paper reached its maximum circulation of 55,000. Golden closed it down in 1968, that *annus horribilis*, the year of the assassinations of Martin Luther King, Jr. and Robert F. Kennedy.

Golden had arrived and then asserted himself in the South just in time to take a hand in the last pure moral campaign this country has known: the struggle to remove from the books those segregationist laws—in health, education, accommodation, transportation and more—that locked in the secondary status of American blacks. His advantage over many other white journalists who covered the civil-rights campaigns of those years was that he actually lived in the South, though he might have been thought, by Southerners, a bit of a carpetbagger. In fact, he rather encouraged the notion of his being so. The title of his paper might be translated: "A Jew, or Stranger, in the South."

Golden used a broad-strokes humor that in its day worked in getting him much attention. He proposed, for example, a Vertical Negro Plan to eliminate segregation, which called for moving all the chairs out of Southern classrooms, since whites and blacks in the South seemed to get along fine until it came to sitting down together. His solution to anti-Semitism was to have Jews threaten to convert to Christianity.

Many of the things Golden wrote in those years were touched with what passed for Jewish sensibility. His timing here, too, could scarcely have been improved, for from the 1950s on Jewish culture—from "Fiddler on the Roof" to the novels of Malamud, Bellow, and Roth—was getting a good press. Golden's contribution to this brief renaissance was a nearly endless flow of nostalgia pieces in the *Carolina Israelite* on Eastern European Jews in the New World, with comedy added. His book titles—*Only in America, For 2¢ Plain, Enjoy! Enjoy!*—partook of this. Golden was called "The Jewish Will Rogers." In 1961 the literary critic Ted Solotaroff, in *Commentary* magazine, attacked Golden's falsely romantic vision of the Lower East Side ghetto life and his self-chosen role as village explainer—explaining blacks to whites, whites to blacks, Jews to Gentiles, Gentiles to Jews, everyone to anyone who would listen. The long assault ended by suggesting that his next book be called "Enough Already!"

The attack never laid a glove on Golden. His readers continued to adore him. Reviewers lined up to laud what they took to be his warmth and honesty. In 1958 *Only in America*, his first collection of essays from the *Carolina Israelite*, sold more than a million copies (in hardcover and paperback) and was on the *New York Times* best-seller list for 66 weeks.

The story is told of the conductor Herbert von Karajan getting into a cab, and when the driver asks where he wishes to go, answering: "It doesn't matter. They want me everywhere." So, too, with Harry Golden. The speaking engagements poured in. Adlai Stevenson was pleased to have him draft speeches for him in his presidential campaigns. John Steinbeck and Henry Miller—a strange combination—were among his admirers. A friendship earlier made with Carl Sandburg, who also lived in North Carolina, deepened. The two men one day sat down, Ms. Hartnett notes, to compile a list of great phonies of the day, on which appeared the names Norman Vincent Peale, Bernard Baruch, Cardinal Francis Spellman, Gen. Douglas MacArthur, and Cecil B. DeMille. Not a bad selection. The only names prominently missing, of course, were those of Carl Sandburg and Harry Golden.

Kimberly Marlowe Hartnett's biography, *Carolina Israelite*, provides a mini-history of the civil-rights movement. Jackie Robinson, Rosa Parks, *Brown v. Board of Education*, the lunch-counter sit-ins, the Freedom Riders, Martin Luther King Jr., the Civil Rights Act of 1964, all come into play in her pages. Through these years and events, when moral clarity was easily established and, with courage on the part of peaceful black protesters, acted upon, Golden flourished.

When the civil-rights movement fell apart, so, soon after, did Harry Golden's high standing as an important figure not only in journalism but in American life. The movement began to collapse, precisely, when in 1966 Stokely Carmichael, then the head of the Student Nonviolent Coordinating Committee, declared for Black Power, which meant that white participation in the movement was no longer wanted. Under a squalid character named H. Rap Brown (currently serving a life sentence for murder), the SNCC would turn anti-Semitic. Enter the Black Panthers—exit the moral cachet that nonviolence gave to the black cause. James Baldwin and a delegation of black artists and intellectuals earlier met with Robert Kennedy, when he was attorney general, and after the meeting Baldwin announced: "Let us not be so pious now as to say that President Kennedy was a great civil-rights fighter."

This remark especially wounded Harry Golden, who had bet all his chips on the Kennedys as great moral leaders. Ms. Hartnett reports that he wrote a book—high on my list of books never to read—called "Mr. Kennedy and the Negroes." Golden wanted President Kennedy to compose an update of "The Emancipation Proclamation." He likened him—sound familiar?—to Lincoln. "He remains the civil rights president," he wrote, when a better case could be made that Kennedy was halting and faltering in his aid to Southern blacks, fearful of moving too quickly lest it cost him politically. Not long after Kennedy's assassination, Golden wrote that Kennedy "was an *idea* to the people of the United States. More than the man he was, and the office he held, was an idea of what we could become; what we could achieve." Amen—and pass the Kool-Aid.

Later Golden would write that Lyndon Johnson was "Kennedy's finest achievement," by which he meant—which is not true—that Kennedy was the spur behind President Johnson's genuinely impressive accomplishments in the realm of civil rights. Golden was out of touch with the militants in the civil-rights movement. His backing of Lyndon Johnson's actions in Vietnam next lost him the young. "The real Iron Curtain," he wrote, "is between adults and kids." He continued to turn out books, but, Ms. Hartnett reports, his son Richard was the chief writer of these, including his autobiography. Wasn't it Charles Barkley, who, when a reporter mentioned a controversial item in his autobiography, replied, "I was misquoted"?

Magazines began rejecting Golden's work. Speaking engagements became fewer. No publisher, Ms. Hartnett writes, was interested in his proposal for a book called "America, I Love You." After he closed down the *Carolina Israelite* in 1968, his occasional writings ran in the *Nation*, that rest home for old socialists. He was asked, and agreed, to serve as a judge for a Miss Nude America contest. Harry Golden died, his fame much muted, in 1981.

Kimberly Marlowe Hartnett's biography of Harry Golden is, at 266 pages of text, the right length. She does not scant any of her subject's faults and brings out his virtues. Like her subject, she is too greatly enamored of the Kennedys. The name of the odious Joseph Kennedy, the founding father, never appears in her book. Her prose is fluent, if sometimes marred by the clichés of the day, among them "reach out," "icons," "shift focus" and "charismatic style." The last phrase she awards to Lyndon Johnson, who may be said to have had the reverse of such a style.

Ms. Hartnett closes *Carolina Israelite* by setting out her subject's contradictions, which were manifold. She tries to revivify him, to bring him into the contemporary age, by suggesting that he was a blogger *avant la lettre*. She claims that he would have loved the Occupy Wall Street movement and thought of himself as "comrade" to all victims. She is doubtless right. Harry Golden was one of those men who never tired of saying how much he loved the people, and like most such men, somewhere along the way he turned a nice profit.

Gershom Scholem

(2017)

IN 1925, AT THE AGE OF TWENTY-EIGHT, Gershom Scholem wrote from Israel to his friend the philosopher Ernst Simon: "I am now busy writing extremely obscure essays, placing my trust in the immortality that comes to those who are not read, only praised." This was a joke, of course, but one that turns out to have a high truth quotient. Fair to say that Gershom Scholem (1897–1979), author of *Major Trends in Jewish Mysticism, The Kabbalah and Its Symbolism, Sabbatai Sevi: The Mystical Messiah,* and other works, owing to the complexity of his arcane subject, has been more lauded than read, let alone understood, but this has not got in the way of his acquiring an international reputation as one of the past century's leading thinkers.

Born among the ill-fated German-Jewish bourgeois—his father was a successful printer in Berlin—Scholem was precocious not alone in his thinking but in his independent spirit. Early in his adolescence he sensed the implausibility of anything resembling serious assimilation among Germany's Jews, and turned to Zionism as not merely an alternative but as a way of life. As he later told an interviewer who asked what motivated him to emigrate to Israel:

> I believe that if there was any prospect of a substantive regeneration of Judaism, of Judaism revealing its latent potential—

this could happen only here, through the Jewish person's reencounter with himself, with his people, with his roots.

Scholem was not observant in his Judaism, and declared that he "never did care for traditional national Jewish theology." He was nonetheless unflagging in his belief in God, claiming that he failed to understand atheism. Morality without religion behind it seemed to him a chimaera. He early discovered a predilection for mysticism, which he made the subject of his life's work. "If humanity should ever lose the feeling that there is mystery—a secret—in the world, then it's all over with us," he told an interviewer. "But I don't believe we'll ever come to that."

The richness of Gershom Scholem's thought, its sometimes paradoxical nature, his impressive erudition, combined to give his writing moral authority. Owing to this authority, during the great controversy in the early 1960s about Hannah Arendt's book on the Adolph Eichmann trial, he, Scholem, crushed the book by accusing its author, formerly his friend, of want of "tact of the heart," love for the Jewish people, and of hatred of Zionism.

As a professor at Hebrew University, Scholem had many brilliant students, but no true disciples. No one has had the combination of wide learning and deep culture required to carry on his scholarship. Since his death, Scholem's reputation has grown greater. Cynthia Ozick, George Steiner, Harold Bloom have written about him and his work in the most elevated language. His friendship with Walter Benjamin, who was five years older than Scholem, and when both were in their twenties was a strong influence upon him, further heightened Scholem's aura as a major twentieth-century thinker. "His work on Jewish mysticism, messianism, and sectarianism, spanning now a half century," wrote Robert Alter in *Commentary* in 1973, "constitutes . . . one of the major achievements of historical imagination in our time."

Little wonder that the figure of Gershom Scholem has inspired younger generations, especially among those with a taste for metaphysics, yearning to find a religious center in their lives. Enter George Prochnik, born in 1961, the author of *Impossible Exile, Stefan Zweig at the End of the World*, and himself something of a specialist in exile. "When I moved to Jerusalem, at the age of twenty-seven, in the summer of 1988," Mr. Prochnik writes,

> I brought with me a battered paperback copy of Scholem's
> *On the Kabbalah and Its Symbolism....* I was one of those
> for whom Scholem loomed as a kind of prophet. I found in
> his work if not faith, yet something closer to revelation than
> anything I could discover in normative Judaism.

The son of a mixed marriage, George Prochnik found no succor in traditional Jewish religious practice—"I hated praying," he notes—and discovered excitement in what he took to be Scholem's religious anarchy. "Gershom Scholem helped plant the seed for this contrarian yearning," he writes, "the wish for a Godless god, and an outlaw's Law, and a revelation that could be stolen from the gilt vaults of orthodoxy, broken up, and redistributed among the poor in faith."

We are here in the realm of theology, that "spurious offspring of faith and reason," as Theodor Mommsen called it, deploring its "tedious prolixity and solemn inanity." Mr. Prochnik has a proclivity for swimming in these muddy waters, which make for the murkiest pages in *Stranger in a Strange Land: Searching for Gershom Scholem and Jerusalem*, his combined biographical portrait of Gershom Scholem and chronicle of his and his wife's own desire "to immerse ourselves in a more Jewish existence on every level...."

Mr. Prochnik's portrait of Gershom Scholem is largely drawn from Scholem's *From Berlin to Jerusalem*, his autobiography of his early years; his *Walter Benjamin: The Story of a Friendship*; and the vast quantity of his letters (he wrote some 16,000 of them). He records Scholem's early passion for all things Jewish, a passion all the more remarkable for its coming from within a strongly assimilationist German-Jewish family in which the flame of Jewishness was guttering. Gershom—then Gerhard—was the youngest of the family's four sons. The two oldest sons went along with the assimilationist program and into their father's business; the third son Werner, became a radical, briefly a Communist, and was murdered in 1940 by the Nazis at Buchenwald.

Off by himself, the young Scholem read Heinrich Graetz's multi-volume *History of the Jews* and Martin Buber, both of whom he would later firmly reject. ("Buber's glory and fame are assured," he wrote, "but he certainly has a talent for making cloudy anything clear.") He learned Hebrew, joined

Zionist youth groups, hunted down ancient Jewish books. He argued with his father over the falsity at the heart of the Jewish assimilationist solution in Germany, holding that Germans viewed Jews as "at best with indifference, at worst with malevolence," noting that no middle-class German gentile had ever visited their home.

Scholem seems never to have been without the polemical spirit. While still a student he wrote a letter opposing Germany's participation in World War I, which caused him to be ejected in his final year from his secondary school. He worked up an act—reminiscent of that portrayed in Thomas Mann's *Confessions of Felix Krull*—pretending to severe mental illness to avoid conscription, and ultimately was able to have himself declared an incurable schizophrenic. His persistent Zionist activities finally caused his father to disown him, announcing the decision in a registered letter containing 100 marks, adding that this was the last money he would receive from him. He was able to sustain himself as a university student, and eventually completed a doctorate at the University of Munich. When in 1923 Scholem finally emigrated to Israel, in what is known as the Third Aliyah, or emigration of Diaspora Jews to Palestine, there were fewer than 100,000 Jews there.

Apart from his engagement with Jewish mysticism, the most decisive event in Gershom Scholem's life was his meeting, in 1915, at the age of eighteen, with Walter Benjamin. Benjamin "put questions to me in his wholly original and unexpected formulations" that caused Scholem to concentrate more intensely than ever before. "What thinking really means," he wrote, "I have experienced through his living example." He described his friendship with Benjamin as "the most important of my life," and later dedicated a book to him as "the friend of a lifetime whose genius united the insight of the Metaphysician, the interpretative powers of the Critic and the erudition of the Scholar." The two exchanged ideas, read each other's work in draft form, and a subtle two-way influence passed between them. In later years Scholem persistently attempted to get Benjamin to emigrate to Israel, but Benjamin dithered and dithered. His fine mind, with its sublime subtlety and depth of perception was toward the end coarsened, in Scholem's view, by Marxism. In 1940, fearful of being returned by Spanish officials to France and the awaiting Nazis, Walter Benjamin committed suicide in Spain at the age of forty-eight.

In 1925, two years after Gershom Sholem's arrival in Israel, he became a professor, specializing in Jewish mysticism, at Hebrew University. The rest, one might say, is history, also historiography, as he went from success to success, strength to strength, acquiring a worldwide reputation solidly based on a large corpus of significant work.

George Prochnik did not fare so well. Israel, the Promised Land, withheld its promise from him. One sees this coming early in his pages on his and his family's life in Israel. Marked by a strong tone of self-dramatization, not free from overwriting, particularly in the descriptions of landscape ("A pomegranate dangled its big red fruit like mumpy cheeks"), these pages are entirely shorn of humor. As soon as Mr. Prochnik begins his account of his own life in Israel, unhappiness sets in, then festers, finally exploding in his and his wife's return to America, where they were divorced. The autobiographical sections of *Stranger in a Strange Land* reveal that it is George Prochnik and not Gershom Scholem who is the true stranger of his book's title.

We first hear of Mr. Prochnik's dissatisfaction with Judaism's "failure to be inclusive of women." The peacenik in him soon enough reveals itself. The Soviet dissent Natan Sharansky is described as having turned into "a right-wing zealot in Israel." He is of course anti-Jabotinsky, the militant revisionist and founder of the Jewish Defense Organization. He is put off by the ultra-orthodox, the sight of whom "left me more and more estranged." Consumerism, which he sees as a strong feature of Israeli life, depresses him. Fancying himself a seeker after the highest truths revealed by religion and philosophy, Mr. Prochnik seems not to have realized that his is the standard outlook of the American progressive, finding as always the world falling short of his utopian standard.

Mr. Prochnik's identification with Palestinians becomes more and more complete. He quotes Edward Said on the wretchedness of the Palestinians' condition as a result of the "Versailles" treaty that gave Palestine to Israel. He describes an idyllic setting in Jerusalem, noting that Palestinians are missing from it and thus from sharing in the enjoyment of it. Of his own economic troubles—he never found a good job, his dissertation at Hebrew University was rejected, he and his wife had three sons—he notes:

> All the little natural pleasures the city offers seem to carry a price tag we can't afford. And I wonder if this sense might be an inkling of what the dispossessed Palestinian would feel.

He profoundly feels the death of Prime Minister Rabin, and with it the squashing of the hope for peace through the Oslo Accords. The gravamen of his complaint is that the Israelis are to blame for "maintaining the exile of another people." The election of Benjamin Netanyahu eventually drove him from the country.

Gershom Scholem remarked that "I share the traditional view that even if we [the Israelis] wish to be a nation like all other nations, we will not succeed. And if we succeed—that will be the end of us." Israel is different from all other nations—in its history, its rebirth, its precarious place in the world—and always will be. To ask it to be better, to ignore its enemies, to exist on a higher moral level than every other nation in the history of the world, which George Prochnik asked of it, is to be certain of the disappointment he found on his misguided sojourn there.

Dreaming of a Jewish Christmas

(2015)

THE FIRST OF THE FEW FIGHTS I ever had with my father was over a Christmas tree. I was five or six years old, he and I were returning from the 400 Theatre on Sheridan Road in Chicago where we saw a movie—I cannot recall its title—that had to do with Christmas. Walking the four or so blocks home, I asked my father if we couldn't have a Christmas tree. I didn't imagine getting one might be a problem. In my memory our conversation went roughly like this:

"That's not possible," he said.

"Why not?" I asked.

"Because we are Jewish," he said, "and Christmas is about the birthday of Jesus Christ in whom we Jews do not believe."

"Why do we need to believe in him to get a tree?" I asked.

I called this a fight, but it was no match, for I lost on a TKO in the first round.

"All I want is a tree," I said.

"Jews don't have Christmas trees," he said. "I don't want to hear anything more about it."

"That's unfair," I said. Kids, then and now and always, are great collectors of injustice, and I was no exception.

"Unfairness has nothing to do with it. Discussion ends here."

I remember walking the rest of the way home in silence, sulking, unable to grasp my father's unreasonableness, when he was always so generous and reasonable about everything else.

Years later my father told me that, on Christmas Eve when he was five-years old, he put up his long white stockings—boys in those days wore knickers, requiring long stockings—on the mantle of his family's apartment in Montreal, and woke the next morning to discover that one of his six older brothers had filled them with coal.

Before going further, I ought to make plain that my father wasn't in the least observant of Jewish ritual. This despite the fact that his father was a Jewish *erudit*, a man who obeyed all the dietary laws of *Kashrut* (or kosher) and prayed with regularity, each morning strapping on his phylacteries, as on various occasions I watched him do when he visited us in Chicago. I don't know what my grandfather thought of his son's want of Jewish observance, which extended to our never having belonged to a synagogue all the years I lived at home, though I and my brother were *bar mitzvahed* and pork was never served in our house.

Later in life my father declared himself, on religious questions, an agnostic; on brave days, he announced himself an atheist. On the large questions he never referred to God but supplanted God with the word Nature. Only Jews, I suspect, can be both atheists and yet be so intensely Jewish on all questions that do not touch directly on God. My father was one of these. God apart, he was chauvinistically, one might almost say relentlessly, Jewish. He gave large sums to Israel and to Jewish charities: the Anti-Defamation League, the Jewish United Fund, Hadassah, B'nai Br'ith, *et alia*. Unobservant in his own life, he nonetheless required, without being tyrannical about it, his two sons go to Hebrew School four afternoons a week, have rabbinically officiated circumcisions for their own male children, themselves remain stalwart in their pride in being Jews. He was always on the *qui vive* for anti-Semitism. "Some people may just hate you for your name," he told me when I was ten or eleven. The notion of avoiding this by changing one's name was beyond unthinkable. Jewishness was a club from which, after all that had happened in Europe, it would be a disgrace to resign. Besides, he was proud of his membership. The club, as he often pointed out, also happened to be filled with an inordinately large proportion of people of extraordinary achievements, and the people themselves had survived against momentous odds.

The problem for me as a kid was that Christmas didn't seem so much a Christian as an American holiday, perhaps *the* American holiday, and to be excluded from it made me feel, somehow, less than fully American. As for Christianity, in those days and perhaps until I was ten or so years old, I thought Christianity and Catholicism were coterminous. This was in good part owing to the neighborhood in which we lived, Rogers Park, where most of the not obviously Jewish kids on our large block went to St. Jerome's and then on either to St. George or St. Scholastica High Schools.

Chicago in those days was a very Catholic city. Ask someone where he lived, and he was likely to mention his parish: St. Nicholas, St. Rita, St. Leo. (Non-Catholics would mention the nearest public park: Chase, Indian Boundary, Green Briar.) Priests and nuns were plentiful and ubiquitous in the 1940s and early 1950s and taught the Catholic schools. Priests in collar and nuns in habit walked the streets, rode the buses, els, and streetcars, and were part of the urban landscape. As a seven- or eight-year old boy, I can remember, on the Sheridan Road bus, asking, "Sister, would you like my seat?" Or: "Morning to you, father?" in unconscious imitation of Barry Fitzgerald.

I mention Barry Fitzgerald because he played a priest in some of the popular movies of my movie-going boyhood years, those of the 1940s and '50s. Movies generally during those years seemed dominated by priestly stories, notably *Going My Way* (1944) and *The Bells of St. Mary's* (1945), in both of which Bing Crosby plays priests. Earlier there was *Boys Town*, with Spencer Tracy straightening out the intransigent Mickey Rooney. In a great many movies the actor Pat O'Brien, in the part of a priest, seemed to be walking killers down the last mile to the electric chair before they offered him a balling confession. Later there was *Miracle on 34th Street* (1947). In 1954 Crosby returned, this time in mufti, in *White Christmas*. In 1959 Audrey Hepburn turned up in *The Nun's Story*. The movie *It's A*

Wonderful Life (1946) is properly described as a Christmas fantasy. One couldn't, in those days, go to the movies without Christmas turning up, with large Christmas trees in supporting roles.

In the building just to the north of ours on Sheridan Road lived the Cowlings. I have heard a stray psychological theory—it's closer to a notion—that at some point in their lives all children believe, however briefly, that their parents cannot be their true parents. What they believe instead is that if they are not in fact royalty, they are surely higher born than to the rather ordinary people with whom they have been assigned to live. I don't give this theory much credence, but I do know that, at age nine, if I were asked to trade my parents for Sam and Dale Cowling I would have done so without the least hesitation, and no kindly uncle to be named later.

Sam Cowling, the father, was a comedian, and appeared every morning on a then nationally famous show called *Don McNeill's The Breakfast Club*, which ran for more than thirty-five years (1933–1968) on ABC radio. He did a regular bit, announced with great fanfare, called "Fiction and Fact and Sam's Almanac." A small man, stocky, handsome, he was kind to everyone and played 16" softball on Sundays on the fields behind our buildings along the lake. Dale Cowling was beautiful, in a motherly way; the very name Dale was pleasing, and also the name, it will be recalled of Roy Rogers's wife. The Cowlings' two sons, Sammy and Billy, were blondish and crew-cutted, and both came to be good basketball players. The boys went to Chicago Catholic schools and then, I believe, to Georgetown. The Cowlings had a Christmas tree that took up a good part of their living room. One year all the lights on the tree were blue. They were a wonderful family, and couldn't have been less Jewish, or should I say more *goyesque?*

Although Jewish kids may have predominated, if very slightly, in the two grammar schools I went to—Eugene Field on Lunt Avenue, later Daniel Boone on Washtenaw Avenue—the understanding was that the country was Christian and Christmas carols—"Silent Night," "Oh, Tannenbaum," "The Little Drummer Boy"—were sung without any Jewish kids asking to be excused. (Some did irreverent Jewish parodies of these songs outside school: "Deck the halls with *schmaltz* and *cholla*..."), but there wasn't the least bad feeling that we had Christianity, by way of music, imposed on us.

I wonder if Christmas carols are sung in public schools today, the age of diversity, without giving equal time to Hanukkah, Kwanza, and other ethnic seasonal songs? I hope they are. I know as a boy I never felt in the least offended by singing Christmas carols. Music is after all the great Christian art, surpassing, in my view, painting and literature. One thinks of Mozart's *Requiem* and the many Bach *chorales* and *cantatas*. Not carols but two of the most popular Christmas songs were of course written by Jews: "I'm Dreaming of a White Christmas" by Irving Berlin and "Chestnuts Roasting on an Open Fire" by Mel Torme. I only regret that Cole Porter didn't write a song about *Simchas Torah* and Johnny Mercer one about *Purim*.

Jews, until the founding of Israel in 1947, have always been strangers in others' lands, and hence assimilationist where possible, in some instances accommodationist. They have also been so within their own religion. I have heard it said that the Conservative wing of Judaism broke away from the Orthodox chiefly over the questions of prohibiting driving on the Sabbath and the elimination of separate seating for women in synagogues. As for Reform Judaism, the latest joke, among non-Reform Jews, is that it is the Democratic Party platform, with holidays added.

The holiday of Hanukkah is an example of Jewish accommodation within the religion itself. For it is fairly evident, and agreed upon by Jewish scholars, that Hanukkah is not in any possible reading a major Jewish holiday. The event it marks, the Maccabean Revolt against the Seleucid Empire in the second century BCE, is post-Biblical, for one thing; and for another it is built on rather a slender and unimpressive miracle, ritual olive oil enough to last only one day lasted for eight, hence the lighting of eight menorah candles. The persuasive explanation about Hanukkah in America is that it was elevated only because it occurred in the winter and could be used by mid-nineteenth-century Jews in America who wished to have a holiday that could if not compete with at least stand alongside Christmas. In more recent years, Jews, or some among them, have added a strong consumer touch to the holiday by presenting children with a gift on each of the eight nights that commemorative Hanukkah candles are lit.

Much followed in the minor sociology of American Jewish life from the emphasis on Hanukah as a Christmas surrogate. Jews send out and receive from Christian friends cards carefully denoting "Season's Greetings." More assimilated Jewish families who still wished to think themselves Jewish bought and set up in their homes Christmas trees, designated Hanukkah bushes. Many Jewish firms and private persons give and attend Christmas parties. There are, of course, Christmas bonuses. All this, of course, is Christmas, with Jesus Christ, or its true cause, subtracted.

As a secular holiday, Christmas has long been under attack. The main line of attack is the accusation that it has come to stand for little more than empty consumerism. So-called "Black-Friday" shopping, whether it be at Target or Wal-Mart or anywhere else can turn ugly. Ravening crowds, screaming, pushing, in some instances punching one another to get a bargain on Play Stations or a toy drone at Best Buy is not, let us agree, America at its best. Yet for a great many people it is more and more what Christmas has become. Bah, one need scarcely bother to add, humbug!

The grand shopping spree that Christmas has increasingly become has lengthened the holiday itself out to roughly a month. Shopping begins in all-too-earnest right after Thanksgiving, if not dab on Thanksgiving day. Shops, supermarkets, elevators are suddenly filled with canned Christmas music. One of the nice things about shopping online is that at least, when doing so, one doesn't have to listen to "Rudolf the Red-Nosed Reindeer." Round late November in recent years I note that I begin signing off e-mails and letters to friends with "Christmas will soon be at our throats."

I have for the most part steered clear of Christmas giving. I pass out a fifty-dollar bill to our UPS man, buy a Christmas lunch for our barber, give the attractive couple who clean our apartment every two weeks two days extra pay, write out a check for $500 for a woman who can use help providing Christmas for her own father-deserted children. My wife and I have long ceased to give each other gifts. Samuel Johnson says that man, foolish fellow, goes in life not from enjoyment to enjoyment but from want to want. Truth is, I am just about out of wants of a palpable kind: I long for no Bentleys, capacious boats, wrist-watches that will tell me how many more days I have to live, exotic travel, exorbitant wines, cashmere underwear, leather goods, lotions, spices off the London East India boat. I am not wise, please understand, merely finished in the line of luxurious acquisition, content and grateful with what I have.

For what percentage of the 300-million or so Americans does Christmas retain its true religious meaning and, with that meaning, its power? A subtler statistician than any I have ever encountered may know. For those of us whom find no religious significance in the holiday, it can carry complicated meanings. Everyone, surely, has heard that suicide rates go up around Christmas, occasioned by those for whom the holiday reminds them of family lost, other unwanted detachments, dead-ended relationships, their own crucial missteps in life.

In recent years, my wife and I have by design eaten our Christmas dinner at home alone. We don't have a good Chinese restaurant in the neighborhood, or should, in traditional Jewish fashion, repair to it. Four or five years ago we used to dine with my wife's dear cousin Patsy and her family—a husband and three daughters and their husbands and daughters' children—in the western Chicago suburb of Oak Brook. On the Eisenhower Expressway, on the way out of the city, as we pass the Mannheim Road exit, now well into the nearly *Judenrein* Chicago western suburbs, my long-suffering wife has had to put up with my annual yuletide joke: "Did you note that sign, dear? Next Jew eighty miles."

The dinner at cousin Patsy's is always excellent and the bonhomie, or in this case holiday cheer, at a perhaps too uniformly high level. Sixteen or seventeen people from the same family, three generations at table, and they all seem genuinely to like one another. No bad feeling, old grudges, resentments, envy, jealousy, hidden malice is ever allowed to leach into the Turkey dressing. Over the years I've studied this extended family carefully, but can find no chink in the façade of their good feeling for one another. Turns out the façade wasn't really a facade; there has never been anything there but a solid structure of family love.

But let us play the old game of what's wrong with this picture: Sixteen or seventeen people, three generations, around a table piled with holiday food. Mistletoe hang from a nearby window. A Christmas tree, gifts beneath it, in the next room. Nordic, also Irish, good looks abound; no paucity of blond hair. Everybody seems to be enjoying him- or herself. Everyone is laughing. Except a man seated there, down table a good bit, toward one of its corners. He is merely smiling, and it is a strange smile, less than wholehearted, with a certain tinge of irony to it. Not a very

Christmassy smile, most would agree. He is, of course, *me*, the odd man out, put out there by himself.

As I was to discover some years ago, I rather like being odd man out. I noticed this, not for the first time, in 1993, in Jerusalem, listening to Shlomo Mintz conduct the Israel Philharmonic Orchestra. Gazing around the hall, I had the following thought: everyone in this room may well be Jewish, and it makes me ever so slightly uncomfortable. I do not wish, apparently ever, to be among the majority; and I enjoy a permanent minority status, and I feel it with greatest intensity as a Jew at Christmas.

But my title promises a Jewish Christmas Dream. Here it is: The night of December 24—I need scarcely add that not a creature was stirring and so forth—I go off to bed. Deep and dreamless sleep comes instantly. The alarm goes off at its usual time of 6:00 a.m. I turn it off, then turn on the radio to discover that it is December 26. I have, lo and behold, slept right through Christmas.

Season's Greetings!

Part Four

Masterpieces

The Brothers Ashkenzai

(2009)

R OBERT LOWELL called Ford Madox Ford's *The Good Soldier* the best French novel in the English language. So, similarly, might one call I. J. Singer's *The Brothers Ashkenazi* the best Russian novel ever written in Yiddish. The book has the grand sweep of Tolstoy, with a vast and wide-ranging cast of characters, a strong feeling for the movement of history, and, playing throughout, the drama of men and women trapped in the machinery of forces much greater than themselves.

I(srael). J(oshua). Singer, born in Bilgorai, Poland, in 1893, was the older brother by nine years of I(saac). B(ashevis). Singer. The Singers' father was a Hasidic rabbi, their mother the daughter of a long line of famous *misnagid* (or non-Hasidic) rabbis. I. J. Singer spent his early years in the shtetl of Leoncin and his adolescent years in Warsaw, where he became caught up in the Haskalah, or Jewish enlightenment, movement. As a young man he worked as a journalist in Kiev, where his early attraction to socialism was punctured by the brute realities of the Russian Revolution. In 1934 he too moved to the US, where he worked for the *Jewish Daily Forward*. He published seven books in all, of which *The Brothers Ashkenazi* (1936) is the best known.

The tension between religious and secular life among Jews born into orthodoxy gave both Singer brothers an inexhaustible literary subject. In much of Isaac Bashevis Singer's fiction, his characters stray from religion and then, after leading lives of dissipation, degradation, and disappointment, return to it, where they find a measure of contentment.

For I. J. Singer, things are more complicated. He did not think much of either traditional religion or the secular life of his time, which didn't leave him, as a novelist, a great deal of room to negotiate. Politics taught I. J. the bitter lesson that, however much the extreme left and the extreme right might disagree, the one common ground upon which they met comfortably was anti-Semitism. The Jew as scapegoat in the dark world of Eastern Europe is more than a leitmotif in *The Brothers Ashkenazi*; it is the underlying moral of the novel. "Don't you know," the wives of the striking Jewish workers cry out to their husbands during a bitter strike in Lodz, "it always ends up with Jewish heads bleeding."

The Brothers Ashkenazi begins not long after the Napoleonic wars, with the arrival of German and Moravian weavers in the Polish town of Lodz. At first excluded, the Jews gradually insinuate themselves into the town. They began as small-time entrepreneurs, setting up minor factories or sometimes working in their homes with handlooms, putting in long hours and grinding out a living. A handful of Jews worked for large-scale German factory owners, as agents, buyers, managers.

One such is Abraham Hersh Ashkenazi, who, soon after the novel begins, is presented by his wife with twin sons, Simha Meir and Jacob Bunem. Abraham Hersh hears the prophecy from his rabbi that his sons will both know great wealth. This prophecy, which will come true, is a disappointment to their father, who would have preferred they be pious and learned.

The brothers turn out very differently, in talent and in temperament. Simha Meir, the first born by a few minutes, is from an early age clever, conniving, a boy and then man concentrated on the main chance. His brother is physically more gifted—strong, handsome, charming—a cynosure. Simha Meir is aflame with ambition; Jacob Bunem, less concentrated, is dedicated to easy living.

At the center of *The Brothers Ashkenazi* is the climb of Simha Meir—who later abandons his religion and becomes Max Ashkenazi—to dominance over the weaving industry of Lodz. The machinations behind his climb are set out in impressive detail. In the background plays the sub-sidiary story of the rivalry and estrangement between the two brothers: Simha Meir, in an arranged marriage, is betrothed and marries the love of his brother's life. Later Jacob Bunem marries into a family of vast wealth, a cause of consternation to Simha Meir.

Conflict is the order of the day in Lodz: between brothers, between owners and workers, between rabbis and miscreants, between Russians and Poles, between Gentiles and Jews, between Polish and Lithuanian Jews. Under capitalism man exploits man, an old saying had it, while under communism just the reverse obtains. So it is in Lodz; no matter who is in command, the city is breeding ground for exploitation, with every kind of hatred polluting the air.

"Simha Meir had the guts of a pickpocket," Singer writes. "In Lodz this was the highest compliment." We learn that "justice isn't a commodity in Lodz," and that "Lodz admired nothing more than wealth." With hundreds of dab touches Singer personifies the city as the sinkhole of men set loose without any guiding principles or goals apart from that of gain: "Lodz knew that with money you could buy anything." When credit dries up and inflation hits Lodz, Singer notes that "even the whores in brothels and the doctors who later treated their venereal diseases were paid off with IOUs."

Such idealism as Singer allows in the novel is given to the few revolutionaries who appear in its pages, but theirs turns out to be a naive revolutionism. Nissan, the son of a poor rabbi, exchanges his father's devotion to Torah for his own to Marxism, into which he invests the same unshakeable faith. He lives to see the revolution he fought for turn into a pogrom, with the corpses of Jews hanging from trees. At one point, Nissan thinks: "Maybe man was essentially evil. Maybe it wasn't the fault of economic circumstances, as he had been taught, but the deficiencies of human character."

Strikes, World War I, the Russian Revolution, the invasion of Lodz first by the Germans, then by the Russians—all are described by Singer, with pitch perfect artistry and pace. Lenin makes a cameo appearance in the novel, as Napoleon does in *War and Peace*, and so do the hapless Czar Nicholas and his Czarina Alexandra. The world turns topsy-turvy, with only Max Ashkenazi's dream of industrial and financial dominance remaining constant, until it, too, is blasted, when, having earlier moved his factory to Russia, he is imprisoned in the new Soviet Union, from which he is saved by his long-despised brother. On the brothers' return to Poland, reconciled at last, Jacob Bunem is killed, in an act of anti-Semitic bullying, by an ignorant Polish officer.

The Brothers Ashkenazi ends on a pogrom, which sends all the city's Jews fleeing: to America, to the new Zion recently created in Palestine, to less cruel countries than Poland. "Lodz," Singer writes, "was like a limb torn from a body that no longer sustained it. It quivered momentarily in its death throes as maggots crawled over it, draining its remaining juices." Max Ashkenazi, intent on personal reform, which he is unable to attain, dies soon afterward.

Masterly, pitiless, this great novel forgoes a happy ending to render instead a just one: The city of Lodz and the characters it spawned get all they deserve.

Civilization of the Renaissance

(2013)

6 6 "THE MOST INSTRUCTIVE of all the books on the Renaissance," Lord Acton called Jacob Burckhardt's *The Civilization of the Renaissance in Italy*. The book was one of the few modern works that Friedrich Nietzsche admired. Burckhardt (1818–1897) and Nietzsche (1844–1900) were colleagues at the University of Basel, in Switzerland. Nietzsche claimed that Burckhardt's were the only lectures he ever enjoyed, and the model for the kind he himself hoped one day to deliver. Burckhardt recognized the younger man's genius, yet was slightly wary of him, knowing how different were their intellectual methods and points of view. Nietzsche was of course a philosopher, of literary bent, trained in the classics. Burckhardt called himself "a contemplative historian."

What a contemplative historian does is on dazzling exhibition in *The Civilization of the Renaissance in Italy*, the pre-eminent work of Burckhardt's career and an unparalleled work of history. He also wrote an introduction to the art of Italy called *Cicerone*, as well as *The Age of Constantine the Great* and *A History of Greek Culture* and a little book on the Flemish painter Peter Paul Rubens. Late in life, he published his lecture notes under the title *Judgments on History and Historians*.

The Civilization of the Renaissance in Italy, despite its formidable title, runs to a mere 341 small pages in my Phaidon Press edition. Burckhardt claimed that he could easily have made it three times as long, and that a larger book would doubtless have earned him "more respect among a lot of people." Instead, as he noted in the first sentence of the book, he had written "an essay in the strictest sense of the word." By this he meant a work that did not aim to be either complete or definitive.

Burckhardt's book is unlike any other historical work in being neither narrative in its construction nor devoted to unraveling historical problems. What it provides is a brilliant survey of those cultural tendencies—and "culture," Burckhardt thought, "always precedes art"—that made the Italian Renaissance "the leader of modern ages." Not least of the book's attractions are its judgments of leading political and literary figures in the period, making it both a work of history and of astute criticism.

The book covers the period bounded by the birth of Dante (c. 1265) to the death of Michelangelo (1564). Although Burckhardt is best known as an art historian, visual artists do not feature prominently in his history. Raphael is mentioned almost in passing. The nature of Leonardo, the great universal genius of the period, is characterized as so rich that it "can never be more than dimly and distantly conceived." Benvenuto Cellini is considered more as an autobiographer than as a visual artist. Giorgio Vasari, the contemporary and indispensable chronicler of Renaissance artists, is appreciatively noted: Without his "all important work, we should perhaps to this day have no history of Northern art, or of the art of modern Europe, at all." Michelangelo goes unmentioned.

Ariosto, Boccaccio, Castiglione, Petrarch, Tasso, and most prominently, Dante weave in and out of Burckhardt's pages. Savonarola, Cesare Borgia, Lorenzo Medici, Machiavelli put in cameo appearances. So, too, do minor figures such as Pietro Aretino, thought to be the father of modern journalism, and as such "not burdened with principles, neither with liberalism nor philanthropy nor any other virtue."

Burckhardt is less interested in biographical portraiture than in trying to capture the spirit of Italians during the Renaissance and how the Italian character, in all its variety, helped create the modern state. He does not scant the villainy of Renaissance despots, governing without morals or principles. Some of the most minor were the most cruel. Among this group was one Pandolfo Petrucci, who exercised power in Siena toward the close of the 15th century. "His pastime in the summer months," Burckhardt writes, "was to roll blocks of stone from the top of Monte Amiata, without caring what or whom they hit."

To grasp what marked off the Renaissance from all that came before, Burckhardt places heavy emphasis on the recovery of the literature and art of antiquity by the Renaissance Italians. "Aristotle," he writes, "became the common property of educated Italians." Cicero was the model among them for prose composition. Arabic and Hebrew texts were studied. The ideal Italian was *l'uomo universale*, the "all-sided man."

The diminished prestige of the church in Italy was a help in freeing men from concentration on the purely celestial. Machiavelli blamed the church for the irreligion and corruption of the Italians. This was a period when popes formed their own dynasties, and dealt in favors and pardons the way a Venetian merchant dealt in glass and silver. With their minds no longer solely on the drama of salvation, mankind, as Burckhardt writes, was "here first thoroughly and profoundly understood. This one single result of the Renaissance is enough to fill us with everlasting thankfulness."

Talent was esteemed more than high birth. Women emerged as more than helpmates. "To understand the higher forms of social intercourse at this period," Burckhardt writes, "we must keep before our minds the fact that women stood on a footing of perfect equality with men." The education afforded upper-class women was no different from that of men. The word "virago," he notes, "then implied nothing but praise."

Burckhardt is splendid on the Italian penchant for vengeance. Honor, which ranked high in the Italian scheme of virtues, was always in peril during the Renaissance. Honor must never be outraged. Burckhardt stresses through his book the role imagination played among Italians of the Renaissance, and writes that "it was to the imagination of the Italians that the peculiar character of their vengeance was due." Avenging of blood was considered a duty. *Vendette* were "handed down from father to son, and extended to friends and distant relations." Revenge "was declared with perfect frankness to be a necessity of human nature." But vengeance must be undertaken with art, and satisfaction achieved through both "the material injury and moral humiliation of the offender." One can find in Burckhardt's pages on vengeance the roots of the modern Mafia.

A good part of the richness of *The Civilization of the Renaissance in Italy* derives from Burckhardt's ability to hold in exquisite balance the corruption and the glory, the squalor and the grandeur, the cruelty and the beauty of Renaissance life. Toward the close of his book, he writes:

> But the Italian of the Renaissance had to bear the first mighty surging of a new age. Through his fits and his passions, he has become the most characteristic representative of all the heights and all the depths of his time. By the side of the profound corruption appeared human personalities of the noblest harmony, and an artistic splendor which shed upon the life of man a lustre which neither antiquity nor mediaevalism could or would bestow upon it.

Burckhardt's sophisticated prose, such as could be commanded only by a man of the deepest culture, brings this to life in the way that no contemporary academic could hope to do.

No one who has read Jacob Burckhardt's masterpiece will ever think to call, say, Woody Allen or Steve Jobs a Renaissance man.

Montesquieu

(2016)

CHARLES-LOUIS DE SECONDAT, Baron de La Brède et de Montesquieu (1689–1755), a leading figure in the French Enlightenment, began his career studying and then practicing law. With the acquisition of his fortune through marriage and inheritance, he settled into the life of a man of letters. He wrote novels, essays (on taste and history among other large subjects), and two books that rendered him famous. *Persian Letters* (1721), a satire on the absurdities of contemporary French society as seen by a visiting Persian, made him a figure of great *réclame* in his own day; and his *The Spirit of the Laws* (1748), on the influence of forms of government and of climate on nations, remains a central work of political philosophy in ours.

Between those two books, Montesquieu published *Considerations on the Causes of the Greatness of the Romans and Their Decline* (1734), a lesser-known work but one deserving the highest acclaim. In it, Montesquieu combines the insights of the historian with those of the political philosopher, set out in brilliant aphoristic style. "At the birth of societies," he writes early in this book, "the leaders of republics create the institutions; thereafter, it is the institutions that create the leaders of republics." Everything Montesquieu wrote was against the background of his pervasive and persuasive views of human nature: "For the occasions which produce great changes are different but, since men have had the same passions at all times, the causes are always the same." Notable among those passions are pride, greed, and the love of glory.

To grasp the quality of Montesquieu's *Considerations*, one has to imagine the 3,000-odd pages of Edward Gibbon's *History of the Decline and Fall of the Roman Empire* condensed to a mere 220 pages and without losing much. Not that the views of the two men are everywhere congruent, but both are proficient in understanding the great sweep of events while simultaneously discerning the role of character in the play of history. Their art consists in balancing the effect of each upon the other.

Of the letters of Cicero, that last Roman republican, Montesquieu writes: "we can see the dejection and despair of the foremost men of the republic at this sudden revolution [the monarchical-minded triumvirate of Caesar, Pompey and Crassus] depriving them of their honors and even their occupations." He finds Cicero's "genius was superb, but his soul was common." Comparing him to Cato, he notes: "Cicero always thought of himself first, Cato always forgot about himself. The latter wanted to save the republic for its own sake, the former in order to boast of it."

Of Roman character in general, Montesquieu is most impressive. "Roman citizens," he writes, "regarded commerce and the arts as the occupations of slaves . . . they knew only the art of war, which was the sole path to magistracies and honors." Pillaging was the chief means of enrichment. Courage, he held, came to the Roman soldier naturally. The advantage the Romans had over the Carthaginians in their three wars was that "the Romans were ambitious from pride, the Carthaginians from avarice; the Romans wanted to command, the Carthaginians to acquire."

Pride lay behind the Roman penchant for suicide, a habit encouraged by the teaching of the Stoics, a philosophy whose first lesson was preparing one for the naturalness and ultimately the negligibility of death. Suicide became among the Romans a point of honor in the face of defeat or public disgrace, and a chance for a redeeming heroism. Suicide allowed each man to put "an end to the part he played in the world whenever he wished." Self-love was the major motive for Roman suicide, for, according to Montesquieu, "such is the value we set on ourselves that we consent to cease living because of a natural and obscure instinct that makes us love ourselves more than our very life."

With the end of the republic ushered in by Augustus, Roman character itself changed. "In the days of the republic," Montesquieu writes, "the principle was to make war continually; under the emperors the maxim was to maintain peace." Political life became secretive. With the Emperor Tiberius, in whom the statesman too often yielded to the paranoid, "flattery, infamy, and crime were the arts necessary to succeed." The march of Roman emperors, with pauses only for the true nobility of Trajan and the Antonines, was a dance of degradation. "All the Roman efforts of conquest ended by satisfying the happiness of five or six monsters," and Roman "citizens were treated as they themselves treated conquered nations."

The gradual but sure debilitation of Roman character ended in the reduction and ultimate defeat of Roman power. Difficult to read Montesquieu on Rome without thinking of the US in our time, as when, for one example among many, he writes that "more states have perished by the violation of their moral customs than by the violation of their laws."

A work of genius, one definition of a masterpiece, makes us see the world differently.

Machiavelli

(2016)

S URELY NO REPUTATION is more locked in, at least in the public mind, than that of Niccolo Machiavelli (1469–1527). Sometimes referred to as the founder of modern political science, he is better known as the progenitor of a policy that everywhere places expediency over morality. As a result, Machiavellism has come to mean immoral actions, and a Machiavel a cunning, utterly self-regarding person, evil incarnate.

The Prince, Machiavelli's most famous—some might say infamous— work, is a manual of instruction to princes on how to capture and retain power. In this manual, a single criterion obtains: what succeeds. The instructions are unstinting in their specificity, often unflinching in their brutality. Apropos of such great leaders as Moses, Cyrus, Theseus, and Romulus, Machiavelli writes: "Hence it comes about that all armed prophets have been successful, and all unarmed prophets have been destroyed." Only Machiavelli could hold up the cruel regime of Cesare Borgia as worthy of emulation. As Isaiah Berlin, in his essay "The Originality of Machiavelli," wrote: "He seems wholly unworried by, indeed scarcely aware of, parting company with traditional western morality."

Yet there is another Machiavelli, and he is to be discovered in a less read, more complexly textured work called *Discourses on Livy*. Livy (c. 59 BCE–CE 17) was the first Roman historian without an earlier career in public office; his history began with the founding of Rome. Machiavelli's purpose in this book is to bring readers to "a right understanding of ancient and modern affairs; so that any who shall read these remarks of mine, may reap from them that profit for the sake of which a knowledge of History is to be sought." Machiavelli restricted his comments in *The Prince* to principalities; here he also considers republics.

The richness of Machiavelli's classical learning is on display throughout the *Discourses*. Early in the book, he sets out the reasons why the laws of the Spartan Lycurgus had a permanence, while those of the Athenian Solon were transient. The chief reason is that laws not supported by good customs are fragile, while good customs stand in need of strong laws for their support. Customs and laws both are required to stay the avarice and rapaciousness of men, who "are, by nature, more prone to evil than to good."

One can scarcely read Machiavelli's *Discourses* without reflecting on their significance for our day. When he writes that "no kingdom can stand when two feeble princes follow in succession," one thinks of recent American history and its string of poor presidents. His explanation of how good men were excluded from office, owing to the valuation of wealth over honor and the insidious influence of corruption, so that men of merit gave way to those with ambition merely, makes one think of current American politics.

The *Discourses* tend to be wider-angled, less instructive and more cautionary than *The Prince*. "A lost freedom," Machiavelli writes, "is defended with more ferocity than a threatened freedom is defended." On the subject of soldiers, he thinks little of mercenaries, and avows "it is not gold, as it is vulgarly supposed, that is the sinews of war, but good soldiers"—iron, in other words, everywhere defeats gold. Evidence of Machiavelli's dazzling mind is shown in his ability to draw useful distinctions. In *The Prince*, he distinguishes between necessary and unnecessary cruelty; in the *Discourses*, between accusations and calumnies, between wars fought for mastery and those fought for life itself (this borrowed from Sallust), and many more.

Machiavelli's great model in the *Discourses* is Rome in its republican years. "For if no commonwealth has ever been found to grow like the Roman, it is because none was ever found so well fitted by its institutions to make that growth." Athens and Sparta may have been governed by better laws, but Rome, by the steady increase of its population through conquest and by admitting strangers to the rights of citizenship, all the while maintaining its military spirit under steady discipline and the need to strive for glory, endured longer than either.

In the *Discourses*, Brutus, Appius Claudius, the Decemvirs, and Julius Caesar play cameo roles. Of Caesar, Machiavelli notes that he was "able to so blind the multitude that it saw not the yoke under which it was to lay its neck." Machiavelli's mastery of Roman history is buttressed by his steady view of human nature with its inability to curb either its ambition or its envy and its need to gratify the desire of the moment. Such, he held, is the general perversity of men, "a sorry lot," that they "may aid fortune but never withstand her."

In the 24th chapter of the *Discourses*, Machiavelli wrote:

> When it is absolutely a question of the safety of one's country, there must be no question of just or unjust, of merciful or cruel, of praiseworthy or disgraceful; instead, setting aside every scruple one must follow to the utmost any plan that will save her life and keep her liberty.

His stringent view of human nature combined with his originality and penetration made Niccolo Machiavelli, in his day and still in ours, the pre-eminent political philosopher of the world not as it ought to be but as it is.

Gogol

(2013)

ONE OF THE ENDURING MYSTERIES of literary history is the appearance in nineteenth-century Russia, that vast and barbarous country, of the greatest writers of fiction in all of literature. Tolstoy and Dostoyevsky are supreme among the novelists of all nations, with Turgenev not far behind. Then there is Chekhov, master of the short story, and Ivan Goncharov, author of *Oblomov* and *The Same Old Story*. Among the Russians, the purest artist is Nikolai Gogol (1809–1852), author of the play *The Inspector General*, some unforgettable stories, and a single novel, *Dead Souls*, which, even though unfinished, is nonetheless a masterpiece.

Gogol is the comic genius among Russian writers, always playful but never shallow. He had a magnificent eye for the bizarre, for the madcap, above all for what was extraordinary in the ordinary. In his story "The Nose" he wrote about a barber who wakes one morning to discover a nose stuffed into his morning loaf of bread. The nose turns out to belong to one of his customers, Collegiate Assessor Kovalyov. How the nose got into the barber's bread and how one morning a few weeks later it reappeared on the face of its owner is never explained. Plots are not Gogol's strong point. Nor was he much interested in ideas.

Dead Souls is a story about Pavel Ivanovich Chichikov, who travels the provincial countryside buying up dead serfs from small landowners.

These serfs remain on the landowners' books until the next census, and, even though dead, are still taxable. Chichikov offers to relieve the landowners of their tax burden. His plan is to install these dead serfs on the tax rolls of a faraway estate, on which he will then be able to get a generous government mortgage, and come away with a small fortune.

The great Russian poet Pushkin was Gogol's friend and supporter, and the man who gave him the idea for *Dead Souls*. Gogol refers to the book not as a novel but as a poem. *Dead Souls* is a poem about Russia, its provincial backwaters, its secondary characters (clerks, minor officials, small landowners), its heartbreaking squalor. "Russia! Russia!" Gogol exclaims midway through the book, ". . . Everything in you is open, desolate and level; your squat towns barely protrude in the midst of the plains like dots, like counters; there is nothing to tempt or enchant the onlooker's gaze. But what is this inscrutable, mysterious force that draws me to you?"

What gives *Dead Souls* its poetic quality is its author's exuberant passion for the detail—one might even say the irrelevant detail—of provincial Russian life. Gogol's eye for such detail is matchless. In his brief, brilliant study *Nikolai Gogol*, Vladimir Nabokov accounts for Gogols's artistry through this and what he calls Gogol's "four dimensional" prose, a sinuous style that captures characters in their inner being. Through his subtle selection of detail and his dazzling prose, Gogol's scenes light up, his characters flame into life, his tragi-comic vision touches the reader's heart.

I write "tragi-comic," for Gogol was far from the mere humorist he is sometimes advertised as being. "I am fated to journey hand in hand with my strange heroes and to survey the surging immensity of life," he wrote in *Dead Souls,* "to survey it through the laughter that all can see and through unknown invisible tears." The book's characters might be thought stock— the miser, the spendthrift, the bearish Russian, and the rest—but for their creator's ability to bring them to life with a shimmering individuality. When Gogol digresses—as he does at nearly every opportunity, sometimes in the middle of a sentence—it is invariably into the realm of comic observation, as in his charming little disquisition on fat men "being better able to conduct their affairs in this world than the thin."

Chichikov, the character at the heart of Gogol's masterpiece, is a lower-echelon civil servant with a corrupt past who specializes in what Gogol calls "blandiloquence," or elaborately empty compliments. Chichikov was brought up by a father whose last words of advice to his son were to please his superiors, not to be seduced by friendship, and to remember that nothing in life is so important as money—advice, notes Gogol, "that remained deeply engraved in his soul."

One of life's "acquirers"—for Gogol a major sin—Chichikov turns out to be an inept acquirer, which makes him quite as interesting as he is detestable. "Wise is the man," Gogol writes, "who does not disdain any character, and instead, examining him with a searching look, plumbs him to the very main-springs of his being." That sentence should stand as the first commandment for every novelist.

Chichikov is a fantast, who imagines himself one day running a plush and productive estate, with a pretty wife and fine children, himself the very model of the perfect Russian citizen. Although Gogol writes, "we have not taken a virtuous man as our hero," he has made Chichikov oddly sympathetic. So that vile and petty in so many ways, Chichikov, when he is caught out at his game, garners our pity. Who cannot feel for the poor wretch, down on his knees, begging forgiveness "in his tailcoat of Narvarino smoke and flame, in his velvet waistcoat and new trousers, with his satin necktie and carefully groomed hair from which emanated the fresh smell of eau de Cologne."

Gogol was contemplating two further volumes to complete *Dead Souls*. The plan was for the first volume to be devoted to Crime, the second to Punishment, and a third to Redemption. He thought of the completed *Dead Souls* as a catechism of sorts that would save the Russian soul. In his second and third volumes, as he wrote to a friend, "the Russian would appear in the fullness of his national nature, in all the rich variety of the inner forces contained within him." Gogol, thank goodness, was never able to get these volumes, with their implicit preachiness, written.

Late in his short life, Gogol simultaneously found religion and promptly lost art. Once Gogol began to think of himself as a Christian reformer, Nabokov writes, "he lost the magic of creating something out of nothing." His genius for devising delicious details disappeared; his powers of invention deserted him. Before he died, he burned what he had written of the second volume of his novel. The last ten years of his life

Gogol suffered greatly from writer's block, and died an excruciating death from anemia of the brain at the age of forty-three.

Dead Souls, meanwhile, is among that small number of uncompleted masterpieces that includes Tchaikovsky's *Unfinished Symphony*, and Robert Musil's *The Man without Qualities*, but with the important qualification that Nikolai Gogol's great work is all the better for remaining unfinished.

Speak, Memory

(2014)

F EW ARE THE TRULY GREAT autobiographies: Benvenuto Cellini's, Jean-Jacques Rousseau's, Ben Franklin's, Edward Gibbon's,
John Stuart Mills's, Henry Adams's, possibly Gertrude Stein's,
and not many more. Nor ought one to be surprised at the paucity of their
number. Of all forms of literature, autobiography is perhaps the most difficult to bring off successfully. Maintaining candor without lapsing into
cant or self-adulation is only one of the difficulties autobiography presents. George Orwell underscored the point:

> Autobiography is only to be trusted when it reveals some-
> thing disgraceful. A man who gives a good account of him-
> self is probably lying, since any life when viewed from the
> inside is simply a series of defeats.

To write superior autobiography one requires not only literary gifts,
which are obtainable with effort, but also an intrinsically interesting life,
which is less frequently available. Those who possess the one are frequently
devoid of the other, and vice versa. Only a fortunate few are able to reimag-
ine their lives, to find themes and patterns that explain a life, in the way successful autobiography requires.

Vladimir Nabokov was among them. Late in *Speak, Memory: An Autobiography Revisited* (1966), he writes that "the spiral is a spiritualized circle,"

and "a colored spiral in a small ball of glass is how I see my own life." This spiral took four twists. The first was the 20 years he spent in aristocratic opulence in his native Russia (1899–1919). This was followed by 21 years of impoverished exile in England, Germany, and France (1919–1940). The third was the years he spent as a teacher in the US (1940–1960). The enormous success of his novel *Lolita*, freeing him to return to Europe—specifically to Montreux, Switzerland—provided the fourth twist, in which he was able to live out his days writing and pursuing butterflies until his death at the age of 78 in 1977.

Speak, Memory does not take up Nabokov's life in the US, the bulk of which he spent teaching literature at Cornell University; nor does it touch on his days in Montreux. The book ends as he, his Jewish wife and their young son, fleeing the Nazis, are about to sail off to America. Much of the greater part of the autobiography is given over to his life in Russia. He writes of his "careful reconstruction of my artificial but beautifully exact Russian past," from which he was brutally severed by the Russian Revolution. He never returned to Russia.

As an autobiographer—and as a novelist, too—Nabokov worked microscopically—rather than telescopically. The miniature was his entrée into the grander scene. "There is, it would seem," he writes, "in the dimensional scale of the world a kind of delicate meeting place between imagination and knowledge, a point, arrived at by diminishing large things and enlarging small ones that is intrinsically artistic." Such was his own method as an artist, and such was the art it produced on which his own international reputation rests.

Nabokov's portraits of his parents in *Speak, Memory* are a reminder of what good luck it is in life to love one's mother and father. Of his mother, he writes: "To love with all one's soul and leave the rest to fate was the simple rule she heeded." *Speak, Memory* provides verbal snapshots of his mother with her brown dachshunds, out hunting mushrooms, listening appreciatively to her son's first overheated poems. With her delicate sensitivity to the illusions of others, she understood what the nurturing of an artistic son required. "She cherished her own past," Nabokov writes, "with the same retrospective fervor that I now do her image and my own past."

Nabokov's father was a man given to good causes, who stood ready to sacrifice, and ultimately to die, for them. A man of learning and culture, he spoke out against government-encouraged pogroms, was against capital punishment, wrote against much that was cruel in the czarist regimes of his day. He served in Alexander Kerensky's cabinet. Nabokov's father lives forever in his son's—and now our—view of him being tossed into the air in gratitude and adulation by the peasants on his estate for justly mediating a dispute among them. "For an instant," Nabokov writes, having viewed this as a boy from a dining-room window, "the figure of my father in his wind-rippled white summer suit would be displayed, gloriously sprawling in midair, his limbs in a curiously casual attitude, his handsome, imperturbable features turned to the sky." He was killed in 1922 in Berlin, while shielding a liberal politician and editor from the pistol-fire of a far-right czarist fanatic.

In *Speak, Memory* Nabokov describes his childhood as "cosmopolitan," which it assuredly was, with four languages spoken in the family. The Nabokovs had not one but two chauffeurs to drive their three cars. Winters, when not in Biarritz, they occupied a mansion on a fashionable street in St. Petersburg. Four Great Danes were loosed at night under the control of a night watchman to guard Vyra, their estate 50 miles from town. Cooks, maids, gardeners, footmen were among the multitudinous household staff. An endless parade of tutors—German, English, French—was entrusted with the early education of the family's six children. What Nabokov calls "the stability and essential completeness" of his young life was of course wiped out by the Bolsheviks.

Speak, Memory is not without its longueurs. A lengthy section is given over to lepidoptery; another to the composition of chess problems. Odd that so great a writer is unable to generate passion in his readers for what were two among his own greatest passions, but it is so. Both, though, touch on his artistic life. Rare butterflies show up in several of his novels and stories. In *The Defense* he wrote one of the great novels about chess, a book whose true theme is obsession.

In his autobiography, Nabokov writes of those "things that one always hopes might survive captivity in the zoo of words." In this zoo one finds, to cite merely half a dozen, such exotic verbal creatures as "karakul," "chamfrained," "intrados," "discarnate" and "intervestibular." Surprising juxtapositions ("flowing nuns" and "the numb fury of verse making") and lilting formulations (a cousin who had "a sense of honor equivalent, morally, to perfect pitch," and "elegant old poets and their smiling similes") arise everywhere. Vladimir Nabokov hadn't it in him to write an uninteresting sentence.

A masterpiece of autobiography ought to capture the spirit of a time and place, be memorably well written, and make a reasonable pass at understanding that greatest of all conundrums, its author's own life. On all three counts, *Speak, Memory* qualifies.

Epictetus

(2016)

CHIEF AMONG THE SCHOOLS of ancient philosophy were the Academics led by Plato, the Peripatetics by Aristotle, the Epicureans by Epicurus, and the Stoics founded by Zeno of Citium. Only Stoicism, now nearly entirely eclipsed, gained a strong footing in the Roman Empire, where it was embraced by Marcus Aurelius, best of all emperors, who, in his Meditations, produced one of the leading Stoic texts. The major Stoic teachers were Chrysippus, Diogenes of Babylon, and, above all, Epictetus (CE 55–135). Cicero and Seneca claimed to be Stoics, but the wavering temperament of the first and the expensive tastes of the second did not permit them to live the philosophy in the quotidian manner Stoicism requires.

Epictetus, the slave of a freedman of Nero named Epaphroditus, who eventually freed him, was Phrygian (from Western Anatolia) by birth and lame in one leg. When in CE 89 the Emperor Domitian banished all philosophers from Rome, Epictetus took up residence in what is now Albania. Like Socrates, whom he much admired, Epictetus committed none of his teachings to writing. He had the good fortune to have among his pupils Arrian, the chronicler of the campaigns of Alexander the Great, who transcribed Epictetus's teachings around CE 108 into a work called the *Encheiridion*, or *Handbook*, but which now carries the overarching title of *Discourses of Epictetus*.

In what has come down to us, Epictetus largely ignores the scientific and metaphysical teachings of the Academics and Peripatetics. He concentrates instead on ethics and the ideal of the virtuous life. Virtue, in Epictetus's philosophy, brings tranquility, leading on to happiness. Unlike the Epicureans, who taught that tranquility resided exclusively outside the life of action, the Stoics were not disdainful of the active life, and in Marcus Aurelius the theme of service not only to individuals but to the wider community is part of the human contract. Epictetus's philosophy is grounded in common sense. How best to meet the requirements of life, or how to live one's life "conformable to nature," is his principal lesson.

The first step on the way to doing this, according to Epictetus, is the scrupulous observation of appearances to form a right judgment of them. "Either things appear as they are," he notes, "or they are not, and do not even appear to be; or they are not, and yet appear to be." Misapprehension of appearances sets one on the track of anguish, frustrated desire, sadness, ruin. This advice of Epictetus is a precursor to Henry James's advice to be a person on whom nothing is lost.

"No man is free unless he is master of himself," claims Epictetus, and self-mastery comes through will. We must will what is right for us, and will the avoidance of what is not. Will is strengthened through accurate observation of appearances. Will operates only on those things within our power.

> In our power are opinion, movement toward a thing, desire, aversion . . . ; and in a word, whatever are our own acts; not in our power are the body, property, reputation, offices . . . , and in a word, whatever are not our own acts.

This distinction anticipates Reinhold Niebuhr's serenity prayer, later adopted by Alcoholics Anonymous: "O God, give us the serenity to accept what cannot be changed, / The courage to change what can be changed, / and the wisdom to know the one from the other."

Desire, for Epictetus, must be carefully monitored. One must not "require a fig in winter." Freedom is gained, he holds, "not by the full possession of the things which are desired, but by removing the desire." Do not "desire many things, and you will have what you want." (This advice, if followed, would close down the consumer society.) All that you truly have need of is "firmness, of a mind which is conformable to nature, of being free from perturbation."

"From your own thoughts," Epictetus states, "cast away sadness, fear, desire, envy, malevolence, avarice, effeminacy, intemperance." Among the things we must not desire is long life. Behind this desire is the fear of death, which is useless since all things in life are transient. Like Montaigne, Epictetus invokes us never to allow death to be long out of mind. Montaigne hoped that death would take him while he was cultivating the cabbages in his garden. "May death take me," Epictetus says, "while I am thinking of these things, while I am thus writing and reading." We know that Montaigne's death was a painful one, of quinsy, which rendered him speechless at the end. How Epictetus died is not known.

Virtue is truly its only reward for Epictetus, for, though he frequently cites God and his greater design of the world, no mention in his work is made of an afterlife. Nor is there any talk of the fate of the soul once departed, if depart it does, from the body. What one gains from the philosophy of Epictetus is awareness, a plan for righteous conduct, and self-mastery of the kind available only to those rare philosophers for whom word and deed are indivisible.

H. W. Fowler

(2017)

AFTER COMPLETING the *Concise Oxford Dictionary*, Henry Watson Fowler suggested to Oxford University Press doing a dictionary that would leave out the obvious words and instead concentrate on those that were confusing and inexact as well as on troubling idioms and obsolete rules. An editor at Oxford referred to it as a "Utopian dictionary," one "that would sell very well—in Utopia." The book, published in 1926 under the title *A Dictionary of Modern English Usage*, was in fact a modest bestseller, and subsequently went through several editions and two revisions.

The book's success was owing entirely to its author, H. W. Fowler, a former English public-school teacher, a failed literary journalist, and a lexicographer extraordinaire. Fowler was magisterial and commonsensical, immensely knowledgeable and understatedly witty, a grammatical moralist whose hatred of humbug made him a moralist on the side of good sense.

A radical in his day, Fowler held that it was no crime to end a sentence with a preposition, that it was better to split an infinitive than to write an awkward sentence attempting to avoid doing so, that common words were to be preferred over foreign and polysyllabic ones. Fowler, as Ernest Gowers, author of *The Complete Plain Words*, wrote, "was an emancipator from the fetters of the grammatical pedants that had bound us for so long."

A Dictionary of Modern English Usage is suffused with the personality and idiosyncrasies of its author, more so perhaps than even Samuel Johnson's famous Dictionary. Fowler had a taste for risky but amusing generalizations. In his entry on "Didacticism," for example, he remarks that "men are as much possessed by the didactic impulse as women by the maternal instinct." By way of usage, he also taught good manners. His entry "French Words" begins:

> Display of superior knowledge is as great a vulgarity as display of superior wealth—greater, indeed, inasmuch as knowledge should tend more definitely than wealth towards discretion and good manners.

One frequently turns to Fowler for advice on useful distinctions: between "forceful" and "forcible," or "intense" and "intensive," or among "finical," "finicking," "finicky" and "finikin." He was excellent at stripping a euphemism or genteelism down to its essential meaning: "'Not to put too fine a point upon it' is an apology for a downright expression, and means 'to put it bluntly.'" On occasion he supplies a brief entry on language change, as in the entry "hair-do": "This now compound noun has reached the dictionaries, and deserves to supersede the alien coiffure and to be written hairdo."

The great gems in *A Dictionary of Modern English Usage* are the lengthier entries sometimes buried under titles that have now themselves become the names for good sense in composition. "Elegant Variation," for example, denoting that habit of "second-rate writers, those more intent on expressing themselves prettily than on conveying their meaning clearly. . ." Elegant variation is the sin in composition of calling the same thing, or naming the same act, by as many different words as possible. The dialogue of amateur writers of fiction, suckers for elegant variation, tends to have their characters not merely "say," but "opine," "allow," "retort," "riposte," and so on into the night.

Other such entries include "Love of the Long Word," "Split Infinitive," "Superiority," "Novelese," "Hybrids and Malformations," "Novelty-Hunting," "Vogue Words," "Slipshod Extensions," and others. One gets a strong sense of Fowler's general tone, wit, and point of view from the opening of his article "Sturdy Indefensibles":

Many idioms are seen, if they are tested by grammar or logic, not to say what they are nevertheless well understood to mean. Fastidious people point out the sin, and easy-going people, who are more numerous, take little notice and go on committing it. Then the fastidious people, if they are foolish, talk of ignorance and solecism, and are laughed at as pedants; or if they are wise, say no more about it and wait. The indefensibles, however sturdy, may not prove to be immortal, and anyway there are much more profitable ways of spending time than baiting them.

Of the two revisions of *Modern English Usage*, Gowers's, published in 1965, 32 years after Fowler's death, is in every way a pleasing supplement to the book, eliminating some overly technical material, adding such new entries as "Worsened Words" and "Abstractitus," but, as Gowers allowed, "chary of making any substantial alterations except for the purpose of bringing [Fowler] up to date." The book was revised a second time in 1996 by R. W. Burchfield, himself earlier the editor of the *Oxford English Dictionary*. "Fowler's name remains on the title page," Burchfield wrote in the preface to his edition, "even though his book has been largely rewritten in this third edition." Sad to report, Burchfield broadened, modernized, streamlined, and along the way essentially destroyed a dazzling book by turning it into a merely useful one.

Those who love language, who view its deployment in speech and in writing as a craft requiring artful care, will continue to rely upon and cherish the original, charming book that is *Modern English Usage* and its irretrievably idiosyncratic author—a masterpiece of personal lexicography in a field dominated by the dull and impersonal.

As a Driven Leaf

(2015)

A HIGH PERCENTAGE of the best historical novels have been written with the classical world as background. One thinks of Marguerite Yourcenar's *Memoirs of Hadrian*, Robert Graves's *I, Claudius*, John Williams's *Augustus*, Steven Pressfield's *Gates of Fire*, and those of Mary Renault's novels set in ancient Greece. Milton Steinberg's *As a Driven Leaf* (1939) is another splendid historical novel, this one set in second century Jerusalem and Antioch, one generation after the destruction of the Jewish Temple (CE 70) and during the rise and suppression of the Bar Kokhba revolt under the Roman rule of the Emperor Trajan.

The author of *As a Driven Leaf* was the rabbi at the Park Avenue Synagogue in New York, where he was famous for his learning and the power of his sermons. A student of the legendary philosopher Morris R. Cohen and for a time the disciple of the rabbi Mordecai Kaplan, founder of Reconstructionist Judaism, Steinberg, who died in 1950 at the age of 46, left behind two nonfiction books—*The Making of the Modern Jew* (1934) and *Basic Judaism* (1947)—still read in our day. A second, unfinished novel, *The Prophet's Wife*, was published posthumously in 2010.

As a Driven Leaf—the title comes from Job 13: 24-25: "Wherefore hidest Thou Thy face . . . / Will Thou harass a driven leaf?"—is a book with something like a cult following. The novelist Chaim Potok remembered how exhilarated he felt, as an adolescent in an Orthodox yeshiva, to find a book that so powerfully captured his own youthful religious turmoil. The other day someone told me that his brother-in-law, after reading the novel 20 or so years ago, decided to go to rabbinical school.

Ambitious in scope, the theme of *As a Driven Leaf* is the conflict between reason and revelation, science and faith that faces Elisha ben Abuyah, Steinberg's protagonist. Handsome, highly intelligent, born to wealth, Elisha is brought up under the guidance of a Greek tutor. When Elisha's father dies, an uncle, orthodox in his Jewish belief, takes responsibility for the boy's upbringing and sends him off to be educated by a learned rabbi, a man whose saintly simplicity and wisdom win Elisha's heart and set him on the path of Jewish learning. He becomes one of the most promising young rabbis of the age, rising to become a member of the Sanhedrin, the supreme court composed of the most learned men in Judea.

Elisha ben Abuyah was a historical character, a Jewish apostate, about whom not all that much is known. He is said to have lapsed into hedonism, replaced Jewish ethics with pagan aesthetics, and betrayed the Jews to the Romans during the Bar Kochba rebellion. With great novelistic skill, Steinberg fleshes out the bare bones of information we have on Elisha ben Abuyah, breathes life into him and into the large cast of characters he encounters in the novel, and gives his story impressive dramatic unity.

In the novel, Elisha contracts a disappointing marriage to a woman of crabbed and conventional views whose miscarriage prevents her from having children. He finds succor in the home of a disciple, whose two young children later die of plague. "It is not in our power," a dictum of the Jewish sages runs, "to explain either the happiness of the wicked nor the suffering of the righteous." The death of these children turns Rabbi Elisha ben Abuyah's mind to doubt, and to searching for answers to the world's mysteries outside the realm of Torah and Jewish learning.

Greek learning is where this search soon leads. A crucial book for Elisha is the geometry of Euclid, in which he discovers what Jewish learning cannot deliver: cold axiomatic proofs set out through a series of indisputable propositions. As Elisha puts it later in the novel, favoring Greek learning over Jewish learning: "Their success, I am convinced, followed from the fact that they started from the foundations. We, on the contrary, have always tried to bolster a pre-established case." Elisha ben Abuyah's intellectual wandering ends in apostasy and eventually with his excommunication from the rabbinate.

The first part of *As a Driven Leaf* is set in Judea; the second, in Antioch in Syria. In Antioch, Elisha's search for certainty takes him further afield—to study Gnosticism, the arguments of the agnostics, the doctrines of the Cynics. Steinberg was learned in Greek and Latin, and steeped in ancient history, and the detailed settings of his novel have a clinching convincingness. In Roman Antioch, Elisha encounters the barbarity of the Roman slave markets, the bloodiness of the gladiatorial arena, where his fellow Jews are put to death at the command of the cruel Roman praetorian prefect, Marcus Tineius Rufus. Elisha's own past reverence for the Pax Romana is wiped out as he sees, "with such fearful clarity, that no society, no matter how great the achievements of its scholars, can be an instrument of human redemption if it despises justice and mercy."

Like the Old Testament God, Steinberg puts Elisha through arduous tests: the temptation of adultery, the seductions of intellectual vanity, and more. Elisha comes to self-knowledge, but the secrets of the universe remain withheld from him. He feels his error in hoping for certainty in life, in abandoning his people and his religion out of intellectual hubris, when he also comes to realize that important truths do not await at the end of a syllogism. Faith and reason, he finally grasps, need not stand opposed. "On the contrary," he tells his old disciple,

> salvation is through the commingling of the two, the former to establish first premises, the latter to purify them of confusion. . . . It is not certainty that one acquires so, only plausibility, but that is the best we can hope for.

In his spiritual wanderings Elisha has gone too far, and can never again accept the authority of his old religion. At the novel's close, his search continues. "Older, sadder, wiser, I go seeking now, through faith and reason combined, the answer to this baffling pageant which is the world, and the little byplay which has been my life."

One imagines that in writing *As a Driven Leaf* Milton Steinberg was writing about his own intellectual conflict over the issue—faith or reason, and in what proportions?—that remains fundamental to thoughtful people to this day. The tension that this conflict stirs in a first-class mind in his novel is compelling, and the incisive portrait of the man caught up in it is what gives *As a Driven Leaf* its standing as a masterpiece.

Joseph and His Brothers

(2012)

ANYONE WITH THE LEAST LITERARY PRETENSIONS has read one or another work by Thomas Mann. Some will have read *Buddenbrooks*, his saga about a Baltic German mercantile family as its energy peters out; others *The Magic Mountain*, that most philosophical of novels and one set in a tuberculosis sanitarium in Switzerland. One is likely to have encountered the novella *Death in Venice* or *Tonio Kroger*, *Mario the Magician*, or one or another of his many splendid short stories. But not many people, I suspect, will have read Mann's tetralogy, *Joseph and His Brothers*, a 1,207-page work of rich and rewarding complexity.

I, a man of extravagant literary pretensions, had not myself read it until only recently. Fifteen or so years ago, I made a run at it, but hit the wall roughly at page 60. What goaded me to take another shot at it was discovering a clean copy on sale at a nearby used-book store. What I discovered is a true masterpiece, but one of a most extraordinary kind. Not the least unusual thing about it is that in this vastly ambitious work Thomas Mann chose to tell a story that everyone already knows.

The story of course is the *Old Testament* account of Jacob, son of Isaac, brother of Esau, and his twelve sons, and of the most impressive of those sons, Joseph, who goes on to become Pharaoh's principal administrator, his Grand Vizier, during the seven fat and seven lean years visited upon

Egypt. The best of all excellent *Old Testament* stories, a story of over-weening vanity, betrayal, reunion, and forgiveness, the biblical version of the Joseph story is used by Mann as in effect an outline, which he filled in, fleshed out, and re-told with the masterly narrative power of the great novelist that he was.

In the *Old Testament*, for example, in a mere half page we are told that Potiphar's wife, enamored of Joseph's good looks, attempts to seduce him, Joseph refuses, she then falsely accuses him of attempted rape, and he is sent off to prison. Mann, or his narrator, claims to be "horrified at the brief-ness and curtness of the original account" in the Bible. In Mann's version, eighty or so pages are spent on the incident, with Potiphar's wife's beauty, cosmetics, handmaidens, seduction methods, and much else described in intricate and perfectly persuasive detail. Where *Old Testament* provides statement of fact, Mann provides heightened and detailed drama.

Thomas Mann took sixteen years to complete *Joseph and His Broth-ers*. (James Joyce took seven to write *Ulysses*, and suggested that readers should take the same length of time to read it.) The years were the tumul-tuous ones between 1926 and 1942—the time of world-wide depression and the rise of Adolf Hitler. Nazism forced Mann and his family into exile, first in Europe, then in the United States. But he pressed on with his novel. In early 1930, he traveled to the Middle East where, as he put it, "with my physical eyes I saw the Nile country from the Delta up (or down) to Nubia and the memorable places of the Holy Land. . ." This book, during these difficult years, was "the undertaking that alone vouch-safed the continuity of my life."

Tour de force, an astonishing feat, is what *Joseph and His Brothers* is, nothing less. This is a book in which an artist, through scholarship and above all through imagination, has worked his way back through time and insinuated himself into the culture of the Biblical Jews and the more elabo-rately exotic culture of the ancient Egyptians. Mann, ever the ironist, at one point early in the book writes: "I do not conceal from myself the difficulty of writing about people who do not precisely know who they are."

Joseph and His Brothers is studded with exquisite touches. Laban, Jacob's exploiting father-in-law, is described as possessing "the hands of a having man." Of Jacob's love for Rachel, Mann writes: "Such is love, when it is complete: feeling and lust together, tenderness and desire." Apropos of Jacob's agedness, he writes of "the touching if unattractive misshapenness of old age." Potiphar's wife, distraught by her passion for Joseph, loses her appetite and is barely able to eat "a bird's liver and a little vegetable." Mann's description of Rachel's labor in giving birth to Joseph is so well done as to leave one exhausted.

Past and present are interwoven throughout this novel. "Men saw through each other in that distant day," Mann writes, "as well as in this." Recurrence is a *leitmotif* that plays through the book. "For we move in the footsteps of others, and all life is but the pouring of the present into the forms of the myth," he notes. Through the novel, Joseph is aware that his is a role in an already written script—a script written by God—and it is this that gives him the courage to carry on: "For let a man once have the idea that God has special plans for him, which he must further by his aid, and he will pluck up his heart and strain his understanding to get the better of all things and be their master. . ." The woman Tamar, who in the disguise of a prostitute allows herself to become pregnant by Joseph's brother Judah, does so because she, too, wants to be inscribed forever in the history of this important family.

One could compose a dazzling little anthology of aphorisms from *Joseph and His Brothers*. "It takes understanding to sin; yes, at bottom, all spirit is nothing else than understanding of sin." And: "We fail to realize the indivisibility of the world when we think of religion and politics as fundamentally separate fields. . . ." Yet again: "No, the agonies of love are set apart; no one has ever repented having suffered them." And finally: "Man, then, was a result of God's curiosity about himself."

In another of the book's aphorisms, Mann writes: "Indeed resolution and patience are probably the same thing." How often must that sentiment, over the sixteen difficult years he spent composing this grand prose epic, have occurred to Thomas Mann himself. At the end of his foreword to the single-volume publication of his tetralogy, Mann wonders if his novel "will perhaps be numbered among the great books?" He cannot know, of course, but as the son of a tradesman he does know that, of the products of human hands, only quality endows them with endurance. "The song of Joseph is good, solid work," Mann writes, "done out of that fellow feeling for which mankind has always been sensitively receptive. A measure of durability is, I think, inherent in it." He was correct. In *Joseph and His Brothers* he created a masterpiece, which is to say, a work built to last.

Life and Fate

(2007)

NO PEOPLE HAVE BEEN PUT TO THE TESTS of suffering the way Russians have. They have never known anything approaching decent government. Czars or commissars, their leaders have always treated them as if they were a conquered nation. Even now, after the fall of communism, things for them remain impressively dreary. I not long ago asked a formidable expert on Russia whom we were supposed to root for among those contending for power in the country. With only thieves, thugs, and former KGB men seeking leadership, he replied, there is no one to root for. Business, in other words, as usual.

Literature has been the only, if of course vastly insufficient, Russian compensation. The barbarity of the nation's conditions has, somehow, produced a great literature studded with magnificent literary subjects. From Pushkin through Solzhenitsyn—with Gogol, Turgenev, Tolstoy, Goncharov, Dostoyevsky, Chekhov, Mandelstam, Babel, Akhmatova, Pasternak, and many others in between—great Russian novelists and poets have never been in short supply.

One Russian writer who until only recently slipped through my own net is Vasily Grossman (1904–1964), author of a novel called *Life and Fate*, which was written under the direct influence of *War and Peace*. The first I had heard of this book was six or so months ago from my friend

Frederic Raphael, the English novelist and screenwriter, a man never given to overstatement. "It's a masterpiece," he said, and, upon investigation, this assessment turns out to be precisely correct.

Grossman was born in Berdichev, in the Ukraine, near Kiev and the scene of one of the first large massacres of Jews before Babi Yar, the infamous mass execution of Jews outside Kiev. A chemist by training, he worked as a mining engineer, and then, following his instincts and talent, became a writer. During World War II, he covered—was "embedded with" we should say today—the Russian army on its eastern front. His dispatches for the publication known in English as *Red Army* were widely read, but nowhere more intensely than by Stalin, who, knowing Grossman had too much integrity to turn hack, was said to have been extremely wary of his ardor for truth-telling.

Like Isaac Babel, author of the *Red Cavalry* stories, Grossman was a Jewish writer with more of a taste than a physique for the military life. As a journalist, he indulged this taste by educating himself on all aspects of weaponry, strategy, and tactics. He wrote about the great battle of Stalingrad and then followed the German army in its retreat, reporting on the extermination camps of Majdanek and Treblinka, arriving with the Soviet army in Berlin. He was unblinking in his accounts of war's devastation and horror, and turned in the most significant account of the bloodiest battle of the 20th century, the attack upon and defense of Stalingrad, which cost 27 million Russian soldiers and civilians and four million troops of the Wehrmacht.

That battle of Stalingrad is at the center of *Life and Fate*. Grossman said that the only book he read—which he read twice—during his time as a journalist was *War and Peace*. The parallel between Napoleon's attack on Russia through Borodino and Hitler's attack on Russia through Stalingrad is obvious. In each, the fate of Europe was at stake; in both battles the losses, but especially those incurred by the Russians, were unprecedented. On each occasion, against all odds, Russia emerged victorious.

To attempt a novel modeled on *War and Peace* is easy; to write one that is unembarrassing by comparison is not. Far from embarrassing, *Life and Fate* is one of the great novels of the 20th century. The book has more than 150 characters, panoramically representing almost all strains of Russian life during the nightmarish Stalin years; various plots and subplots are neatly interwoven with detailed descriptions of battles and penetrating excursuses on totalitarianism, on the history of the persecution of the Jews ("anti-Semitism," Grossman writes, "is . . . an expression of lack of talent, an inability to win a contest on equal terms"), on the evolution of morality and kindness. The novel is rich in apercus. Viktor Shtrum, one of its central characters, is an experimental physicist who claims that "the value of science is the happiness it brings to people," but he also holds that "science today should be entrusted to men of spiritual understanding, to prophets and saints. But instead it's left to chess players and scientists."

Like almost all first-order imaginative literature produced in the Soviet Union, the book could not be published there. Mikhail Suslov, a powerful member of the Politburo, said that it was unlikely to be published for another 200 or 300 years. History intervened to squash this prediction, yet in sad fact Grossman, who died of stomach cancer, did not live to see his great novel in print.

As Tolstoy did in *War and Peace*, Grossman in *Life and Fate* does not hesitate to bring in historical characters: Adolf Eichmann, Josef Stalin, Adolf Hitler, and actual German and Russian generals appear in the novel's pages. An unforgettable two chapters in the middle of the book describe, in an all but unbearable yet utterly persuasive way, the experience of going to the gas chambers.

In this novel, Grossman is able to keep two large balls in the air at all times: the conduct of the war and life under the two fascisms, German and Russian, so that throughout the spiritual confrontation of the fragile soul of the individual and the colossus that is the State plays out. This confrontation at the heart of *Life and Fate* is what gives the novel its grandeur.

Life and Fate is a novel of 871 pages in its American edition (translated by Robert Chandler, *New York Review of Books Classics*), over the course of which there are many bitter smiles, but no laughs whatsoever. A chronicle of the past century's two evil engines of destruction—Soviet communism and German fascism—the novel is dark yet earns its right to depression. But it depresses in the way that all genuinely great art does—

through an unflinching view of the truth, which includes all the awfulness of which human beings are capable and also the splendor to which in crises they can attain. A great book, *Life and Fate* is a book only a Russian could write.

Memoirs of Hadrian

(2010)

IN 1982, WHEN I FIRST READ Marguerite Yourcenar's *The Memoirs of Hadrian*, I asked Arnaldo Momigliano, the great scholar of the ancient world, what he thought of the novel. Italian to the highest power, he put all five fingers of his right hand to his mouth, kissed them, and announced, "Pure masterpiece." Now, nearly 30 years later, I have reread the work and find it even better than before. A book that improves on rereading, that seems even grander the older one gets—surely, this is yet another sign of a masterpiece.

Its author was born in Belgium, wrote in French, and lived much of her adult life in Maine with her excellent translator and companion, Grace Frick. As such, Mme. Yourcenar (1903–1987) was, in effect, a writer without a country, though she was the first woman elected to the *Académie Française* (in 1980). She was the last aristocratic novelist of the 20th century, and not only in the sense that her father was of aristocratic descent. She did not ask in her fiction the contemporary middle-class questions of what is happiness and why have I (or my characters) not found it, concerning herself instead with something larger—the meaning of human destiny as it plays out on a historical stage.

Mme. Yourcenar wrote a good deal of fiction, but her imperishable work is *Memoirs of Hadrian*, first published in French in 1951. The novel is in the form of a lengthy letter written by the aged and ill Emperor Hadrian, who ruled from CE 117 to 138, to the 17-year-old but already thoughtful Marcus Aurelius.

Roman emperors seem to be divided between monsters and mediocrities, with an occasional near-genius, like Hadrian, thrown in to break the monotony. Highly intelligent and cultivated, he was a Grecophile, always a good sign in the ancient world. As emperor, he attempted to pull back from the imperialist expansion of his predecessor Trajan and wanted, as the chronicler Aelius Spartianus put it, to "administer the republic [so that] it would know that the state belonged to the people and was not his property."

And yet Hadrian was also a Roman emperor, which meant living amid dangerous intrigue, wielding enormous power, and being able to fulfill his erotic impulses at whim. He was, Spartianus writes, "both stern and cheerful, affable and harsh, impetuous and hesitant, mean and generous, hypocritical and straightforward, cruel and merciful, and always in all things changeable"—in short, not a god but a man.

Mme. Yourcenar has taken what we know of the life of Hadrian and from this sketchy knowledge produced an utterly convincing full-blown portrait. One feels that one is reading a remarkable historical document, an account of the intricate meanings of power by a man who has held vast power. Imagine Machiavelli's *The Prince* written not by an Italian theorist but by a true prince. Imagine, further, that he also let you in on his desires, his fears, his aesthetic, his sensuality, his feelings about death—in a manner at once *haute* and intimate, and in a prose any emperor would be pleased to possess.

"I see an objection to every effort toward ameliorating man's condition, on earth," Hadrian writes, setting out the political philosophy that will inform his reign,

> namely that mankind is perhaps not worthy of such exertion. But I meet the objection easily enough: so long as Caligula's dream remains impossible of fulfillment, and the entire human race is not reduced to a single head destined for the axe, we shall have to bear with humanity, keeping it within bounds but utilizing it to the utmost; our interest, in the best sense of the term, will be to serve it.

Part of the mastery of *Memoirs of Hadrian* is in its reminder that the emperor, like the rest of us, remains imprisoned in a perishable human body. Hadrian's letter to young Marcus is being written at the end of his life, and so with a sure grasp of the inexorability of "Time, the Devourer." Hadrian has come into his wisdom only after manifold errors and tragic mistakes; not least among the latter, contriving, through thoughtlessness, in the death of his great love, the Bithynian youth Antinous. He is writing "when my harvests are in." The letter lets Hadrian take his own measure.

"I liked to feel that I was above all a continuator," Hadrian writes. He notes that he looked "to those twelve Caesars so mistreated by Suetonius," in the hope of emulating the best of each:

> the clear-sightedness of Tiberius, without his harshness; the learning of Claudius without his weakness; Nero's taste for the arts, but stripped of all foolish vanity; the kindness of Titus, stopping short of his sentimentality; Vespasian's thrift, but not his absurd miserliness.

Mme. Yourcenar has Hadrian compare himself, favorably, with Alcibiades, who "had seduced everyone and everything, even History herself." Unlike Alcibiades, who had brought destruction everywhere, he, Hadrian,

> had governed a world infinitely larger . . . and had kept pace therein; I had rigged it like a fair ship made ready for a voyage which might last for centuries; I had striven my utmost to encourage in man the sense of the divine but without at the same time sacrificing to it what is essentially human. My bliss was my reward.

Like most of our lives, Hadrian's—and so Mme. Yourcenar's novel—is plotless. What keeps the reader thoroughly engaged is not drama but the high quality of Hadrian's thought and powers of observation. Hadrian, through the sheer force of his mind, comes alive. That this most virile of characters has been written by a woman might be worth remarking were it not the case that the greatest novelists have always been androgynous in their powers of creation. With the dab hand of literary genius, Mme. Yourcenar has taken one of the great figures of history and turned him into one of the most memorable characters in literature.

Charnwood's *Lincoln*

(2014)

BOOKS ABOUT ABRAHAM LINCOLN are legion and usually lengthy. The most famous of these books and the longest is perhaps also the worst: Carl Sandburg's multivolumed biography, a repository of folklore and myth-making that Edmund Wilson called "the cruelest thing that happened to Lincoln since he was shot by Booth." Lincoln books continually—one is tempted to write "continuously"—appear. Such is the appetite for these books that an old joke among publishers had it that a sure-fire American best-seller would have the title "Lincoln's Mother's Doctor's Dog."

The best book about Lincoln was written not by an American but by an Englishman named Lord Charnwood. His *Abraham Lincoln* (1916) is a work in the distinguished tradition of brilliant books by foreign writers on American subjects. Alexis de Tocqueville's *Democracy in America*, Lord Bryce's *The American Commonwealth* and George Santayana's *Character and Opinion in the United States* are books in this line. These foreign observers were able to tell us things about ourselves that we Americans were likely to overlook or perhaps did not wish to know.

Born Godfrey Rathbone Benson (1864–1945), later a member of Parliament and an Oxford don, Lord Charnwood was something of an Americanophile, having also written a book on Theodore Roosevelt. He wrote his Lincoln biography in the middle of World War I, a time when the world seemed to be coming apart, as it had seemed to Americans during the Civil War some 60 years earlier.

Lord Charnwood's *Abraham Lincoln* has a universal appeal, though it was originally written for an English audience. The English much admired Lincoln. True, at the time of the American Civil War, many aristocratic Englishmen sided with the South owing to the region's aristocratic pretensions, with Charles Darwin and Lord Tennyson being two notable exceptions. But workers in the English textile industry, feeling a kinship with the slaves of the South, sided with the North in the war, even though it was against their self-interest to do so.

Lord Charnwood's main emphasis in *Abraham Lincoln* is on character analysis and political philosophy. His decision to place it there was a wise one, for it enlarges the biography's scope and lends it a Plutarchian gravity that helps give the book its standing as a masterpiece.

The concise portraits of the subsidiary players in the drama that was the Civil War are not the least of the book's pleasures. Lord Charnwood writes of Millard Fillmore that he

> had an appearance of grave and benign wisdom . . . but he was a pattern of that outwardly dignified, yet nerveless and gutless and heartless respectability, which was more dangerous to America at that period than political recklessness or want of scruple.

Franklin Pierce he finds a figure of "sheer, deleterious insignificance." Salmon P. Chase, Lincoln's Secretary of the Treasury, "must have been a good man before he fell in love with his goodness." Horace Greeley, the influential editor of the *New York Tribune* during the Civil War years, is described as "too opinionated to be quite honest," a formulation worth contemplating by all who hold unshakably firm opinions.

Lincoln was a moral hero for Lord Charnwood and his cause the only right one. The biographer believed the South's "enduring heroism in a mistaken cause" to be nothing less than a "pathetic spectacle." Yet he considered both Robert E. Lee and Stonewall Jackson "men of genius," and superior to any military leaders on the other side. He recognized the high quality of Alexander Stephens, vice president of the Confederacy, but held a low opinion of Jefferson Davis, whose "fanatical narrowness" condemned him to a "progressive warping of his determined character."

Great as Lord Charnwood's admiration for Lincoln was, he never portrays him as an unvarnished hero, refraining from what he calls "frigid perfections." He examines in careful detail Lincoln's weaknesses, his small vanities and deficiencies. At the same time, he defends him against what he deems unjust criticisms. Lincoln's law partner and biographer William Herndon refers to Lincoln's ambition as "a little engine that knew no rest." Lord Charnwood counters this by arguing that Lincoln was finally ambitious for the public weal. He writes:

> If ambition means the eager desire for great opportunities, the depreciation of it, which has long been a commonplace of literature, and which may be traced back to the Epicureans, is a piece of cant which ought to be withdrawn from currency, and ambition, commensurate with the powers which each man can discover in himself, should be frankly recognized as a part of Christian duty.

Lord Charnwood's *Abraham Lincoln* efficiently recounts Lincoln's youth and largely self-administered education, improbable rise in politics, complex relations with military commanders and cabinet members, and assassination, without neglecting his serene temperament and the philosophical outlook that governed his conduct through the Civil War. He devotes many pages to scrutiny of Lincoln's letters, debates and speeches. Rightly so, for Lincoln's prose style, which he acquired through careful reading of Shakespeare, Euclid, and the Bible, made him one of the great American writers.

Of the power of Lincoln's speeches, Lord Charnwood writes:

> It was the distinction of Lincoln—a man lacking much of the knowledge which statesmen are supposed to possess, and capable of blundering and hesitation about details—first, that ... he was free from ambiguity of thought or faltering of will, and further, that upon his difficult path, amid bewildering and terrifying circumstances, he was able to take with him the minds of very many very ordinary men.

The grandeur of Abraham Lincoln, in Lord Charnwood's view, is that he put the need to preserve the union before his party, his family, his own ambitions. He prosecuted a war in which 1/32nd of the nation's population was killed without ever showing hatred for the other side. It was not men but slavery he hated. Yet his hatred, as Lord Charnwood writes, "left him quite without the passion of moral indignation against the slave owners, in whose guilt the whole country, North and South, seemed to him an accomplice." Malice wasn't available to Lincoln; mercy came naturally to him. His magnanimity in forgiveness was another sign of his superiority. He was magnificent in his lofty impersonality.

These words from the concluding paragraph of Lord Charnwood's masterly biography capture Abraham Lincoln better than any I know:

> For he was a citizen of that far country where there is neither aristocrat nor democrat. No political theory stands out from his words or actions; but they show a most unusual sense of the possible dignity of common men and common things. . . . If he had a theory of democracy it was contained in this condensed note which he wrote, perhaps as an autograph, a year or two before his presidency: "As I would not be a slave, so I would not be a master. This expresses my idea of democracy. Whatever differs from this, to the extent of the difference, is no democracy."

Great men and women do not always get the biographers they deserve. In Lord Charnwood, Abraham Lincoln found his.

Book of the Courtier

(2013)

THE *BOOK OF THE COURTIER* was an international bestseller from its publication in 1528 until the end of the eighteenth century. Going through no fewer than 150 editions, it was translated into French, Spanish, Dutch, English, German, Polish, and Latin. Twenty years in gestation, put through many revisions, the book, whose subject is the proper behavior of men and women at the courts of Renaissance princes, was written by Baldesar Castiglione, an aristocrat, soldier, and diplomat who died, at age fifty, less than a year after publication of his magnum opus.

Born into a wealthy family residing near Mantua, Castiglione was a contemporary and friend of Raphael, who painted a famous portrait of him. After serving at the court of Francesco Gonzaga, Castiglione took up residence at the court of Urbino, ruled by Duke Guidobaldo da Montrefeltro. Known for its concerts, plays, poetry readings, and festivals, the richness and refinement of Urbino's cultural life was overseen by the Duke's wife Elizebetta.

The Book of the Courtier is set on four different nights at the court of Urbino. Several people, all drawn from life, have gathered for a discussion of the qualities the ideal courtier should possess. The only two people conspicuously missing from the proceedings are the author, Castiglione, and the prince himself, Duke Guidobaldo. The mistress of ceremonies, directing the flow of talk, is the Duchess.

Set out in dialogue form, the book does not always, as we should say today, stay on message. Often it veers into lengthy digressions on the nature of women, on what constitutes perfect love, and on the true meaning of a kiss. Castiglione informs us that his book merely "rehearses some discussions which took place among men singularly qualified in such matters." Many of those who hold the floor have conflicting perspectives, even opposing views. Little is definitively settled. Often Castiglione leaves complex questions, issues, problems to be settled only in the mind of his readers.

In *The Civilization of the Renaissance in Italy*, the great Swiss historian Jacob Burckhardt claims that the true subject of *The Book of the Courtier* is the perfection of the nobleman at court. He summarizes the skills the courtier must acquire. Apart from mastering the arts of war, which are primary, "the courtier," in Burckhardt's summary, "must be at home in all noble sports, among them running, leaping, swimming and wrestling; he must, above all things, be a good dancer and, as a matter of course, an accomplished rider." For Castiglione, the courtier should be acquainted with great literature, know music to the point of being able to play an instrument, be steeped in the arts of oratory, and in conversation employ exquisite tact and apply the art, in his memorable phrase, of "cheating expectations."

Not only must the courtier acquire all these skills, but he must also avoid any suggestion of exhibitionism or braggadocio in his demonstration of them. He must display them with a casual air of easy mastery. The ideal courtier, Castiglione writes, "must put every effort and diligence into outstripping others a little, so that he may be always recognized as better than the rest." But he must do so without showing the least strain or hint of affectation. He is to accomplish this through *sprezzatura,* the art of artlessness, or the art that hides art.

The Book of the Courtier is in part a manual of advice on such subjects as seduction, the behavior required of women at court, practical jokes, how to keep love secret, why it is a mistake to learn chess, and more. Some of this advice has a cold Machiavellian flavor. Castiglione writes:

There is an adage which says that when our enemy is in the water up to his waist, we must offer him our hand and rescue him from peril; but when he is up to his chin, we must put our foot on his head and drown him forthwith.

At other times, *The Book of the Courtier* reads like the anti-Machiavelli, at least the Machiavelli of *The Prince*, with its stern lessons on attaining and retaining power at all costs. In the fourth and final section of *The Book of the Courtier*, Castiglione, contra Machiavelli, addresses himself to the courtier's role as moral adviser to princes.

Here it becomes clear that Castiglione intends for his ideal courtier to be more much than a fop, a Renaissance dandy, a connoisseur in the art of self-presentation, but above all that an instructor to his prince on the subject of righteous rule. The point of the courtier making himself so charming, and of his elegant display of mastery of the arts, is that through them he will raise himself in the prince's esteem, thereby seducing him into heeding his advice. If the excellence of the courtier's cultural attainments is "the flower" of his training, "the fruit" lies in helping his prince "toward what is right and to warn him against what is wrong." The courtier, Castiglione holds, is "the whetstone," the prince "the knife"; as the physician is concerned with his patient's health, so the courtier is concerned with the prince's virtue.

Castiglione was not a trained philosopher, but like most educated men of his day, he had read Plato and Aristotle with care. Plato and Aristotle were themselves courtiers—not philosopher-kings, as Plato had it in *The Republic*, but philosophers who instructed kings. Plato, alas, failed in his abortive attempt to council the incorrigible Dionysius of Sicily. Aristotle was more successful in his tutelage of Alexander the Great.

Renaissance Italy, though in many ways one of great ages of mankind, was also an age of despotic princes with vast treasure and unlimited power. The too greatly rich, in Castiglione's view, "often become proud and insolent." Power applied without reflection and training in virtue, he felt, was a certain formula for disaster. Castiglione's courtier, in his function as court philosopher, was to curb the insolence and do all he could to forestall the disaster by instilling virtue in his prince.

What gives *The Book of the Courtier* its standing as a masterpiece is not alone the brilliance of its detail and cogency of its arguments but how pertinent so many of its pages seem in our day—and are likely to seem in any other day. The right relation of virtue to power will always be the key political issue, and few writers in the nearly five centuries since he wrote *The Book of the Courtier* understood this more profoundly than Baldesar Castiglione.

Ronald Syme

(2016)

I**N HIS STUDY** of the Roman historian Sallust (86–35 BCE), Ronald Syme writes that "historians are selective, dramatic, impressionistic." Later in the same work he notes that "systems and doctrines decay or ossify, whereas poetry and drama live on, also style and narrative." These words apply to Syme himself, a man generally considered the greatest modern historian of Rome. Syme wrote biographies of Sallust and Tacitus and much else, but his reputation rests on *The Roman Revolution*. Published in 1939 when the specter of fascism clouded Europe, it was soon recognized as the magnificent book it is.

Ronald Syme (1903–1989) was a New Zealander who studied at and settled in Oxford. His specialty was prosopography, or the study of collective biographies to find common characteristics of historical social classes or groups. This was invaluable for *The Roman Revolution*, which is a compelling account of the decline of the Roman oligarchy in favor of a principate, or monarchy, quietly but implacably put in place by Augustus, the first of the Roman emperors. If historians had Rolodexes, none could be more complete than Syme's on the Romans in the last years of the Republic. "In any age in the history of the Roman Republic," he notes, "about twenty or thirty men, drawn from a dozen dominant families, hold a monopoly of office and power." An intramural, nearly incestuous, affair was Roman political life. Consider Servilia, "Cato's half-sister, Brutus's mother, Caesar's mistress."

A man who sees beneath every surface, demolishing all pretenses, Syme, early in his great book, writes: "The Roman constitution was a screen and a sham." Of the idealism of the Republic, he notes: "Liberty and law are high-sounding words. They will often be rendered, on a cool estimate, as privilege and vested interest." No cooler estimator existed than Syme. "The career of Pompeius," he writes, "opened in fraud and violence. It was prosecuted, in war and peace, through illegality and treachery."

Once the Triumvirs—Julius Caesar, Pompeius, Lepidus—were in ascendance, the Roman Republic's day was done. "From a triumvirate it was but a short step to a dictatorship," Syme writes. Julius Caesar, who emerged as dictator, before his assassination adopted Octavianus, whom Syme regularly refers to as "Caesar's heir." Octavianus would subsequently become Augustus, who, after his victories over Caesar's assassins and later Marcus Antonius, ruled for 40 years. Augustus, Syme writes, possessed "an inborn and Roman distrust of theory, and an acute sense of the difference between words and facts."

Syme was a master of the brief character sketch, not infrequently followed by a sharp observation. The mixture of good and evil in the same people fascinated him. After toting up Marcus Antonius's many flaws, he writes that "a blameless life is not the whole of virtue, and inflexible rectitude may prove a menace to the Commonwealth." Cicero, he says, "had lent his eloquence to all political causes in turn, was sincere in one thing only, loyalty to the established order. His past career showed that he could not be depended on for action or statesmanship."

Augustus succeeded owing to his ambition and cunning, and to his awareness that, after long years of civil war, Romans were willing to surrender liberty for peace and concord. Concord meant rule by one man—monarchy—whose worst feature, along with the loss of liberty, "was the growth of servility and adulation."

Unsurpassed in his erudition, relentless in his perspicacity, Syme combined these merits with a historical style in the tradition of Thucydides, Sallust, Tacitus, and Gibbon, great disillusionists all. The interjection of the short, deadly sentence is among the hallmarks of this style. "Two days of diplomacy divided the Roman world," is but one example from Syme. The murder of Cicero "disgraced the Triumvirs and enriched literature with an immortal theme" is another. Accounting for the rise of Octavianus, he writes: "Accident blended with design."

With a single sentence he fills in long spans of time. "From first to last the dynasty of the Julii and the Claudii ran true to form, despotic and murderous." He writes of Antonius and Cleopatra in Egypt that they "spent nearly a year after the disaster [of the battle of Actium] in the last revels, the last illusory plans, and the last despondency before death." He specializes in the risky yet authoritative generalization: "Lacking any perception of the dogma of progress—for it had not yet been invented—the Romans regarded novelty with distrust and aversion." Sometimes this style turns aphoristic: "Politics can be controlled but not abolished, ambition curbed but not crushed." Again: "It is not enough to acquire power and wealth; men wish to appear virtuous and to feel virtuous."

Toward the close of *The Roman Revolution* Syme writes: "To explain the fall of the Roman Republic, historians invoke a variety of converging forces or movements, political, social and economic, where antiquity was prone to see only the ambition and agency of individuals." As with all historical masterpieces, one comes away from *The Roman Revolution* feeling unblinkered and intellectually rejuvenated.

Quest for Corvo

(2009)

"ALL I CAN TELL YOU about the book, my dear fellow," A. J. A. Symons wrote to his brother Julian in mid-composition of *The Quest for Corvo*, "is that it will be unlike any other biography ever written." He was right. Symons, 34 when he published the book in 1934, never wrote another. (He died at 41.) One begins the *The Quest for Corvo* in delight and ends it in satisfaction—one definition, surely, of a masterpiece.

Symons's biography of a little-known writer named Frederick Rolfe (1860–1913) is unique in biographical literature in bringing the reader in on how the biographer knows what he knows about his subject; and in owning up to what he doesn't know or feels cannot be known. *The Quest for Corvo* is biography in the form of a detective story, and as such it is riveting.

The surest formula for a masterpiece biography—of which there are not that many—is an extraordinary human being writing about a great one. In *The Quest for Corvo*, we have an utterly charming man writing on a madly eccentric one. "Charlatan or Genius?" is the book's subtitle, and when one has finished reading it one is inclined to conclude that Rolfe was fully both.

Rolfe was a failed painter, photographer, musician, and, most devastatingly of all to him, a born Anglican who failed to achieve priesthood in the

Catholic Church. (He claimed never to have met an honest Catholic, yet, in a characteristic touch, added, "if I were not Catholic I shouldn't be anything at all.") Toward the end of his life, he signed himself Fr. Rolfe, hoping to be mistaken for a priest.

What Rolfe was, indisputably, was an immensely talented writer. He wrote no great books, though his *Hadrian the Seventh*, a brilliant fantasy in which he imagines a character obviously based on himself being made Pope after the College of Cardinals can't decide on a worthy candidate, has gone through many printings since his death. A remarkable stylist, Rolfe wrote with precision and high comic flourish. He had a strong taste for magniloquence and was a master of vituperation.

The Quest for Corvo begins with Symons chatting with a friend who tells him about Rolfe's *Hadrian the Seventh*. Symons reads it and is so struck by it that he is determined to learn more about its author and to search out anything else by him. At the time, Symons was working on a book of his own—A Select Bibliography and History of the Books of the Nineties, with Notes on Their Authors, which he never completed—and was the secretary of the First Edition Club in London. Later, with the French gourmet and wine merchant André Simon, he founded the Wine and Food Society. Symons was dedicated to elegant acquisitions and good living. At his life's end he said, "No one so poor has lived so well." Good living and self-doubt prevented him from writing another book, while Rolfe continued to produce under the most penurious conditions.

Symons's biography takes the form of a continual connecting of the dots, filling in gaps through Symons's encounters with Rolfe's former friends and those with whom he had business dealings. Chance plays a large role, as Symons is led from one to another of Rolfe's connections. "Mr. Pirie-Gordon was the missing link between Rolfe's middle and his later years," Symons writes. "I was able to piece the story together, to watch another rotation of the wheel to which Rolfe was bound."

One of the book's special pleasures is in Symons's portraits of the extraordinary characters who offered their hands to Rolfe only, inevitably, to have them bitten. Among these are splendid miniatures of now-forgotten but once-important English men of letters and publishers, among them Shane Leslie and the religious novelist Robert Hugh Benson. Most extraordinary of all is the astonishing Maundy Gregory, who buys a Rolfe letter from Symons and later himself turns up several of Rolfe's missing manuscripts. The mysteriously wealthy Gregory, though Symons was unaware of it, was a bagman for David Lloyd George, selling knighthoods and other honors for the right price.

The Quest for Corvo, as Symons notes, is in part a story of human benevolence. Men and women were attracted to Rolfe, despite all that was off-putting about him. The Duchess of Sforza-Cesarini, who gave him an allowance, also conferred upon Rolfe, or so he claimed, the title of Baron Corvo. But Rolfe was a genuine paranoid—a paranoid who made his own enemies, and did his utmost to keep them.

He was a sponger, a liar, a homosexual dedicated to suborning the innocent, a fantasist ever ready, as Symons has it, to add "new turrets" to "his castles in the air," yet in his dedication to his pretensions, in his utter friendlessness—he dedicated one of his books to "the Divine Friend much desired," a want ad if ever there was one—Rolfe was also unspeakably sad.

Refreshingly un-Freudian, *The Quest for Corvo* makes scant reference to Rolfe's parents, his upbringing, the formation of his character. Rolfe enters Symons's book fully formed, a monster not in the least sacred. "Though the peculiar inner energy which possessed Fr. Rolfe is beyond analysis," Symons writes, "the external events of his life, and his reactions to them, can be collated and made comprehensible."

Rolfe's troubles began, Symons concludes, with his homosexuality, his knowledge that he was not like most men, which fed into his paranoia. "His forbidden love," Symons writes, "was a source of weakness, but hate could make him strong." Rolfe was hard to do justice to, but Symons, out of the largeness of his imagination, in the end finds him a figure from whom "it is unjust . . . to withhold admiration and pity," a judgment that seems exactly right.

A slender book, an odd book, a completely original book, *The Quest for Corvo* also represents a new method of writing biography that has never been copied. That it hasn't been, that perhaps it cannot be without the keen mind that Symons brought to it, is but another mark of its standing as a masterpiece.

The Old Bunch

(2012)

MEYER LEVIN IS BEST REMEMBERED, if at all, as the author of the novel *Compulsion* (1956), based on the Leopold and Loeb murder case of the 1920s. But Mr. Levin (1905–1981) wrote several novels, and one of them, *The Old Bunch* (1937), retains great power. *The Old Bunch* is long—964 pages in the Citadel Press reprint edition—but not in the least sprawling. The chronicle of the lives of 19 late adolescents, all Jewish, living on the West Side of Chicago, it is beautifully orchestrated, flowing from the life of one character to another. Lest this seem parochial, some of the characters travel to New York, Paris, Palestine (not yet Israel).

The story's timeline runs from the early '20s to 1934, ending at the close of the World's Fair in Chicago. Franklin Delano Roosevelt is in office. The destinies of the characters, now in their 30s, are settled.

Destiny is Mr. Levin's larger subject. Each character plays out his or her fate in the pages of *The Old Bunch*. Not one is heroic. The roster includes two physicians, a hat maker, a furniture manufacturer, a fellow-traveling lawyer, a small-time criminal lawyer, a corrupt (in the best Chicago tradition) lawyer, a high-school teacher, a sculptor, an unsuccessful inventor, and a sad loser who rides the rails during the Depression. The women are of the era when the only serious career offering was a husband

and children, and in the novel all of them marry, except for a grammar-school teacher who is unable to find the right man and another woman who ends up a bit of a floozy. Mr. Levin fills in the details so artfully that the reader is caught up in all the characters' lives, feeling the sting of their defeats, engaged in their small but touching dramas.

The method is that of realism. Details add up to form character, and character becomes destiny. For example, young Sam Eisen's strain of nonconformity impels him first to leave the boyhood club of friends because of its want of seriousness; later he will drop out of the University of Illinois because of his repugnance toward compulsory ROTC service; the bourgeois spirit of his wife drives him to divorce; and he ends up a lawyer whose career is devoted to idealistic but ultimately empty radical causes.

The central characters' parents—some immigrant and impoverished, others here for a generation and flourishing—work as button makers, have small factories, run flop houses, are fur-workers, real-estate operators, cigar makers, grocery- and furniture-store proprietors, and, in one notable instance, the political boss of the Jewish West Side.

The Old Bunch is an excellent corrective to *The World of Our Fathers*, Irving Howe's historical account of the Jews of (mostly) New York, with their labor-union and socialist backgrounds. American Jews at the turn of the past century were more various than one might think based on Mr. Howe's book.

Mr. Levin sets his characters in their time by having them talk about the pop culture of the age. The names Jack Dempsey, Babe Ruth, Red Grange, Fatty Arbuckle, Sophie Tucker, Charles Lindbergh, Walter Winchell, Sally Rand, Leopold and Loeb play through the novel's pages. Snatches of popular songs of the time—"Nothing but blue birds all day long"; "You've got the cutest little baby face"—serve as refrains, commenting, often ironically, on the novel's action.

Corruption—of unions, of judges, of the police, of politicians—is central to the novel. With the right connections, everyone is buyable, everything fixable. Judges are on the take, cops beat up unionists, the utilities and railroad magnate Samuel Insull perhaps the biggest crook of all. No city has ever been a greater deterrent to idealism than Chicago, and Mr. Levin neatly captures this.

The novelist refers to his characters as "a lucky generation." Too young for World War I, they will later be too old for World War II. But they are not too young or too old for the Depression, to which some of the most stirring pages of "The Old Bunch" are devoted. Most of the characters watch their lives unravel under the pressure of the complete economic breakdown.

Many things mark the tradition of realism—one that includes among its masters Honoré de Balzac, Émile Zola, Theodore Dreiser, and John Dos Passos—but it is distinguished above all by illustrating the pressure that social arrangements bring to bear on individual character.

The novelists who wrote under realism's banner had to know more than psychology, the heart and mind in all their wanderings. They also had to understand how institutions function, and to understand it in detail. Their very method made these novelists worldly. To write *The Old Bunch*, Mr. Levin had to know how the Chicago courts worked, how unionizing and union busting were undertaken, how kibbutz life in Palestine was lived, how medical research and practice are conducted, sculpture created and sold, and much more.

The Old Bunch is a reminder of why novelists were once regarded as gods—gods in the sense of being omniscient. It also reminds us that novelists of any earlier time had larger ambitions than they do in our day, when they are often content to write about people who, like themselves, live more in their minds than in the world. One Levin character, the sculptor Joe Freedman, asks, "Why did one get sidetracked with some shred of truth, with religion or love, politics or surrealism, but so few seemed to keep themselves open for the whole bitter truth of the human race?" *The Old Bunch*, Meyer Levin's neglected masterpiece, is, finally, a reminder that nothing less than "the whole bitter truth of the human race" was once the subject of the novel.

Life of Johnson

(2015)

THE WORLD'S GREATEST BIOGRAPHY was composed by a depressive, a heavy drinker, an inconstant husband and a neglectful father who suffered at least seventeen bouts of gonorrhea. The biography is of course James Boswell's *Life of Johnson*. Biography is its genre but *sui generis* is its form and content. Nothing like it came before and nothing like it has appeared since. Biography we call it, but in some ways it also qualifies as an autobiography of its author, who regularly obtrudes in its pages and may even be said to be its secondary subject. Donald Greene, the American scholar of eighteenth-century literature, proposed that the book's true title should have been *Memoirs of James Boswell, concerning his acquaintance with Samuel Johnson*.

Adam Sisman ends his excellent book *Boswell's Presumptuous Task* by noting that "though the *Life of Johnson* was a pioneering work which opened up new possibilities for biography, it was also unique: never again will there be such a combination of subject, author, and opportunity." Boswell was twenty-two, Johnson fifty-four when they met in 1763. Johnson was widowed from his beloved, nineteen-years-older-than-he wife Tetty; Boswell was the unanchored and still disappointing oldest son of the Scottish laird and magistrate Lord Auchinleck. Famous both as a talker and as the author of the *Rambler* and *Rasselas* and his *Dictionary*, Johnson was already everywhere recognized as a great man. Upon meeting him, Boswell must have sensed that this large, strange, twitch-and-tic ridden man was his passage to a permanent place in literary history.

Boswell saw not merely a great subject in Samuel Johnson, but an exemplar, a teacher, a reality instructor, for the two men were vastly different in outlook, stability, and above all good sense. Johnson came to love Boswell—he called him "a clubbable man"—without ever quite treating him as an equal. "You are longer a boy than others," he told him when Boswell was in his mid-thirties. In Johnson's eyes, he would remain a boy, always in need of straightening out, through their twenty-one-year-long relationship, which ended with Johnson's death in 1784 at seventy-five.

An habitual keeper of journals, Boswell wrote down nearly everything he heard Johnson say or that was said about him. Before setting out to write the biography of Johnson, Boswell, in 1785, published his *Tour of the Hebrides*, his trip to the western islands of Scotland with Johnson, at the end of which he announced that he was planning to write a full life of Johnson. Boswell had been collecting Johnsoniana—journals, notebooks, letters, anecdotes supplied by friends—for years. He also wrote under the lash of two competing biographers, that of Sir John Hawkins, who was Johnson's official biographer, and that of Mrs. Hester Thrale Piozzi, in whose home Johnson was long a welcomed and intimate guest.

Boswell's *Life of Johnson* was the first biography to attempt to probe the inner life of its subject, while also considering his writings and his standing as a public figure. Johnson himself, who wrote *Lives of the Poets*, felt that the inner failings of a biographical subject should not be ignored. Boswell set out to write not a panegyric but a full portrait of the great man in all his weaknesses, failings, faults, and oddities, of which Johnson offered a rich smorgasbord. He did so, however, only against the larger view of his subject's grandeur. Boswell adored Johnson, and his self-appointed assignment in writing his biography was to show that he was greater than his intellectual bullying—his so-called "bow-wow way"—prejudices, lassitude, general slovenliness, and sometime crushing temper. He claimed, correctly, that in his book Johnson was seen "more completely than any man who has ever yet lived."

At the heart of Boswell's biography was Johnson's conversation, both that to which Boswell was privy and that reported by others. Over the twenty-one years of their relationship, Mr. Sisman speculates, Boswell met with Johnson on roughly four hundred days. Whenever he did, he prodded, he fairly goaded him into conversation on what he hoped would be propitious topics. Well worth the effort it was, for Johnson was studded with "genuine vigour and viviacity" and larded with "the exuberant variety of his wit and wisdom." In its slightly less than half-million words, the best things in Boswell's biography are Johnson's many *mots*. So greatly did these capture the fancy of Boswell's readers that he was accused of having people "talk Johnson." To this he replied: "Yes, I may add, I have Johnsonised the land, and I trust that they will not only talk, but think, Johnson."

One encounters all the famous Johnsonisms in Boswell's biography, from "When a man is tired of London, he is tired of life." to "One of the disadvantages of wine is that it makes a man mistake words for thought." to "Patriotism is the last refuge of a scoundrel." Anthologies of Johnson's sayings have been published. In Boswell, though, one sees the great talker *dans combat*.

Johnson's many distinctions are always of interest, such as that between intuition and sagacity, or between talk and conversation, or between doctrine contrary to reason and doctrine above reason. He prefers the Irish over the Scottish because "the Irish are a very fair people—they never speak well of one another." He regularly pulls back the curtain on pretense: "Depend upon it," he tells Boswell, "that if a man *talks* of his misfortunes, there is something in them that is not disagreeable to him." He thought the situation of the Prince of Wales "the happiest of any person's in the kingdom," for he had "the enjoyment of hope, the high superiority of rank, without the anxious cares of government. . . ." He lambasts Swift, Hume, Gibbon, Voltaire, Rousseau, and prefers Richardson's novels over Fielding's.

Oliver Goldsmith said that "there is no arguing with Johnson; for if his pistol misses fire, he knocks you down with the butt end of it." Although not said in response to this, Johnson held that "every man has the right to utter what he thinks truth, and every man has a right to knock him down for it. Martyrdom is the test." Alexander Pope, Boswell notes, is said to have been a less than brilliant conversationalist, adding: "In this respect

Pope differed widely from Johnson, whose conversation was, perhaps, more admirable than even his writings, however excellent."

Early in his biography, Boswell remarks that he is firmly of the opinion "that minute particulars are frequently characteristick, and always amusing, when they relate to a distinguished man." In the hands of an artful biographer, these minute particulars, like so many well-placed dots in a pointillist painting, conduce to provide a satisfyingly full picture. So it is with the *Life of Johnson*. Boswell shows us his gruff table manners, how he walked, his laugh (like that of a rhinoceros), his terror of death, his immense, one can only call it his Christian, generosity to the poor and those defeated by life.

Some have found Boswell slavish in his admiration of Johnson. Macaulay called him "servile and impertinent, shallow and pedantic . . . always laying himself at the feet of some eminent man, and begging to be spat upon and trampeled." Boswell's wife said of the relationship: "I have seen many a bear led by a man; but I never before saw a man led by a bear." If Johnson put up with Boswell's sometimes doubtless cloying sycophancy—"Sir," he at one point tells him, "you have but two topicks, yourself and me. I am sick of them both"—his doing so paid off handsomely. Without James Boswell's biography, Johnson's reputation would not stand anywhere near as high as it does today. A great biographer was required to show us how great a man Samuel Johnson was.

Part Five

Hitting Eighty

Hitting Eighty

(2017)

Not to be born is best, when all is reckoned,
But when a man has seen the light of day
The next best thing by far is to go back
Where he came from, and as quick as he can.
Once youth is past, with all its follies,
Every affliction comes on him,
Envy, confrontation, conflict, battle, blood,
And last of all, old age, lies in wait to besiege him,
Humiliated, cantankerous,
Friendless, sick and weak,
Worst evil of all.

—Oedipus at Colonus, SOPHOCLES*

I SHALL SOON BE HITTING 80. Or perhaps it is more precise to say that 80 will soon be hitting me. Eighty, a stately, an august age, but a preposterous number nonetheless. Beginning a job at *Encyclopaedia Britannica* in 1965, a document from the Personnel—not yet Human Resources—Department informed me that my retirement date would be 2002. The date, 2002, with its ridiculous futurity, caused me to smile. Well, 2002 is long since here and gone. The minutes, the hours, the days, the weeks, the months, even the years pass by at roughly the same pace. It's only the decades that seem to fly by.

Mine has been an immensely fortunate life, though, as Solon warned Croesus, never declare your good fortune until your last breath is drawn.

---

* Translation by David Grene.

This richest of men, king of Lydia, Croesus lived long enough to see the death of his son, the suicide of his wife, and the fall of his kingdom to the Persians. I have no kingdom to lose, and though I have over the years undergone some of the standard sadness—divorce, early death in the family—I have much for which to be grateful. Still, as Polybius, the Greek historian of Rome, had it: "Fortune is envious of mortal men, and is most apt to display her power at the very point where a man believes that he has been most blessed and successful in life." This is why I remain a fully paid-up subscriber to the Knock-Wood Insurance Company, from which I carry a long-term policy. If you're interested in such a policy yourself, contact my agent, Keina Hura.

I drew excellent cards in life, both personal and historical. Personally, I was born to generous, intelligent, and honorable parents, who provided economic security and early gave me the gift of freedom to discover the world on my own. Historically, my generation was too young for the Korean War, too old for the Vietnam war, and lived through a period of continuous economic prosperity in the most interesting country in the world. Ours was a low-population generation—children born toward the end of the Depression—so that colleges and universities wanted us, and we evaded the mad, sad scramble to gain admission to those schools that the world, great ninny that it is, mistakenly takes to be superior.

Ours was also the last generation to grow up eager for adulthood. After us, thanks to the cultural revolution of the late 1960s, staying youthful, forever youthful, was the desideratum; juvenility, not senility, as Tom Wolfe (a member in good standing of our generation) noted, was to be the chief age-related disease of the future. We, though, wanted to grow up, some of us perhaps too quickly. Many of us entered into marriages and had children in our early twenties. Philip Larkin spoke for us when he said that he gave up on Christianity upon learning that, in the afterlife, Christians would return to childly state. Larkin's own childhood was less than happy; besides, he wanted the accoutrements of adulthood: long-play records, liquor, beautiful women, keys.

My generation grew up with memories of the country's one good war— World War II—hummed the sophisticated music of the Gershwin brothers, Rodgers and Hart, and Cole Porter, and found rock 'n' roll trivial, if not laughable. We learned about charm, our ideal of sophistication, and much else from the movies. We smoked cigarettes, drank Scotch and bourbon, and ordered dry martinis, went to work in suits, a small number of the men among us wore serious hats. We carried handkerchiefs. No one born after 1942, a contemporary of mine declared in a generalization that has held up nicely under my random sampling, carries a handkerchief. In the early 1970s, when I began teaching at a university, after the sixties had brought down the wall of formality, the first decision I faced was whether to teach in tie and jacket or jeans and open-collar shirt. I went for the tie and jacket; it felt more natural. Besides, by my thirties I owned no jeans.

My generation also had the good fortune to be around for the impressive advantages in technology, not least medical technology, which has led to the prolongation of life. Among these advances, none has been more radical than the advent of the so-called Digital Age, that most mixed of mixed blessings. I have friends, contemporaries, who have decided to take a pass on everything to do with computers, tablets, smartphones—who needs a car, is their reasoning, a horse is good enough—and live, so to say, pre-digitally.

I am not among them, yet I remain impressed by the sheer goofiness of much that appears online, which I have seen described as "a vanity press for the demented," and where the law of contradictions has been banished. One day, Googling myself (that new and necessary and slightly obscene-sounding verb when used reflexively) I discovered that I was simultaneously a homophobe and an old poof.

I'll accept the "old" part. One of the dangers of being old—for the moment setting death aside—is that one tends to overvalue the past. Machiavelli, in his *Discourses on Livy*, writes: "Men do always, but not always with reason, commend the past and condemn the present . . . [and] extol the days when they remember their youth to have been spent." Santayana holds that the reason the old have nothing but foreboding about the future is that they cannot imagine a world that is any good without their being in it. The temptation, when among contemporaries, is to lapse into what I call crank, in which everything in the past turns out to have been superior to anything in the present. Not true, of course, but oddly pleasant to indulge—even though one knows, as Noel Coward, who later in his life himself indulged in crank, had it, "There is no future in the past."

The detractions of old age are obvious: The lessening capacity for the active life, the weakening of the body, the diminution of sensual pleasure, the irrefutable nearness of death. Toss in memory loss and you get diminishment generally. Cicero, whose own old age was not lived at the Ritz—he was forced into exile and murdered by order of Marcus Antonius, his decapitated head and right hand hung up in the Forum—claimed that "older people who are reasonable, good-tempered, and gracious bear aging well. Those who are mean-spirited and irritable will be unhappy at every stage of their lives." Yet Schopenhauer, that never-less-than-impressive grouch, held that "we shall do best to think of life as a *desengaño*, as a process of disillusionment: since this is, clearly enough, what everything that happens to us is calculated to produce."

At 80, I remain, if not I trust entirely illusioned, still amused by the world. I find myself more impressed than ever by the mysteries of life, not least among them unmotivated altruism. In its elusiveness, human nature remains for me endlessly fascinating. No greater spectacle exists than watching it play out at endeavors high and low. I have a friend who reports that, every morning, his 88-year-old mother-in-law wakes and mutters "shit," cursing because she hadn't died in her sleep. I once read a letter from a man of 71, sent to my physician, saying that he had had enough of life and had decided to forego chemotherapy for stomach cancer. At 80 I find I haven't had nearly enough of life, and each morning upon waking, mutter "Thank you."

Part of my good fortune has been my health. ("So long as you have your health," the old Jews used to say—correctly, it turns out.) Several years ago I had heart-bypass surgery, and occasionally my immune system, betraying its name, lets me down. The most recent instance was my contracting a skin-blistering condition called (and best pronounced in a W. C. Fields accent) Bullous Pemphigoid. Apart from a five-minute stretching exercise in the shower, and the normal walking-about on errands, I do no formal exercise. I have friends my age contemplating triathlons, or who play tennis, singles, for 90-minute stretches. My own greatest athletic accomplishment at 80 is that I can still put on my trousers while standing up. When others speak of staying in shape, I wonder what shape it is precisely they have in mind.

Gradual loss of memory, short- and long-term, is a well-advertised part of the deal in aging. Isaiah Berlin, in a letter to a friend on his forthcoming 80th birthday, writes: "But 80 is enough—now the decline—the order is one forgets names, then nouns, then everything: gagahood—the end."

This, however, if my own experience is any guide, is to make things appear more drastic than they are. True, one occasionally walks into a room in one's own apartment and requires a few seconds to remind oneself what it was, again, that brought one there. The title of a movie, the name of the author of a book, the quarterback who succeeded Joe Montana for the San Francisco 49ers elude one, though through the good offices of Google they may be recaptured quickly enough. One of the side benefits of memory loss is that, after a five-or-so-year hiatus, one forgets the plots of most movies and can see them again as if afresh.

Still, evidence regularly crops up suggesting my generation is about to hear the Great Publican's call, "Time, gentlemen, time." I go to lunch with a friend who tells me that he has had a pacemaker installed. Another friend is recovering from bypass surgery. An old college roommate informs me that he has been diagnosed with Parkinson's. A boyhood pal has had two unsuccessful spinal surgeries and a prostate operation. We grow old, we grow old, we shall soon wear a lot more than our trousers rolled.

In our twenties, at lunches, my male friends and I talked a fair amount about sports and sex; in our thirties and forties and fifties, food and movies and politics were the main subjects. Since our seventies, health has taken over as topic number one. Sleep is a big item: No one seems to sleep through the night without having to get up two or three or more times. The fortunate ones among us are those who can get back to sleep. The old brutish masculine question of our twenties—"Getting much?"—now refers not to sex but to sleep.

I appear moderately fit, I am neither over- nor underweight, I have a respectable amount of hair (most of it gray) on my head and none whatsoever on my legs. I have not yet developed a walk sufficiently odd to put in for a grant from *Monty Python*'s Ministry of Silly Walks. When alone, I find it difficult to think of myself as soon to be 80. I am, I suppose, a youthful 80—an oxymoron if ever I heard one. I don't think of myself as 26, mind you, or 38. If pressed, what I think of myself as is a squishy middling age—57, say. One would prefer to look ageless. The truth is that, on a good day, I might pass for 74.

Still, there it is, that rude number 80. Eighty, it occurs to me, might make one too aged even to qualify as a dirty old man. I was never a Casanova-like seducer, nor claimed to be a champion sack artist, yet it is saddening to consider oneself entirely out of contention in the sexual realm. Yet the knowledge that the beautiful young girl one finds oneself staring at is likely to consider you, sexually, out of the question *does* take the air out of one's fantasies.

On the other, not-yet-palsied hand, near 80 I find (small compensation though it may seem) that I am able to compliment women on their beauty without their feeling that I am hitting on them. "Were I a mere forty years younger," I found myself saying to a cheerful waitress not long ago, "I should pursue you with all the cunning currently at my disposal." Perhaps she can fantasize about me when I was 40— make that, to be safe, 50—years younger. Perhaps, more important, my dear wife can forgive me for this necessary but awkward paragraph. But then men, as I used regularly to tell my beautiful granddaughter, are brutes.

Within a block of where I live there are two retirement homes, and two blocks in the other direction is Northwestern University. The majority of pedestrians I encounter on the street are bent over—the elderly on their walkers, the young over their smartphones. The spectacle reminds me of a passage in *Time Regained*, the final volume of Proust's great novel:

> Life at such moments seems to us a theatrical pageant in which from one to another we see the baby turn into a youth and the youth into a mature man, who in the next act totters toward the grave.

Eighty is not without its pleasures. One is that one sees the trajectory of others' lives and careers—"the trajectory from life to death, with the final vertical plunge not far away," Proust called it in *Time Regained*. One thinks here of those prodigies who came whirring out of the gate but lost ground on the second turn, with nothing left for the home stretch. Or those who were good at school but, as it turned out, nothing else. Or those who made all the predictably correct career and personal moves and yet ended up with supremely boring lives. Or those whose success, given their utter absence of talent and paucity of charm, remind one that the world is not an entirely just place.

Again, I think of my own good luck through life. Going to the University of Chicago, which I did in a blindly stumbling way, turned out to be a crucial step, giving me a primitive but genuine sense of a high culture foreign to my upbringing but which nonetheless seemed worth attempting to attain. I sometimes think I decided on a career as a writer because there was nothing else I could do: I was too squeamish for medicine, insufficiently bright for higher science, too heedless of close detail for law, too easily bored for business.

I was lucky (again) to have come of age when there was still a military draft, which gave me two years between leaving school and having to go out into the world. I began writing in earnest in the Army and published my first bits of journalism while there at the age of 22. In the Army, too, while at dreary Fort Hood in Texas, I put in for the job of clerk typist at a recruiting station either in Little Rock, Arkansas, or Shreveport, Louisiana. I was told by a gruff first sergeant that one of these jobs was mine and that I had a choice, Shreveport or Little Rock. With perhaps a half-second to answer, I blurted out, "Little Rock, Sergeant." In Little Rock, I met and married my first wife with whom I had my two sons. What, I have often wondered, if I had said "Shreveport, Sergeant"?

After the Army, I moved to New York, where I worked on a now-forgotten political magazine, whose chief benefit was meeting Hilton Kramer, another editor there who, though nine years older and vastly more sophisticated than I, befriended me. Several years later, Hilton put up my name, and wrote a strong recommendation on my behalf, as a candidate for the editorship of the *American Scholar*, the quarterly published by Phi Beta Kappa. Not a member of Phi Beta Kappa, nor ever even a good student, I was sublimely confident I had no chance for the job, even though I was put on the short list of candidates. I saw the interview as an expense-paid day in New York.

All I can remember of the interview itself is that a man on the hiring committee named Edgar Shannon, then president of the University of Virginia, asked me what I would do for young readers if I were made editor of the journal. "Let them grow older," I answered—which must have rung the gong, for I was chosen for the job. I edited the *American Scholar* from my home in Evanston, aided by two splendid sub-editors, Jean Stipicevic and Sandra Costich, in Washington. As I explained to them on numerous occasions, the division of labor here was clear: They did all the work and I took all the credit, which is pretty much how things worked out.

Acquiring the editorship of the *American Scholar* was a lovely bit of luck, but then so was my other job, teaching in the English Department at Northwestern. This came about earlier, through the offices of the literary critic Irving Howe, for whose magazine *Dissent* I (then a freelancer) wrote two essays. Howe, an eminence in his day, instructed the head of the English department that there was a fellow in town named Joseph Epstein who someday figured to have a strong reputation as a writer and that he ought to hire him. *Mirabile dictu*, the man did, even though I have no advanced degrees, or ever acquired any. Better yet, my Northwestern job was without tenure—each year, for 30 years, I was asked if I should like to stay on for another year—so that I never had to attend any faculty meetings and listen to the petty squabbles of my colleagues. If the reigning sin of capitalism is greed, and that of socialism is envy, from their conversation I grasped that that of academic life is resentment.

So there I was, with two relatively cushy jobs, both sounding more prestige-laden than they truly were, the two together not requiring anything like my full energy. I am a man who has made a respectable living without having had to go into an office regularly since 1970, and owing to these jobs I am, today, a thing I'd never thought I'd be: a pensioner. To fill in the time, and to evade boredom, I have been able to write and edit 30 or so books. My luck seems to have held out, for thus far I haven't run out of things to write about or editors who agree to publish and, most astonishing of all, pay me for my various scribblings. We are all autodidacts. The only difference is that I, because of a certain small skill acquired over the years at constructing sentences, happen to have conducted my self-education in public.

I should like to say that my current age has mellowed me, made me calmer and wiser, more thoughtful generally. Alas, it is not so. I find myself as easily ticked off as ever at inefficiency, bad manners, what I take to be stupidity in high places. Seeing those I take to be the wrong people vaunted can also tick me off—though no longer to the max, since I have come to understand that this is the way of the world. I do not allow myself to get as worked up about political subjects as formerly, my patience having lengthened a notch or two. If there is any reason behind these modest improvements in self-deportment, it is perhaps to be found in my reminding myself (as if any reminder is required) that I shall before long be departing the planet, and there is no point in spending any of the time remaining to me with a red face. The thought lends me a certain detachment, though nothing, mind you, approaching serenity.

THE MOST DIFFICULT THING about aging is time—the obvious fact that one is running out of it. At 80, one is obviously playing well into the fourth quarter, if not in overtime. To change from a basketball to a gambling metaphor, at 80 one is also playing on house money. That, though, doesn't diminish one's greed for more time still. From roughly 60 on, the obituary columns of the *New York Times* have become the first thing I check, partly to see if anyone I know has pegged out but also to discover how old the newly dead were. A fine morning is when the subjects of the paper's main obituaries are all over 90; a dreary one is when most were still in their 70s, or younger.

Life at 80 is marked by a sense of delimitation. Santayana wrote that whatever one's age, one should always assume that one still has a decade left to live. In one of his letters he noted that, in his early 80s, his physician wanted him to lose 15 pounds, adding that he apparently desired him in perfect health just in time for his death. (He lived to 88.) In his 80s my friend Edward Shils still bought dishes and other new household items: "It gives one a sense of futurity," he explained.

I find the English phrase "This should see me out" more and more coming to mind. I shall probably not, in my lifetime, buy another suit. (A friend in the clothing business tells me that only lawyers buy suits nowadays.) I own two good overcoats. I may have enough shoes to play on through. I have some 40-odd neckties, no fewer than seven scarves, and a single ascot, which I may work up the nerve to wear if I make it to 85. These should see me out.

If one is fortunate enough to make it into one's 90s, the problem, outside health, figures to be friendlessness. I have myself felt the loss of dear friends for at least a decade now. I happen to have had many friends seven and eight years older than I, and a few much older than that, most of whom are gone. Some among them were also important to me as sources of approval. The good opinion of my writing by Hilton Kramer, John Gross, Dan Jacobson, and Edward Shils—four men notable for their intellectual penetration and lovely sense of humor—meant a great deal to me. Their approval boosted my self-esteem, or as I prefer to think it, my self-Epstein. I know precisely what Sybille Bedford means when, in her book *Jigsaw*, she wrote: "Hope of approval by a handful of elders and betters: yes; aiming at sales, fashion, success: no." In his letters, Isaiah Berlin begins at 60 to complain that there is no one left for him to look up to. Berlin himself, of course, was a man up to whom a great many younger men looked, and even now, long after his death in 1997, still do. Yet the world seems impoverished without people inhabiting it one admires without qualification.

At 80, I wonder if I have already reached the status of back number. Some years ago Murray Kempton wrote about Arthur J. Goldberg who, some will recall, was the former attorney for the AFL-CIO, the former Secretary of Labor under John F. Kennedy, the former Supreme Court Justice, the former Ambassador to the United Nations. Kempton gave his article the title "The Former Arthur Goldberg." For some years now, I have begun to sniff something of this same odor of formeraldehyde about myself. I have seen myself described as the former editor of the *American Scholar*. I am, officially, a Lecturer Emeritus at Northwestern, and people no longer address me (wrongly) as Dr. Epstein. When they did, I had to restrain myself from saying, "Read two chapters of Henry James and get right into bed; I'll be over as soon as I can."

Five or six years ago, a famous journalist told a friend of mine that that very day was his 80th birthday, but he wasn't telling anyone. He, the journalist, specialized in the status life and on being with-it in a high-powered way, and 80, by its very nature, carried with it more than a mere suggestion of being out of it. I have no such problem. I rather like the notion of being out of it and am closing in on achieving the blessed state. I know the names of fewer and fewer movie stars and, on the street, could not distinguish Cate Blanchett from Keira Knightley. Once a regular moviegoer, I now almost never go to the movies and am content to wait six months, a year, or longer, for the arrival of a promising (of which there seem to be fewer and fewer) movie to come out in DVD. I have scant interest in any movie about people under 40. I have almost arrived at the condition of a friend who, emerging from another disappointing contemporary movie, announced, "I never want to see another movie I haven't seen before."

In politics, I seem to have arrived at the same position, if not the same politics, as the British historian A. J. P. Taylor, who once claimed for himself "extreme views, weakly held." Most of my views these days are backed up by very few facts. At 80, is one really supposed to take time out to read up on the trade bill, know the name of the Indian minister of defense, or have a clear position on the safe-road amendment currently up before the Illinois legislature? I don't believe so. My current interest in travel is nil. I shall die content not having seen Khartoum or Patagonia. I'll be all right without another trip to Europe. "When a man is tired of London," Samuel Johnson pronounced, "he is tired of life." But then, Johnson knew London, and England with it, before its leading figures were those two knights of doleful countenance, Sir Elton and Sir Mick.

As for books, I mentioned to someone the other day that I was slowly reading my way through Theodor Mommsen's majestic four-volume *History of Rome*. "You don't read any crappy books, do you?" he said. With the grave yawning, I replied, why would I? As a literary man, I used to make an effort to keep up with contemporary novels and poetry, but no longer feel it worth the effort. No more 500- and 600-page novels for me written by guys whose first name is Jonathan. I have given the current batch of English novelists—Martin Amis, Ian McEwan, Julian Barnes, Salman Rushdie—a fair enough shot to realize I need read no more of them; their novels never spoke to me, and are less likely than ever to do so now. I glimpse poems in the *New Yorker*, the *Times Literary Supplement*, and in the few literary quarterlies to which I still subscribe; but none stick in the mind, and poor poetry itself has come to seem little more than an intramural sport, restricted in interest largely to those people who continue to write the stuff.

About visual artists, whereas once I would have been ashamed not to know the names Frank Stella, Robert Motherwell, and Fairfield Porter, today I shamelessly acknowledge I cannot name a single working painter or sculptor. About installation and performance artists, don't even ask. Out of it, nicely, happily out it.

"There is," says Sophocles, "no one without suffering; the happy are those who have the least of it." The reliably cheerful Schopenhauer adds: "No man is happy but strives his whole life long after a supposed happiness which he seldom attains, and even if he does it is only to be disappointed with it; as a rule, however, he finally enters harbor shipwrecked and dismasted."

Schopenhauer is, of course, correct: Happiness is a fool's goal; contentment is a more reasonable expectation. Measurements for contentment are not easily established, but the one I prefer is the absence of regrets. Here I count myself fortunate yet again. I have only two regrets in what is now my lengthy life: That I did not study classics and learn Latin and Greek when young, and less serious, that I do not live in a place where I look out on water. As regrets go, these are trivial stuff—pathetic, really. I am a man who found the right work, married (the second time) the right woman, live in the right place. Such disappointments as I have known I have brought on myself by not working hard enough, or being thoughtful enough. A lucky life, mine, touch wood, and may the evil eye not visit me.

FOR A THOROUGHLY LUCKY LIFE, one would need to die a painless death not preceded by an illness. Not so easy to arrange. The Greeks, Jacob Burckhardt reports, spent their days "in perpetual contemplation of approaching death." Socrates's was the most admirable death history provides: self-imposed in the presence of friends. Seneca talks a big game about death, noting that every journey has its end, that "life itself is slavery if the courage to die be absent," and insisting that it's best to remember that you didn't exist before you were born and you will return to that state when you die. Yet Seneca, Nero's tutor and later advisor, and history's first speechwriter, in the end underwent an enforced and sadly botched suicide, his veins too desiccated to allow the blood from his cut wrists to flow quickly, a death Tacitus describes in crushing detail.

Montaigne was perhaps the most death-minded of all great writers. He deals with the subject in a number of his essays, chief among them "On Fear," "That We Should Not Be Deemed Happy Until After Our

Death," and "To Philosophize Is to Learn How to Die." Life, Montaigne felt, must be tried "on the touchstone of this final deed."

> In judging another's life, I always see how its end was borne: and one of my main concerns for my own is that it be borne well—that is, in a quiet and muted manner.

Wisdom, Montaigne held, ought to teach us not to be afraid of dying. Therefore, it follows that the best way of dealing with death is not to put it out of mind—"what brutish insensitivity can produce so gross a blindness"—but to think almost relentlessly about it, "to educate and train [our souls] for their encounter with that adversary, death." He himself claimed to have always been besieged by thoughts of death, "even in the most licentious period of my life." Montaigne wished to die while working on the cabbages in his garden. Instead he died, at 59, an arbitrary and tortured death by quinsy, an abscess that chokes off breathing.

I have never been able to take Montaigne's advice. While I was never so naïve as to ignore that death was the second main fact—after birth—of life, even now I have not been able to brood upon it. I have a short attention span—lucky again—that has never allowed me to undergo serious depression or even to linger for long on unpleasant thoughts. Suicide has never entered my mind.

Unlike the woman mentioned earlier who each morning arises to say "shit" because she's still here, I wake grateful that I am and hope my visit can be extended. I still like it here, still find much to amuse, and a few things yet to charm, me. I understand the longing for death at the close of a long life, especially if the end is accompanied by pain, or even if it is accompanied by disappointment or fatigue. I do not ignore the supreme fact of death, and I can easily imagine a world without my insignificant presence in it. The utter nullity after death, though, I find difficult to grasp. I envy people with strong religious faith, for whom the death question has been put to rest, but have never myself been able, and now expect ever, to find it.

I have few hopes of being remembered beyond the lifespans of my three grandchildren. I have left instructions not to have a memorial after I vacate the premises, having attended too many where the wrong people arrange to speak and, in their remarks, get the recently dead person impressively out of focus. I have left instructions to be cremated, my ashes buried in a plot next to my parents, a simple gravestone, like theirs, setting out my name, birth, and death dates.

I have friends in their mid- and late-80s, and even a few in their early 90s, who still find much pleasure in life and bring pleasure to others. With the continued support of the Knock-Wood Insurance Company and modern medicine, I hope to emulate them. I realize that I may be served an eviction notice at any time. I suppose I am as prepared as any normally disorderly fellow can be, though one thing I haven't taken care of, if my death turns out to be a peaceful one, is the matter of last words. Goethe has already taken "More light." Beethoven has used up "Applaud, my friends, the comedy is finished." I prefer something more in the mode of Lope de Vega (1562–1635), the Spanish playwright and poet, who on his deathbed asked his physician if he thought he would make it through the night, and when told he was unlikely to do so, remarked, "Very well, then, Dante's a bore." As for myself, thus far the best I have been able to come up with is, "I should have ordered the Mongolian beef."

A perhaps too relentless self-chronicler, I seem to have written essays on turning 50 ("An Older Dude"), 60 ("Will You Still Feed Me?"), 70 ("Kid Turns Seventy"), and now this. If only I can get to 130 or 140— who knows, there just might be a book in it.

Original Publication
Information for Essays
in this Book

Part One : The Culture

"The Ideal of Culture," originally published as "The Cultured Life," the *Weekly Standard*, March 20, 2017.

"From Parent to Parenthood," originally published as "From Parent to Parenting," *Commentary*, May 1, 2015.

"Death Takes No Holiday," *Commentary*, June 1, 2014.

"Wit," originally published as "From Wit to Twit(ter)," *Commentary*, January 1, 2015.

"Genius," originally published as "I Dream of Genius," *Commentary*, September 1, 2013.

"Cowardice," originally published as "Who You Calling a Coward?," *Commentary*, April 1, 2015.

"Old Age and Other Laughs," *Commentary*, March 1, 2012.

"What's So Funny?," originally published as "Notes on What's So Damn Funny," *Commentary*, September 1, 2014.

"The Fall of the WASPs," originally published as "The Late, Great American WASP," the *Wall Street Journal*, December 23, 2013.

"The Virtue of Victims," originally published as "The Unassailable Virtue of Victims," the *Weekly Standard*, May 18, 2015.

"Cool," originally published as "How Cool Was That?," the *Weekly Standard*, May 17, 2017.

"The Sixties," originally published as "Hope I Die Before I Get Young," *Commentary*, January 13, 2017.

"University of Chicago Days," *Claremont Review of Books*, Summer 2017.

Part Two: Literary

"Erich Auerbach," originally published as "An Uncommon Reader," the *Weekly Standard*, June 16, 2014.

"Kafka," originally published as "Is Franz Kafka Overrated?," the *Atlantic*, July/August 2013.

"Orwell" originally published as "The Big O: The Reputation of George Orwell," the *New Criterion*, May 1990.

"Proust," originally published as "The Proustian Solution," the *Weekly Standard*, May 28, 2012.

"C. K. Scott Moncrieff," originally published as "A Proustian Character," the *Wall Street Journal*, March 6, 2015.

"The Young T. S. Eliot," originally published as "From Tom to T. S.," *Claremont Review of Books*, Summer 2015.

"Philip Larkin," originally published as "The Real Philip Larkin," the *Wall Street Journal*, November 28, 2014.

"Willa Cather," originally published as "The Heart of the Heartland," the *American Spectator*, September 2013.

"George Kennan," originally published as "The Cracked Vessel," the *American Spectator*, April 2014.

"Isaiah Berlin," originally published as "A Thinker, I Suppose," *Claremont Review of Books*, Summer 2016.

"Michael Oakeshott," originally published as "The Conversationalist," the *Weekly Standard*, June 15, 2015.

"John O'Hara," originally published as "A Rage to Write," the *Weekly Standard*, December 12, 2016.

"F. Scott Fitzgerald, a Most Successful Failure," originally published as "A Most Successful Failure," the *Wall Street Journal*, June 2, 2017.

"Wolcott Gibbs," originally published as "There at the New Yorker," the *Weekly Standard*, December 12, 2011.

"Evelyn Waugh," originally published as "White Mischief," *Claremont Review of Books*, Spring 2017.

"J. F. Powers," originally published as "A Writer's Daily Bread," the *Wall Street Journal*, August 16, 2013.

"Edward Gibbon," originally published as "The Best of Scribblers," *Commentary*, September 1, 2015.

"Herodotus," originally published as "Father of History," the *Weekly Standard*, October 20, 2014.

"Tacitus," originally published as "Tacitus the Great," the *Weekly Standard*, January 11, 2016.

"*Encyclopaedia Britannica*—The Eleventh," originally published as "Wisdom on the Installment Plan, the *Wall Street Journal*, June 17, 2016.

"Grammar," originally published as "Gwynne's Grammar by N. M. Gwynne & The Sense of Style by Steven Pinker," the *Wall Street Journal*, September 26, 2014.

"Clichés," originally published as "Sound Familiar?," the *Weekly Standard*, January 26, 2015.

"Literary Rivals," originally published as "'You Stink,' He Explained," *Commentary*, December 1, 2015.

"Why Read Biography," originally published as "Life Within Lives," the *Weekly Standard*, April 11, 2016.

Part Three: Jewish

"Sholem Aleichem," originally published as "The Jewish Sholem Aleichem," *Commentary*, January 1, 2014.

"Jokes A Genre of Thought," *Jewish Review of Books*, Winter 2017.

"Jews on the Loose," *Jewish Review of Books*, Spring 2016.

"Jewish Pugs," *Jewish Review of Books*, Fall 2016.

"Harry Golden," originally published as "The First Talking Head," the *Wall Street Journal*, August 14, 2015."

"Gershom Scholem," originally published as "Gershom Scholem: Modern Mystic," the *Wall Street Journal*, March 17, 2017.

"Dreaming of a Jewish Christmas," originally published as "I'm Dreaming of a Jewish Christmas: Celebrating a Day You Don't Really Share," in Jonathan V. Last, ed., *The Christmas Virtues: A Treasury of Conservative Tales for the Holidays* (West Conshohocken, PA, 2015).

Part Four: Masterpieces

"The Brothers Ashkenazi," originally published as "A Yiddish Novel with Tolstoyan Sweep," the *Wall Street Journal*, February 7, 2009.

"Civilization of the Renaissance," originally published as "Mankind Turns to Understanding Himself," the *Wall Street Journal*, November 1, 2013.

"Montesquieu," originally published as "In Montesquieu a Historian Blended With a Political Philosopher," the *Wall Street Journal*, June 10, 2016.

"Machiavelli," originally published as "Machiavelli Explains What Makes Republics Tick," the *Wall Street Journal*, July 29, 2016.

"Gogol," originally published as "Surveying the Surging Immensity of Life," the *Wall Street Journal*, May 3, 2013.

"Speak, Memory," originally published as "Nabokov Looks Back at Life Before 'Lolita,'" the *Wall Street Journal*, June 13, 2014.

"Epictetus," originally published as "Virtue As Its Own Reward," the *Wall Street Journal*, January 8, 2016.

"H. W. Fowler," originally published as "Parsing the Weightiness of Words," the *Wall Street Journal*, January 20, 2017.

"As a Driven Leaf," originally published as "Balancing Faith and Reason," the *Wall Street Journal*, January 2, 2015.

"Joseph and His Brothers," originally published as "Putting Literary Flesh on Biblical Bones," the *Wall Street Journal*, August 24, 2012.

"Life and Fate," originally published as "Tolstoy's Heir," the *Wall Street Journal*, May 5, 2007.

"Memoirs of Hadrian," originally published as "Portrait of Power Embodied in a Roman Emperor," the *Wall Street Journal*, October 9, 2010.

"Charnwood's Lincoln," originally published as "The Biography He Deserved," the *Wall Street Journal*, February 14, 2014.

"Book of the Courtier," originally published as "The Prince's Man," the *Wall Street Journal*, July 26, 2013.

"Ronald Syme," originally published as "A Short Step to Dictatorship," the *Wall Street Journal*, April 15, 2016.

"Quest for Corvo," originally published as "A Biography Like No Other," the *Wall Street Journal*, December 4, 2009.

"The Old Bunch," originally published as "Destiny's Children," the *Wall Street Journal*, January 28, 2012.

"Life of Johnson," originally published as "A Biography as Great as Its Subject," the *Wall Street Journal*, September 11, 2015.

Part Five: Hitting Eighty

"Hitting Eighty," the *Weekly Standard*, January 2, 2017.

Index

P